Golf Courses of the U.S. Open

Golf Courses of the U.S. Open

David Barrett

Foreword by Rees Jones

Abrams, New York

Contents

PAGE 1: WINGED FOOT, 9TH HOLE.   PAGE 2: 2002 OPEN AT BETHPAGE.   OPPOSITE: CONGRESSIONAL, 9TH HOLE

FOREWORD

BY REES JONES

Some of my favorite childhood memories are from the U.S. Open. I went to my first in 1950 when I was eight and stood right behind Ben Hogan when he accepted the winner's trophy at Merion Golf Club. In 1955, I remember standing on top of a station wagon (there were no stands) near the 18th green of the Olympic Club to watch Jack Fleck make his putt on the 72nd hole to tie Hogan. (Fleck won the playoff.)

My father, Robert Trent Jones Sr., was already a well-known golf-course architect when he began his involvement in remodeling and renovating courses for the United States Golf Association's biggest championship, the U.S. Open. As a result, our family got to travel to almost every championship. In the more than 50 years since, I think I have missed a dozen Opens.

I did more than watch during those childhood visits. During the 1954 Open at Baltusrol Golf Club, I measured the length of the drives hit by the players, which helped Dad to reposition Olympic's bunkers in preparation for the following year's Open.

I did not attend the 1951 Open at Oakland Hills Country Club, but I remember the controversy over my father's redesign. Dad had been hired by the club to bring the course back to its pre-Depression glory and to modernize it for the upcoming championship. Even then, Dad was concerned about the implications of improvements in golf equipment, so he lengthened and toughened the layout.

Some would say he made it *too* tough. There were only two rounds under par. The winner, Hogan, passed my mother in the crowd after his final-round 67. She congratulated him on his score, and he replied, "Mrs. Jones, if your husband had to play his courses for a living, you'd be in the bread line."

The Oakland Hills Open was a milestone in the history of the championship. It was now evident that the classic courses, venerable though they were, would require at least a little updating against the onslaught of technological advances in the design of balls and clubs. I understood even then that the U.S. Open was the ultimate examination in American golf, and, as such, the host course would have to keep up with the times. Although every golf course at that mid-century point had undergone its share of tweaking, changes for a layout selected for the championship had become a given.

Between 1951 and 1962, I watched closely as my father prepared Oakland Hills, Baltusrol, Olympic, Oak Hill Country Club ('56), Southern Hills Country Club ('58), and Oakmont Country Club ('62) for Opens. After that, the USGA

selected two courses with nine holes of his original design—Congressional Country Club's Blue Course ('64) and Atlanta Athletic Club's Highlands Course ('76). The USGA also selected two of his original 18-hole designs, Bellerive Country Club ('65) and Hazeltine National Golf Club ('70).

Since those courses have held Opens, all of them have been renovated to varying degrees. That's the influence of advancing equipment technology, as well as athlete training and conditioning.

In 1985, I had headed my own golf course architecture firm for 11 years when I got a call from The Country Club. They wanted to restore and modernize their revered old course in Brookline, Massachusetts, in preparation for the 1988 U.S. Open. That was my first Open redesign; I was 46, the same age my father was when he redesigned Oakland Hills.

Between then and now, I've had the good fortune to renovate 12 of the 50 courses in this book, continuing the efforts begun by my father to make U.S. Open sites championship-worthy for contemporary players. (And in some cases, my renovations came on top of my father's own redesign work.)

Five of the 12 were remodeled *after* being selected to host the Open: The Country Club, Hazeltine National ('91), Baltusrol ('93), Pinehurst No. 2 ('99), and Bethpage State Park's Black Course ('02). Two opted to remodel, hoping (successfully, it turned out) to attract the tournament: Congressional ('97) and Torrey Pines South ('08). Five courses had previously hosted an Open, and some entertained the possibility of attracting a future Open: Atlanta Athletic Club, Bellerive Country Club, Medinah Country Club (No. 3), Oakland Hills Country Club, and Skokie Country Club.

Each experience was another step toward the redesign of the next course. A friend once asked me which players I followed during a recent Open. I answered that I wasn't just watching a player; I was watching the course. The interaction of player and course helps me understand the routing, strategy, and design features that factor into a championship-caliber layout.

While working on the different courses, I researched and read about the original course architects, trying to get inside their heads to understand their styles and strategies, studying why their courses were regarded highly enough to be selected as U.S. Open sites in the first place. I also watched competitions on courses that I came to know quite well.

Every renovation is a different process. I approach each course on its own merits: strengths and weaknesses, flexibility, ability to withstand changes without compromising its character. I delve into the club archives, scrutinize old photos and aerial maps, and track down historic references.

The designers at Rees Jones Inc. never go to a course to simply and automatically add length. We do add yardage to challenge the awesomely long drives today's pros are capable of hitting. But we also sometimes eliminate a blind hole, reposition fairway bunkers, add greenside bunkers, change the green size (at The Country Club, we enlarged one green and made three smaller), take out trees, add a pond, or change the angle of a tee box.

We redesign so that when the USGA sets up the course, the players believe that the course is a fair test of golf skills. We try to make the player use every club in his bag and penalize a shot only to the degree that it is missed.

And the process is not a singular effort. The host club, the USGA, and the consulting architect become a team. Whatever changes our design firm makes, we first submit them to the USGA for approval. This cooperation is crucial. Quite often, the USGA provides input that is implemented in the design.

I remember standing with USGA Executive Director David Fay on the 18th fairway at Bethpage Black during the renovation prior to the 2002 Open. He said, "Let's add a bunker at this green," and I immediately saw his point and agreed. Once our remodeling is done, the USGA takes it from there for the championship. It is the USGA, not the architect, that determines the narrowness of the fairway, the height of the rough, the hole locations, the speed of the greens, and other playing characteristics.

In 1954 at Baltusrol, gallery ropes were introduced for the U.S. Open. The primary reason was not to control the gallery; it was to protect the course setup, because when the crowd walks and tramples the grass, the rough becomes much less effective as a penalty for players missing the fairway. I remember a big discussion among the club officials and the USGA about how they were going to pay for this new expense. My father even suggested putting advertising on the support posts to raise the money. (That's probably when, at 12 years of age, I learned the importance of course setup.)

Today the ropes are being moved even farther away from the centerline of the fairway. Each year, the USGA makes choices in order to present the ultimate—but fair—test given the unique qualities of each course. No more "monsters" in the vein of the 1951 Oakland Hills Open.

David Barrett, by the way, tells the truth behind the quote—"I am glad to have brought this course, this monster, to its knees"—about that event that had been attributed to Hogan for decades. You can read that story—and my father's involvement in the plot—in the Oakland Hills chapter.

For nearly two decades, David brought readers this kind of insider information as the man responsible for overseeing the major-championship previews for *Golf Magazine*. Now his intimate knowledge of the courses and his insights, coupled with his thorough research, enable him to write skillfully and smoothly about these 50 illustrious courses and their championships—past, present, and upcoming.

In *Golf Courses of the U.S. Open*, David perfectly integrates the story of the golf course with accounts of the championship, painting a colorful and informative panorama. I wanted to read it slowly to savor every detail, but I was so caught up in the stories, I found I couldn't turn the pages fast enough. His anecdotes are so lively that I felt as if I were right there in the gallery at Myopia for the 1901 Open, which "set the all-time standard for misery." As immersed in the game of golf as I am, I was fascinated by golf lore that I had never heard before, about a subject that is so close to me.

Besides telling a colorful story, David has a historian's gift for interesting details that shed light on the early Opens, years when golf professionals were regarded as second-class citizens and tournaments were attended by hundreds, not tens of thousands, of spectators. He delves thoroughly into the architectural history of the courses, describing the evolution of their designs over more than a century. In doing this, David also brings the golf-course architects to life, especially those giants of "The Golden Age of Architecture" who designed most of the courses that have hosted the Open.

The U.S. Open takes place only once a year, and the title of champion is a coveted one. David gets inside the players' heads and brings the reader an understanding of the mental challenges in this pressure-packed competition.

Golf Courses of the U.S. Open will be interesting reading for all golfers who have watched the Open on television or have been lucky enough to attend the event itself, as I have. It is a great contest between the golf course and each golfer. This book will change the way you view the U.S. Open Championship.

BOBBY JONES. OPPOSITE: 18TH HOLE

ATLANTA ATHLETIC CLUB (HIGHLANDS COURSE) DULUTH, GEORGIA 1976

The USGA had a lot of reasons *not* to select Atlanta Athletic Club to host the 1976 U.S. Open. All those cons, however, were trumped by the one argument in favor: Bobby Jones wanted it. ¶ On November 16, 1971, Jones, his body so riddled by a long bout with the neurological disease syringomyelia that he was down to 60 pounds, dictated a letter. "My home club, the Atlanta Athletic Club, has recently built a new country club," the letter stated. "Our membership is most eager to be awarded the privilege of entertaining the USGA Open Championship … and I should be most happy if my old club should become the host for my favorite golf tournament." ¶ Jones died 31 days after completing that letter, but the words of the game's greatest amateur and four-time U.S. Open champion would carry much weight posthumously. In September 1972, the USGA awarded the 1976 Open to the Athletic Club, despite a litany of factors that would have eliminated most courses.

challenge the awesomely long drives today's pros are capable of hitting. But we also sometimes eliminate a blind hole, reposition fairway bunkers, add greenside bunkers, change the green size (at The Country Club, we enlarged one green and made three smaller), take out trees, add a pond, or change the angle of a tee box.

We redesign so that when the USGA sets up the course, the players believe that the course is a fair test of golf skills. We try to make the player use every club in his bag and penalize a shot only to the degree that it is missed.

And the process is not a singular effort. The host club, the USGA, and the consulting architect become a team. Whatever changes our design firm makes, we first submit them to the USGA for approval. This cooperation is crucial. Quite often, the USGA provides input that is implemented in the design.

I remember standing with USGA Executive Director David Fay on the 18th fairway at Bethpage Black during the renovation prior to the 2002 Open. He said, "Let's add a bunker at this green," and I immediately saw his point and agreed. Once our remodeling is done, the USGA takes it from there for the championship. It is the USGA, not the architect, that determines the narrowness of the fairway, the height of the rough, the hole locations, the speed of the greens, and other playing characteristics.

In 1954 at Baltusrol, gallery ropes were introduced for the U.S. Open. The primary reason was not to control the gallery; it was to protect the course setup, because when the crowd walks and tramples the grass, the rough becomes much less effective as a penalty for players missing the fairway. I remember a big discussion among the club officials and the USGA about how they were going to pay for this new expense. My father even suggested putting advertising on the support posts to raise the money. (That's probably when, at 12 years of age, I learned the importance of course setup.)

Today the ropes are being moved even farther away from the centerline of the fairway. Each year, the USGA makes choices in order to present the ultimate—but fair—test given the unique qualities of each course. No more "monsters" in the vein of the 1951 Oakland Hills Open.

David Barrett, by the way, tells the truth behind the quote—"I am glad to have brought this course, this monster, to its knees"—about that event that had been attributed to Hogan for decades. You can read that story—and my father's involvement in the plot—in the Oakland Hills chapter.

For nearly two decades, David brought readers this kind of insider information as the man responsible for overseeing the major-championship previews for *Golf Magazine*. Now his intimate knowledge of the courses and his insights, coupled with his thorough research, enable him to write skillfully and smoothly about these 50 illustrious courses and their championships—past, present, and upcoming.

In *Golf Courses of the U.S. Open*, David perfectly integrates the story of the golf course with accounts of the championship, painting a colorful and informative panorama. I wanted to read it slowly to savor every detail, but I was so caught up in the stories, I found I couldn't turn the pages fast enough. His anecdotes are so lively that I felt as if I were right there in the gallery at Myopia for the 1901 Open, which "set the all-time standard for misery." As immersed in the game of golf as I am, I was fascinated by golf lore that I had never heard before, about a subject that is so close to me.

Besides telling a colorful story, David has a historian's gift for interesting details that shed light on the early Opens, years when golf professionals were regarded as second-class citizens and tournaments were attended by hundreds, not tens of thousands, of spectators. He delves thoroughly into the architectural history of the courses, describing the evolution of their designs over more than a century. In doing this, David also brings the golf-course architects to life, especially those giants of "The Golden Age of Architecture" who designed most of the courses that have hosted the Open.

The U.S. Open takes place only once a year, and the title of champion is a coveted one. David gets inside the players' heads and brings the reader an understanding of the mental challenges in this pressure-packed competition.

Golf Courses of the U.S. Open will be interesting reading for all golfers who have watched the Open on television or have been lucky enough to attend the event itself, as I have. It is a great contest between the golf course and each golfer. This book will change the way you view the U.S. Open Championship.

INTRODUCTION

Just as winning the U.S. Open is the ultimate accomplishment for a player, being selected to host the U.S. Open has become the ultimate honor for a golf course, serving as recognition that it is one of the best—and toughest—courses in the country.

Since the first Open in 1895, 49 private clubs and public facilities have served as sites for the championship that is run by the the United States Golf Association. In 2008, Torrey Pines in San Diego will join that list. This book covers all 50 courses, offering insight from both historical and architectural perspectives.

The U.S. Open has become a huge event, with courses lining up to be chosen and sites selected six or seven years in advance. That wasn't the case in the early years of golf in this country, when the U.S. Amateur was considered a more prestigious tournament. For the Open, courses were picked a few months in advance and drew small galleries and sparse fields of mostly Scottish-born professionals.

The design of some of the early courses was rather primitive. Golf architecture didn't really develop in this country until after 1910. Of the early sites, perhaps only Myopia Hunt Club was of the quality of courses found in the British Isles. That changed rapidly when such designers as Donald Ross and A.W. Tillinghast began to fill the American landscape with outstanding courses during the Golden Age of Architecture, from the mid-teens through about 1930. To this day, most of the courses that host the Open were built in that era.

Eight Open courses no longer exist. Four are original courses that have been replaced by new layouts on the same and/or adjacent land: Newport, Shinnecock Hills, Chicago Golf Club, and Baltusrol. Another, Philadelphia Cricket Club's St. Martins Course, was reduced to a redesigned short nine when the club built a new course at another site. In three cases, the land on which the golf course sat was sold for development: Baltimore Country Club's Roland Park Course, Fresh Meadow, and Englewood. (Baltimore and Fresh Meadow moved to different sites; Englewood disbanded.)

The championship has outgrown some Open courses, either because they are too short to test the game's best players or because they don't have enough space to accommodate the crowds, corporate tents, and television compounds that are part of a modern Open.

On the other hand, a number of Golden Age courses have recently been unveiled as Open sites. Pebble Beach, once considered too remote, hosted its first Open in 1972; Shinnecock Hills, for the same reason, waited until 1986, more than 50 years after its essentially new course was built. Pinehurst No.

2 in North Carolina had to wait for developments in air conditioning and agronomy before hosting in 1999, and Bethpage Black needed a change in philosophy to bring the Open to a truly public course and the funding to improve its condition before it could join the party in 2002.

This new blood has been beneficial for the Open. In fact, many observers consider the four courses mentioned above to be the best Open sites of all.

This changing of the guard brings up a surprising truth about the Open. The common perception is that the championship returns to the same courses decade after decade. Actually, there are only three courses that have hosted more than four Opens—Oakmont with seven, Oakland Hills with six, and Winged Foot with five. (Baltusrol has hosted seven, but at three different courses, with four at the Lower Course.)

Although the roster is ever-changing, it is true that the Open has stuck mainly to the classic courses, at least since a largely unsuccessful flirtation in the 1960s and '70s with courses that had been built only a few years before.

"I think the reason we tend to go back to the older courses is that with our setup, they offer more of a challenge," says Mike Davis, the USGA's senior director of competitions. "They tend to have smaller greens, and that's going to make it a test for modern players. The greens tend to have more severe undulations, so with modern green speeds they are tougher to putt and to get the ball up and down. And they tend to have more sloping fairways. If you put any golfer, even Tiger Woods, on an unlevel lie, that adds to the challenge. They tend to make the modern courses flatter because of the machinery."

David Fay, the executive director of the USGA, says the association puts an emphasis on history, which gives a natural advantage to courses such as Oakmont and Winged Foot. "Going forward, I would hate to give up on returning to places like that," he says.

Nonetheless, Fay spearheaded the move to Bethpage Black, the first non-resort public course to host the Open, and has an eye on sprinkling in a course or two of more modern vintage. "I'd like to believe that before I leave the USGA, we will at least have identified a golf course for an Open that was built since Richard Nixon was president," he says.

Indeed, the most recently constructed Open site is Atlanta Athletic Club, with nine holes of its Highlands Course completed in 1967 and nine in 1971. There is not a single living architect who designed a U.S. Open course.

Of course, there are contemporary architects who are almost perennially redesigning U.S. Open courses, most notably Rees Jones, who has become known as the "Open Doctor." Some of his work has been restoration, and some of it has been modernizing. He brought Bethpage Black back to what A.W. Tillinghast had in mind, but at Torrey Pines, he came very close to building an entirely new course.

Classic courses that stand still do not have a chance of hosting future Opens in this era of rapidly advancing equipment technology. That has always been true, but it has been particularly so in the last decade, as distance increases have accelerated. Bethpage, for example, was redesigned in 1997, but several new tees had to be added even before the 2002 Open. Long par fours have always been part of the Open tradition—and these days that means par fours of more than 500 yards.

"The courses that stay in the rotation and keep getting championships are the ones that are progressive," Jones says. "With the advances in equipment, you basically have to rethink a golf course every five years now. And it's not only length. For example, front bunkers became less effective when players started spinning the ball. Then we put some back hole locations with terraces that were hard to access if you're spinning the ball. Now they can use a different ball that doesn't spin as much."

Difficulty is one of the requirements for Open courses. And with an Open setup—narrow fairways, long rough, firm and fast greens—the difficulty increases exponentially.

"The Open has long had the imprimatur of being the world's toughest golf tournament and that's a moniker I hope it never loses," says Fay. "As a fan, you wouldn't necessarily want to see a steady diet of it, but I think once a year the fans expect—and sort of enjoy—seeing the players feel like they've been in a fistfight. You see the strain on their faces in a way that you might not see in other golf tournaments."

In recent years, the USGA has done its best to see that the Open doesn't lose the "toughest" label. Scoring actually has gone up in the years 1995 to 2006 compared with the period immediately preceding. The only other time that happened was in the 1950s, when the USGA established its standard, highly punitive, Open setup. The best-remembered of those championships is the Oakland Hills "monster" of 1951, but that was only one of three championships in the decade in which the winning score was seven-over par.

"Those days are long gone," says Fay. "Today if you had a winning score like that it would be because of some mess-up, either by nature or man."

Advances in agronomy, which allow greens to be maintained firmer and faster than ever, are largely behind the recent challenges. Bringing courses so close to the edge has led to some "mess-ups," such as the second-round hole location on the 18th at Olympic in 1998—the ball sometimes refused to come to rest near the hole. Or the dried-out, impossible-to-hold greens at Shinnecock Hills in 2004. Neither the 18th at Olympic nor the seventh at Shinnecock—the most daunting of the greens in 2004—presented a problem in Opens held a decade earlier at each site.

As the greens have become firmer, the USGA has for the most part decided to cut back on the rough since 1999. The idea is to give players a chance to go for the green from the rough rather than automatically having to pitch back to the fairway with a sand wedge. That makes for more interesting golf, and is still a challenge because it's so difficult to hit a concrete-like green on a shot from the rough, where a player can't control the spin.

That change, along with technology, has spawned another concern: When players can bomb their drives and hit a wedge into the green even on a 450-yard par four, there is less concern about driving into the rough unless it is really nasty.

Like the courses themselves, U.S. Open setup philosophies are constantly changing. Davis, who took over the primary U.S. Open course-setup responsibility from Tom Meeks in 2006, notes, "It used to be that complaints about an Open involved getting the ball to the green, a lot of it about the rough. Now the complaints are more about the greens—hole locations or green speeds. Maybe we shouldn't make the greens quite so firm and fast, so we can avoid the situation like Shinnecock in 2004, and maybe go back to making it a little harder to get to the green."

A new idea that was implemented in 2006 was to move the gallery ropes farther away from the fairways to eliminate the situation of a wild drive ending up in a good lie where spectators have trampled the grass. Another idea called for graduated rough, less severe close to the fairway and more severe for shots that were farther off-line.

One thing that won't change is the trend toward narrower fairways. Whereas once U.S. Open fairway widths were 35 to 40 yards, they are now 25 to 30. For example, Winged Foot's fairways in 2006 averaged nine yards narrower than during its previous Open, in 1984.

"I'm not crazy about it from a purely architectural standpoint," says Davis. "When you have a wider fairway, you are creating angles for approach shots. By narrowing the fairways, you might be taking away a feature that the architect wanted to have. The fact is, though, that with technology players are not only hitting the ball farther, but also straighter. If the fairways were 40 yards wide today, nobody would miss a fairway."

On the other hand, lengthening a course by moving the tees back brings the landing zones for drives that the architect intended. Fortunately, most of the Golden Age architects left room to stretch the holes, though in some cases the limits have been reached.

In any case, don't expect the Open ever to become player-friendly. "We're not nearly as fixated on par as some would claim we are," says Fay. "But we want it so that making pars in a U.S. Open is a good score."

To accomplish that goal, the U.S. Open will continue to be played on some of the country's strongest courses.

BOBBY JONES. OPPOSITE: 18TH HOLE

ATLANTA ATHLETIC CLUB (HIGHLANDS COURSE) DULUTH, GEORGIA 1976

The USGA had a lot of reasons *not* to select Atlanta Athletic Club to host the 1976 U.S. Open. All those cons, however, were trumped by the one argument in favor: Bobby Jones wanted it. ¶ On November 16, 1971, Jones, his body so riddled by a long bout with the neurological disease syringomyelia that he was down to 60 pounds, dictated a letter. "My home club, the Atlanta Athletic Club, has recently built a new country club," the letter stated. "Our membership is most eager to be awarded the privilege of entertaining the USGA Open Championship … and I should be most happy if my old club should become the host for my favorite golf tournament." ¶ Jones died 31 days after completing that letter, but the words of the game's greatest amateur and four-time U.S. Open champion would carry much weight posthumously. In September 1972, the USGA awarded the 1976 Open to the Athletic Club, despite a litany of factors that would have eliminated most courses.

First, the two nines at the 36-hole complex that would be combined as the Open course had just been completed in 1967 and 1971. (Jones had never seen the new course.) Second, the USGA felt the course needed considerable work. Finally, Atlanta weather is not conducive to the firm, fast greens the USGA prefers for an Open, which is why the championship previously had never been played in the Southeast.

Ultimately, it didn't matter because of the shadow one man cast over the game. "We are here because of [Jones]," tournament manager Nancy Jupp conceded.

This was only fitting, because Jones and the club grew up together at the beginning of the 20th century. In 1908, the downtown Atlanta Athletic Club decided to get into golf and founded East Lake Golf Club six miles down the streetcar line from the city center. Jones took up the game there shortly after.

By the time it hosted the Ryder Cup in 1963, the club was running into problems. East Lake had been swallowed up by Atlanta's growth, the surrounding neighborhood had become a high-crime area, and many members were living in the northern suburbs.

That year, East Lake resolved to sell 18 of its 36 holes to finance a new course and clubhouse in Duluth, well north of the city. Four years later, with 27 holes designed by Robert Trent Jones Sr., a majority of members decided on a complete break with East Lake. A group of members who didn't want to move bought the East Lake property and formed their own club, which retained the East Lake name.

The new club was first known as Riverbend Country Club, before adopting the rather unwieldy moniker of Atlanta Athletic Club Country Club. When the Athletic Club closed its downtown operation in 1971, leaving Duluth as the club's lone site, it became simply Atlanta Athletic Club. That same year, it opened nine more holes, designed by Joe Finger, which would be combined with nine of Trent Jones's holes to form the Open-hosting Highlands Course. (Riverside is the other course.)

The USGA and the club embarked on a program of changes to make the course worthy of the national championship. From 1973 to 1975, Highlands received a $400,000 makeover—a hefty sum considering the original 27 holes were built for $650,000.

7TH HOLE

Trent Jones had redesigned a number of courses to prepare them for U.S. Opens. Now his own course would be on the receiving end of a redesign by the uncle-nephew team of George and Tom Fazio. Believing he would get a chance to strengthen his nine, Finger made detailed renovations and was surprised by the hiring of Team Fazio.

"It was like having one attorney argue a case all the way up the line and then hiring another to present it to the Supreme Court," Finger said.

Finger's nine, the front side of Highlands, was on more open terrain, whereas Trent Jones's holes were more wooded. The reasons for choosing Highlands over the Riverside Course as the Open site are murky, although the last two holes of the original Riverside were borrowed permanently to become the 17th and 18th of Highlands.

The choice seems even odder considering Finger designed his nine for membership play while Trent Jones was building a demanding test. "I felt the property available for my nine was too wide open for tournament play, and the holes lacked the needed length," Finger said. "At the time, I indicated where traps might later be installed for a major."

The Fazios carried out most of those recommendations—and much more. Originally expecting to make only minor alterations, they stayed two years, rebuilding or relocating every bunker. In addition, the Fazios shortened the 10th from 450 to 370 yards and shrank the green, changed the 11th from what USGA chief executive P.J. Boatwright called a "Mickey Mouse" par five into a controversial 480-

yard par four, and turned the 12th from a par four to a par five. A new tee on the finishing hole turned a relatively easy par five into a bear of a par four at 460 yards.

When the alterations, more extensive than any Open course in history, were finished, Boatwright termed the Athletic Club "a good course. It's not a great course, although it could become one with further modifications. At this moment, it probably doesn't measure up to the courses that have held the Open the last five years."

Even considering the previous five Opens had been played at Merion, Pebble Beach, Oakmont, Winged Foot, and Medinah, Boatwright's comments were lukewarm.

But Boatwright's view was the prevailing one. In his *Confidential Guide to Golf Courses,* golf architect Tom Doak wrote that the Athletic Club is "one of those 1970s 'championship courses' that is more difficult than charming." It certainly had the long par fours that the USGA wants for an Open, but it didn't have a lot of character. After three architects had put their stamps on it, the course reminded one player of "warmed-over hash."

In *Sports Illustrated,* Dan Jenkins even had unkind words for the clubhouse. "The tournament did not have the classic Open look or atmosphere," he wrote. "For one thing, the AAC looks more like a modern resort hotel than the traditional coun-

try club with proper aging. It was weird to see the USGA committeemen in their blue coats, striped ties and armbands wandering around at a place where, through various clumps of trees, one could find a health spa, tennis facilities and an aquatic center."

But, in the end, the Atlanta Athletic Club provided a memorable finish. The championship would have belonged to John Mahaffey if he had been able to handle the last few holes on Saturday and Sunday. Mahaffey, who had lost in a playoff the year before, led by six strokes after nine holes of the third round, but finished the day with just a two-stroke lead over PGA Tour rookie Jerry Pate.

On Sunday, the final two twosomes came to the 18th hole separated by one stroke. In the penultimate group, Al Geiberger and Tom Weiskopf were both at one-under; in the final group, Pate was two-under and Mahaffey one-under (having bogeyed 16 and 17).

The 18th was one of the Open's toughest finishing holes. Water guarded the left side on the tee shot and the front of the green. All four players avoided the cardinal sin of driving into the water, but found the right rough. Weiskopf and Geiberger laid up short of the pond with their second shots. Impressively, both made par—Geiberger holing a 15-footer and Weiskopf a six-footer.

In the final group, Mahaffey had a poor lie in the rough, more than 200 yards to the green. Decid-

JERRY PATE

An Open Moment

As Jerry Pate walked toward the green after his second shot on the 18th hole in the opening round in 1976, he heard a mixture of laughter and groans from the gallery. His ball had stopped on the bank of the water hazard, just above the water, but a frog hopped onto the ball and knocked it into the water. Pate took a penalty drop, got up and down for bogey, and said he wasn't disconcerted by the mishap because he likely would have made a bogey from where the ball originally perched anyway. On Sunday, Pate would put his approach shot two feet from the hole, where no frog could get it.

ing he couldn't count on Pate's making a mistake, Mahaffey attempted a fairway wood, a no-hope shot that dived into the water. He would bogey and finish fourth.

Pate caught a good lie in the Bermuda rough, which had been difficult to hit from all week. With 190 yards to the hole, he wanted to hit a 4-iron. His caddie, John Considine, talked him into hitting a 5-iron, believing it would carry the hazard. It was a 5-iron for the ages, flying straight at the hole and finishing two feet away. After twice asking USGA official Harry Easterly whether he could two-putt and still win, Pate tapped in the birdie for a two-stroke margin and an Open title at age 22.

Despite the doubts as a championship test, the course had held up reasonably well in a rainy week that softened the greens but made an already stout 7,015-yard layout play even longer. Pate scored in the 60s in the final three rounds for a winning total of three-under 277, but nobody managed better than 67 all week.

Just five years later, the Athletic Club landed the 1981 PGA Championship, won by local boy Larry Nelson going away. David Graham, who had won the U.S. Open at Merion earlier that summer, compared the two courses by saying, "Merion is a classy lady. This course is a rough bitch."

The club then hosted a rather unsatisfying 1990 U.S. Women's Open on the Riverside Course, and seemed to be on the way to the dustbin of major championship history. Then in 1995, Trent Jones's son Rees helped bring the club back onto the national scene.

Rees Jones is known for his redesigns of several U.S. Open courses, but it was his work at East Lake that really got the Atlanta Athletic Club members' attention. His redesign in the early 1990s had turned East Lake into a regular host of the Tour Championship.

Jones turned Highlands into a better members' course by reducing the size of many bunkers and eliminating others, especially those front-

15TH HOLE

ing greens, which had bothered the members but hardly had given the pros a second thought. Jones rebuilt every green and extended seven holes, bringing the total yardage to 7,213.

Most importantly, by completely redoing all of the green complexes, he gave the course a consistent feel, instead of the quadraphenic personality it had received from the work of four architects (including that done by the team of Arnold Palmer and Ed Seay in the 1980s).

Jones actually shortened four holes, including the 11th, which he shrank from an awkward and controversial 480-yard par four to a fair test at 454 yards. Among the holes getting longer, the 15th grew to 227 and the 18th to a 490-yard par four.

Those two holes, the toughest and the best on the course, played key roles when the club hosted the 2001 PGA Championship. The 15th, with water hugging the right of the green, is a hard hole to par, but champion David Toms made a hole-in-one with a 5-wood in the third round.

As in 1976, the 18th was again decisive. Toms drove into the first cut of rough but unlike Pate, elected to lay up. The strategy paid off when he holed a 12-foot par putt for a one-stroke victory over Phil Mickelson.

If not quite as spectacular as Pate's finish, it was stirring nonetheless. Perhaps more importantly for Atlanta Athletic Club, the now mature course was more praised than panned. After a shaky major debut, the club had finally established itself as a major player and soon was awarded the 2011 PGA.

Jones has given the course another reworking in preparation for that event. His 1990s changes were aimed to a large degree at member play and the overall feel of the course, while the recent ones are designed to strengthen it as a championship test. (Toms won with a record 265 total in 2001.) New tees have been built on 14 holes, bringing the total yardage to about 7,500. Greenside bunkers were made deeper and moved closer to the greens. Water was brought more into play on a couple of holes, and a new trick has been employed in the battle against driving distance—lowering some of the tees.

"That's the latest thing," Jones says. "We can't water the infield the way the Dodgers did when they had bad infielders."

1976 TOP FINISHERS

Jerry Pate	71-69-69-68—277
Tom Weiskopf	73-70-68-68—279
Al Geiberger	70-69-71-69—279
John Mahaffey	70-68-69-73—280
Butch Baird	71-71-71-67—280
Hubert Green	72-70-71-69—282
Tom Watson	74-72-68-70—284
Lyn Lott	71-71-70-73—285
Ben Crenshaw	72-68-72-73—285
Johnny Miller	74-72-69-71—286

Low round: Baird, Mike Reid, 67

Scorecard

HOLE	PAR	YARDAGE 1976 OPEN	YARDAGE TODAY
1	4	455	438
2	4/5	450	545
3	4	460	475
4	3	205	220
5	5	540	560
6	4	440	425
7	3	175	190
8	4	420	485
9	4	415	430
Out	35/36	3560	3768
10	4	370	439
11	4	480	464
12	5	510	550
13	4	390	387
14	4	415	470
15	3	215	240
16	4	410	460
17	3	205	207
18	4/5	460	573
In	35/36	3455	3790
Total	70/72	7015	7558

Note: For majors, the second and 18th holes are expected to be par fours of 505–510 yards

1ST HOLE AT ROLAND PARK IN THE 1920S

BALTIMORE COUNTRY CLUB (ROLAND PARK COURSE)

BALTIMORE, MARYLAND 1899

Golf as a selling point for real estate is hardly a new idea. Back in 1897, the developers of Baltimore's Roland Park neighborhood found that home sales were lagging, so they decided to entice buyers by building the first 18-hole golf course in Maryland. It worked. More than 500 people responded to the invitation to join the Baltimore Country Club, lured no doubt by the waived entrance fee for charter members and annual dues of $20 for men and $10 for women and juniors. ¶ Home sales picked up for Roland Park, a 550-acre community that was one of the first planned garden suburbs, partly laid out by Frederick Law Olmsted Jr. and featuring one of the nation's first shopping centers, which still survives at the corner of Roland Avenue and Upland Road. The course, designed by transplanted Scotsman Willie Dunn, was built in 1898 and hosted the U.S. Open just a year later. ¶ Built on hilly terrain, Roland Park provided challenges for golfers both on their shots and in walking from shot to shot. "The first drive seemed to take one off the roof of the world, and the last one was a tough grind uphill, particularly

Scorecard

1899 U.S. Open

Hole	Yardage
1	354
2	150
3	484
4	280
5	185
6	335
7	310
8	450
9	277
Out	2825
10	488
11	147
12	328
13	305
14	248
15	515
16	222
17	339
18	239
In	2831
Total	5656

punishing on a hot day," wrote A.W. Tillinghast, who designed the club's Five Farms East Course in 1926. "As the work [on the new course] progressed, some of [the members] talked to me and the burden of their inquiries was invariably hill climbing. They wanted to be assured that the new holes would be somewhat less arduous."

At 5,288 yards when it opened, the Roland Park course was short even by turn-of-the-century standards. A number of tees were moved back 25 to 35 yards for the Open to make it play 5,656 yards, still on the short side. The difficulties created by the hills made up for the lack of length. "There is considerably much more golf in it than you get on many courses that are much longer," said one observer.

Many players accustomed to flatter courses didn't play their best, but one man had no trouble at all. Willie Smith, one of five brothers who had emigrated from Carnoustie, Scotland, just a year earlier, won by 11 strokes with a 315 total for four rounds. That victory margin would stand as the Open record for 101 years until Tiger Woods romped to a 15-stroke win in 2000. Willie Anderson led after two rounds, but faded badly on the 36-hole final day with rounds of 85 and 84 to finish 12 shots behind Smith.

The author of an article in *Golf* reporting on the championship wrote, "When I heard on Thursday night at dinner [after the first 36 holes] that [Anderson] had been in bed for two hours already, my friends will give me credit for advising them that Will Smith would be easily able to hold him in check on the following day. Directly I hear a man going to extremes, either in the direction of abstemiousness or the reverse, when preparing for the effort of his life, my suspicions are immediately aroused as to the amount of confidence he has in his own ability."

That proved to be true, but Anderson recovered his confidence and went on to win four Open titles, a record he shares with Bobby Jones, Ben Hogan, and Jack Nicklaus.

One interesting note from the championship is that players recorded the number of putts on the scorecards. Of the 3,978 holes played by the competitors, there were two shots holed from off the green, 487 one-putts, 2,392 two-putts, and 1,097 three-putts or worse. Of course, that was on greens that were plagued by crabgrass until a welcome rain 10 days before the championship.

Twenty-seven years later, Tillinghast gave Baltimore a longer and stronger course at Five Farms,

about eight miles north in the town of Timonium. The Roland Park area was annexed by the city in 1918, and members were unhappy with increased traffic and high taxes. By that time, Falls Road had transformed from a dirt path that two holes played across to a busy road separating the first, 17th, and 18th holes from the rest of the course. Still, the Roland Park course remained open until 1962, when the West Course at Five Farms joined Tillinghast's course.

The club hasn't abandoned Roland Park. The clubhouse, tennis courts, and other recreational facilities are still used, and three holes are preserved, with a plaque honoring Smith. The land across the road that used to be part of the course is now occupied by a gated community and a complex of two high schools.

Five Farms East has never hosted a U.S. Open, but it is a fine course that is ranked in the top 100 in the country and was the site of the 1928 PGA Championship and 1988 U.S. Women's Open.

1899 TOP FINISHERS

Willie Smith	77-82-79-77	315
Val Fitzjohn	85-80-79-82	326
George Low	82-79-89-76	326
W.H. Way	80-85-80-81	326
Willie Anderson	77-81-85-84	327

Low round: Jack Park, 75

ROLAND PARK CLUBHOUSE TODAY

10TH HOLE, OLD COURSE, IN 1915. OPPOSITE TOP: LOWER
COURSE 4TH HOLE. OPPOSITE BOTTOM: 7TH HOLE

BALTUSROL GOLF CLUB

SPRINGFIELD, NEW JERSEY OLD COURSE 1903, 1915; UPPER COURSE 1936; LOWER COURSE 1954, 1967, 1980, 1993

Baltusrol Golf Club, one of the most storied and traditional of all U.S. Open sites, was founded by a man who didn't play golf. However, he did have connections with those who did. ¶ The man behind Baltusrol was Louis Keller, who in 1887 started the *New York Social Register*, a publication that listed the 400 most prominent families in society—as determined solely by Keller. In the 1890s, when golf began to take hold in America, many of his subjects began to play. Keller never caught the bug himself, but he did enjoy the prospect of starting a club for his friends. ¶ In April 1895, Keller sent letters to selected acquaintances inviting them to join his new club. He had already gone to the trouble of hiring an Englishman named George Hunter to design nine holes on property Keller owned near the base of a "mountain," actually more of a ridge, in northern New Jersey. What's more, the initiation fee would be only $20, yearly dues $10. Not surprisingly, he received a strong response.

Soon Baltusrol, along with 14 other clubs, joined the five charter members in the USGA. In 1903, with its course expanded to 18 holes, the club hosted its first U.S. Open. In all, Baltusrol has hosted seven Opens, a total matched only by Oakmont, which will host its eighth in 2007.

In addition, Baltusrol is the only club to have hosted the Open on three different courses. The first two were on the Old Course, which was abandoned when A.W. Tillinghast built the Lower and Upper Courses in the early 1920s. The Upper got the nod in 1936, but the brawnier Lower Course has hosted four championships since, in 1954, '67, '80, and '93.

The Lower Course is certainly a fine course, although it is perhaps not as dramatic or punishing as some of the other Open sites. Jack Nicklaus wrote in a *Sports Illustrated* article in 1967 that the Lower Course is "marvelously fair. ... In many Opens, fear has been the dominant emotion. ... That will not be the case at Baltusrol, because the course, while not easy by any means, has a good balance between the opportunities of success and the chances of getting into trouble."

Rees Jones, called in to touch up the Lower Course for the 1993 Open, just as his father, Robert Trent Jones Sr., had done in preparation for the 1954 event, says the course "proves you don't have to overcook a design to have championship-caliber golf. It lulls you to sleep because it doesn't look as hard as it really is."

Actually, the Lower Course hasn't been that hard compared with other Open sites. The last three times it has hosted the championship, the course has produced scoring records. Nicklaus won in 1967 with a 72-hole record of 275. He then set another standard with a 272 in 1980, matched by Lee Janzen in 1993. (Tiger Woods in 2000 and Jim Furyk in 2003 also shot 272.)

In addition, Nicklaus and Tom Weiskopf tied the 18-hole scoring record of 63 in 1980. As much as

17TH HOLE

the course, the weather has been a factor for the low scores, because none of the Baltusrol Opens have featured rock-hard greens or extreme rough.

Given that relatively benign history, it is ironic that Baltusrol was named after a murder. On the night of February 22, 1831, a prosperous farmer named Baltus Roll was murdered by thieves. The mountain became known as Baltusrol Mountain and the rutted road leading to property was called Baltusrol Way, so it was natural for the club to take the name.

As was often the case with American courses built in the 1890s, the original course was rather haphazardly laid out—maybe even more than most. On the original 2,372-yard nine-hole layout, most of the holes were shorter than 300 yards, but the ninth stretched 517 yards. It seems Hunter found himself with a layout in which the eighth green was far from the clubhouse. Rather than change his plans, he built a long ninth hole. The course was quickly expanded

to 18 holes and lengthened to 6,000 yards in 1898; further refinements in 1900 resulted in what is now referred to as the Old Course.

Willie Anderson, who would be the top player of the next decade, was hired as the pro in 1898. He stayed only a year, but when the Open came to his old course in 1903, Anderson claimed the title, the second of his four championships and the first of three in a row, a feat still unmatched.

Anderson entered the final round with a six-stroke lead, but blew it all in the closing 18 of regulation. In fact, he lost most of it on one hole, taking an eight on the 182-yard ninth. After pulling his tee shot into a clump of trees, Anderson's next stroke ricocheted off a branch, back nearly to where he was standing, and the ball lodged in some stones. But after he three-putted for his eight, Anderson regained his form.

Pars on eight of the last nine holes got Anderson into a playoff with fellow Scot David Brown, who

18TH HOLE

had won the 1886 British Open before immigrating to America. The playoff was held in sloppy, rainy conditions, under the protest of Brown, who was ordered to start by the USGA. ("It's na gowf, the water's sure to stop the roll of the ball," Brown is reported to have said.) Anderson won the 18-hole mess-fest by two, 82-84.

George Low, a Scotsman with a proclivity for course design, took over as Baltusrol's pro in 1903 and supervised many changes during the next decade, including turning the 10th hole into a short par of 314 yards and building a new green with a moat around it, creating what might have been the first island green.

In the 1915 Open, this green was the setting for the tournament's key shot, by Jerome Travers, a four-time U.S. Amateur champion from nearby Upper Montclair Country Club. Travers wasn't considered much of a threat at stroke play, but he was playing a familiar course and was in the thick of it when he came to the 10th hole in the final round.

There, it appeared that his old bugaboo, wild driving, would cost him the championship. He sliced his tee shot out of bounds, then overcompensated and badly hooked his next. His third shot (the out-of-bounds penalty was then distance only) was a stroke of genius, carrying the water in front and stopping five feet from the hole. Travers made the putt for a par. He went on to play the final six holes in an extraordinary (for the times) one-under for a one-stroke victory over Tom McNamara. The 28-year-old Travers never played in another Open, concentrating instead on his career as a Wall Street broker.

The course received some criticism after the Open, especially for its short par fours. The club decided it needed a stronger layout, so the growing membership bought land for a second course, hiring Tillinghast in 1918.

Tillinghast, who already had produced notable layouts at San Francisco Golf Club and nearby Somerset Hills in New Jersey, went beyond the original budget of $100,000 and the two-year timetable. The project, 36 new holes, ended up costing $180,000 and taking six years, though Tillinghast found a way to keep 18 holes open at all times.

Many holes on the Old Course had gone up and down the mountain, but Tillinghast did not like holes that play straight uphill. So the Upper Course, which plays along the bottom part of the mountain, features mostly sidehill slopes. The Lower Course occupies flatter ground below.

Tillinghast kept certain features of the Old Course: The first and second holes of the Lower and five holes of the Upper follow the same routing as holes on the Old Course, and the third, fifth, 15th, and 16th greens of the Lower occupy green sites from the Old Course.

A good player, Tillinghast had competed in the 1904 U.S. Amateur at Baltusrol. In that event, his opponent, Chandler Egan, had hit a shot that received a lucky bounce off a tree on the 12th hole of the Old Course on his way to winning his match. During construction of the new courses, Tillinghast gleefully chopped that tree down.

Both courses were first-class tests. The Upper Course joins the Lower in the top-100 rankings of U.S. courses, and is a favorite of many members.

18TH HOLE, OLD COURSE

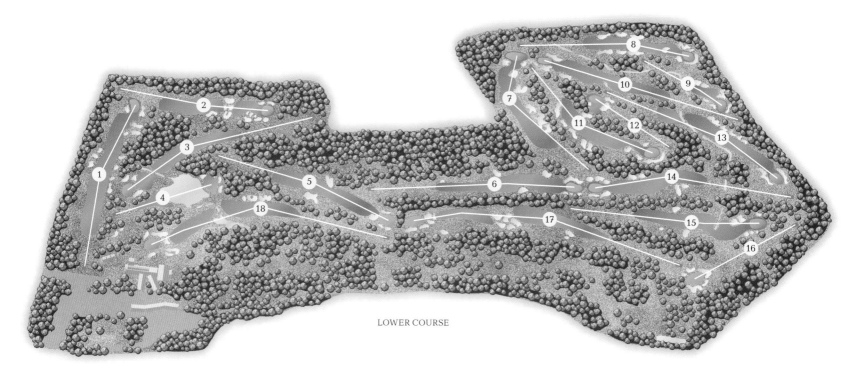

LOWER COURSE

Its greens are notoriously difficult and it has many outstanding holes. When the USGA was deciding which course would host the 1936 U.S. Open, a delegation that included Bobby Jones and Francis Ouimet chose the Upper.

That championship was won by dark horse Tony Manero, who stole the title from hard-luck story Harry Cooper, perhaps the best player of all time never to win a major championship.

When Cooper grabbed the lead with rounds of 71-71-70, fellow pro Willie Hunter said in the locker room in the break between the third and fourth rounds, "Nobody can stop Harry now, but maybe he'll stop himself. If I had his game, nothing could worry me, yet Harry frets and fumes and fights himself all the way around."

Cooper contained his demons through 13 holes, but on the 14th, he three-putted from 10 feet. Shaken, the man known as "Lighthorse Harry" walked to the next tee, where he didn't wait long enough for the gallery to clear the green after the group in front finished. His tee shot bounced off a spectator into a bunker. Another bogey. On the 18th, there was a delay of 10 minutes after Cooper's playing partner, Leslie Madison, had his pocket picked as spectators swarmed around the players on the way to the green. It couldn't have helped Cooper's nerves, and he made his third bogey on the last five holes.

Still, Cooper finished with a 284 total, which represented a 72-hole record for the Open. A radio announcer thrust a microphone into Cooper's face and asked him how it felt to be a champion. "I haven't won this thing yet," he said. "There are sev-eral men out there on the course who may catch me."

Manero did, with a stunning round. Four strokes behind entering the final round, Manero birdied the 12th and 13th holes to go five-under. Facing a 20-minute delay on the 18th tee, Manero stayed calm as he received a pep talk from two-time Open champ Gene Sarazen, who had requested to play with his boyhood pal and fellow Italian-American for the 36-hole final day. Manero finished with a par for a 67 and a total of 282 to beat Cooper's short-lived record.

When thoughts turned to another Open after World War II, the members hired Trent Jones to remodel the Lower. He added 400 yards, bringing the total yardage to 7,027.

The Lower made its Open debut in 1954, three years after the infamous Open at Oakland Hills where Trent Jones's redesign was called a "mon-ster." His approach at Baltusrol was more friendly.

Jones's biggest change was turning the over-water par-three fourth into a much more formi-dable challenge by moving the tee back 70 yards, making it 194 yards to an expanded green. During one of Trent Jones's visits, a member told him the new fourth was too difficult. The architect took the critic, another member, and club pro Johnny Farrell to the fourth tee, which is near the clubhouse. After the other three put their tee shots on the green, Trent Jones knocked his into the hole on the first bounce. "Gentlemen," he said, "I think the hole is eminently fair."

The redesign wasn't Trent Jones's only contribu-tion to the 1954 U.S. Open. He wanted to install gal-lery ropes on the entire course to keep the fans off the fairways—a first in golf. (Augusta National and the Old Course at St. Andrews had roped off parts of the course.) "I felt it needed to be done, not only for the protection of the players, but also, from an architect's point of view, to keep the rough that was in play from being trampled down," he later wrote in *Golf's Magnificent Challenge*. With tournaments drawing larger and larger galleries, the concept caught on—no doubt Cooper wished it had been tried 18 years earlier.

Although the Lower Course was the host of the 1954 Open, the Upper played a role in the outcome. On the 72nd hole, leader Ed Furgol hooked his tee shot so deep into the trees that he had no shot back to the proper fairway, but he did have a narrow opening to the parallel Upper 18th. Remembering that Ben Hogan had hit his second shot to that fairway from a similar position in the second round, Furgol took out an 8-iron and got back into play.

Not that his par five was easy from there. Furgol missed the green with his third shot and needed to make an eight-footer. When it fell, he become an even more unlikely winner than Manero. The 37-year-old Furgol, whose left arm was permanently bent and six inches shorter than his right due to a boyhood accident, had won only once on tour and the previous winter had taken a club pro job.

Whereas big names Hogan and Sam Snead weren't factors in 1954, the situation was decidedly different when the Open returned to the Lower Course in 1967. Superstars Nicklaus and Arnold Palmer engaged in a head-to-head battle, playing together for the final 36 holes.

They entered the final round tied for second with Billy Casper, one stroke behind the surprise 54-hole leader, amateur Marty Fleckman. When Fleckman and Casper, playing in the final group, faded quickly on Sunday, it was down to Nicklaus and Palmer.

There was little doubt about the spectators' allegiance. Besides greeting Palmer's best shots with throaty cheers and Nicklaus's with polite applause or silence, some fans went further. A couple toted a life-size cardboard cutout of Palmer, with the sign "Go Arnie Go!" Others, standing in the rough, unfurled a banner that read, "Hit It Here, Jack!"

Unfazed, Nicklaus methodically demolished the hopes of Palmer and his supporters. Five birdies in a six-hole stretch gave Nicklaus a 31 on the front nine and a four-stroke lead he would hold to the finish as he closed with a 65, the best round of the week.

JACK NICKLAUS AND ARNOLD PALMER

Thirteen years later, Nicklaus was at it again. This time the biggest scoring fireworks came in the first round, when he and Weiskopf tied each other and the championship record of 63, with Nicklaus missing a three-foot putt on the 18th for 62. That first round still accounts for half the 63s shot in Open history (Johnny Miller in 1973 and Vijay Singh in 2003 shot the others), as greens softened by rain took some of the teeth out of the Lower Course.

As in 1967, the Open was a head-to-head battle. This time it was between Nicklaus and Isao Aoki, a man with an unconventional swing and an even odder-looking putting stroke who was trying to become the first Japanese player to win a major. They were paired for all 72 holes, the first 36 by luck of the draw, and entered the final round tied for the lead.

Aoki trailed by two when he put his third shot five feet from the hole on the par-five 17th. Nicklaus rammed home his own birdie from 20 feet, then won by two as both birdied the 18th. The fan reaction was 180 degrees different from what it had been in 1967. Nicklaus, now 40 and something of an underdog, was received warmly. After his victory, the scoreboard operators on the 18th spelled out: "Jack is Back." Not only was he back, but he also became the first player to win two Opens at the same course since Willie Anderson at Myopia in 1901 and 1905.

The every-13th-year sequence of Baltusrol Opens continued in 1993, when Janzen became the second player (after Lee Trevino in 1968) to shoot four rounds in the 60s at an Open. The key shot was a chip-in birdie on the 16th hole, which gave Janzen a two-stroke lead over runner-up Payne Stewart.

A straightforward test, the Lower has a single quirk—pacing. The last two holes are par fives, both good ones and very different. The 17th, which played at 630 yards in 1993 and since has been stretched to 650, was the longest hole in Open history. The 18th is reachable in two (542 yards in 1993, now 554), providing the opportunity for a birdie or eagle at the finish.

In championship play, the two front-nine par fives are par fours, leaving the 17th and 18th as the only par fives on the course. It makes for a difficult start, as the four longest par fours come in the first seven holes. The back nine, with no monster par fours and the two par fives, is the place to make up ground.

The 16th, a par three that now plays 230 yards, is one of the tougher holes on the back nine. Its green, on the site of the 10th green of the Old Course, is now ringed by sand instead of a moat. All the greens on the Lower have subtle slopes that are hard to read, but the 16th is especially tricky because the mountain is close enough to influence the break. Gene Littler essentially blew the 1954

Open here when a seemingly straight three-foot putt broke away from the hole.

Tillinghast was a believer in par fives that could not be reached in two. In fact, he believed the ideal par five shouldn't be reached in three if a player missed either his drive or second shot. "The most effectual method, and I believe the only satisfactory one, is the location of a truly formidable hazard across the fairway," he wrote. "This must be carried with the second shot if the green is to be gained with the third. Obviously, this break in the fairway must be great, let us say 100 yards, for it not only has to be crossed with the second, but also keep any shot short of it from getting home."

The hole that best epitomizes this idea is the Lower's 17th, with its formidable cross bunkers 400 yards from the tee (originally one large bunker called "Sahara"). They are difficult even for a pro to carry with his second shot if his drive finds heavy rough. But the hole isn't quite untouchable in two—Billy Farrell, the son of longtime Baltusrol head pro Johnny Farrell, did it in 1967 when the hole played 623 yards, and John Daly has done it twice—at 630 yards in 1993 and 650 yards at the 2005 PGA Championship.

JACK NICKLAUS SINKS A KEY PUTT ON THE 17TH HOLE ON THE WAY TO WINNING IN 1980.

The 18th wasn't reachable when Tillinghast built it, but it certainly is now. Nonetheless, it has been tougher than expected down the stretch, mostly because of trouble off the tee. Furgol escaped from the left side in 1954, but Dick Mayer wasn't so fortunate when he strayed into the trees on the right. He had to take an unplayable lie, made a double bogey, and lost by two.

Nicklaus in 1967 and Janzen in 1993 both sprayed their drives to the right and ended up with long-iron third shots after laying up short of a creek that seldom comes into play, but both ended up making birdie. Nicklaus hit his lay-up second embarrassingly fat, then hit what he calls the best pressure shot of his career to that point, a 1-iron from 240 yards. Janzen, leading by two, thought about trying to clear the creek from a bad lie but changed his mind because "if I hit it in the water, it would probably be the dumbest decision in the history of golf." He laid up then bounced a 4-iron onto the green eight feet from the hole.

The 1993 Open might have been the last at Baltusrol, at least for a while. With Bethpage Black making its Open debut in 2002, Winged Foot returning in 2006, and Shinnecock Hills a successful site, the club that has been a USGA favorite could get squeezed out by other New York City-area courses. So Baltusrol snatched up the 2005 PGA Championship when it became available. In an effort to keep pace with the prodigious distance gains by tour players, the Lower Course was pumped up by Rees Jones to 7,376 yards for that event, won by Phil Mickelson with a four-under total.

Though it played tougher in 2005, which could boost the Lower Course's future Open prospects,

TONY MANERO (RIGHT) RECEIVES THE TROPHY IN 1936; HARRY COOPER (LEFT) WAS SECOND.

the record scoring in past Opens at Baltusrol isn't a reason for the USGA not to return. As Tillinghast once wrote, "Any great course will now and then take a good beating from good men, and there is nothing that can be done fairly to stop it, nor any reason why there should."

1903 TOP FINISHERS
•Willie Anderson	73-76-76-82—307
David Brown	79-77-75-76—307
Stewart Gardner	77-77-82-79—315
Alex Smith	77-77-81-81—316
Donald Ross	79-79-78-82—318

•Anderson won playoff, 82-84
Low round: Anderson, 73

1915 TOP FINISHERS
Jerome Travers	76-72-73-76—297
Tom McNamara	78-71-74-75—298
Bob MacDonald	72-77-73-78—300
James Barnes	71-75-76-79—301
Louis Tellier	75-71-76-79—301

Low round: James Donaldson, 70

1936 TOP FINISHERS
Tony Manero	73-69-73-67—282
Harry Cooper	71-70-70-73—284
Clarence Clark	69-75-71-72—287
Macdonald Smith	73-73-72-70—288
Wiffy Cox	74-74-69-72—289
Ky Laffoon	71-74-70-74—289
Henry Picard	70-71-74-74—289

Low round: Manero, 67

An Open Moment

Sam Snead never won the U.S. Open, but he was considered one of the favorites in 1954 after winning the Masters that year. Things went sour on his first shot, a snap-hook that ended up nearly against the out-of-bounds fence that separates the Lower Course from Shunpike Road. "Lawdy me, what a way to start a tournament," Snead was heard to moan. With no stance on the normal side of the ball, Snead grabbed an 8-iron, turned the clubhead upside down, took a left-handed stance, and hit a remarkable shot 160 yards down the fairway. Despite the recovery, he still bogeyed the hole, and finished 11th.

1954 TOP FINISHERS

Ed Furgol	71-70-71-72—284
Gene Littler	70-69-76-70—285
Lloyd Mangrum	72-71-72-71—286
Dick Mayer	72-71-70-73—286
Bobby Locke	74-70-74-70—288
Tommy Bolt	72-72-73-72—289
Fred Haas	73-73-71-72—289
Ben Hogan	71-70-76-72—289
Shelley Mayfield	73-75-72-69—289
Billy Joe Patton	69-76-71-73—289

Low round: Dick Chapman, 67

1967 TOP FINISHERS

Jack Nicklaus	71-67-72-65—275
Arnold Palmer	69-68-73-69—279
Don January	69-72-70-70—281
Billy Casper	69-70-71-72—282
Lee Trevino	72-70-71-70—283
Deane Beman	69-71-71-73—284
Gardner Dickinson	70-73-68-73—284
Bob Goalby	72-71-70-71—284
Dave Marr	70-74-70-71—285
Kel Nagle	70-72-72-71—285
Art Wall	69-73-72-71—285

Low round: Nicklaus, 65

1980 TOP FINISHERS

Jack Nicklaus	63-71-70-68—272
Isao Aoki	68-68-68-70—274
Keith Fergus	66-70-70-70—276
Lon Hinkle	66-70-69-71—276
Tom Watson	71-68-67-70—276
Mark Hayes	66-71-69-74—280
Mike Reid	69-67-75-69—280
Hale Irwin	70-70-73-69—282
Mike Morley	73-68-69-72—282
Andy North	68-75-72-67—282
Ed Sneed	72-70-70-70—282

Low round: Nicklaus, Tom Weiskopf, 63

1993 TOP FINISHERS

Lee Janzen	67-67-69-69—272
Payne Stewart	70-66-68-70—274
Paul Azinger	71-68-69-69—277
Craig Parry	66-74-69-68—277
Scott Hoch	66-72-72-68—278
Tom Watson	70-66-73-69—278
Ernie Els	71-73-68-67—279
Raymond Floyd	68-73-70-68—279
Fred Funk	70-72-67-70—279
Nolan Henke	72-71-67-69—279

Low round: Hoch, Parry, Stewart, Watson, John Cook, David Edwards, Steve Lowery, Nick Price, Joey Sindelar, 66

Scorecard

Hole	Par	Yardage 1993 Open	Yardage 2005 PGA	Average*	Rank*
1	4	470	478	4.34	2
2	4	381	378	4.12	T10
3	4	466	503	4.28	4
4	3	194	200	3.08	14
5	4	413	423	4.18	9
6	4	470	482	4.29	3
7	4	470	505	4.37	1
8	4	374	364	4.05	16
9	3	205	212	3.19	8
Out	34	3443	3546	35.90	
10	4	454	454	4.23	7
11	4	428	440	4.27	5
12	3	193	218	3.12	T10
13	4	401	424	4.06	15
14	4	415	430	4.11	13
15	4	430	430	4.24	6
16	3	216	230	3.12	T10
17	5	630	650	5.02	17
18	5	542	554	4.81	18
In	36	3709	3830	36.98	
Total	70	7152	7376	72.88	

*Cumulative average and rank from 1980 and 1993 Opens

GARY PLAYER. OPPOSITE TOP: 1ST HOLE.
OPPOSITE BOTTOM: 6TH HOLE

BELLERIVE COUNTRY CLUB ST. LOUIS, MISSOURI 1965

The awarding of the U.S. Open to Bellerive Country Club marked the beginning of what

proved to be an unsuccessful experiment in bringing Opens to recent-vintage sites. The Robert

Trent Jones Sr.-designed Bellerive, located in the western suburbs of St. Louis, had been open

for only five years when Gary Player won the 1965 Open. ¶ In coming years, Champions

(1969), Hazeltine National (1970), and Atlanta Athletic Club (1976) would host Opens within

a decade or so of building their courses. Including Bellerive, those proved to be four of the least

aesthetically satisfying championships. The Open has not returned to Bellerive, Champions,

or Atlanta, and went back to Hazeltine only after an extensive redesign. ¶ Immaturity had as

much to do with the unimpressive debuts of this trio of courses as any design flaws. None was

in the great condition expected for an Open, and all had an unfinished appearance. Bellerive

(1992) and Atlanta Athletic Club (2001) received better reviews after hosting PGA Champion-

ships in more mature states, and Hazeltine is a regular site for golf's majors, having hosted the

Open and PGA, with a Ryder Cup on the way.

Bellerive is a poster child for 1960s-era championship golf—plenty long and challenging with large greens but lacking the character of Golden Age designs such as Winged Foot and Oakmont. Trent Jones had become a favorite of the USGA by redesigning some of those classic courses, particularly Oakland Hills and Baltusrol, for the new era of improved equipment, so it was natural that when they decided to go modern, they chose one of his original designs.

Bellerive was a new course but an old club, founded in 1910 and named for the last French governor of St. Louis. The club decided in the 1950s to move west of the city, where most of its members were living, rather than undertake a costly remodeling of the deteriorating clubhouse. One of the members behind the move was Hord Hardin, an 11-time club champion who went on to become president of the USGA in 1968–69 and Masters chairman from 1980 to 1991. Hardin was instrumental in landing the U.S. Open, a task assigned him by St. Louis mayor Raymond Tucker as a way of celebrating the city's bicentennial.

The competitors were greeted by a course that was brutally long at 7,191 yards with a par of 70. It wasn't until three decades later that the Open went to a longer par-70 track, Congressional in 1997. The prognosticators forecasted that only a long hitter could handle Bellerive, but that's not the way it turned out. The 5-foot-7 Player, though a fitness fanatic, was not a bomber. His playoff opponent, 44-year-old Australian Kel Nagle, was one of the shortest hitters in the field.

One reason the longer hitters didn't have an edge was that much of the length came from the par-five eighth and 17th holes, unreachable in two at 580 and 606 yards, which negated the long hitters' advantage.

The large, undulating greens made approach putting an important factor. "Because of the putting problems, the remaining areas of the greens [besides where the hole is located] are just as much a part of the hazards of the hole as are the traps, the rough and the water," Trent Jones wrote in the championship program.

Three-putts, ball-swallowing rough, unreachable par fives, and six par fours of more than 450 yards added up to a bear of a test at Bellerive. There were only eight sub-par rounds all week and the lowest score was two-under 68. Arthur Daley in the *New York Times* wrote that the lack of legitimate birdie opportunities made for "the dullest Open

ever" and that Bellerive was not a proper course for the Open because it was "too new, too long, too unfair, too inflexible."

For his part, Trent Jones would later write that at Bellerive, "par was the standard that the USGA and I, along with a lot of other purists, feel it should be."

Arnold Palmer and Jack Nicklaus couldn't come close to that standard. Palmer shot a birdie-less 76-76 to miss the cut and Nicklaus opened with a 78 and barely made the cut. But Player, the final member of golf's Big Three, held up his end, and was the most consistent player in the field with two rounds of 70 followed by a pair of 71s for a total of two-over 282.

The toughest hole was the sixth, a 195-yard par three with a narrow green 140 feet long and a pond guarding the front and right. A total of 98 balls found the pond (a dozen from play on the adjacent fifth hole), and the field averaged 3.62 strokes, making it one of the toughest par threes in Open history.

Contributing to that average was the strange adventure of Bob Panasiuk, who hit the green in regulation in the first round but made a nine. He putted his ball off the green and into the water, then forgot about the stroke-and-distance option of replaying the putt. Instead, he dropped on the other side of the hazard and dumped his next shot into the pond.

Nagle's spot in the playoff was partly due to another strange situation in the third round, when a ruling was reversed, saving him a stroke. His drive on the 12th hole ended up 30 yards left of the fair-

17TH HOLE

way in an area he thought might be ground under repair. Officials ruled it wasn't, and Nagle made an apparent bogey with a one-stroke penalty for an unplayable lie. However, officials later discovered that the previous day, Ray Floyd hit a drive that landed within inches of Nagle's and received relief from a burrowing animal hole. They returned to the spot and noticed Nagle's ball had rested against the cast made by that burrowing animal, which should have entitled him to relief. The five became a four.

Player also helped Nagle get into the extra round. Leading by three strokes after Nagle double bogeyed the 15th in the final round, Player gave two shots back with a double bogey of his own on the par-three 16th. At virtually the same time, Nagle birdied the 17th to tie Player and injected some drama into the first color telecast of the U.S. Open. (The 17th was one of the spotty-looking fairways the members dyed green to look better on television, an action that made USGA officials apoplectic.)

Fittingly, the playoff was a dull affair, with Player leading from start to finish. He shot a wonderful 33 on the front nine, winning by three strokes with a 71 after meaningless bogeys on the last two holes. Nagle was never in it after the fifth hole, where his hooked drive hit a woman spectator. When Nagle arrived, she was lying on the ground, bleeding from the head and being attended to by medical staff. Shaken, Nagle badly pulled his next shot, which traveled only 20 yards before striking another fan on the leg, leading to a double bogey. Neither spectator was seriously injured, but Nagle's chances were.

When the PGA Championship came to Bellerive 27 years later, trees that were saplings in 1965 had matured. Oddly enough, the course was shorter at 7,148 yards, even with par increased to 71. The par-four 12th was shortened by 50 yards to relieve gallery congestion and the par-five 17th was reduced from 606 yards to 536, giving players the option of going for the pond-guarded green in two.

The par-three sixth claimed another victim. Gene Sauers, the pace-setter through the first three rounds, dunked his tee shot and made a double bogey to lose the lead for good as Nick Price shot 278 to win by three on a course that was still plenty tough.

Bellerive has just undergone a revision by Trent Jones's son Rees, who also redesigned his father's work at Congressional and Oakland Hills. A pond was added at the second hole while the pond at the 17th was eliminated, a number of tees were moved back, and all the green complexes rebuilt.

That was the second step taken with an eye on landing a future Open. The first was hosting the 2004 U.S. Senior Open, which Peter Jacobsen took after Tom Kite lost the lead by playing the last four holes in four-over, including a double bogey on the 18th. Once again at merciless Bellerive, double bogeys had as much to do with the outcome as birdies.

1965 TOP FINISHERS

•Gary Player	70-70-71-71—282
Kel Nagle	68-73-72-69—282
Frank Beard	74-69-70-71—284
Julius Boros	72-75-70-70—287
Al Geiberger	70-76-70-71—287
Bruce Devlin	72-73-72-71—288
Raymond Floyd	72-72-76-68—288
Tony Lema	72-74-73-70—289
Gene Littler	73-71-73-72—289
Dudley Wysong	72-75-70-72—289

•Player won playoff, 71-74
Low round: Nagle, Floyd, 68

Scorecard

Hole	Par	Yardage 1965 Open	Yardage 1992 PGA	Yardage• Today
1	4	435	434	435
2	4	436	437	411
3	3	164	165	187
4	4/5/5	470	556	570
5	4	465	453	475
6	3	195	195	210
7	4	401	381	380
8	5	580	581	620
9	4	416	426	445
Out	35/36/36	3562	3628	3733
10	4/4/5	460	485	522
11	4	373	373	376
12	4	460	404	485
13	3	198	179	184
14	4	405	411	415
15	4	456	456	498
16	3	218	222	235
17	5	606	536	605
18	4	453	435	464
In	35/35/36	3629	3520	3784
Total	70/71/72	7191	7148	7517

• Nos. 4 and 10 could play as par fours of approximately 500 yards for championships, resulting in a par-70 course of some 7,425 yards.

5TH HOLE. OPPOSITE: 4TH HOLE

BETHPAGE STATE PARK (BLACK COURSE) FARMINGDALE, NEW YORK 2002, 2009

It was certainly the loudest site in U.S. Open history. But the enthusiastic gallery that brought Open decibel levels to new heights really did have something to shout about. When all the reviews were in, Long Island's Bethpage Black, the first truly public course to host the championship, had moved near the top of the unofficial list of best Open sites. Its 2002 debut was so successful the USGA waited only a few months before announcing its return in 2009. ¶ Such a scenario would hardly have seemed likely to anyone playing the course as recently as the early 1990s. It's not that the Black wasn't a worthy design. A.W. Tillinghast created a masterful layout much admired among golf's cognoscenti. The problem was that whereas other Tillinghast courses such as Winged Foot and Baltusrol were polished gems, Bethpage was a diamond very much in the rough. The course, part of the New York State Parks system, suffered from an inadequate maintenance budget. Calling it scruffy is being kind.

Enter David Fay, executive director of the USGA and a strong proponent of playing the U.S. Open on a public course. "You look at the landscape of American golf, and most of the people who play the game play at public facilities," he said. The USGA was trying to change its image from an organization for the private clubs. What better way than with a "People's Open"?

The Open had been to a couple of courses that are open to the public. But Pebble Beach and Pinehurst No. 2 are resorts with lofty green fees and restricted access. No true daily-fee or government-owned facility had ever hosted, in no small part because none was considered challenging or well-groomed enough.

Bethpage Black was certainly tough enough. "Without doubt, were the other three courses at Bethpage as severe as Black, the place would not enjoy the great popularity it has known," Tillinghast wrote a couple of years after the course opened. "If they had to play under such punishing conditions week in and out, they'd probably chuck their clubs into the lake and take to pitching horseshoes." In fact, a sign by the first tee warns that it is "recommended only for highly skilled golfers."

Fay, who grew up in the New York City area and was familiar with Black, thought it Open-worthy. A couple of people whose judgment he trusted backed up his opinion. Jay Mottola, executive director of the Metropolitan Golf Association and a friend of Fay's since childhood, told him after the MGA held its Met Open at the Black in 1989 that the course could host the U.S. Open. George Zahringer, one of the area's top amateurs, expressed the same sentiment.

Zahringer, who would win the 2002 U.S. Mid-Amateur Championship, had played most of the great private courses in the New York area. "Whatever I had heard about [Bethpage Black] couldn't begin to do justice to the real thing," Zahringer later said. "It was sensational. Sure, it was beat up. But to me, it was like looking at a great house that's fallen into disrepair."

10TH HOLE

Fay let those suggestions simmer until the spring of 1995, when he arranged for an outing at the Black for three foursomes of key USGA personnel plus a few special guests, including Rees Jones, known as the "Open Doctor" because of his redesign and restoration work on several U.S. Open courses.

The group found tees with more dirt than grass, patchy fairways, bumpy greens, and bunkers into which so much sand had been dumped it was almost like quicksand. There were few rakes, but with Tom Meeks, one of the organization's top Rules men, on hand, nobody dared move his ball out of a footprint. The verdict? They all loved it.

"You could see that architecturally, it was way above and beyond any public course that I'd ever seen," said Meeks, who came away with a favorable impression despite a bad experience in a greenside bunker at the third hole, where he took several swings and was unable to escape the soft sand.

They knew money would take care of the conditioning. But they also knew it would take a *lot* of money. Realistically, the only way to get the course in U.S. Open condition would be for the USGA to fund the improvements itself.

"I knew the state couldn't pay for it," Fay said. "Some guy in Syracuse wasn't going to feel warm and fuzzy about the state dumping $3 million into some golf course on Long Island."

Since 1986, the USGA had become more involved in the operations aspect of the championship, which also meant netting more of the profits. USGA officials knew an Open so close to New York City would attract plenty of corporate support, enabling them to recoup their investment. Also, Fay believed that holding the Open at a truly public course was an idea worth spending some money on.

Fay met with state officials and promised $2.7 million for the course renovation. (The final tab was close to $4 million.) In return, the state promised it would increase its budget to maintain the course properly after the Open and would not unreasonably raise green fees. (Currently they run $31 on weekdays and $39 on weekends for state residents.)

The deal wasn't quite done, though, because Fay and his staff don't actually select Open courses. They just make recommendations to the executive committee. In another outing arranged by Fay, the Black again was its own best salesman. Once the committee saw the course, any skepticism melted away.

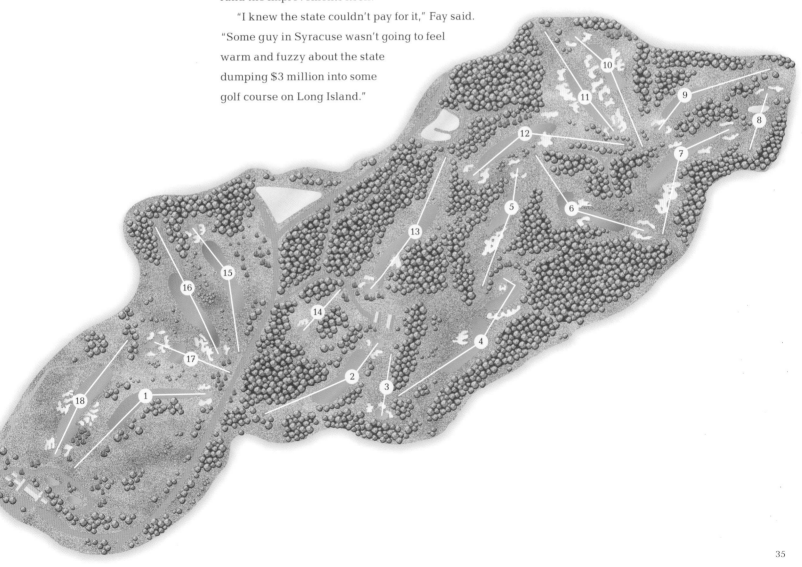

The renovation would have carried an even larger price tag had Jones, a big fan of Tillinghast's work, not agreed to work for free. "It's more of an honor than a job," he said.

In a way, Jones felt he was completing the task Tillinghast had started more than 60 years previously. Built during the Depression, the courses at Bethpage were the Golden Age architect's last project. Unlike most of his earlier designs, Tillinghast was not involved at the construction stage, so his personal stamp was not as strong at Bethpage as it was at other Open courses like Baltusrol and Winged Foot.

Instead, the construction work was carried out by Joseph Burbeck, the superintendent of Bethpage State Park. A 2002 article in *Golf Digest* even suggested Burbeck was the real designer, while Tillinghast was just a consultant, despite a lack of proof other than Burbeck family lore. In fact, the original plans for the course are missing. Nearly all the experts, however, believe Tillinghast was responsible for the design and its brilliant routing. Tillinghast himself gave credit to Burbeck for the idea of making the Black an extremely challenging course, and, as the man on the scene, Burbeck certainly had some influence on the finished product.

The four courses at Bethpage (a fifth was built later) were a major Work Relief project, employing 1,800 people. Black was the last of the four to open, in 1936, and was an immediate hit. It hosted

big names for two exhibitions within its first few years, both involving Sam Snead. (Contrary to local legend, he didn't walk off the course in disgust at either.) But over the years, the course began to deteriorate, especially during the budget crunch of the 1970s and afterward given the small maintenance staff.

When Jones began his work, his guide was a 1938 aerial photo, which showed that neglect had caused changes. Some bunkers, including the large ones between the 10th and 11th fairways, had been overgrown with scrub or even saplings. Other large bunkers had transformed into several small bunkers, perhaps due to rain damage. Artfully sculpted bunkers had become rounded off and dull.

The redesign focused on the vast bunkers, the most striking visual feature and the most important strategic element of the course. The original greenside bunkers were a bit away from the greens. Nobody is quite sure if this was because it was a public course, or even whether it was Tillinghast's intention at all. But if the course were to host the U.S. Open, the bunkers needed to be moved right up against the greens, and the fingers and noses that made them so interesting restored. Jones's crew visited Winged Foot to get an idea of Tillinghast's bunker style.

The fairway bunkers were moved forward and the tees backward to bring the sand into play as much as possible. In fact, lengthening the course

14TH HOLE

15TH HOLE

was a two-step process. A couple of years after the 1997–98 renovation, driving distance increased dramatically on the PGA Tour. Black always had been considered a long course, but it now didn't seem so long, even after every tee but the first had been moved back. So Jones built new tees on several holes to replace those built just a couple of years earlier, resulting in a 7,214-yard layout, the longest in Open history at the time.

Still, there was concern in some quarters that the pros would burn up the Black Course with record scoring. Even USGA officials were predicting a below-normal winning score of six- to eight-under par, partly because the bunkers, such an intimidating feature for amateurs, don't scare the pros. But mostly it was due to the greens, which are relatively flat compared to other Open—and Tillinghast—courses.

Again, it's not certain to what degree this was originally intended. If Tillinghast had been present, or if there had been more money for construction, would more slopes have been built into them? It's impossible to know. In any case, the USGA decided to leave the greens pretty much alone in the redesign.

It proved to be a wise decision. In fact, the relatively gentle slopes on the greens were a perfect match for modern agronomy. The USGA and superintendent Craig Currier were able to make the greens as fast as they wanted without worrying about balls trickling 30 feet down a slope after nearly stopping close to the hole. Open courses

with undulating greens have a "speed limit." At the Black, green speeds started at about 12 on the Stimpmeter in the first round and, by all accounts, were approaching 15 by Sunday. At those speeds, even level putts were treacherous.

Instead of being one of the easiest Open courses ever, the Black won raves as one of the most challenging. Only the winner, Tiger Woods, broke par for 72 holes, shooting three-under 277 to finish three ahead of Phil Mickelson.

There was another significant factor in the Black's resistance to scoring. The rough was the thickest and nastiest in years, making it nearly impossible to reach the green after a wayward drive on the long par fours. It was a measure of how much the players liked the course that there were few complaints about the severity of the rough.

There was some justifiable criticism about the USGA's inflexibility in setting up the 10th and 12th holes, especially during a cold, rainy second round. The championship tee on the 10th called for a 250-yard carry just to reach the fairway. In the second round, when the ball was not flying well in the cold and the hole played into the breeze, a significant portion of the field wasn't able to reach the fairway. Similarly, the USGA decided to play the 12th at its full 499 yards all four days.

USGA officials later admitted the tees should have been moved up on the 10th and 12th holes, at least in the second round, and the 10th has since been changed with the fairway now beginning 20 yards closer to the tee. But that pair of holes aside,

17TH HOLE

Bethpage was one of the fairest tests of driving ability in Open history, rewarding length (because of the long par fours) and accuracy (because of the unfriendly rough) in equal measure.

While the first three holes are fine, the fourth tee is where most golfers have their "Wow!" moment. The view is dominated by an impressive cross bunker about 360 yards out on a slope separating the lower fairway from the upper portion on the 517-yard par five. The 100-yard-wide bunker is artfully shaped with grass fingers and noses.

In addition to being visually appealing, the fourth is impeccably designed. The mid-handicapper needs to hit a good drive and solid second to carry the cross bunker, but the pros usually have no problem with the bunker even if they miss the fairway. The challenge for the pros lies in holding the firm, shallow green with the second shot. Tillinghast has provided a fairway to the right of the green that provides an easy pitch for those who can avoid the temptation of trying to get home in two.

The 451-yard fifth is another of the Black's great holes, both visually and strategically, with a huge bunker to the right of the fairway and trees jutting out on the left between the landing area and the green, which sits on a hill. In truth, it's a better and tougher hole for amateurs than it was for the pros in the 2002 Open, simply because the bunker wasn't in play for most of them. But the hole still ranked as the fifth toughest and likely will be more difficult in 2009, as a new tee will bring the bunker into play.

The 2002 Open was the first in which players started from both the first and 10th tees, and starting on No. 10, with its 250-yard carry to the fairway, was no fun at all. This hole and the parallel 11th have a links-like feel with dunes and bunkers between them on the left on each hole—the ones that had been abandoned before being restored by Jones.

The 12th raised concerns when USGA officials watched the New York State Open at Bethpage in 2001. Players at that event—local club pros and amateurs—were flying the bunker at the dogleg and hitting short irons into what was supposed to be a tough hole, so the tee was extended back to make it play 499 yards, the longest par four in U.S. Open history. This created a 243-yard carry over a bunker with a tall face that guarded almost the entire corner of the dogleg. For short hitters unable to carry that bunker, there is no good way to play the hole—they have to lay up with a 3-wood to the right of the bunker to avoid going through the fairway, from where it is virtually unreachable in two.

The 554-yard 13th and 161-yard 14th are breathers. Long to medium hitters can get home in two at the 13th, as Woods did in the final round to make a key birdie that gave him a cushion. The downhill 161-yard 14th is a rarity, a par three that played as the easiest hole with a 2.903 average.

"You don't want to make every hole impossible, you want to have an ebb and flow," Jones says. "Bethpage is a good example. A third of the holes are hard to par, a third are swing holes, and on the other third you have good birdie opportunities."

The easiest hole is followed by the toughest. The 459-yard 15th played to a 4.6 average in 2002, even though there is a tee 20 yards farther back the USGA didn't use. The green is elevated and unlike most on the course, has a severe slope, effectively reducing the target area because the ball won't stay on the front half of the green.

The 16th is 20 yards longer but plays shorter because it is downhill. Sand is the dominant feature on the 207-yard 17th, a visually arresting par three. It's the widest green on the course, but also the shallowest.

Jones made more changes to the 18th than any other hole. Not only short at 360 yards, it also was bland. Jones stretched it to 411 yards, still not particularly long, but turned it into a photogenic, narrow driving hole by building no fewer than 12 irregularly shaped fairway bunkers close to the landing area.

An Open Moment

Playing out of the rough was no picnic at Bethpage, but leave it to champion Tiger Woods to make it look easy. In the second round, Woods's tee shot on the par-three 17th bounced over the green into a terrible lie in the long stuff—the ball was only visible from directly over it—facing a delicate downhill shot. Somehow he lofted it so high that it managed to land softly and trickle to the hole, nearly going in before settling a couple of feet away for an unlikely par. The shot was so good that Woods's caddie, Steve Williams, gave him a hug. Woods went on to birdie the 18th for a 68 in the cold, wet conditions, a round that gave him a three-stroke lead over second place Padraig Harrington and a seven-stroke margin on the rest of the field.

TIGER WOODS

Players have the option of laying up short of all the bunkers, leaving a 170-yard shot to an elevated green shrunk to just over half its original size, or hitting a 3-wood to leave a slightly shorter approach. With the fairway narrowing to a skinny neck at 290 yards, hitting driver is not really an option. Although not the ultra-demanding finish seen at many Open sites, it's enough to keep a player on his toes—and also give him a chance for a birdie.

It never hurts the reputation of a course to have the best player in the world win there. Woods's victory was his seventh in a span of 11 majors. But there was more to the event's success than his win or the quality of the course. There was also the enthusiasm of the fans, sparked in part by watching the pros tackle a course anyone can play.

The atmosphere, unlike any golf tournament ever, was more like a football game, with not only deafening roars for birdies, but also chants and shouts encouraging fan favorites as they walked to the greens or tees. The most beloved player was Mickelson, then still chasing that elusive first major title he would finally capture at the 2004 Masters, who was spurred on by chants of "Let's Go Mick-el-son!"

There were surprisingly few incidents of fans crossing the line and bothering players, though they did wage a battle of sorts with Sergio Garcia in the second round. Impatient with his habit of regripping the club numerous times before each shot, some fans began to count out the "milking" maneuvers. Garcia eventually responded with an obscene gesture, then compounded his image problem by complaining after the round that officials

Scorecard

2002 U.S. Open

Hole	Par	Yardage	Avg.	Rank	Fwy.%	Green%	Putts
1	4	430	4.259	9	52.7	46.4	1.65
2	4	389	4.204	13	67.6	55.8	1.69
3	3	205	3.211	12		55.4	1.70
4	5	517	5.011	16	60.0	67.9	1.63
5	4	451	4.422	5	63.3	36.7	1.64
6	4	408	4.202	14	62.9	54.1	1.67
7	4	489	4.479	4	62.2	27.1	1.64
8	3	210	3.334	8		65.3	1.91
9	4	418	4.086	15	60.4	60.7	1.64
Out	35	3517	37.208		61.3	52.1	1.68
10	4	492	4.499	3	58.5	27.9	1.63
11	4	435	4.376	7	54.5	38.9	1.59
12	4	499	4.523	2	56.0	38.0	1.59
13	5	554	4.941	17	56.0	73.2	1.69
14	3	161	2.903	18		77.4	1.65
15	4	459	4.600	1	58.0	38.0	1.80
16	4	479	4.411	6	57.8	38.7	1.72
17	3	207	3.224	10		57.5	1.73
18	4	411	4.220	11	58.9	53.4	1.67
In	35	3697	37.697		57.1	49.2	1.70
Total	70	7214	74.905		59.2	50.7	1.69

would have stopped play because of the rain if Woods had still been on the course. (Woods, who played in the morning, essentially won the championship with a 68 in Friday's terrible conditions.)

Play wasn't halted despite the steady rain because the sandy soil of Bethpage drains so well—the same reason the greens were so firm and fast for the weekend despite Friday's rain. Garcia, who finished fourth, apologized to Woods, good-naturedly took the fans' barbs on Saturday, and smiled with them by Sunday. On such a feel-good week, there was no reason for anyone to leave Bethpage on a sour note.

2002 TOP FINISHERS

Tiger Woods	67-68-70-72—277
Phil Mickelson	70-73-67-70—280
Jeff Maggert	69-73-68-72—282
Sergio Garcia	68-74-67-74—283
Scott Hoch	71-75-70-69—285
Billy Mayfair	69-74-68-74—285
Nick Faldo	70-76-66-73—285
Tom Byrum	72-72-70-72—286
Nick Price	72-75-69-70—286
Padraig Harrington	70-68-73-75—286

Low round: Faldo, 66

18TH HOLE

WALTER HAGEN HOLES OUT ON 18 TO BEAT MIKE BRADY IN A PLAYOFF. OPPOSITE: 8TH HOLE

BRAE BURN COUNTRY CLUB WEST NEWTON, MASSACHUSETTS 1919

The 1919 U.S. Open at Brae Burn was the first of many to be contested on a course designed or redesigned by Donald Ross. In fact, it started a string of eight of 13 Opens played on Ross courses through 1931. ¶ Ross immigrated to the United States from Scotland in 1899 and for many years lived in Massachusetts during the summer and North Carolina in the winter. He already had designed several courses in the Boston area when he was called on by Brae Burn to redesign its course in 1912. The club was founded in 1897 as a nine-hole course and expanded to 18 holes in 1902. ¶ The land was rather challenging for designing a golf course because it was marked by a number of steep slopes. As Brad Klein points out in *Discovering Donald Ross*, the architect employed the strategy of using the flatter ground for long par fours and par fives and steeper ground for short par fours and par threes. Ross retained nine holes from the original 18-hole course and built nine new ones. ¶ The course is noteworthy for a number of short, well-designed par fours, many of which are difficult for their length. There

are a couple of very long par threes, the 225-yard eighth and 255-yard 17th, but the overall lack of length (currently 6,527 yards from the back tees) is the main reason the club has hosted only one Open. Brae Burn was the site of the 1928 U.S. Amateur won by Bobby Jones and, more recently, the 1975 and 1997 U.S. Women's Amateurs. Ross redesigned four holes for the 1928 U.S. Amateur and made some minor changes in 1947, the year before he died.

The 1919 win marked the second of Walter Hagen's two U.S. Open victories, but, frankly, it should really be remembered as the Open that Mike Brady lost. For Brady, a local favorite from nearby Oakley Country Club, this was the best of several chances to win an Open, but he was destined never to come through. He lost in a playoff to John McDermott in 1911, squandered a three-stroke lead in the final round in 1912, and entered the final round in 1915 one stroke back before faltering.

This time he took a five-stroke lead with an outstanding 73 in the third round, but closed with an 80 to let Hagen catch him at 301 for 72 holes before losing the playoff the next day, 77-78. It's the largest 54-hole lead ever squandered at the Open.

A. Linde Fowler, reporting on the championship for *The American Golfer,* wrote, "if the brilliant-playing Boston professional could have kept his mind free of all thought of what his rivals were doing, especially Hagen, it is almost certain that he could have won." But Brady spent much of the final round asking his friends how other leading contenders were doing and even trying to see some of their shots, and "a man cannot do these things and concentrate thoroughly on his own game."

Hagen teed off well behind Brady on the 36-hole final day, finishing his third round just before Brady finished his last. Hagen would shoot a 37 on the final nine to Brady's 41, with pars on the last six holes when he knew that was what he needed to do to force a tie. "His courage was best shown on those putts which try the golfer's soul, the three to five footers which had been missed so frequently by nearly every man in the field," wrote Fowler.

Hagen hit a wonderful approach to eight feet on the 18th and had a birdie putt to beat Brady. Legend has it that master showman Hagen called for Brady to come out of the clubhouse to watch him putt, but the attempt rimmed the hole and stayed out.

More Hagen tales from the playoff, told by Hagen himself in *The Walter Hagen Story*, had Sir Walter partying all night with singer Al Jolson and heading straight to the course, then telling Brady on the second tee to roll down his sleeves, "so the gallery won't see your arms shaking." It should be remembered, though, that Hagen wasn't above embellishing his own legend.

It's hard to determine precisely what happened at a key moment in the playoff, when Hagen found his ball buried deep in the muck on the 17th hole. Contemporary accounts report that an official turned the ball for identification, loosening it slightly. Hagen, in his book, wrote that he lifted the ball to identify it and replaced it gently in the hole so that it didn't fall all the way to the bottom.

17TH HOLE

Through time, others have exaggerated that version to say Hagen replaced the ball to give himself a nice lie. The latter version certainly isn't true, as Hagen had to take a mighty swipe, sending mud flying, to extricate the ball. He ended up making a five on the 255-yard hole to take a one-stroke lead to the final hole.

There, Hagen topped his drive, barely clearing a creek 80 yards in front of the tee, but nailed a fairway wood close to the green, chipped on, and holed a three-footer for par after Brady nearly holed his chip shot for birdie.

The playoff was marked by another odd Rules incident. Hagen was cruising with a four-stroke lead on the 11th hole when a Brady supporter noticed Hagen moving a match cover more than a club-length from his ball in the fairway. A player was then allowed to move a loose impediment only from *within* a club-length (a match cover was then considered a loose impediment instead of a moveable obstruction).

When Brady holed a long birdie putt and Hagen was penalized two strokes, the margin was suddenly cut to one. Brady birdied the 12th, and it was now even—or so it seemed. In the meanwhile, a Hagen supporter said he noticed Brady move a stone on a previous hole in violation of the same Rule. On the 13th hole came word that neither penalty would be enforced, and Hagen was back ahead by two.

In the first round, a Scotsman named Willie Chisholm made the second-highest score on a hole in U.S. Open history, an 18 on the par-three eighth. (Ray Ainsley made a 19 on the par-four 16th at Cherry Hills in 1938.) Chisholm hit his tee shot into a rocky ravine and had trouble getting out of it. The story goes that when his fellow competitor and marker Jim Barnes told him he counted 18 strokes, Chisholm replied, "Oh, Jim, that can't be! You must have been counting the echoes." Chisholm withdrew without turning in his scorecard. In the 1970s, the club cleaned out the ravine, so it is now all grass.

1919 TOP FINISHERS

*Walter Hagen	78-73-75-75—301
Mike Brady	74-74-73-80—301
Jock Hutchison	78-76-76-76—306
Tom McNamara	80-73-79-74—306
George McLean	81-75-76-76—308
Louis Tellier	73-78-82-75—308

*Hagen won playoff, 77-78

Low round: Charles Hoffner, 72

Scorecard

HOLE	PAR	YARDAGE 1919 OPEN	YARDAGE TODAY
1	4	337	320
2	4	293	308
3	4	375	365
4	4	393	437
5	5	558	568
6	3	150	159
7	4	394	405
8	3	203	225
9	4	299	293
Out	35	3002	3080
10	5	491	482
11	4	442	445
12	4/3	385	169
13	3/5	190	470
14	5	550	555
15	4	311	310
16	4	409	358
17	3	255	255
18	4	400	403
In	36/37	3433	3447
Total	71/72	6435	6527

GROVER CLEVELAND PARK, 18TH HOLE

COUNTRY CLUB OF BUFFALO   BUFFALO, NEW YORK   1912

Want to play a U.S. Open course for $14? The place to go is Grover Cleveland Park on the border

of the city of Buffalo and the town of Amherst. Of course, you won't be playing *exactly* the same

course. For the 1912 U.S. Open, this was the Country Club of Buffalo course, playing to 6,250

yards. It's now an Erie County facility that measures 5,621 yards. The Country Club of Buffalo

moved from the site in 1926, when it opened a Donald Ross course at a new location. ¶ The club,

inspired by The Country Club outside Boston, opened in 1889, though golf did not start until

1894. The first course was a rudimentary nine-holer, but three of its holes were redesigned on

the suggestion of C.B. Macdonald, one of the pioneers of golf-course design in America. In 1901,

that course was abandoned when the organizers of the Pan-American Exposition secured

the property. ¶ So the club purchased land at the corner of Main Street and Bailey Avenue,

with nine holes opening in 1901 and nine more in 1905. Ganson Depew, a local man, laid

out the course, and by 1910, Walter J. Travis was brought in to improve it with an eye on

Scorecard

1912 U.S. Open

Hole	Par	Yardage
1	4	345
2	4	315
3	4	380
4	4	380
5	5	455
6	4	300
7	3	125
8	5	430
9	4	300
Out	37	3030
10	6	606
11	4	350
12	4	340
13	3	210
14	3	170
15	5	516
16	3	155
17	5	540
18	4	333
In	37	3220
Total	74	6250

Scorecard

Today
Grover Cleveland Park

Hole*	Par	Yardage
1 (1)	4	350
2 (2)	4	422
3	3	160
4 (5)	4	415
5 (6)	4	320
6	3	230
7	3	194
8 (10)	5	483
9 (11)	4	380
Out	34	2954
10 (12)	4	312
11 (13, 14)	4	339
12 (15)	5	524
13 (16)	3	142
14	4	319
15	4	300
16	4	260
17	3	146
18 (18)	4	325
In	35	2667
Total	69	5621

*Hole numbers from 1912 in parentheses

luring the U.S. Open. Travis was a three-time U.S. Amateur champion who, along with Macdonald, was one of the first American golf architects. The plan worked, and Travis finished 10th and was low amateur at the 1912 Open.

The championship was won by John McDermott, who had become the first American-born player to take the title the previous year. Although he was only 21 when he won his second championship, McDermott played in only two more Opens and suffered an emotional breakdown in 1915, spending the rest of his life in institutions. McDermott had a disastrous start to the 36-hole final day in 1912, pulling his first two tee shots out of bounds on the first hole. Fortunately, an out-of-bounds shot called for a distance-only penalty in those days, and he managed a double-bogey six. McDermott shot rounds of 74-71 to finish at two-under 294, and held off Tom McNamara, who closed with a course-record 69 but ended up two back.

This was the first year that par became an official standard at the Open. As such, the Country Club of Buffalo played to a par of 74 and the 606-yard 10th was the only par six in the history of the U.S. Open. But McDermott made a mockery of that tag, playing the hole in 4-5-4-5, six-under over four rounds.

Major Jay J. Morrow, writing in the September 1913 issue of *The American Golfer,* pointed out that, based on statistics from the 1912 Open, par was wrong on a couple of holes at Buffalo, including the 10th. The scorecards of the top 12 finishers showed that they made seven fours, 32 fives, and only nine

scores of six or higher on the 10th. Obviously, the determination of par was still a work in progress.

There have been two redesigns of the course since it hosted the Open. In 1918, land that was formerly a polo field was incorporated into the course and several holes were redesigned to reduce congestion, bringing par to a more modern 71. But within a decade the club decided to purchase land farther from the city, in Williamsville, and build a bigger course. The site at Main and Bailey was sold to the City of Buffalo for $800,000 in 1926 to become part of Grover Cleveland Park, which was later taken over by the county.

The newly public course hosted the 1926 U.S. Public Links Championship. Unfortunately for the course, land that contained two holes and part of a third was sold for the construction of a Veteran Affairs hospital in 1950, and the course shrank to its current size. The ground that was lost included the first portion of the old 606-yard 10th, which now plays as the 483-yard eighth. Ten holes of today's course cover the same route as holes from the 1912 Open, with another hole combining two holes.

1912 TOP FINISHERS

John McDermott	74-75-74-71—294
Tom McNamara	74-80-73-69—296
Mike Brady	72-75-73-79—299
Alex Smith	77-70-77-75—299
Alex Campbell	74-77-80-71—302

Low round: McNamara, 69

CLUBHOUSE IN ABOUT 1913

LLOYD MANGRUM (SECOND FROM RIGHT) CELEBRATES HIS 1946 WIN TWO DAYS LATER AT TOOTS SHORS IN NEW YORK. OPPOSITE TOP: 15TH HOLE. OPPOSITE BOTTOM: 18TH HOLE

CANTERBURY GOLF CLUB CLEVELAND, OHIO 1940, 1946

For a brief stretch, it looked as if the USGA couldn't stay away from Canterbury Golf Club, which hosted two U.S. Opens practically back-to-back in the 1940s. Oddly enough, those were the only two Opens ever hosted by the Cleveland club. ¶ The 1940 Open at Canterbury was the next-to-last played before World War II—Colonial Country Club in Fort Worth, Texas, hosted in 1941 before the event took a hiatus until 1946, when it came right back to Canterbury. The club hasn't stayed completely out of the limelight since, hosting the 1973 PGA Champion-ship, the 1964 and 1979 U.S. Amateurs, and the 1996 U.S. Senior Open. And it's still ranked on lists of the top 100 courses in the country. ¶ Canterbury opened in 1922, designed by Herbert Strong, an English professional who gravitated into golf design after immigrating to the United States. The club's crest is based on that of the city of Canterbury in England, but there is a degree of separation. The club was actually named after the town in Connecticut that was the birthplace of Moses Cleaveland, who founded the city of Cleveland in 1796.

Extensive changes to the back nine were made in 1927–28, for which Jack Way, who was then the pro, receives much of the credit. Since then, the course has remained largely unchanged. It currently measures 6,942 yards, just 21 yards longer than it did for the 1946 Open.

Canterbury was built on high ground 600 feet above Lake Erie, so the wind can be a factor. The land is rolling and the green complexes are designed to punish inaccurate approach shots. Henry Picard, who played in both Canterbury Opens, called it a course with 12 "backbreakers," the first nine holes and especially the last three.

When it was played at 615 yards in 1946, the 16th was then the longest par five in Open history. In fact, the back tee was considered too long in 1940 and the hole was set up at 588 yards, but the committee did not feel so kind six years later. Virtually unchanged, the 16th is now officially listed at 611 yards, still a three-shot hole. The first shot is downhill, the second uphill on the rollercoaster fairway, which proceeds straight for 470 yards before making a slight dogleg to the right.

Nos. 17 and 18 are the two toughest holes on the course. The 229-yard 17th called for a wood from most of the Open competitors, with the hole playing over a valley back up to a green that is slightly higher than the tee. The 18th is difficult both to walk and to play at 439 uphill yards. Standing on the tee of this hole during a driving rainstorm in a three-man playoff in 1946, eventual winner Lloyd Mangrum said, "Anyone who gets a four here is a miracle man." Byron Nelson did get a four, but he came to the hole with a two-stroke deficit; Mangrum and Vic Ghezzi both made fives as Mangrum won by one.

The 1940 Open was won by Lawson Little, who had created a sensation earlier by sweeping the U.S. and British Amateurs in 1934 and 1935, an unprecedented feat. The burly Little turned pro in 1936 and is widely "credited" with being responsible for a 1938 Rules change limiting players to 14 clubs, as he was known to carry more than 20 clubs, with an implement for every type of shot he might face around the green.

Little's title was almost stolen by Gene Sarazen, who at 38 was looking for a third Open to go with the ones he had captured in 1922 and 1932. Sarazen, with a late starting time, knew he needed a 34 on the back nine to catch Little—an unlikely prospect. But he did just that, holing a 30-foot putt for a par on the 17th and nearly sinking a 60-footer for a birdie on 18.

In the playoff, however, Little was razor-sharp, seldom missing a green, while Sarazen, according to the *New York Times*, after playing 10 years younger than his age at the end of regulation, "was his age, with a few years added." Spraying the ball all over the course, Sarazen holed three shots from off the greens but still lost 70-73.

9TH HOLE AT THE 1940 U.S. OPEN

There was plenty of heartbreak in this Open. Ed "Porky" Oliver, a likeable 230-pounder, was disqualified, along with five others, for starting the final round before his scheduled tee time in advance of an approaching storm. The players were on the first fairway when they were disqualified, but they finished the round, hoping for a reversal. Oliver ended up with a 287 total that would have put him in the playoff, but the ruling stood.

And Sam Snead, who had blown the Open the previous year by making an eight on the 72nd hole, came crashing down again. This time he led after the first round with a 67 and trailed by one after three rounds, only to close with an 81 to finish 16th.

The 1946 Open also was marked by sad tales, particularly regarding Ben Hogan and Byron Nelson, the pre-tournament favorites. Hogan, who would win 13 times in 1946, three-putted the 18th from 18 feet, failing on the second from two feet, to finish one shot out of the playoff. Nelson, winner of a record 18 tournaments the year before and playing in the last full season of his career, stumbled into the playoff with bogeys on the last two holes, including a missed three-footer on the 17th.

Even worse, Nelson suffered a one-stroke penalty on the 13th hole of the third round when his caddie accidentally kicked his ball, although it wasn't really his fault. There were no fixed gallery ropes, and the marshals who held a rope to keep fans away from the area of Nelson's shot were too close to the ball, so that as soon as his caddie fought through the crowd and ducked under the rope, he kicked the ball without seeing it.

The playoff was tense and ended up lasting all day, with Mangrum, Nelson, and Ghezzi almost never separated by more than two strokes. All shot even-par 72 in the morning and headed out for another 18-hole playoff. It was a lingering death for Nelson and Ghezzi, as each held a fleeting share of the lead during the second playoff round.

Mangrum stayed alive by holing a 60-foot putt for a bogey after driving out of bounds on the par-five ninth, gained control with three birdies in a four-hole stretch on the back, and held on despite bogeys on the last two holes for another 72, to 73 each for Nelson and Ghezzi. It was a surreal finish, as hard rain pelted down and lightning flashed all around—a kind of potential sudden-death that they apparently weren't worried about in those days.

1940 TOP FINISHERS

*Lawson Little	72-69-73-73—287
Gene Sarazen	71-74-70-72—287
Horton Smith	69-72-78-69—288
Craig Wood	72-73-72-72—289
Ralph Guldahl	73-71-76-70—290
Ben Hogan	70-73-74-73—290
Lloyd Mangrum	75-70-71-74—290
Byron Nelson	72-74-70-74—290

*Little won playoff, 70-73
Low round: Sam Snead, 67

1946 TOP FINISHERS

*Lloyd Mangrum	74-70-68-72—284
Vic Ghezzi	71-69-72-72—284
Byron Nelson	71-71-69-73—284
Herman Barron	72-72-72-69—285
Ben Hogan	72-68-73-72—285
Jimmy Demaret	71-74-73-68—286
Edward Oliver	71-71-74-70—286
Chick Harbert	72-78-67-70—287
Dick Metz	76-70-72-69—287
Dutch Harrison	75-71-72-70—288
Lawson Little	72-69-76-71—288

*Mangrum won playoff with 72-72, Ghezzi 72-73, Nelson 72-73
Low round: Harbert, Chandler Harper, 67

Scorecard

Hole	Par	Yardage 1946 Open	Yardage Today
1	4	430	432
2	4	369	367
3	3	176	177
4	4	440	452
5	4	410	412
6	5	477	522
7	3	200	201
8	4	412	410
9	5	553	552
Out	36	3467	3525
10	4	367	344
11	3	170	180
12	4	374	373
13	5	483	490
14	4	403	384
15	4	371	367
16	5	615	611
17	3	230	229
18	4	441	439
In	36	3454	3417
Total	72	6921	6942

ORVILLE MOODY SET TO STROKE HIS FINAL PUTT.
OPPOSITE TOP: 1ST HOLE. OPPOSITE BOTTOM: 4TH HOLE.

CHAMPIONS GOLF CLUB (CYPRESS CREEK COURSE) HOUSTON, TEXAS 1969

The champions behind Champions were Jimmy Demaret and Jack Burke Jr., a pair of successful pros from Houston who traveled together in the 1940s and 1950s when the automobile was the mode of transportation on the PGA Tour. To ease their boredom on drives that stretched for many hours, they would speculate about the types of golf holes they could build on the land they were passing. ¶ By 1956, the 46-year-old Demaret was looking to retire, while Burke, though only 33, was looking to spend more time at home with his growing family. So they decided to put their ideas into practice and build a golf course in their hometown. Well, not exactly "in." The land they acquired was perfect for golf, but it was 25 miles from downtown. Moreover, it was northwest of the city, the wrong side of town for an upscale development. ¶ But Demaret and Burke proved to be visionary developers. They knew a new international airport was coming to that side of Houston, along with freeways. Land was cheap because their site was remote, so they and their investors also were able to develop housing. Soon, the area began to boom, in which Champions played no small part.

One of the key men in the project was a young Houston advertising executive named Jack Valenti, who would later become an advisor to Lyndon Johnson and then the president of the Motion Picture Association of America. He helped recruit members and also suggested the name Champions, which Demaret and Burke didn't like it at first, thinking it sounded too immodest.

The colorful, gregarious Demaret and the opinionated, sometimes irascible Burke made an odd couple. Demaret first caddied then became an assistant pro at age 16 at River Oaks Country Club, where Burke's father was the head pro. Demaret spend a lot of time at the Burke house, and young Jackie knew him as "Uncle Jim." Together, they accounted for 48 victories (31 by Demaret, 17 by Burke) and five majors (three Masters for Demaret, the 1956 Masters and PGA Championship for Burke).

They became heavily involved in all aspects of building, then running, Champions, which was—and is—very much a golf club, not a country club, with a membership of serious players and an unusually high proportion of low handicappers.

For designing the golf course, they selected Texas architect Ralph Plummer, a former protégé of Colonial designer John Bredemus. The course had to be cleared out of a dense pine forest. "I couldn't see more than six feet ahead of me when I first laid eyes on the property," Burke said. Trees, bunkers, and a liberal dose of water come into play on the Cypress Creek Course, which opened in 1958 and features huge greens in the style of that time. The club later added the Jackrabbit Course.

This champion-sized course was built with tournament play in mind. The club hosted the 1967 Ryder Cup, along with the PGA Tour's Houston Champions International starting in 1966. In a five-year run, with a year off for the 1969 U.S. Open, the event boasted a strong group of champions: Arnold Palmer, Frank Beard, Roberto de Vicenzo, Gibby Gilbert, and Hubert Green.

Alas, the U.S. Open was not so successful. Attendance was disappointing, with many would-be spectators apparently deciding not to make the long drive north, and there was little buzz about an Open played on a course that hosted a regular Tour event—to the locals it seemed like just another Champions International.

Part of the disappointment was the course itself. In his *The World of Professional Golf* annual, Mark McCormack wrote, "It was not up to U.S. Open standards. The Open has been held on the great courses of the United States…courses with character and history, courses where each hole was memorable. But, sometimes it was difficult to distinguish the holes at Champions. Was that par three with water in front of the green the eighth, or the 12th; the 10th and 11th, now which is which?"

Finally, the action lacked excitement. Defending champion Lee Trevino and Gene Littler, the year's leading money winner at that point, missed the cut, while Jack Nicklaus finished 25th. Arnold Palmer was a factor in the final round, but not all the way to the final hole.

The stage belonged mostly to players like Miller Barber, who had never won a major and blew a three-stroke lead with a 78 in the final round, and Bob Rosburg, a 42-year-old who hadn't won since 1961 and had taken a club-pro job. Rosburg missed a three-foot par putt on the 72nd hole to finish one stroke back, tied for second with Al Geiberger and future PGA Tour Commissioner Deane Beman.

The winner was Orville Moody, who had spent 14 years in the Army and had joined the Tour only the previous year. "Sarge" was unknown to everyone except Trevino, who had met him in the Army and presciently had predicted a victory for Moody, who was very accurate off the tee. But Moody was also one of the Tour's worst putters—and one of the first to putt cross-handed—and the victory at Champions would be the only one of his PGA Tour career.

8TH HOLE

Moody's winning score was one-over 281, despite Bermuda rough that hadn't grow in and wasn't up to U.S. Open standards. The course, which played 7,166 yards for the Ryder Cup, was shortened to 6,967 yards for the Open. The USGA converted the fifth hole from a par five to a par four (making a par 70), and reduced yardage on three of the par threes. But the greens were given very little water and became very firm. And the wind in the final round blew from a completely different direction, the north, confusing the field, of which only one player broke par.

The toughest hole at Champions in the Open was the 14th, a 430-yard uphill par four that Moody bogeyed in the final round. His key stroke came on another toughie, the 213-yard 12th, where he and Barber, avoiding water to the left, both hit their tee shots onto hardpan well right of the green. Barber dumped his second shot into a bunker and made a crushing double bogey, but Moody somehow nipped his ball cleanly and hit it to three feet for an unexpected par.

If the par-three fourth had been played to its full length of 228 yards instead of being shortened to 193 for the Open, it might have been the most difficult.

Two years later, during the 1971 Champions International, this hole humbled Ben Hogan and caused him to give up competitive golf. Hogan was then 58 and mostly retired, but he had finished ninth the year before. This time, though, in the first round he hooked three tee shots onto the steep, rocky bank of the wide creek guarding the fourth green, with only the third ending up in a playable position. Scrambling down the bank, he hurt first his leg, then his pride, making a nine on the hole. After hitting his second shot on the 11th hole, apparently satisfied that his last two shots in competition were a drive in the fairway and an iron on the green, Hogan turned to his playing companions, said, "Never get old," and headed back to the clubhouse, never to play on Tour again.

That was also the last year of the Champions International. The Tour returned to Champions for the Tour Championship in 1990, 1997, 1999, 2001, and 2003, when Chad Campbell shot an extraordinary 61 on the way to winning the event.

Scorecard

Hole	Par	Yardage 1969 Open	Yardage 2003 Tour Champ.
1	4	435	455
2	4	444	450
3	4	379	421
4	3	193	221
5	4/5	451	514
6	4	418	449
7	4	417	462
8	3	180	186
9	5	505	512
Out	35/36	3422	3674
10	4	448	453
11	4	450	460
12	3	213	232
13	5	544	540
14	4	430	431
15	4	418	416
16	3	175	181
17	4	436	455
18	4	431	459
In	35	3545	3627
Total	70/71	6967	7301

1969 TOP FINISHERS

Orville Moody	71-70-68-72—281
Deane Beman	68-69-73-72—282
Al Geiberger	68-72-72-70—282
Bob Rosburg	70-69-72-71—282
Bob Murphy	66-72-74-71—283
Miller Barber	67-71-68-78—284
Bruce Crampton	73-72-68-71—284
Arnold Palmer	70-73-69-72—284
Bunky Henry	70-72-68-75—285
George Archer	69-74-73-70—286
Bruce Devlin	73-74-70-69—286
Dave Marr	75-69-71-71—286

Low round: Murphy, Bobby Mitchell, 66

TOMMY BOLT GETS SET TO THROW HIS DRIVER IN THE WATER ON THE 18TH HOLE IN 1960.
OPPOSITE TOP: 1ST HOLE. OPPOSITE BOTTOM: 14TH HOLE

CHERRY HILLS COUNTRY CLUB CHERRY HILLS VILLAGE, COLORADO 1938, 1960, 1978

Arnold Palmer made a career out of going for broke, and he cemented his image on the first tee at Cherry Hills Country Club in the 1960 U.S. Open. ¶ At 346 yards, the first hole was downhill and a reasonably long hitter could hit a drive onto the green, especially in the thin air of mile-high Denver. It was a gamble, however, because rough in front and a creek to the right guarded the putting surface. This suited Palmer perfectly. Trailing by seven strokes entering the final round, he unleashed a mighty, accurate blow that finished on the green. Filled with adrenaline, he went on to birdie the first four holes and six of the first seven to spark a front-nine 30 before surviving the more treacherous back nine for a 65 that gave him his only U.S. Open title. ¶ Of course, earlier in the championship, the first hole revealed the downside of Palmer's hell-bent-for-leather approach. He also tried to drive the green in the first three rounds, with mixed results. He found the creek in the first round and made double bogey. Palmer made a birdie in the second round, but the hole cost him a bogey in the third round

when he chunked a chip from the rough near the green. For the week, Palmer played the first in one-over.

Galleries and television audiences loved Palmer for his attacking style, so much so that the charismatic son of a club pro from western Pennsylvania is rightfully credited with the boom in PGA Tour purses and television exposure in the 1960s. But the U.S. Open encourages cautious play on demanding courses made more difficult by heavy rough and fast greens. Palmer finished his career with four runner-up finishes in the Open—three in playoffs—and it's likely his boldness cost him an Open or two.

However, the first nine at Cherry Hills was an exception to the Open rule, offering a rare opportunity for low scoring. At another site, Palmer's famous charge might never have materialized.

The back nine more than makes up for the front side, despite speculation about low scores prior to the last two Opens there. In fact, Andy North's one-over 285 in 1978 marked the last time an Open was won with an over-par score until 2006.

Cherry Hills was founded in 1922 by members of Denver Country Club who felt the course was becoming overcrowded and wanted to form a club where golf, rather than social functions or family activities, would be the focus. In the early years, women were not allowed.

The course, which got its name because a cherry orchard occupied part of the site, was designed by Philadelphia architect William Flynn, who built back-to-back par fives at the finish, although the 18th has always been played as a demanding par four in major championships.

16TH HOLE

ARNOLD PALMER CELEBRATES HIS VICTORY IN 1960.

That the 1938 U.S. Open was held at Cherry Hills is remarkable considering the club nearly went under earlier that decade. During the Great Depression, many members who had retained their Denver Country Club memberships had to choose one of the two clubs. With Denver offering more for families, wives were often adamant that their husbands drop Cherry Hills.

The property-holding corporation for the club went broke, and the club remained solvent only through the formation of a new land company. Cherry Hills hosted the U.S. Open largely through

the efforts of member Will Nicholson, a member of the USGA's executive committee. Still, the USGA made an unprecedented demand of a $10,000 bond to assure a profitable return for the championship.

Replied Nicholson, "Hell, we don't even have enough in our treasury to buy a case of ketchup!" That, of course, is precisely why the USGA wanted the guarantee, ultimately raised by members of the Denver business community.

The championship wound up turning a profit. The winner was Ralph Guldahl, who became the fourth player to defend the title. He went on to win the Masters in 1939 at age 26, and at that stage in his career had accomplished more than Sam Snead, Byron Nelson, or Ben Hogan, all born the same year he was. But Guldahl's game mysteriously left him in 1941, and he never returned to the Tour when it resumed in 1944 after a one-year war hiatus.

Guldahl trailed by four strokes entering the final round but won by six when the two players ahead of him, Dick Metz and Jimmy Hines, skied to 79 and 83, respectively. Those weren't the only high numbers during the week. Ray Ainsley set a record high score on a single hole with a 19 on the 16th. His second shot found the inaptly named Little Dry Creek, and he kept thrashing and splashing until he finally got the ball out. When a USGA official asked why he didn't take a penalty drop, Ainsley responded, "I thought I had to play the ball as it lies at all times."

The 1960 Open also saw some water adventures, this time on the 18th, where a large pond starts in front of the tee and guards the left side of the fairway. Doug Sanders could have tied for the first-round lead with a par on the 18th, but as he was about to hit his tee shot, a fish jumped out of the water 30 feet from the tee, distracting him. He hesitated before sending the shot into the hazard for a double bogey. Later in the day, terrible-tempered Tommy Bolt sent two drives, and then his driver, into the hazard. A boy from the gallery retrieved the club from the water and ran off with it.

Mike Souchak would have led by four strokes entering the final round if not for his own misadventure on 18 in the third round. Distracted by the click of a camera that had been smuggled in by a spectator, Souchak sent his drive out of bounds to the right and made a double bogey that cut his lead to two.

If Souchak was steamed after the third round, so was Palmer, tied for 15th despite solid ball-striking but settling for scores of 72-71-72 because of shaky putting. He was even angrier after asking a writer friend from Pittsburgh, Bob Drum, what he thought a 65 in the final round would accomplish. "Nothing," Drum dismissively replied. "You're too far back."

17TH HOLE

"I'll show him," Palmer thought as he stalked off. After his heroic birdie on the first hole, Palmer chipped in to birdie the second, tried to drive the green on the 328-yard third and got up and down from the rough for birdie, and holed a 20-foot birdie putt at the fourth. After a disappointing par five at the fifth, he sank a 25-footer for birdie at the sixth and a six-footer at the seventh. Only a bogey at the eighth prevented a record 29 on the front nine.

Souchak also tried to drive the first green in the final round. But he found the water and made bogey. Souchak continued to fade and others made their moves on the vulnerable front nine, turning the final round into one of the Open's wildest shootouts. At one point, nine different players held at least a share of the lead within a 15-minute span.

Two of them, a legend and a legend-to-be, were paired together: 48-year-old Hogan and 20-year-old amateur Jack Nicklaus. The youngster three-putted consecutive holes on the back nine, eventually claiming second place. Hogan, feeling he needed a birdie at the par-five 17th, tried to get close to the

pin on his third shot with a wedge and watched the ball drop into the water in front of the green to drown his chances. (He then drove into the water on 18 and made a triple bogey.)

Over the demanding closing holes, all the contenders fell away except Palmer, who proved Drum wrong and won by two at four-under thanks to an even-par 35 on the back nine that was every bit as vital as his spectacular start.

Ironically, Palmer himself took away the option of a spectacular opening to the round at the next Open at Cherry Hills. Palmer, who received a lifetime membership to the club after his win, was hired to make changes in preparation for the 1978 event. He and design partner Ed Seay built new tees on five holes, including the first, added 12 bunkers, and redesigned the 13th green.

Palmer moved the first tee back 50 yards and left, turning the hole into a 399-yard dogleg. While the idea was to strengthen the opening stretch, it turned a fascinating risk/reward hole into a dull, straightforward one, not to mention taking away an

18TH HOLE

An Open Moment

Jack Nicklaus, in the final pairing with Andy North in the third round in 1978, was two strokes back as they played the 13th hole, and had gained momentum after an eagle on 11. After a good tee shot on the relatively easy 382-yard par four, Nicklaus felt the call of nature and visited a portable toilet next to the fairway.

He then hit one of the worst shots of his career, a fat sand wedge from 103 yards that plunked into a creek 30 yards short of the green that shouldn't even have been in play. He hit his next shot into a bunker and made a triple bogey that sent him reeling toward an eventual sixth-place finish. "I don't know how this will appear in the newspapers, but I never got my mind back on what I was doing after I went to the portable toilet," he said after the round. Asked if he regretted the side trip, he replied, "No, I had to go."

element of nostalgia. (During the 1985 PGA Championship, the original first tee was used.)

Cherry Hills measured 7,083 yards in 1978, plenty long on paper. But adjusted for the altitude, the course was equivalent to about 6,500 yards, and there was a fear the players might tear it up.

Instead, the course tore them up. One reason was the extremely punitive rough. A dry winter left the rough rather thin, but the application of fertilizer in late May, followed by 10 straight days of rain, created a monster. In the third round, 18-year-old amateur Bobby Clampett, just three strokes off the lead, whiffed two pitch shots from the long rough near the first green, his club slipping right under the ball.

The rough led players to lay back off the tee for control—most used driver no more than four times a round. But that left the problem of hitting the small greens, especially in windy conditions.

The 480-yard par-four 18th was one of the fiercest holes in Open history, playing to an average of 4.74. Its fairway effectively narrowed by a right-to-left slope toward the water, many players hit a fairway wood or 1-iron off the tee to avoid either driving through the fairway or into the hazard, then used a similar club for the second shot.

There were only 11 birdies all week on the 18th, and the only player to birdie the hole twice was

North, the champion. He holed long putts for birdies in the second and third rounds, but it was a three-and-a-half foot putt for a bogey in the final round that gave him the title.

It was a strange Sunday. After winning the Masters, Gary Player had the second leg of the Grand Slam in sight when he entered the final round trailing North by one shot, but he faded with a 77. North, a 28-year-old with just one Tour win, handled the tough conditions well through 13 holes, playing them in even par to take a five-stroke lead. He then staggered home, going four-over on the last five holes to win by one over J.C. Snead and Dave Stockton.

North pulled his approach shot on the 486-yard 14th, the second most difficult hole, and was lucky not to end up in a creek. He bogeyed that one and double bogeyed the par-three 15th, where he took two to escape a greenside bunker.

When Stockton made a birdie ahead of him, North's lead had gone from five to one in 15 minutes. But Stockton couldn't par the brutal 18th, and sat in the clubhouse tied at two-over with Snead, whose tee shot on 18 skipped off the water and into the fairway for a very fortunate par. North needed a bogey to win, and that's what he got by veering from the right rough to the left rough, then dumping his third into a greenside bunker before getting up and down. He added drama before his short putt to win by stepping away after a gust of wind.

There also have been two PGA Championships at Cherry Hills. In 1941, Vic Ghezzi won the extra-hole final (the PGA was match play then) over Byron Nelson. In 1985, Hubert Green won a battle against Lee Trevino.

With PGA Tour players averaging 30 yards longer than in 1978, Cherry Hills plays too short for a men's major championship today, although it did host the 1993 U.S. Senior Open and 2005 U.S. Women's Open. Cherry Hills remains a stiff challenge for anyone who doesn't belt the ball Tour distances, and it has a strong finishing stretch.

Ben Hogan once included the 14th among his best holes in America. It's a dogleg left now at 480 yards from the back tee, with trees right of the fairway and the green guarded by a large bunker to the right and Little Dry Creek to the left. The same creek comes into play on the 215-yard 15th and the 433-yard 16th.

In fact, there is water on each of the last five holes. No. 17, a par five of 555 yards, features a green surrounded by water on all sides—a lake to the back and left and a moat wrapping around very close to the green on the front and right.

Finally, there's the 18th, a hole that has humbled the greatest players in the world. Not Palmer, though. When he won in 1960, he missed the green but chipped to five feet and made the par putt. A round that started with a memorable drive ended with a memorable celebration, as an elated Palmer took off his visor and flung it into the gallery.

1938 TOP FINISHERS

Ralph Guldahl	74-70-71-69—284
Dick Metz	73-68-70-79—290
Harry Cooper	76-69-76-71—292
Toney Penna	78-72-74-68—292
Byron Nelson	77-71-74-72—294
Emery Zimmerman	72-71-73-78—294

Low round: Harold McSpaden, 67

1960 TOP FINISHERS

Arnold Palmer	72-71-72-65—280
Jack Nicklaus	71-71-69-71—282
Julius Boros	73-69-68-73—283
Dow Finsterwald	71-69-70-73—283
Jack Fleck	70-70-72-71—283
Dutch Harrison	74-70-70-69—283
Ted Kroll	72-69-75-67—283
Mike Souchak	68-67-73-75—283
Jerry Barber	69-71-70-74—284
Don Cherry	70-71-71-72—284
Ben Hogan	75-67-69-73—284

Low round: Palmer, 65

1978 TOP FINISHERS

Andy North	70-70-71-74—285
J.C. Snead	70-72-72-72—286
Dave Stockton	71-73-70-72—286
Hale Irwin	69-74-75-70—288
Tom Weiskopf	77-73-70-68—288
Tom Watson	74-75-70-70—289
Andy Bean	72-72-71-74—289
Jack Nicklaus	73-69-74-73—289
Bill Kratzert	72-74-70-73—289
Johnny Miller	78-69-68-74—289
Gary Player	71-71-70-77—289

Low round: Miller, Weiskopf, Mike McCullough, 68

Scorecard

1978 U.S. Open

HOLE	PAR	YARDAGE	AVERAGE	RANK
1	4	399	4.30	6
2	4	419	4.28	7
3	4	323	4.09	15
4	4	429	4.26	9
5	5	543	5.03	17
6	3	166	3.18	14
7	4	384	4.06	16
8	3	229	3.35	5
9	4	432	4.46	3
Out	35	3324	37.01	
10	4	437	4.44	4
11	5	594	5.01	18
12	3	203	3.26	11
13	4	382	4.27	8
14	4	486	4.51	2
15	3	208	3.24	12
16	4	419	4.26	10
17	5	550	5.20	13
18	4	480	4.74	1
In	36	3759	38.93	
Total	71	7083	75.94	

Note: The course is little changed today, playing to a total of 7,160 yards.

ANDY NORTH

CHARLES BLAIR MACDONALD. OPPOSITE TOP: 7TH HOLE.
OPPOSITE BOTTOM: 10TH HOLE

CHICAGO GOLF CLUB WHEATON, ILLINOIS 1897, 1900, 1911

Charles Blair Macdonald, the founder of Chicago Golf Club, was a towering figure in early American golf, literally and figuratively. A big man, Macdonald was opinionated, egotistical, and often irascible, with a passion for golf that drove him to be one of the game's greatest proselytizers. Macdonald saw himself as the guardian of the true interests of the game as it spread in the late 19th century. As a golf-course designer, he was determined to build courses in the U.S. that were of the same quality as those in Scotland and England. ¶ Macdonald, it must be said, really did have a feel for the game as it existed in the land of its origin. In 1872, at the age of 16, he went to Scotland for two years to study at the University of St. Andrews, staying with his grandfather, a member of the Royal and Ancient Golf Club. William Macdonald introduced his grandson to the golf sage of St. Andrews, Old Tom Morris, and Charles took to the game like a duck to water. Soon, he was playing every day, with companions that included Young Tom Morris, who had just won a fourth straight Open Championship.

Returning to Chicago, Macdonald had nowhere to play because golf didn't then exist in the United States. But on a trip to England in 1878, he played at Royal Liverpool and continued to do so on annual visits.

He ached to start a golf club in Chicago and bored his friends by constantly talking up the game, but the poor state of the national and local economy made his wishes unfeasible. The time was finally right in 1892, when the city started gaining momentum with the successful hosting of the World's Fair. In the spring, Macdonald laid out seven rudimentary holes at the estate of Senator C.B. Farwell in Lake Forest to demonstrate the game to some friends. No hole was longer than 250 yards and several were less than 100, but the demonstration was effective enough that Macdonald's friends started putting in money to start a real golf course—Chicago Golf Club.

The site was a farm in Belmont, 20 miles west of the city, offered by farmer A. Haddow Smith, a Scotsman by birth. While Macdonald writes in his 1928 book, *Scotland's Gift: Golf*, that the Belmont course was ready for play in 1892, turn-of-the-century Chicago publications state that it opened in 1893. Another disputed point is whether Belmont expanded from nine holes to 18 before the club moved to a new site in Wheaton. Macdonald contended it did, but other sources disagree.

Sequence notwithstanding, the club purchased a 200-acre farm in Wheaton, 25 miles west of the city, in the spring of 1894 and Macdonald set about designing a course that would be "comparable with the best inland courses abroad." The course was ready in the spring of 1895, which probably made it the first 18-hole course in the United States (if Belmont didn't have 18 earlier).

Macdonald was busy in 1894. In those early days of golf in America, he was one of the best amateur players in the country, and in his mind he was *the* best. In September 1894, Newport Country Club in Rhode Island held what it billed as a national championship. Macdonald, the favorite, lost by one stroke and complained loudly about what he claimed was an unjust two-stroke penalty for a ball resting against a stone wall. He also complained that a true championship should be at match play. Macdonald was so influential that a match-play championship was hastily arranged for the next month at St. Andrew's Golf Club in New York. Macdonald lost there, too, in the final; his excuse this time was that he was up most of the night at a party

given in his honor by Stanford White, the famous architect.

In the weeks following his second defeat, Macdonald continued serving up a fine whine. Now his position was that an event run by an individual club couldn't be considered a national championship, for which a truly national organization needed to be formed. Thus, the Amateur Golf Association of the United States (soon to be renamed the United States Golf Association) was born in December 1894, with Chicago joining Newport, St. Andrew's, Shinnecock Hills, and The Country Club as founding members. In 1895, Macdonald won the first U.S. Amateur at Newport.

The USGA was responsible for running the U.S. Open as well as the Amateur. As a charter member, Chicago was naturally in line to host. After the first two Opens were held at Newport and Long Island's Shinnecock Hills, the event came west to the Windy City in 1897, the last time the Open and Amateur were held back-to-back at the same venue, as well as the last time the Open was contested at 36 holes.

The course was certainly stronger than the relatively primitive layouts Newport and Shinnecock Hills had at the time. Chicago was somewhat like St. Andrews's Old Course in Scotland in that most of the holes had an adjacent twin running the other direction, though the greens were separate instead of double as at the Old Course.

But instead of going out and back like St. Andrews, the front nine formed a clockwise circle to come back to the clubhouse, with the back nine running counter-clockwise inside it. Critics said that since Macdonald tended to slice, this routing was no coincidence: A slice was always in play on the adjacent hole, whereas a hook meant big trouble, finishing either on a neighboring farm or on a field of long grass on the interior of the course. It wouldn't be the last time that a designer tailored a course to his own game.

Joe Lloyd, an Englishman who had a club job in Massachusetts in the summer and another in France in the winter, won the 1897 Open. He owed his one-stroke victory to making a three on the 18th, an impressive feat considering the hole played 466 yards in this era of the lifeless gutta percha ball. It gave him a final-round 79 for a 162 total. Willie Anderson, then just 17 years old, was second with rounds of 79 and 84.

Anderson went on to win four Opens, a record he shares with Ben Hogan and Jack Nicklaus; if not for Lloyd's heroics, Anderson would be the young-

HARRY VARDON

15TH HOLE

est winner as well as the sole record holder for most Open wins.

Macdonald shot 85-89 to finish 11th and was nipped for low amateur by one stroke by his future son-in-law, H.J. Whigham. Macdonald also failed to win the U.S. Amateur on his home course. He was the medalist in stroke play, but lost in the semifinals as Whigham took the title.

Early members of Chicago Golf Club included such notable figures as Robert Todd Lincoln (son of the president), Marshall Field, and George Pullman. Although the course was well outside the city,

there were frequent trains to Wheaton, and a coach met members at the station, a mile from the club. The members were fanatics, as this item from the 1897 Green Rules indicates: "When ice or snow lies on the putting greens, players are recommended to make their own agreements as to removing it or not before commencing their match."

Three years later, the 1900 Open at Chicago was noteworthy mostly for the presence of English greats Harry Vardon and John H. Taylor, who were in the midst of a barnstorming tour of the United States. (Vardon was promoting a new ball, the

"Vardon Flyer.") The Open demonstrated that the duo was far better than any of the top golfers living in America, most of whom were actually transplanted Scotsmen. Vardon won with a 72-hole total of 313, two shots better than Taylor and seven shots ahead of third-place David Bell.

Taylor gave the course his stamp of approval, saying it might have been the best he had ever seen away from the true links of the seashore. Players' only complaint was of the greens, which were wiry in part due to the mechanical brushing machines. Vardon even whiffed on a short putt in the first round, when his putter got caught in the grass just behind the ball.

The quality of the putting surfaces improved greatly for the third and final Open at Chicago in 1911. But the new bentgrass greens also posed some difficulty because they were extremely fast. So putting again was blamed for the high scoring, at least in the first two rounds. The 36-hole final day was played mostly in the rain, with a hardy band of about 100 spectators braving the conditions to follow the feature group of Fred McLeod and John McDermott.

McLeod, the 54-hole leader, fell back with a closing 83, leaving McDermott in a three-way playoff with Mike Brady and George Simpson. The 20-year-old McDermott, who had lost in a playoff a year earlier, prevailed to become the first native of the U.S. to win the title.

Macdonald was gone from the Chicago scene by this time, having moved to New York in 1900. His next project was the National Golf Links of America on Long Island, for which he prepared by extensively studying courses in Scotland and England. National created a sensation when it opened in 1910, and was instantly considered the best course in America.

Around that time, the members of Chicago realized that their course, although ahead of its time when it opened, was in danger of becoming outdated in the rapidly evolving American golf scene. In 1913, they asked British architect Harry S. Colt to make suggestions, but did not implement most of them.

In 1922–23, Seth Raynor, Macdonald's right-hand man, built essentially a new layout, which remains today. The redesign is credited strictly to Raynor—Macdonald was not so active in course design at that point, though it's hard to believe he didn't have some influence.

The current course has only six holes that follow the routing of holes on the original course—the first, 17th, and 18th retaining the same numbers,

17TH HOLE

the new 10th matching the old ninth, the new 14th the old seventh, and the new 15th the old eighth. Even those holes are different lengths than the old ones and all have new greens (Raynor built 18 new putting surfaces) and hazards. The double fairways were mostly eliminated, some of the previously unused land on the interior was utilized, and three par threes added—the original course had only two true one-shotters and ended up with only one when some of the holes were redesigned between 1900 and 1911.

As a testimony to the quality of the design, Chicago Golf Club is currently ranked 20th in the U.S. by *Golf Magazine* and 39th by *Golf Digest* despite not hosting a national event between the 1928 and 2005 Walker Cups.

When the Western Open moved permanently to Chicago in 1962, there was some talk about using Chicago Golf Club as part of a rotation, but it has never hosted the event. At 6,782 yards, Chicago has become a bit short for today's pros. But it still remains an excellent course and one of the seminal addresses of American golf.

1897 TOP FINISHERS

Joe Lloyd	83-79—162
Willie Anderson	79-84—163
Willie Dunn	87-81—168
James Foulis	80-88—168
W.T. Hoare	82-87—169

Low round: Anderson, Lloyd, 79

1900 TOP FINISHERS

Harry Vardon	79-78-76-80—313
J.H. Taylor	76-82-79-78—315
David Bell	78-83-83-78—322
Laurie Auchterlonie	84-82-80-81—327
Willie Smith	82-83-79-83—327

Low round: Taylor, Vardon, 76

1911 TOP FINISHERS

*John McDermott	81-72-75-79—307
Mike Brady	76-77-79-75—307
George Simpson	76-77-79-75—307
Fred McLeod	77-72-76-83—308
Jock Hutchison	80-77-73-79—309
Gilbert Nicholls	76-78-74-81—309

*McDermott won playoff with an 80, Brady 82, Simpson 86

Low round: McDermott, McLeod, Alex Campbell, 72

Scorecard
Original Course

Hole	Par	Yardage 1900 Open	Yardage 1911 Open
1	5	460	468
2	4	330	358
3	4	340	337
4	4	415	418
5	4	320	334
6	5	520	568
7	4	300	310
8	4	260	315
9	3	160	140
Out	37	3235	3344
10	3/4	140	241
11	4/5	270	510
12	4	330	330
13	5	500	519
14	4	300	300
15	4	350	364
16	4	310	318
17	4	320	348
18	4	422	427
In	36/38	2942	3357
Total	73/75	6032	6605

Scorecard
Today

Hole*	Par	Yardage
1 (1)	4	450
2	4	450
3	3	219
4	5	550
5	4	328
6	4	395
7	3	211
8	4	445
9	4	409
Out	35	3457
10 (9)	3	149
11	4	414
12	4	442
13	3	149
14 (7)	4	356
15 (8)	4	400
16	5	525
17 (17)	4	465
18 (18)	4	425
In	35	3325
Total	70	6782

*Holes on original course in parentheses

13TH HOLE. OPPOSITE: 18TH HOLE.

COLONIAL COUNTRY CLUB FORT WORTH, TEXAS 1941

Marvin Leonard, the founder of Colonial Country Club, might never have built a golf course

if his old club, Rivercrest Country Club in Fort Worth, had agreed to experiment with bent-

grass greens. ¶ Leonard, who along with his brother ran a successful discount store, was

an avid golfer with an interest in course design and agronomy. On vacations in California,

Leonard enjoyed putting on smoother bentgrass greens instead of the grainy, bumpy Ber-

muda used in Fort Worth and across the South. The prevailing wisdom was that bent couldn't

stand the summer heat. Leonard told the Rivercrest board he would pay to convert two or

three greens to bentgrass. If it didn't work, he would pay for conversion back to Bermuda.

The board turned him down, and the story goes that the club president said, "If you're so sold

on bentgrass greens, why don't you go ahead and build your own course and put them in?"

¶ That's just what he did. In 1934, Leonard bought 157 acres near Texas Christian University.

John Bredemus is generally given credit for the design, but the Colonial Country Club

history, *The Legacy Continues: A 50-Year History of Colonial Country Club,* says that after asking for plans from both Bredemus and Perry Maxwell, Leonard "borrowed from both designers to mold the Colonial tapestry." The greens were planted with seaside bentgrass, mixed with sand and cow manure, and watered frequently to combat the heat.

The course opened in January 1936 to positive local reviews, but Leonard had a higher goal: the U.S. Open, which seemed like a pipedream since it had never been played in the South.

An intense lobbying effort—plus a personal guarantee of $25,000 by Leonard—made the dream a reality in 1941. It didn't hurt that the bentgrass greens held up well and indeed made for smoother putting surfaces.

The USGA did recommend some changes to the fourth and fifth holes, so Leonard bought a few neighboring acres, reportedly at several times the market value. He then hired Maxwell to lengthen the third, fourth, and fifth holes, a stretch that came to be known as the "Horrible Horseshoe" because of its collective difficulty.

At 7,005 yards and a par of 70, Colonial was long for the pre-World War II era. It also demanded accuracy to avoid trees, a winding creek, and the Trinity River. But nobody quite knew how it would play for the Open. Wrote William Richardson in the *New York Times*, "One school of thought [holds] that it is one of the most difficult ever selected for the championship and that the winning score will be between 286 and 290, while others hold to the opinion that the record of 281 will be broken."

Neither camp had it right, but the ones predicting difficulty were closer. Craig Wood shot 284 to win by three strokes as only four players bettered 290.

It was a sweet victory for Wood, who had lost playoffs in all four majors, a dubious feat matched only by Greg Norman. Like Norman, Wood was often the victim of unlikely heroics, such as Gene

CRAIG WOOD

3RD HOLE

Sarazen's double eagle at the 1935 Masters and Byron Nelson's holed 1-iron during the 1939 U.S. Open playoff.

Today we would say that Wood, then 39, finally won his first major at the 1941 Masters. But the Masters hadn't really obtained that status yet, so for most observers at the time, the 1941 Open was the win that turned the bridesmaid into a bride.

It almost didn't happen. Wood had hurt his back the month before and played the Open wearing a heavy corset. When he started with a double bogey, Wood considered withdrawing before playing partner Tommy Armour talked him out of it. Wood was tied for the lead at the halfway point. A long hitter, his driving was very accurate on the 36-hole Saturday as he shot 70-70 and wasn't seriously threatened.

That was Colonial's sole U.S. Open, mainly because Leonard decided to bring the pros to town every year. The Colonial National Invitation started in 1946 and is the longest-running PGA Tour event held continuously at the same site. Fort Worth native Ben Hogan won the event five times and remains linked to the course.

The course has been lengthened very little since opening and is a favorite of many Tour players. While it now plays relatively short for 21st-century pros, Colonial rewards accuracy off the tee, one reason Annika Sorenstam chose it as the site of her PGA Tour appearance in 2003.

The only significant redesign was involuntary—the state mandated changes to the flow of the Trinity River for flood control in 1968. In all, nine holes were redesigned, most significantly a pair of strong par threes, the eighth and 13th. Each had played over a bend in the river that was straightened out, so those holes had to be redesigned.

Byron Nelson called the old eighth hole "the hardest par three I ever saw with the possible exception of the 16th at Cypress Point…If you pushed it a hair or didn't hit it exactly solid, you'd go in the river. And you had to hit again from the tee, there wasn't any drop area."

Neither new par three carries the same fire. Now the banner for Colonial is carried by the fifth hole, one of the toughest holes on the PGA Tour. It's 470 yards, but practically requires a left-to-right shot off the tee to avoid going through the fairway of the dogleg right. Stray right and you're under some huge trees; farther right, the Trinity River awaits.

1941 TOP FINISHERS

Craig Wood	73-71-70-70—284
Denny Shute	69-75-72-71—287
Johnny Bulla	75-71-72-71—289
Ben Hogan	74-77-68-70—289
Herman Barron	75-71-74-71—291
Paul Runyan	73-72-71-75—291

Low round: Hogan, 68

Scorecard

Hole	Par	Yardage 1941 Open	Yardage Today
1	5	569	565
2	4	395	400
3	4	468	476
4	3	220	246
5	4	469	470
6	4	395	393
7	4	418	427
8	3	198	192
9	4	343	402
Out	35	3475	3571
10	4	403	404
11	5	593	609
12	4	400	433
13	3	192	178
14	4	455	457
15	4	447	430
16	3	207	188
17	4	406	383
18	4	427	427
In	35	3530	3509
Total	70	7005	7080

PRESIDENT WARREN G. HARDING PRESENTS THE TROPHY TO JIM BARNES. OPPOSITE: 18TH HOLE.

COLUMBIA COUNTRY CLUB CHEVY CHASE, MARYLAND 1921

Columbia Country Club was at the forefront of turf-grass development in the U.S. One of its founders, Dr. Walter Harban, persuaded the U.S. Department of Agriculture to begin turf-grass research and to use the course for its field work. So it's ironic that the only time the U.S. Open was played there, in 1921, the course was struck by a combination of blight and drought the month before, turning greens that had been praised earlier that year for being the truest in the land into spotty putting surfaces. ¶ "Dr. Harban is deserving of much sympathy," wrote J. Lewis Brown in *Golf Illustrated*. "He did everything in his power and no one knows better than I, what splendid condition the course was in but a few weeks before the championship." ¶ Jim Barnes didn't mind. The man known as "Long Jim" because of his 6-foot-3 frame put together one of the most dominating performances in U.S. Open history, opening with a 69 and going on to a nine-stroke victory with a 289 total. A native of England, Barnes moved to the U.S. at age 19 in 1906 and was one of the top players of his era.

In addition to the 1921 Open, he captured two PGA Championships, one British Open, and three Western Opens, considered a major in those pre-Masters days.

Barnes played well for all four rounds, but one shot stands out. After driving into the rough on the short par-four second hole during the third round, Barnes lofted his second shot over a tree, watched it land on the right side of the green, roll down a slope across the green to the left side, and drop into the hole for an eagle. The final round was a victory march—literally so on the last hole, where the Marine Band played as Barnes walked up the fairway. President Warren G. Harding made the eight-mile trip from the White House and presented Barnes with the trophy.

The Marine Band, incidentally, was somewhat lacking in golf etiquette. It erupted in music just as Fred McLeod, Columbia's head pro from 1912 to 1967, stroked a 10-foot birdie putt on the 72nd hole that would have given him solo second. (He missed.)

The original Columbia club dated from 1898, but moved to its Chevy Chase premises in 1911 after being told the land it had been leasing was to be sold for residential development. Strangely enough, the new owner had a change of heart and kept the land as a golf course—it's now Woodmont Country Club.

The club then set out to build the finest course in the country on its new site. The architect was Herbert Barker, an English pro who designed about 10 courses while living in the U.S. from 1908 to 1915. Dr. Harban, a fine amateur player who had laid out Columbia's previous course, assisted Barker.

The members were very disappointed in 1915 when they consulted with Walter J. Travis, the U.S. Amateur champion-turned-golf architect, who informed them that their course wasn't of championship caliber after all. They hired Travis to make some changes, and when English greats Harry Vardon and Ted Ray played the course on a 1920 tour of the U.S., they proclaimed it one of the best in the country. In short order, Columbia was awarded the 1921 Open.

The course was best known at the time for the fifth hole, a 560-yard par five. The tee shot played over a ravine and the second over a vast array of

16TH HOLE

bunkers that covered the width of the fairway and extended 100 yards down the hole, starting at the 300-yard mark. The hazard that proved more dangerous in the championship, however, was the out of bounds that hugged the left side.

In the final round, 19-year-old Bobby Jones was two-under par for four holes before hitting two shots out of bounds and making a quadruple bogey. He would still manage to finish fifth, but lost low amateur honors to Chick Evans by one stroke. In the second round, Leo Diegel fared even worse, taking an 11 with three shots out of bounds, the first by only six inches.

The routing is unchanged since 1921 and has been lengthened only slightly, from 6,380 yards to 6,586, though several architects have done renovation work through the years. While it would no longer be a particularly difficult test for the best golfers in the world, it's still a tough track for amateurs, especially since hilly terrain makes for difficult lies and causes many holes, including the 18th, play longer than the yardage. In 2003, Columbia rejoined the national tournament scene, hosting the U.S. Junior Amateur.

1921 TOP FINISHERS

James Barnes	69-75-73-72—289
Walter Hagen	79-73-72-74—298
Fred McLeod	74-74-76-74—298
Charles Evans Jr.	73-78-76-75—302
Emmett French	75-77-74-77—303
Bobby Jones	78-71-77-77—303
Alex Smith	75-75-79-74—303

Low round: Barnes, Alfred Hackbarth, 69

Scorecard

Hole	Par	Yardage 1921 Open	Yardage Today
1	4	362	374
2	4	309	459
3	4	365	357
4	3	214	212
5	5	560	534
6	4	460	455
7	4	332	325
8	3	193	186
9	4	440	442
Out	35	3235	3344
10	4	438	430
11	4	436	431
12	5	502	503
13	3	163	168
14	4	408	423
15	4	365	374
16	3	141	160
17	4	285	320
18	4	407	433
In	35	3145	3242
Total	70	6380	6586

ERNIE ELS. OPPOSITE: 10TH HOLE

CONGRESSIONAL COUNTRY CLUB (BLUE COURSE)

BETHESDA, MARYLAND 1964, 1997, 2011

Golf at Congressional Country Club was born in 1922, when Devereux Emmet was hired to design 18 holes. As the club pertains to the U.S. Open, however, Congressional really only dates back to 1957, when Robert Trent Jones Sr. was hired to design a new nine. Four years later, he redid one of Emmet's nines, nearly obliterating any remnants of the original to complete the course that would host the 1964 Open. ¶ While that Open was held on essentially a Trent Jones course, the same couldn't be said for the 1997 championship. By that time the course had been given a thorough makeover by his son Rees. ¶ Although the pre-1950s history of Congressional means little to the Blue Course that hosts the U.S. Open (a fourth nine was completed in 1979, giving the club a second 18 called the Gold Course), it is nonetheless a fascinating tale. ¶ The club got its name for a good reason—it was the brainchild of two Congressmen from Indiana, Oscar E. Bland and O.R. Luhring. At the time, Washington's top clubs, Columbia and Chevy Chase,

weren't particularly hospitable to politicians. The grand idea of Congressional was to create a place for members of government and gentlemen of business to relax and trade ideas to their mutual benefit. In later years, such coziness would have been viewed with suspicion, but the 1920s were an era in which President Calvin Coolidge, an honorary member of Congressional, said, "The business of the nation is business."

Politicians didn't have as much money as businessmen, so the original funding came from selling more than 800 life memberships at $1,000 each to capitalists like Vincent Astor, John D. Rockefeller Sr. and Jr., Pierre Dupont, Harvey Firestone, and Walter Chrysler. Meanwhile, William Howard Taft, Woodrow Wilson, Warren G. Harding, Calvin Coolidge, and Herbert Hoover, all former, current, or future Presidents, were "founding life members."

The club had one of the grandest openings ever in 1924, presided over by President Coolidge—the occasion marked the opening of the clubhouse, as

the course had been open for a year—and attended by some 7,000 "guests from every circle of Washington's cosmopolitan society," according to the *Washington Times.*

Despite its grand ambitions—or maybe because of them—Congressional lost money from the outset, even during the Roaring Twenties. Its life members didn't have to pay dues, and its politician members paid dues but no initiation fee, so there was not enough incoming cash.

The financial situation got worse during the Depression. Membership dropped and in 1940, the club's mortgage was foreclosed and sold at public auction. Although not as bad as it sounds since the only bidder was a group made up of club members, the reconstituted club continued to struggle. The club's board authorized a search for a government lease, and quickly found a taker in the Office of Strategic Services, the forerunner of the CIA. The organization rented the property to train spies for $4,000 a month, with an obligation to restore the grounds at the end of the lease.

6TH HOLE

KEN VENTURI

Congressional now became Area F. An obstacle course was built from the swimming pool down over the golf course, and climbing ropes hung from the tall trees near the clubhouse. The area that would become the third nine was used for intense training: From near the site of what is now Blue's 15th tee, live machine-gun rounds were fired over the heads of crawling trainees. When the war ended, the fairways were crisscrossed with roads and barbed-wire obstacles, and 50 Quonset huts covered the tennis courts.

Like the rest of the country, Congressional rebounded quickly after the war. In fact, thanks to the revenue from the lease, the club's finances were better than they ever had been and the club could proceed with a long-planned expansion.

In the mid-1950s, Congressional hired Trent Jones, the game's most prominent architect, to design the third nine, which was opened by Vice President Richard M. Nixon in 1957. Trent Jones delivered a brawny test that quickly earned acclaim and had Congressional members thinking about

the U.S. Open. They hired Trent Jones back to bring one of Emmet's nines to the same championship standard.

Donald Ross had worked on Emmet's layout in 1930, but that was just a tweaking. Trent Jones performed major surgery on what would become the front nine of the Blue Course. A few holes kept the same fairways, but others were rerouted. There were new green sites, new tees, and more severe bunkering, a Trent Jones trademark in preparing an Open course. The biggest change was on the sixth hole, where a pond was put in front of the green and par reduced from five to four for the Open. The USGA almost immediately awarded the 1964 Open to Congressional.

Trent Jones even ended up toughening two holes on Congressional's third nine that were pressed into Open service to avoid finishing on a par three. The 18th was taken out of play, and the 17th, a strong par four with a peninsula green and amphitheater setting, became the finishing hole. A par three on the third nine replaced the missing hole, becom-

15TH HOLE

ERNIE ELS CELEBRATES HIS VICTORY ON THE OLD 18TH GREEN.

An Open Moment

In the sweltering conditions of the 1964 U.S. Open, the USGA didn't put out water containers for the players at the tees, and bottled water hadn't yet come into vogue. Players relied on their caddies or friends to grab a drink at a concession stand, but that was a problem for Jack Nicklaus. The only soft drink sold on the grounds was Pepsi, which came in Pepsi cups. Nicklaus endorsed Coke, so he had his Pepsi poured into beer cups. "No wonder he can't putt," a spectator was overheard to say during the second round. "That's his fourth beer this nine."

ing the 16th hole on the Open course, with another "stand-in" hole serving as No. 17 because of the routing.

At 7,053 yards, Congressional was at the time the longest course ever to host an Open, even with a par of 70. That might not seem intimidating in today's terms, but in an era of persimmon woods and aerodynamically simplistic balls, the distance assured players would post few red numbers. With the average drive that week measuring 252 yards, many players were hitting long irons, even woods, into heavily defended, elevated greens.

In writing about the first round in which only one player broke par, *New York Times* columnist Arthur Daley wrote that Congressional "had none of the trickery of so many of the recent courses. It [protected par] because it is big and has all the proper muscles in the right places."

After the round, Tony Lema, who a month later would win the British Open, said, "It's so tough out there, I don't see any how any of us will last 36 holes on Saturday. We'll need oxygen and ambulances."

Though he was talking only about difficulty of the course, Lema would be unwittingly prophetic of how the final day played out in temperatures very close to 100 degrees.

But in the second round, 29-year-old Tommy Jacobs showed that Congressional was vulnerable if a player was really on his game. He became only the second player to shoot a 64 in the Open, tying the record set by Lee Mackey in 1950. The final 36 holes, to be played on one day, shaped up as a two-man race between Jacobs (136) and Arnold Palmer

(137), who had opened a four-stroke gap on the rest of the field. For most, that meant the title surely would belong to Palmer, who had won that year's Masters for his seventh major title.

Not so fast. Palmer inexplicably came out firing blanks, missing the first five greens in the third round on the way to a 75-74 finish. The final day would be a two-man battle, all right, but the unlikely protagonists would be Jacobs and Ken Venturi.

Venturi had been a fine player in the late 1950s, almost winning the Masters as an amateur and finding success as a pro. But he had played poorly starting in 1961 due to a series of injuries, most notably a bad back. He hadn't even qualified for the Open the previous three years. In 1963, his confidence utterly shot, Venturi hit the low point of his career, earning less than $4,000.

His game had shown improvement in early 1964 with finishes of third and sixth, but that hardly stamped him as a serious threat in a major. But Father Francis Murray, a priest Venturi had befriended in San Francisco, was a believer. Before the Open, Venturi received a letter from Murray that read, in part, "If you should win, Ken, you would prove, I believe, to millions everywhere that they, too, can be victorious over doubt, misfortune and despair."

After opening with 72-70, Venturi shot 66 in the third round. The score could have been lower, but the northern California native forgot about the importance of drinking fluids in the hot weather and succumbed to the heat during the back nine. Feeling dizzy on the 17th green, he missed a putt of less than two feet. Another miss from just a little longer on No. 18 left him two strokes behind Jacobs with 18 holes remaining.

When Venturi staggered into the locker room, he was beginning to suffer from heat exhaustion, and there was doubt about whether he would be able to come out for the final round in 45 minutes. John Everett, a doctor and Congressional member, gave him salt tablets and iced tea. While others ate lunch, Venturi could only lie down.

Venturi resolved to give it a go, Everett following him every step to monitor his condition and ply him with liquids and salt tablets (12 during the round). Those steps got slower and slower, and by the back nine Venturi's twosome had fallen a couple of holes behind. The USGA wasn't about to penalize him for slow play, however.

Strangely however, Venturi held his game together even though he looked like a zombie. His final round included 14 pars, two birdies, and only two bogeys, worthy of commendation in the U.S. Open under any circumstances but a near miracle considering his condition. "I wasn't trying to make things happen, I was *letting* things happen, which is the key to playing well," he later said.

Jacobs would be the one to wilt, shooting 76, which opened the way to a four-stroke victory for Venturi. In the scorer's tent, a dazed Venturi sat nearly paralyzed, unable even to read his scorecard and fearful of signing it in case it was incorrect. Finally, Joe Dey, the USGA executive director, who had walked the final 36 holes with Venturi as an official, leaned over and said, "Sign it, Ken. It's correct."

The next year, the USGA decided to do away with the 36-hole Saturday finish, instead playing 18 holes each on Saturday and Sunday. Venturi's long march was a factor in the decision; so was the additional television revenue that could be derived from a second weekend day.

Congressional played host to the 1976 PGA Championship, won by Dave Stockton in dramatic fashion. Thinking he led by two when it was actually one, he hit a 3-wood off the 18th tee. Stockton hit a 2-iron approach after finding out he had only a one-stroke margin but came up short. He then pitched on and holed a 12-foot putt to edge Don January and Ray Floyd.

The club then hosted the Kemper Open from 1980 through 1986. After seven years of giving up their course for a week every year, the members decided to drop the Kemper and go after another major.

First, they needed to address a couple of problems. The Washington, D.C., area, smack between the North and South, is a notoriously difficult place to grow grass, and Congressional's greens needed to be rebuilt. After consulting with Rees Jones and the USGA's P.J. Boatwright, the members decided even more work was in order to attract another Open.

Trent Jones's course was full of blind and semi-blind shots, with greens that were not only elevated but also fronted by bunkers, obscuring the view from the fairway. This style of architecture is no longer in vogue; today's player wants to see what he's shooting at. The younger Jones prescribed full cosmetic surgery.

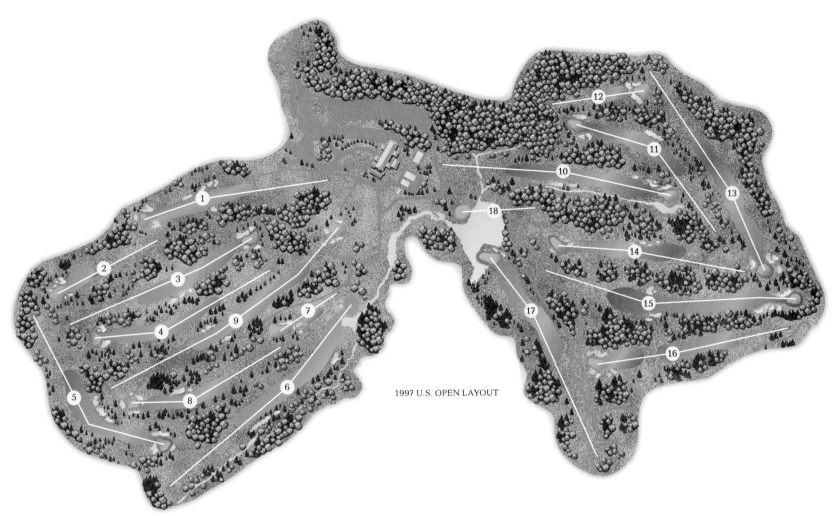

1997 U.S. OPEN LAYOUT

"The course had a lot of brawn, but it didn't have a lot of beauty," he says. "We kept the brawn, but enhanced the beauty."

The Blue Course was closed from June 1989 to July 1990, and when the work was finished Jones had retained only the routing—he not only rebuilt and recontoured all 18 greens, he also lowered 17 of them. He then elevated several tees and regraded several fairways to bring the landing areas into view.

He changed the bunkering around the greens, placed fairway bunkers in tiers to challenge short, medium, and long hitters alike, and added mounding to give the fairways and greens definition. He also made the greens more receptive, while placing many of them diagonally to the fairway to enhance strategy. While longer, it was no longer as fearsomely long for the pros as it was in 1964, considering the increase in driving distance.

The new Congressional was an immediate hit with members, who found it more user-friendly, and with the USGA, which liked the added definition but saw no reduction in the challenge and almost immediately selected to club the 1995 U.S. Senior Open and 1997 U.S. Open.

This time, though, the Blue Course would be used in its entirety, including the par-three 18th hole—against the wishes of many members—marking

the first time since 1909 that the U.S. Open would finish on a par three. Jones redesigned Congressional's finishing hole to bring water to the left more into play.

The drama never got that far in the 1997 Open. In the final round, the climax took place on 17, the old finishing hole. Ernie Els and Colin Montgomerie, in the next-to-last pairing, came to that hole tied for the lead. Tom Lehman, playing behind them, was also tied until he bogeyed 16.

The downhill 17th had been extended to 480 yards, and both Els and Montgomerie faced middle irons to a hole location on the back left of the green, in precarious proximity to water left and more water long. Els played first and struck a magnificent 5-iron shot that finished 15 feet directly behind the hole. Then Montgomerie flinched. Aiming for the middle of the green with a 6-iron, he steered it even farther away from the water and missed the green right and short.

Montgomerie chipped to five feet, Els missed his birdie try, and then with the drama building—nothing happened. The setting at the final two holes was unique, with a large crowd on a hillside able to watch both of the final holes. Unfortunately, one of the protagonists in the final act was a player who lets crowd noise bother him perhaps more than anyone else in the game, which naturally has made him a target for hecklers.

In the second round, Montgomerie let a few comments from the gallery bother him as he spoiled a superb opening 65 with an ugly 76. There were no taunts in the final round, but with Montgomerie facing the biggest putt of his life, the crowd wasn't as quiet as he wanted. Jay Haas and Tommy Tolles, on the 18th green, were ready to wait for Montgomerie and Els to finish. Instead, he waved for them to play out the hole, which took several minutes.

"I felt that we could have played the hole without waiting so long," said Els, who eventually parred the hole. "You're not going to get 20,000 people to be quiet with a couple of international boys leading the U.S. Open." It was like calling a timeout to ice the field-goal kicker—only Montgomerie was icing himself. Who knows what was going through his mind when he finally hit the putt? In any case, Monty missed.

Els twice could point to No. 17 as the key to his victory, having hit two superb approaches on Sunday. In the completion of the rain-delayed third round in the morning, he nearly holed a 4-iron, making a birdie. Montgomerie, on the other hand, bogeyed 17 all four rounds.

Lehman, the first man to hold the 54-hole lead at three straight Opens since Bobby Jones from 1928 to 1930, came to 17 clinging to a chance for an elusive first title, but he needed a birdie on one of the last two holes. He caught the approach shot a bit heavy, sending the ball left. It landed on the bank and kicked into the water, ending his hopes. "I would give anything in the world for a mulligan," he said after the round.

Although the 17th was decisive, it wasn't the hardest hole at Congressional. Just as in 1964, that distinction belonged to No. 6. A par five for members, the sixth has played as a par four-and-a-half for the pros thanks to water guarding the front of the green. Drive it into the rough under U.S. Open conditions, and reaching the green was out of the question.

There are only three water holes at the Blue Course, but they are the three longest par fours on the course for championships. In addition to Nos. 6 and 17 (now the 18th) there is what is now the 494-yard 11th, another par five for members, which has a stream running down the right side, feeding a pond that sits to the right of the green. In 1997, when it played as the 10th, Els came up short and left with his approach in the final round but chipped in for birdie.

CONGRESSIONAL'S MOST FAMOUS HOLE PLAYED AS THE 18TH IN 1964, THE 17TH IN 1997, AND WILL BE THE 18TH IN 2011.

Pros usually look to par fives to make up ground, but that hasn't been the case at Congressional. The 15th (now the 16th) is 583 yards and uphill. The ninth is one of the most striking holes at Congressional, a 607-yarder with an up-and-down fairway and a rough-filled ravine in front of the green. When the Open returns to Congressional in 2011, however, preliminary plans are for the pond-fronted sixth to play as a par five and the 15th as a par four. Mike Davis, the USGA's new course setup man, suggested the change because it restores No. 6 as a risk/reward hole by giving players the option to go for it in two or lay up.

A bigger change, representing a return to the past, already has been implemented. The hole where Venturi took his slow victory walk in 1964, will once again be the 18th in 2011. The difference is that it is now the finishing hole for normal play, too. Going back to the drawing board, Jones and the club changed the routing so the 18th hole became the 10th, with the positions of the tee and green reversed. The hole was lengthened to 220 yards by building the new tee where the halfway house used to be located.

1964 TOP FINISHERS

Ken Venturi	72-70-66-70—278
Tommy Jacobs	72-64-70-76—282
Bob Charles	72-72-71-68—283
Billy Casper	71-74-69-71—284
Gay Brewer	76-69-73-68—286
Arnold Palmer	68-69-75-74—286
Bill Collins	70-71-74-72—287
Dow Finsterwald	73-72-71-72—288
Johnny Pott	71-73-73-72—289
Bob Rosburg	73-73-70-73—289

Low round: Jacobs, 64

1997 TOP FINISHERS

Ernie Els	71-67-69-69—276
Colin Montgomerie	65-76-67-69—277
Tom Lehman	67-70-68-73—278
Jeff Maggert	73-66-68-74—281
Jay Haas	73-69-68-72—282
Jim Furyk	74-68-69-71—282
Olin Browne	71-71-69-71—282
Tommy Tolles	74-67-69-72—282
Bob Tway	71-71-70-70—282
Scott McCarron	73-71-69-70—283
David Ogrin	70-69-71-73—283
Scott Hoch	71-68-72-72—283

Low round: Montgomerie, 65

Scorecard

1997 U.S. Open

HOLE	PAR	YARDAGE	AVG.	RANK
1	4	402	4.07	13
2	3	235	3.34	5
3	4	455	4.24	8
4	4	434	4.30	6
5	4	407	4.04	15
6	4	475	4.53	1
7	3	174	3.05	14
8	4	362	3.94	18
9	5	607	5.00	17
Out	35	3551	36.51	
10	4	466	4.48	2
11	4	415	4.11	11
12	3	187	3.13	10
13	4	461	4.37	4
14	4	439	4.23	9
15	5	583	5.01	16
16	4	441	4.30	7
17	4	480	4.41	3
18	3	190	3.11	12
In	35	3662	37.14	
Total	70	7213	73.65	

Scorecard

2011 U.S. Open (expected)

HOLE	PAR	YARDAGE
1	4	402
2	3	250
3	4	470
4	4	469
5	4	407
6	5	560
7	3	205
8	4	354
9	5	635
Out	36	3752
10	3	220
11	4	494
12	4	469
13	3	191
14	4	466
15	4	474
16	4	515
17	4	437
18	4	518
In	34	3784
Total	70	7536

JULIUS BOROS. OPPOSITE : 9TH HOLE

THE COUNTRY CLUB BROOKLINE, MASSACHUSETTS CLYDE COURSE 1913; COMPOSITE COURSE 1963, 1988

It's said that nothing good ever comes from work by committee. The composite golf course at

The Country Club is an exception, the one great American course that can't be credited to

any one or two designers. Several members, a couple of pros, and finally (after the course had

existed for more than 30 years), one professional architect had their fingerprints on the origi-

nal design of the holes that now make up the Composite Course used for major events at The

Country Club. ¶ In the absence of a single designer, it is tempting to say nature designed The

Country Club, but that is hardly true except in the sense that without heavy earthmoving equip-

ment, those who laid out the holes had to follow the ups and downs of the terrain to find the

best natural green sites while skirting the site's many rocky outcroppings and marshy areas.

¶ "If the Good Lord himself had ever gone out of his way to find a place less suitable for a golf

course than Brookline, I do not think he could possibly have found it," recalled G. Herbert

Windeler, an early golf chairman at The Country Club. "We had, however, one thing. We did

have the traditions of our Pilgrim fathers, and all the historical facts of how they landed on rocks

and developed land around them, which stood us in good need, because when it came to clearing and blasting and finishing the country, there was nothing that ever fazed us."

The club had to make do with land ill-suited for golf because it when it bought the land in 1882, golf was virtually non-existent in the United States. The idea was to have a place for social and family gatherings that was out in the "country," but close enough to be reached easily by horse-drawn transportation for a one-day outing. Indeed, horses were one of the main attractions: The club chose this site on Clyde Street because it already had a track for horse racing.

The reason for the generic name is that this really was the first country club in the nation. The inspiration for golf at The Country Club came in 1893, from France of all places. Florence Boit, a niece of Country Club member Arthur Hunnewell,

had played golf at Pau, France, where she lived, and brought her clubs on a visit to the U.S.

Watching her hit the ball inspired Hunnewell and a neighbor to lay out a seven-hole course on their estates, and another Country Club member, Laurence Curtis, became so enamored by the game that he suggested the club construct a course. It would be six holes, laid out by Curtis, Hunnewell, and Robert Bacon. Their authorized expenditure was $50.

The story goes that while demonstrating the game to the other members, Hunnewell holed his first shot, a feat that failed to elicit the wild enthusiasm he expected. After all, the onlookers thought to themselves, isn't hitting the ball in the hole the idea of the game?

Those early holes were short and very close to the clubhouse. Some criss-crossed the race track and the polo field inside it, creating friction

13TH HOLE

FRANCIS OUIMET

between the golfers and equestrians. "Golfers were voted, I think by a majority of the members, a nuisance, and were looked upon somewhat as the untouchables are in India," Windeler recalled.

Still, golf became popular, and polo was abandoned in 1901, although horse racing and riding continued. (Racing eventually stopped in 1935.) By 1894, golf was so entrenched there that The Country Club became one of the five founding member clubs of the USGA. Also that year, it hired Scotsman Willie Campbell as professional and greenskeeper, and he helped expand the course to nine holes.

Campbell is named in most sources as the designer of The Country Club, which gives him too much credit. His was not the lone voice, as the members who had laid out the original six holes also had their say. Also, he was gone by 1899, when the second nine was laid out.

Moreover, all those original versions didn't survive even the first decade of the 20th century. The course was lengthened in 1904, followed by another redesign in 1909—again, most of the work was done by the members.

Several of them, including Windeler and Herbert Jaques, tried to convince the club to buy 30 acres adjoining the club for three new holes. After being turned down, they bought it themselves with money raised from members who believed in the project. Four years later, the three holes known as "Windeler's Folly" were completed; the group then gave the land to the club, providing only that the club assume the mortgage that had been taken out to complete the work.

Those holes comprised the ninth, 10th, and 11th holes in the 1913 U.S. Open. On the current Composite Course, the middle hole of the trio, a par three, is not used, and the others play as Nos. 9 and 10.

With the course upgraded and lengthened to 6,245 yards by 1909, it was finally ready to host its first U.S. Open, in 1913. It was a tournament that would help shape the future of golf in America.

In one of the most storied championships in the history of the game, 20-year-old amateur Francis Ouimet upset English greats Harry Vardon and Ted Ray, igniting a surge of interest in the game in the United States. Not only that, it was a tale that even a scriptwriter might find hard to conceive—the hero, Ouimet, grew up across Clyde Street from the 17th hole at The Country Club and still resided there with his parents.

No amateur had won the Open to that point, and Ouimet seemed an unlikely candidate. No patrician amateur, he had gotten into the game by caddying. He almost didn't enter, thinking he already had taken too much time from work to play in the U.S. Amateur, but his boss convinced him otherwise. Meanwhile, Vardon was making his first trip to America since 1900, when he won the U.S. Open. The five-time British Open champion (he would add a sixth in 1914) was a strong favorite, followed closely by the long-hitting Ray, who had claimed the British Open a year earlier.

After two rounds, Vardon and another Englishman, Wilfrid Reid, were tied for the lead at 147, with Ray two behind. Ouimet made a good showing at 151, generating enough local interest to draw a large crowd for the 36-hole final day, even in the rain. With a 74 in the third round, Ouimet pulled even with Vardon and Ray entering the final round. (Reid, who reportedly got into a fight with Ray at dinner the night before, faded badly.)

With the rain turning the course into a quagmire, scores soared in the final round. Ouimet made the turn in 43, followed by a double bogey on the par-three 10th. Vardon and Ray had already finished with 79s, so Ouimet needed to play the last six holes in two-under par to tie. Given the sloppy conditions and the difficulty of the course, it seemed an impossible task. But Ouimet's birdie at the 13th drew a shout from the gallery, drawing nearly everyone on the premises, including Vardon and Ray, to watch the youngster play the closing holes.

Ouimet made a par five on the 14th despite a half-topped second shot, got up and down for a par four on the 15th, and made a routine par three on No. 16. On 17, a 360-yard par four, he hit his second shot to about 15 feet and holed the downhill, curling birdie putt, sending the crowd into a frenzy.

"[The spectators] could not control themselves," Herbert Warren Wind wrote in *The Story of American Golf*. "They yelled, pummeled each other joyously, swatted their friends with umbrellas, and shouted delirious phrases they had not thought of since boyhood."

Ouimet remained calm, knowing he needed a four on the 410-yard 18th. His second shot cleared the front bunker but came up just short of the green. He chipped to five feet and proved impervious to pressure by holing the putt. This time the cheer could be heard in downtown Boston, and Ouimet was carried to the clubhouse on the shoulders of the crowd. "Many not realizing that Ouimet was an amateur and not a professional, thrust bills of large denominations at him only to be met with a smile and a shake of the head," read the next day's *New York Times*.

Ouimet was, of course, a heavy underdog in the playoff. But playing with a preternatural calm, he shot an extraordinary 72 on another rainy day to beat Vardon by five strokes and Ray by six. "Mr. Ouimet's 72 in that weather and on that muddy course was just about as good a single round as was ever played," wrote esteemed British golf writer Bernard Darwin, who served as Ouimet's marker that day.

Once again, No. 17 was a key hole. Trailing by only one, Vardon, apparently trying to cut the corner, drove into a bunker at the elbow of the dogleg left and made a bogey. Ouimet again birdied the hole that sat directly across from his house.

For the second straight day, the gallery of several thousand carried Ouimet off the 18th green on their shoulders. Ironically, events that transpired at the nation's first and most emblematic private club helped expand the game beyond the country-club set. In 1913, there were 350,000 golfers in America; a decade later, there were two million.

The Open returned to The Country Club in 1963 to commemorate the 50th anniversary of Ouimet's victory. By then, a second golf boom was well under way, thanks to another man-of-the-people hero, Arnold Palmer. And the game itself was vastly different, thanks mostly to equipment advances. Many wondered if The Country Club could stand up to the assault of the modern players.

Oddly enough, the scoring in the 1963 Open resembled that of the hickory-shaft era; Julius Boros's winning total of 293 was the highest since 1935. That anomaly was caused by a couple of factors. First, an extremely cold winter had left spongy, patchy fairways and greens that were not as smooth as usual for an Open. But the biggest factor was strong winds that not only affected ball flight, but also dried out the greens, making The Country Club's small putting surfaces difficult targets.

As in 1913, the 17th hole was crucial in a tight finish. Boros, coming from behind with a 72 that matched the best score of the fourth round, birdied it with a 20-foot putt. Palmer, battling for the lead, missed an 18-inch putt on 17 and also finished at 293. Jacky Cupit had a two-stroke lead going to

ARNOLD PALMER HITS A SHOT FROM A TREE STUMP ON THE 11TH HOLE OF THE PLAYOFF IN 1963.

the 17th, but he drove with a 3-wood into the rough near the Vardon bunker, came out short, pitched on, and three-putted for double bogey. The next day, Boros won the 18-hole playoff with a 70 to Cupit's 73 and Palmer's 76.

The course had been toughened considerably by using holes from the Primrose Nine designed by William Flynn in 1927. In the Composite Course used for the Open, the Primrose holes were the 11th, 12th, and 13th. The 11th actually combined two holes on the Primrose nine, creating a 445-yard par four with a pond in front of the green. This hole cost Palmer the Open. In the third round, his 2-iron approach dived into the pond and he made a triple bogey. In the playoff, his drive ended up in a tree stump and he ended up with another triple.

But before the championship, Palmer's biggest complaints were about the 12th, calling it "ridiculous." He might have been right. A par five for the members, it played as a 470-yard par four, with the blind, uphill second shot required to carry a 30-foot bluff. In those days when the average drive wasn't much more than 250 yards, it was almost too long.

Another change was that the second hole, a short par four in normal play, became a 190-yard par three. All those changes have become permanent in the Composite Course used for major events.

Continuing with the anniversary theme, the Open next came to The Country Club in 1988, marking 75 years since Ouimet's win. This time, Rees Jones gave the course a thorough makeover, which was so well received that it stamped him as the "go-to" architect for Open preparation.

Jones's work wasn't so much a redesign as a restoration, bringing back features that had been lost through the years while also updating the course for the modern game. By looking at photographs from the 1930s, Jones determined that many of the greens had shrunk. Restoring them to their original size brought back some difficult hole locations. He also rebuilt them, re-creating subtle contours in keeping with the character of the course. Some bunkers that had been abandoned over the years were restored.

The changes were so subtle that they were barely perceptible. Says Jones, "The greatest compliment I got was, 'What did you do?'"

However, there's little subtlety about the back tier of the 17th green, which Jones rebuilt. The small shelf has a nasty back-to-front slope that turns this short par four into a severe challenge when the hole is located there. The shelf is tough to hit, even with a wedge, and it's even tougher to get up and down from behind the green.

The 17th has continued to play a starring role in championships. Curtis Strange nearly blew the 1988 U.S. Open there, three-putting from 15 feet on that treacherous back tier to fall into a tie for the lead with Nick Faldo in the final round. Strange preserved a spot in a playoff with a difficult up-and-down from the front bunker on 18, then won the title on Monday, 71-75.

It was another case of an American beating an Englishman. The same scenario was played out en masse in the 1999 Ryder Cup, with the U.S. stag-

CURTIS STRANGE

ing a thrilling rally to defeat Europe on the final day, culminating with the "putt heard 'round the world," a 45-footer by Justin Leonard on (where else?) the 17th green, awakening the ghosts of Ouimet.

Although it has stolen a lot of the attention, No. 17 isn't the only strong hole at The Country Club. The first hole is a stout opener at 452 yards, but No. 3 is even tougher. The 448-yarder has a fairway that snakes through some of The Country Club's distinctive rock outcroppings before reaching a green well protected by bunkers and a water hazard behind.

The front nine also has a couple of clever short par fours, the 338-yard fourth and 312-yard

17TH HOLE

An Open Moment

Paul Azinger began the final round nine strokes out of the lead in 1988, but when he played the front nine in 30, a Johnny-Miller-at-Oakmont type of comeback seemed like a possibility. Through 16 holes, Azinger had picked up one more birdie to stand at six-under for the day, and he still had a chance if he could pick up a birdie or two on the last two holes. He played safe with a 2-iron off the 17th tee, leaving a 7-iron to the flag perched on the tiny back left shelf. But his approach skittered over the back of the green and he couldn't stop his pitch shot, which rolled all the way to the front of the green. He made a bogey that ended his chances.

sixth. Trying to drive the fourth green, tucked at the end of a short but sharp dogleg, is a risky proposition. The straightaway sixth is more tempting, but there's only a narrow opening between bunkers front right and front left.

The seventh, a 201-yard par three that is the only hole remaining from the 1893 layout, was the third toughest hole at the 1988 Open. The reachable par-five ninth is one of the "folly" holes from 1909, and is little changed from when Windeler and the others hacked it out of the wilderness. The prominent feature is a large, rough-covered rock outcropping located at the landing area for tee shots, though these days some players can try to fly it and shorten the hole.

Holes 10 through 13, represent the hardest stretch on the course; Ben Crenshaw named these holes "The Wall." The 439-yard 10th is another "folly" hole back up the hill. As Palmer's misadventures in 1963 show, No. 11, now 453 yards, is exacting.

The USGA eased up on the players in 1988 and set up the 12th, with its severely uphill second shot, at 450 yards, 20 shorter than in 1963. It still ranked as the toughest hole on the course. (In the 1999 Ryder Cup, it was a brutal 486 yards.) The last of three holes borrowed from the Primrose Nine, the 13th is a 433-yarder with a pond to the right of the drive zone. In 1988, Strange made a birdie here in the playoff for a key two-stroke swing.

The Composite Course (and, for that matter, the Clyde Course that forms the regular 18) has only two par fives, and both are reachable in two—the back nine's representative is the 527-yard 14th. Finally, No. 18, which plays across the old racetrack, has been lengthened substantially in the past 40 years. At 385 yards in 1963, it was actually shorter than in Ouimet's day, but it played to 438 yards for the 1988 Open, with three fairway bunkers on the left restored by Jones. It provides a bit more chance for birdie than many Open finishers, but with its elevated, sloping green, it can be a hard par.

In addition to the three U.S. Opens and the Ryder Cup, The Country Club has hosted five U.S.

18TH HOLE

Amateurs, three U.S. Women's Amateurs, two Walker Cups, a U.S. Junior Amateur, and a U.S. Girls' Junior. Many expected the club to be named to host the 2013 U.S. Open on the 100th anniversary of Ouimet's triumph. But due to various problems with hosting a modern major, with all its trappings and traffic, at the club's Brookline location, the USGA decided against it. It is quite possible that the U.S. Amateur will be played there instead.

One thing is certain: The golf course itself is still worthy of a major competition, and that's a testament to its original designers—whoever they may have been.

1913 TOP FINISHERS

*Francis Ouimet	77-74-74-79—304
Harry Vardon	75-72-78-79—304
Ted Ray	79-70-76-79—304
James Barnes	74-76-78-79—307
Walter Hagen	73-78-76-80—307
Macdonald Smith	71-79-80-77—307
Louis Tellier	76-76-79-76—307

Ouimet won playoff with a 72, Vardon 77, Ray 78
Low round: Ray, 70

1963 TOP FINISHERS

*Julius Boros	71-74-76-72—293
Jacky Cupit	70-72-76-75—293
Arnold Palmer	73-69-77-74—293
Paul Harney	78-70-73-73—294
Bruce Crampton	74-72-75-74—295
Tony Lema	71-74-74-76—295
Billy Maxwell	73-73-75-74—295
Walter Burkemo	72-71-76-77—296
Gary Player	74-75-75-72—296
Dan Sikes	77-73-73-74—297

*Boros won playoff with a 70, Cupit 73, Palmer 76
Low round: Palmer, Dow Finsterwald, Bob Gajda, 69

1988 TOP FINISHERS

*Curtis Strange	70-67-69-72—278
Nick Faldo	72-67-68-71—278
Mark O'Meara	71-72-66-71—280
Steve Pate	72-69-72-67—280
D.A. Weibring	71-69-68-72—280
Paul Azinger	69-70-76-66—281
Scott Simpson	69-66-72-74—281
Bob Gilder	68-69-70-75—282
Fuzzy Zoeller	73-72-71-66—282
Fred Couples	72-67-71-73—283
Payne Stewart	73-73-70-67—283

*Strange won playoff, 71-75
Low round: Peter Jacobsen, 64

Scorecard

1913 U.S. Open

Hole	Par*	Yardage
1	5	430
2	4	300
3	5	435
4	4	300
5	4	420
6	4	275
7	3	185
8	4	380
9	5	520
Out	38	3245
10	3	140
11	4	390
12	4	415
13	4	420
14	5	470
15	4	370
16	3	125
17	4	360
18	4	410
In	35	3000
Total	73	6245

*Par is estimated

Today (Composite Course)

Hole*	Par	Yardage	Avg.**	Rank**
1 (1)	4	452	4.25	5
2 (2)	3	185	3.24	7
3 (3)	4	448	4.25	5
4 (4)	4	338	4.00	15
5 (5)	4	439	4.21	10
6 (6)	4	312	3.90	16
7 (7)	3	201	3.30	3
8 (8)	4	385	4.04	14
9 (9)	5	510	4.81	18
Out	35	3270	36.00	
10 (11)	4	439	4.27	4
11	4	453	4.34	2
12	4	450	4.42	1
13	4	433	4.24	7
14 (14)	5	527	4.86	17
15 (15)	4	434	4.20	11
16 (16)	3	185	3.11	13
17 (17)	4	381	4.23	9
18 (18)	4	438	4.19	12
In	36	3740	37.86	
Total	71	7010	73.86	

*Hole numbers from 1913 course in parentheses
**Average score and rank from 1988 Open

GENE SARAZEN

FRESH MEADOW COUNTRY CLUB FLUSHING, NEW YORK 1932

It's hard to imagine today, but the U.S. Open was once held in New York City. It was near the far edge of the borough of Queens, in an area that still had a rural flavor of neighboring Long Island when Fresh Meadow Country Club opened in 1922. In fact, the land was a farm before the golf course was built. ¶ But the A.W. Tillinghast course lasted only 24 years before being overtaken by rapid expansion, replaced by the Fresh Meadows housing development, a mixture of high-rise apartments and row houses, along with a shopping center, cinema, and schools. ¶ Fresh Meadow was founded by members of the Unity Club, a social club formed by the Jewish community in Brooklyn. The group thought big from the start. It hired Tilling-hast, one of the top architects of the day, to lay out the course and, two years after it opened, hired Gene Sarazen, one of the game's top players, as its pro. In short order, Fresh Meadow landed the 1930 PGA Championship and 1932 U.S. Open. ¶ Sarazen made it to the final of the 1930 PGA, which was then held at match play, losing to Tommy Armour on the 36th hole. Feeling that he was a victim of the "host pro jinx," Sarazen left in 1931 for a similar position at the nearby Lakeville Club so he wouldn't suffer a similar fate in the 1932 U.S. Open.

It worked—barely. Sarazen, generally a bold player, decided on a conservative strategy, partly because he was worn out after winning the British Open a couple of weeks earlier and partly because of local knowledge of the course's dangers. "Fresh Meadow was not a great course, but it was a tough one to score on," he later wrote in *Thirty Years of Championship Golf*. "Like nearly all courses designed by A.W. Tillinghast, it featured bottleneck greens guarded on both the right and left by unusually deep bunkers. I didn't want to tangle with those brutal traps any more than I had to."

Sarazen trailed by five after shooting 74-76 and wasn't any better after eight holes of the third round. But over the final 28 holes, he began attacking, a strategy that paid off with perhaps the finest sustained stretch of play ever in the Open. He followed a birdie two on the ninth hole of the third round with nine-hole scores of 32-32-34. His final-round 66 was an Open record and yielded a three-stroke victory.

The club weathered the economic difficulties of the Great Depression and World War II, but the end of the war brought new challenges. Housing developments were spreading rapidly in Queens, and the club's real-estate taxes were rising with the trajectory of a wedge shot. The city wanted to build a sewer line under the course and the initial plans for a projected school placed it in the course's fifth fairway.

The club's board found a way out in 1946. Lakeville, the same club where Sarazen had taken a position 15 years earlier, had gone bankrupt. It wasn't far away but offered a quieter setting outside the city in the town of Great Neck. It also had a fine course, designed by another top golf architect, Charles H. Alison, in 1925. Fresh Meadow was able to buy Lakeville for $650,000 (renaming it

Fresh Meadow, which still exists) and sell its own property to the New York Life Insurance Company for $1.075 million. The club's financial dilemma was solved, but the world lost a very good Tillinghast course.

1932 TOP FINISHERS

Gene Sarazen	74-76-70-66—286
Bobby Cruickshank	78-74-69-68—289
Philip Perkins	76-69-74-70—289
Leo Diegel	73-74-73-74—294
Wiffy Cox	80-73-70-72—295

Low round: Sarazen, 66

Scorecard

1932 U.S. Open

HOLE	PAR	YARDAGE
1	4	437
2	4	395
3	4	391
4	3	188
5	5	578
6	4	428
7	4	412
8	4	435
9	3	143
Out	35	3407
10	4	385
11	4	413
12	3	155
13	4	448
14	3	219
15	4	424
16	5	587
17	4	373
18	4	404
In	35	3408
Total	70	6815

1932 U.S. OPEN

WALTER TRAVIS. OPPOSITE TOP: 2ND HOLE. OPPOSITE BOTTOM: 14TH HOLE

GARDEN CITY GOLF CLUB GARDEN CITY, NEW YORK 1902

Garden City Golf Club is a great course that helped ruin a wonderful friendship. The Long Island course is the work of Devereux Emmet and Walter J. Travis, two of the most influential figures in course design in the early days of American golf. Both were Garden City members, but Travis's constant criticisms and re-workings of Emmet's original design inevitably led to friction between the two. ¶ Garden City was Emmet's first design; he laid out nine holes in 1897 and nine more the following year. He wasn't really a golf-course architect at the time; in fact, the profession didn't yet exist in the United States. He was simply a man who traveled in high social circles and was a very good golfer. ¶ Emmet was also a friend of George L. Hubbell, general manager of the Garden City Company. When Hubbell decided to build a golf course for his company's hotel and community, he turned to Emmet for his knowledge of the great courses of England and Scotland.

Travis, a native of Australia, immigrated to the U.S. and took up golf in 1896 at age 35, quickly becoming a top amateur. When Garden City became a private club in 1899 (it had been public), Travis was quickly persuaded to join.

Garden City would be good to Travis. In 1900, he claimed the first of his three U.S. Amateur titles there, defeating Findlay Douglas two-up in a bizarre finish to a 36-hole final completed in a raging storm. The 18th green was under water, and attempts to mop it up were unsuccessful. Since it was impossible to putt, both players had to hit pitch shots from the putting surface; Travis knocked his dead to wrap up the title.

The U.S. Open came to Garden City in 1902, and Travis overcame a slow start to finish second, six strokes behind Laurie Auchterlonie, a Scotsman playing out of Chicago.

Travis and Emmet were friends and golf companions in those years, with Emmet persuading the "Old Man" (as the 40-plus Travis was known) to enter the 1904 British Amateur, where Travis created a sensation by becoming the first player from America to win, while Emmet reached the quarter-finals.

Their relationship changed in 1905, when Travis went public with criticism of his home course. Something of a Renaissance man, Travis was a writer and also had gotten into golf design in 1899 by laying out Ekwanok in Vermont. In an article in *Country Life* about American courses, Travis, after writing that "Garden City is one of the best courses in the country," proceeded to detail suggested changes to almost every hole. The next year, the club commissioned him to carry out some of those changes.

Travis had two main problems not only with Garden City but also other early American courses. The first was an excessive use of cross bunkers, which adversely affected the "duffer" but did not

18TH HOLE

sufficiently challenge the expert, who could carry them easily. The second was that the greens were flat and uninteresting.

The most noteworthy change at Garden City was the addition of bunkers to the sides of the fairways to catch errant drives, which Travis felt was a better challenge of good players' skills. These small, deep bunkers were hard to escape, and to this day are one of the salient features of the course. In addition to adding length to several holes, Travis also built some pot bunkers around greens and undulations into the large putting surfaces. The owner of a great short game, his courses always challenged players around the greens.

Ironically, Travis ended up being the victim of one of his own bunkers. The U.S. Amateur returned to Garden City in 1908, and Travis was one down in his semifinal match against Jerry Travers coming to No. 18. The finishing hole is a memorable par three, over a pond to a well-bunkered green. Travis's tee shot found one of his deepest bunkers. He slashed at the ball twice without escaping before emerging to concede the match.

By this time, despite Travis's tinkering with his layout at Garden City, Emmet had become an established golf architect. He ultimately designed more than 70 courses—most were in the New York area, but his portfolio also included Congressional near Washington, D.C. In *The Old Man: the Biography of Walter J. Travis,* author Bob Labbance reveals that after years of strained relations with Travis, Emmet sent a 1921 letter saying, "My dear Travis. We were friends so long and I have always regretted our estrangement. Cannot we be friends again?"

It's not known whether the two reconciled. Still, however contentiously, they left a combined legacy at Garden City. Emmet's original routing is basically unchanged more than a century later, and Travis's changes give the course much of its character.

Garden City remains highly regarded by architecture aficionados and is ranked 39th in the U.S. by *Golf Magazine.* Though not close to the ocean, its terrain on the Hempstead Plain is reminiscent of a Scottish links, with sand-based soil, brown fescue in the rough, and greens that are level with the fairways rather than sculpted above them. It's a course where the average player can get around nicely if he hits it straight, but it has plenty of strategic interest for the low handicapper and severe penalties in the form of deep rough and nasty bunkers for those who stray off line.

Tom Doak, one of today's leading architects and a consultant at Garden City, wrote in a recent club history that the simplicity of the design and naturalness of its appearance, "[reminds] me about the essence of golf—the joy of being outdoors, of hitting the ball and chasing after it, the difficulty of getting it into a tiny hole afar."

1902 TOP FINISHERS

Laurie Auchterlonie	78-78-74-77—307
Stewart Gardner	82-76-77-78—313
Walter Travis	82-82-75-74—313
Willie Smith	82-79-80-75—316
Willie Anderson	79-82-76-81—318
John Shippen	83-81-75-79—318

Low round: Gilbert Nicholls, 73

Scorecard

HOLE	PAR*	YARDAGE 1902 OPEN	YARDAGE TODAY
1	4	289	302
2	3	140	137
3	4	355	407
4	5	493	523
5	4	266	360
6	4	294	440
7	4/5	339	550
8	4	408	418
9	4	312	323
Out	36/37	2928	3460
10	4	338	414
11	4	389	426
12	4/3	260	193
13	5	500	538
14	4	333	343
15	4	382	447
16	5/4	456	405
17	5	434	495
18	3	150	190
In	38/36	3242	3451
Total	74/73	6170	6911

*1902 par is estimated

1904 U.S. OPEN

GLEN VIEW CLUB   GOLF, ILLINOIS 1904

How do you get to the Glen View Club? Take Golf Road to the village of Golf—or perhaps take the railroad to Golf station. ¶ The combination of the course and railroad gave the suburban Chicago village its name. The chairman of the Chicago, Milwaukee & St. Paul was a founding member of Glen View, which opened in 1898. His method of getting to the course was to take a private car on his train line and have the engineer drop him off and pick him up at a spot close to the course. Engineers called the spot the golf station, though there was no station. ¶ A few years later, the railroad did build a station, officially named "Golf." By then, the post office was also known as Golf. When the tiny village incorporated in 1928, it became Golf. Today, the village of Golf has fewer than 400 residents. ¶ The club might have been located more prosaically within the town of Evanston if that municipality hadn't been "dry" at the time of Glen View's founding. The club was the brainchild of William Campbell, a Scotsman and Northwestern University professor who made sure the club was outside the town limits.

Famous Chicago architect Daniel H. Burnham discovered the site. He, in turn, enlisted landscape architect Ossian Cole Simonds, a protégé of Frederick Law Olmsted, to lay out the grounds. The course was designed by its first pro, Richard Leslie. He must have done a good job, because in 1922 when the club brought in William Flynn, he rerouted only two holes, the 13th and 17th, while modernizing the rest of the course.

Hewn out of a forest at a time when most courses were being built on farmland, the course wasn't easy to build. In the *1903 Book of Sport*, Joseph E. Ryan wrote, "When [C.B.] Macdonald and [H.J.] Whigham [then well known golfers, the former was the founder of the Chicago Golf Club] said it would take a fortune to make the Glen View wilderness into a golf course, the indomitable founders of Glen View said: 'We have $90,000 to begin with, and lots more in sight.'"

Glen View hosted the first Western Open in 1899 and the 1902 U.S. Amateur, won by the club's own Louis N. James. When the U.S. Open came to Glen View, James, just back from college and feeling he wasn't in good form, withdrew rather than risk a poor showing in front of the home folks.

With a branch of the Chicago River running through the course and a reservoir on the eighth and ninth holes, Glen View had more water trouble than most courses around the turn of the century. Through three rounds of the Open, the leader was Fred MacKenzie, who had recently left St. Andrews, Scotland, to become the professional at Chicago's Onwentsia Club. At the 460-yard eighth hole, named "Trouble," MacKenzie found it. His second shot just failed to clear the bank of the reservoir and, after a penalty drop, his next stroke found bushes near the green.

He ended up with an eight on the hole and an 80 on the round. Willie Anderson blew right past him with a final-round 72, matching the best round in Open history to that point, for the third of his four Open titles.

1904 TOP FINISHERS

Willie Anderson	75-78-78-72—303
Gilbert Nichols	80-76-79-73—308
Fred MacKenzie	76-79-74-80—309
Laurie Auchterlonie	80-81-75-78—314
Bernard Nicholls	80-77-79-78—314

Low round: Anderson, Alex Campbell, 72

18TH HOLE

Scorecard

HOLE	PAR*	YARDAGE 1904 OPEN	YARDAGE TODAY
1	4	440	430
2	4/3	230	182
3	4	375	435
4	4	360	395
5	4	330	375
6	5	560	550
7	3	180	168
8	5	460	490
9	4	250	350
Out	37/36	3,185	3,375
10	4	440	432
11	3	210	153
12	4	235	325
13	4/5	356	537
14	3	170	162
15	5	512	505
16	4	335	388
17	4	285	350
18	4	323	338
In	35/36	2,866	3,190
Total	72	6,051	6,565

*Par is estimated for 1904

TONY JACKLIN. OPPOSITE TOP: 6TH HOLE.
OPPOSITE BOTTOM: 8TH HOLE

HAZELTINE NATIONAL GOLF CLUB CHASKA, MINNESOTA 1970, 1991

What was the best comeback in U.S. Open history? Was it Arnold Palmer in 1960? Billy Casper

in 1966? Johnny Miller in 1973? Arguably, the greatest comeback wasn't by a player but by a

course: Hazeltine National Golf Club in 1991. ¶ In 1970, the first U.S. Open at Hazeltine was

a disaster. The course, built just eight years earlier, wasn't ready for an Open. Its design was

widely criticized by the players. To make matters worse, a fierce wind whipped through the

Minnesota prairie in the first round, causing some of the greatest players in the game to strug-

gle to break 80. The only happy person at the end of the week was England's Tony Jacklin,

whose seven-under 281 gave him a seven-stroke victory. ¶ The runner-up was Dave Hill, but

he isn't remembered for finishing second. Hill and Hazeltine will forever be linked because

of one of the most bizarre press conferences in golf history. In half-joking terms but with criti-

cism that was deadly serious, Hill lit into Hazeltine and its designer, Robert Trent Jones Sr.,

after the second round.

7TH HOLE

12TH HOLE

16TH HOLE

Hill had the clubhouse lead when he finished the round (Jacklin was still on the course), but at first declined to come to the press tent. After eating lunch with a friend and downing a couple of drinks, Hill obliged the media—and gave them great copy.

"If I had to play this course every day for fun, I'd find another game," he said. A reporter asked what the course lacked. "Eighty acres of corn and a few cows," Hill answered. "They ruined a good farm when they built this course. Just because you cut the grass and put up a few flags doesn't mean you have a golf course." His recommendation: "Plow it up and start over again."

One of the more outspoken pros of his era, Hill was merely saying what other pros were thinking. They didn't like the course when the 1967 Minnesota Classic was played there (with a winning score of two-under by Lou Graham) and hated it under U.S. Open conditions.

The criticisms involved the glut of doglegs (nearly every hole that wasn't a par three was a dogleg), numerous blind shots, and unreceptive greens (some of them sloped away toward the back). It was also exceptionally long, though it was set up at 7,151 yards instead of the 7,400 it could stretch to.

When he played the course in 1967, Bob Rosburg said the course had so many doglegs it must have been laid out in a kennel. Don January didn't enter the 1970 Open even though he was exempt, saying, "There is no way to line up a drive at Hazeltine unless you do so by the clouds." In a tournament preview in Sports Illustrated titled "Blind Man's Bluff at Hazeltine," Jack Nicklaus wrote that the course "lacks definition."

Indeed, the first hole set the tone for Hazeltine. The tee was well above a fairway that couldn't be seen, and the green was hidden from view around a corner. It was an unsettling start to an unsettling course.

There were explanations for some of the course's features. The club's founder, Totton P. Heffelfinger, insisted on having a children's par-three course close to the clubhouse, between the first and ninth holes. That led directly to two doglegs and indirectly to two more. The blind shots resulted largely because earthmoving wasn't then done on such a large scale as it is today. (Trent Jones challenged the assertion that the course was really so full of blind shots, saying, "Maybe Nicklaus is blind.")

In any case, the question needs to be asked: Was the course *that* bad? There is nothing inherently wrong with doglegs, which are usually more interesting and more strategic than straightaway holes. Blind shots shouldn't be a big problem in a tournament—that's one reason for practice rounds. It's not unreasonable for the best players in the world to hit shots into greens that aren't entirely receptive. Even in those days, pros were known to cry "Unfair!" when faced with really challenging courses.

During his own press conference the day after Hill's remarks, Trent Jones shot back with, "If you built the kind of course the pros would really like, you would have dead flat greens and dead flat fairways, very little rough, and very few traps. That kind of course wouldn't require an architect; you could order it from the Sears Roebuck catalog."

Still, the players had a legitimate point in asserting that the course got tiresome when *every* hole was a dogleg, many of them severe. For instance, what was the point of the 90-degree dogleg on the par-five seventh? Why make it a three-shot hole when the pond near the green would have made it a perfect risk/reward reachable par five? Even the par-three 16th was almost a dogleg when the flag was on the back left of the green, thanks to trees at the left front.

The USGA also had some problems with the course—as did the PGA, which rejected Hazeltine's overtures for hosting a PGA Championship in the 1970s. In 1970, P.J. Boatwright, then the executive director of the USGA, called Hazeltine "a very hard course, but not great architecturally."

Hazeltine carried out some modifications, mostly softening the undulations in the greens, and was given a U.S. Women's Open in 1977. Shortly after that championship, a couple of key Hazeltine members met with Boatwright about hosting a future U.S. Open. They were stunned by his reply. "If you want another Open," he said, "get rid of that 17th hole."

Most members were actually fond of No. 17, a par four of 344 yards that they felt had character. And with the way Jacklin played it, the hole had provided some excitement in an otherwise dull 1970 Open. After a double bogey in the first round, he made birdies in both the second and third rounds after errant drives, hitting stellar second shots, once from the woods and another over a tree. But the USGA didn't like a hole that required a lay-up tee shot with an iron so late in the round.

The USGA originally gave Hazeltine the Open largely because of Heffelfinger, who had been USGA president from 1952 to '53. The championship had outgrown the Minneapolis area's two previous U.S. Open sites, Minikahda (1916) and Interlachen (1930)—Heffelfinger also was a member of the former.

But after an unsuccessful debut, no amount of influence could lure back the Open without a major facelift to the course. So a trio of members, future USGA President Reed Mackenzie, Minnesota Golf Association Executive Director Warren Rebholz, and Robert Fischer, set about finding a solution. A logical step seemed to be to turn No. 17 into a par three, but what to do about the 16th, a par three played with Lake Hazeltine as a backdrop? Back-to-back par threes wouldn't do.

One day, Mackenzie was tramping through some bushes behind the 15th green and found a flat spot near the shore of the lake. In a "Eureka!" moment, he realized that it could be the tee for a par-four 16th. Thus was born a hole that many now consider one of the best in America.

Trent Jones came to town in 1978 to work on some other changes. When Mackenzie and the others told him of their idea, Trent Jones made a sketch on a napkin. But the redesign of 16 and 17 was mostly the work of the members. Trent Jones's idea was for the par-three 17th to follow the path of the tee shot on the old 17th, but the members didn't want to lose the 17th green, so they built the new hole to correspond roughly to the approach shot on the old one (but longer).

The new 16th required a tee shot of some 200 yards over lake and marsh to reach the fairway. The green was placed on a peninsula built into the lake. It left a very long uphill walk to the 17th tee, but the new layout was worth the inconvenience.

No. 16 played at 384 yards for the 1991 Open, with Trent Jones's son Rees providing the finishing touch by turning a drainage ditch on the left of the fairway into a clearly defined hazard. Ironically, many players used irons from the tee, but it was a much better hole than the old 17th and at least offered the option of hitting a 3-wood. When the 16th played into a strong headwind in the third round, it required a 3-wood or driver from the tee and turned into a terror, extracting an average score of 4.938.

The new holes were decisive in that Open. Scott Simpson held a two-stroke lead on Sunday when his 1-iron tee shot on 16 drifted left into the rough, leading to a bogey. When he also bogeyed 18, he fell into a playoff with Payne Stewart.

"There is no reason why I can't make birdies over those last three holes tomorrow [in the play-off]," said Simpson, who had bogeyed 16 and 17 in the third round. Instead, he came to 16 with a two-stroke lead and bogeyed the final three to lose by two. Stewart forced a tie by holing a 20-foot birdie putt on 16 as Simpson three-putted from 30 feet, then took the lead for good on 17 when Simpson pulled his tee shot into the water.

There were other big changes in 1978, mostly eliminating or softening doglegs. So you might say the course lost its bark, while retaining its bite.

The parallel ninth and 18th were turned from sharp left doglegs to gentle ones. The first half of the ninth hole became the 18th, playing to a new green, while a new ninth hole was built to the left of the old one, and the children's course reduced from nine holes to three. The first, yet another dogleg left, became nearly straight.

After the changes, the USGA still wasn't sure about Hazeltine as a U.S. Open course but awarded it the 1983 U.S. Senior Open, then a fairly new event. Many of the competitors had played in the 1970 Open, and they endorsed the changes. Even Dave Hill liked it. He hadn't turned 50 and wasn't eligible for the Senior Open, but had a chance to

An Open Moment

Jack Nicklaus stood on the sixth tee at two-over par for the first round of the 1970 U.S. Open. He observed the wind whipping at 35 miles per hour and said to playing companion Orville Moody, "You know, anything in the 70s would be a good score today. I wouldn't be embarrassed to shoot an 80." He did worse. Nicklaus triple bogeyed the sixth, pulling his second shot into a pond and missing a two-foot putt. He followed that with bogeys on the seventh and eighth for a 43 on the front nine. After the round, Tony Jacklin, who'd been four-under before making a bogey and a double bogey on the last three holes for a 71, ran into Nicklaus and said, "I blew it. I had it, but I blew it. What did you shoot?" "Eighty-one," replied Nicklaus. "And I played well on the back to get it."

16TH HOLE

see the course around that time. A successful event prompted the USGA to award Hazeltine its second-chance Open in 1991. The club then hired the younger Jones to make more changes. With a major redesign already done in the previous decade, Rees Jones's work was more of a refinement. He got rid of most of the remaining blind shots, changed some bunkering, built a new back tee on the 18th, and made the aforementioned change to the hazard to the left of 16. He finalized a redesign of the par-five seventh, building a new tee to reduce the dogleg and reduce the yardage to bring the water next to the green more in play on the second shot.

The course played to almost exactly the same yardage in 1991 as in 1970—7,149 yards to 7,151. Otherwise, Hazeltine was almost completely different. So was the reaction.

"There's not a bad hole out there," said Lanny Wadkins, providing the prevailing sentiment. "It's a fair course, the way an Open course is supposed to be."

Hazeltine's strong suit now is its variety, resulting in part from its terrain, which was part farmland, part forest, and part lakefront before the course was built. The woodland holes are some of the least changed and some of the best, including the sixth, a dogleg (there still are a few) medium-length par four with a pond to the left of the green. On the back nine are the 12th, a longer par four framed by trees, and the short par-four 14th, where Tiger Woods made a costly bogey in the 2002 PGA Championship before rallying with birdies on the last four holes to finish one behind Rich Beem.

After record attendance of 40,000 per day, favorable reaction to the course, and a suspenseful finish at the 1991 U.S. Open, the club was relieved. "I'll be honest," said Rebholz. "If things had gone the other way in 1991, we'd have been toast. I don't think we would have gotten another chance to host a major championship."

Although USGA officials spoke favorably about returning, they delayed the process just enough for

17TH HOLE

PAYNE STEWART

the PGA of America to offer Hazeltine the 2002 and 2009 PGAs and the 2016 Ryder Cup—a deal the club couldn't refuse.

What did they do to prepare? Bring in Jones for another redesign, of course. This time he built five new tees to add 211 yards. For good measure, he overhauled every bunker. A few years later, he made further modifications in preparation for the 2006 U.S. Amateur. Such willingness to constantly change and update their course, unmatched by any club except perhaps Augusta National, has led some members to joke that the club's logo should include a bulldozer.

"Dad took a real beating in 1970," Jones says, "which created sort of a Jones family mission to bring Hazeltine up to today's standards."

1970 TOP FINISHERS

Tony Jacklin	71-70-70-70—281
Dave Hill	75-69-71-73—288
Bob Charles	76-71-75-67—289
Bob Lunn	77-72-70-70—289
Ken Still	78-71-71-71—291
Miller Barber	75-75-72-70—292
Gay Brewer	75-71-71-76—293
Billy Casper	75-75-71-73—294
Bruce Devlin	75-75-71-73—294
Lee Trevino	77-73-74-70—294
Larry Ziegler	75-73-73-73—294

Low round: Charles, Randy Wolff, 67

1991 TOP FINISHERS

*Payne Stewart	67-70-73-72—282
Scott Simpson	70-68-72-72—282
Fred Couples	70-70-75-70—285
Larry Nelson	73-72-72-68—285
Fuzzy Zoeller	72-73-74-67—286
Scott Hoch	69-71-74-73—287
Nolan Henke	67-71-77-73—288
Ray Floyd	73-72-76-68—289
Jose Maria Olazabal	73-71-75-70—289
Corey Pavin	71-67-79-72—289

*Stewart won playoff, 75-77

Low round: Henke, Pavin, Stewart, Zoeller, 67

Scorecard

Hole	Par	Yardage 1970 Open	Yardage 1991 Open	Yardage Today	Average*	Rank*
1	4	456	440	462	4.25	5
2	4	424	435	435	4.06	14
3	5	585	580	633	5.04	16
4	3	196	194	194	3.11	12
5	4	394	412	412	4.19	9
6	4	408	405	405	4.22	7
7	5	563	518	543	4.77	18
8	3	185	166	176	3.22	8
9	4	400	432	432	4.23	6
Out	36	3611	3582	3692	37.09	
10	4	414	410	410	4.08	13
11	5	590	556	606	4.97	17
12	4	426	432	466	4.26	4
13	3	172	204	247	3.28	3
14	4	355	357	352	4.15	11
15	5	592	590	642	5.05	15
16	3/4	214	384	402	4.40	1
17	4/3	344	182	182	3.18	10
18	4	433	452	474	4.33	2
In	36	3540	3567	3781	37.69	
Total	72	7151	7149	7473	74.79	

*Average score and rank from 1991 Open

9TH HOLE. OPPOSITE: 5TH HOLE

INTERLACHEN COUNTRY CLUB EDINA, MINNESOTA 1930

Interlachen Country Club has held only one U.S. Open, but it was of the highest historic sig-

nificance: Bobby Jones won the third leg of his 1930 Grand Slam there. ¶ Although history

remembers the championship primarily for three shots by Jones, all of which had an element

of luck, the real key to his victory was the third round, in which the greatest amateur in the

game's history was firing on all cylinders and opened a huge lead. ¶ First, the memorable

shots. In the second round, Jones hit the "lily pad shot" on the ninth hole, a reachable par five

with a pond fronting the green. Jones semi-topped his second shot, which skipped across the

water (it didn't actually hit any lily pads) and finished on the bank on the other side. He got

up and down for a birdie. Later, in his book *Golf is My Game*, Jones revealed he was distracted

as he was starting his downswing—two girls in the gallery moved as if they were about to run

across the fairway.

18TH HOLE

The other two shots came on the last two holes of the championship. Struggling to hold his lead, Jones hit his tee shot on the 17th, a monster par three of 262 yards, off a tree and toward an area to the right that was normally a water hazard but had turned into a dry marsh because of a drought. The ball was not found, but USGA official Prescott Bush (grandfather of President George H.W. Bush) ruled that it was in a parallel hazard and allowed Jones to drop in the fairway. Jones made a double bogey, but it might have been worse if he had to go back to the tee under the stroke-and-distance penalty.

Jones then put an exclamation point on the championship by holing a 40-foot birdie putt on the 18th hole. The huge roar echoed back to Macdonald Smith, mounting a final-round challenge several groups behind. Ultimately, Jones won by two.

For all his good fortune, though, Jones effectively won the championship with a third-round 68 that was one of his best ever. He hit three approach shots within one foot of the hole and didn't make a putt longer than 10 feet.

"I have never seen him as keen to rip into par, as deeply concentrated on one big round, as he was when he marched to the tee that forenoon for the third round," wrote Grantland Rice in *The American Golfer.*

In *Golf is My Game*, Jones wrote, "I felt as I think a good halfback must feel when he bursts through a line of scrimmage…sees an open field ahead of him, and feels confident he has the speed to reach the goal."

Jones opened up a five-stroke lead, enough cushion to win despite a final-round 75. "If I had been that halfback in an open field," he went on to finish his analogy, "I stumbled so many times before I got to the goal line that I am sure my coach would have made me turn in my uniform."

Interlachen certainly provided enough obstacles: rolling terrain, ankle-high rough, water hazards, and a couple of outsized holes that would stand up even today in terms of yardage. In fact, the 262-yard 17th still ranks as the longest par three in Open history. The first hole was a par four of 478 yards that

Scorecard

HOLE	PAR	YARDAGE 1930 OPEN	YARDAGE TODAY
1	4/5	478	531
2	4	370	355
3	3	180	200
4	5	506	525
5	3	178	176
6	4	343	345
7	4	352	360
8	4	397	430
9	5	485	530
Out	36/37	3289	3450
10	4	344	347
11	5	484	475
12	5	530	557
13	3	194	190
14	4	444	440
15	4	408	414
16	4	315	318
17	3	262	225
18	4	402	413
In	36	3383	3379
Total	72/73	6672	6829

required two wood shots. (Both are easier today: No. 17 is shorter while No. 1 is longer but is now a par five.) On the other hand, a number of short par fours and par fives offered birdie chances—if a player could keep the ball in the fairway.

Designed in 1911, Interlachen was the first solo project for Willie Watson, who later moved to California and built a number of courses, including San Francisco's Olympic Club. In 1919, Interlachen brought in Donald Ross, the leading architect at the time, for an extensive remodeling. Before the 1930 Open, the club's pro, Willie Kidd, changed the 16th and 17th holes.

Interlachen was scheduled to host the 1942 U.S. Open, which was cancelled because of World War II. After the war, the club wasn't in financial position to hold an Open. Later, the championship's logistic needs outgrew the club's ability to host it.

Robert Trent Jones Sr. changed two holes in 1962 and Geoffrey Cornish did some bunker work in 1984, but they didn't change the essence of the historic course. Still highly regarded and ranked 44th in the U.S. by *Golf Digest*, Interlachen was the site of the 1993 Walker Cup and 2002 Solheim Cup, and is getting ready for the 2008 U.S. Women's Open.

While the U.S. Open may have left Interlachen behind, for one week the course was the canvas for one of the greatest players ever at his peak. Before the 1930 Open, Walter Hagen, the greatest professional of the era, stated, "This championship will be the hardest championship that any man has ever won…it is the field against one man—Bobby Jones." If the best pros couldn't beat Jones, it was unlikely any amateur would, and two months later the Georgian won the U.S. Amateur at Merion to complete the Grand Slam, already having swept the British Open and Amateur. Afterward, feeling he had accomplished all he could, Jones retired from competition at age 28.

1930 TOP FINISHERS
Bobby Jones   71-73-68-75—287
Macdonald Smith   70-75-74-70—289
Horton Smith   72-70-76-74—292
Harry Cooper   72-72-73-76—293
Johnny Golden   74-73-71-76—294
Low round: Jones, 68

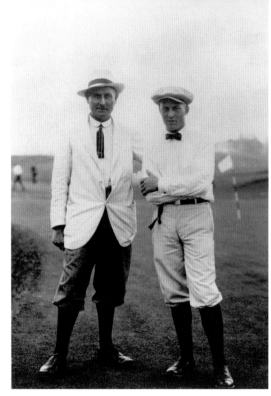

HARRY VARDON AND BOBBY JONES. OPPOSITE TOP: 5TH
HOLE. OPPOSITE BOTTOM: 7TH HOLE

INVERNESS CLUB TOLEDO, OHIO 1920, 1931, 1957, 1979

The Inverness Club is considered to be one of the master works of architect Donald Ross. But

nobody knows exactly how much of it he actually was responsible for. ¶ Ross wasn't the

original architect; the club opened with nine holes in 1903 and he was called in for a rede-

sign in 1916. It was long thought that Ross was hired to build a second nine and to upgrade the

existing nine, but research for the recent club history by Dave Hackenberg reveals references

to an 18-hole course in place before Ross's arrival—although the mentions are hardly defini-

tive. ¶ The ambiguity surrounding Inverness's early years does not end there. According to

the records, Bernard Nichols was the original architect. Since many courses of the era were

designed by Scottish golf professionals, this may have been a misspelling of Bernard Nicholls,

a noted pro around the turn of the century. On the other hand, there's no other evidence that

Nicholls designed courses.

Whoever the designer was, his math wasn't good. At the last minute, it was discovered that his original plans consisted of only eight holes, so a par three was hastily squeezed into the layout.

By bringing in Ross, the members showed they were determined to possess a course worthy of hosting tournaments. Ross devised a plan in 1916, but it is not known to what extent his layout used existing holes. There aren't even any records or drawings to show which of the current holes correspond to the original nine or 18.

But Ross did make several visits to the site, which makes Inverness one of the few "hands-on" courses for a prolific architect who sometimes did

his designing from a distance. Most of the work was carried out in 1917–18.

The routing takes advantage of the rolling topography and its main feature, a depression that cuts perpendicularly across eight holes. A stream runs intermittently through that depression and sometimes dives underground, helping give the course its early name of "Innerness," or "inner stream." Later, founder S.P. Jermain's wife looked at a map of Great Britain and suggested naming it after the Scottish town.

Ross's stamps are his bunkering and green complexes, though how much he rebuilt them is unclear. But it is known that Ross built a new green

8TH HOLE

for the 18th hole and created two holes on newly acquired property. These holes are the fourth and seventh, and they were the two hardest holes on Ross's course.

The seventh hole (the fifth in Ross's design) is considered one of the architect's classics. It doesn't have any bunkers and doesn't need them. At 438 uphill yards, it played long for 1920. It recently has been extended to 481 yards. A brook runs along the right of a narrow fairway, but the biggest challenge is the green, difficult to hit in regulation and tricky to putt. Its slope is so severe a putt from above the hole can easily trickle off the green.

A number of architects have tinkered with the course since Ross, mostly in preparation for champi-

onships. A.W. Tillinghast made some modest touch-ups before the 1931 Open. Dick Wilson lengthened the course for the 1957 Open and did extensive bunker work, but said, "Anyone who changes this Rembrandt is crazy."

A couple of decades later, some thought the uncle-nephew team of George and Tom Fazio was guilty of drawing moustaches on the masterpiece when they built four new holes before the 1979 U.S. Open. Originally, they were brought in to moder-ate the slope on the 17th green, which was too severe for modern green speeds. The members soon wanted the Fazios to look into another concern, congestion.

The 17th green and the 16th and 18th tees, as well as the seventh green and eighth tee, were within just yards of each other. The Fazios envi-sioned a massive gallery bottleneck on this spot, along with two other areas.

Inverness already had bought property on which the possibility of building new holes had been discussed, and Team Fazio came up with a plan that included three holes on the new property and a new par five that would use land occupied by the current sixth, seventh, and eighth holes. It also called for the elimination of the 13th, the one that had been crammed in on the original nine.

In many ways, the Fazios took great care to make sure the new holes didn't change the exist-ing mix. The par-three eighth was replaced by a par-three sixth of similar length. The new par-four fifth was a dogleg left, as was the old seventh. The 13th was replaced by another par three, the new third, slightly longer.

The new eighth hole added a par five to the championship course, a bonus since there had been only one par five in the 1957 U.S. Open, after the ninth was converted to a par four. But the total par remained the same for regular play: No. 9, a par five for members, lost some yardage and became a par four. The changes to that corner of the course also enabled a new 18th tee, stretching the hole from a too-short 330 yards to 354.

The green contours were copied from the origi-nals. What's more, the turf was actually removed from the old greens and replanted on the new ones, because the German bentgrass used for the greens was no longer available.

Why, then, did critics lambaste the new holes for being out of character with the rest of the course? Mainly because two of the new greens, the third

and fifth, were guarded closely by ponds. Although Ross was not averse to using water hazards when they naturally presented themselves, he refrained from creating them.

Arthur Hills, a golf architect and Inverness member, has done the most recent work at the club. To better integrate the Fazio holes, he turned the pond at the fifth hole back into a natural stream before the 1986 PGA Championship. More recently, he made some significant changes that were equal parts restoration and modernization. Hills's study of old photographs led him to expand some greens, and also to redo some bunkers more in Ross's original style. Meanwhile, he built new tees on seven holes to increase the course to a more formidable 7,255 yards.

Inverness has not hosted an Open since 1979 or a major since the 1993 PGA Championship, but the recent changes increase the club's chances of hopping back onto the Open carousel.

A return to Inverness would be welcome if the course were to produce the kind of drama, intrigue, and occasional wackiness that marked its four prior Opens.

The first Inverness Open in 1920 saw top-10 finishes from 18-year-old Bobby Jones, playing in his first U.S. Open, and 50-year-old Harry Vardon, playing in his third and last. Vardon, owner of six British Open titles, had entered the 1900 and 1913 Opens, winning the first and losing a playoff to Francis Ouimet in the second. Now he embarked on a final U.S. tour along with Ted Ray, the third man in the 1913 playoff.

This time, Vardon wasn't expected to win. But he summoned the form of his prime and held a four-stroke lead on the 12th tee in the final round. But a storm suddenly arose, and the ending was bitter. The wind, fatigue, and an unreliable putting stroke combined to sink Vardon. He played the last seven holes in seven-over and finished one behind the champion, Ray.

"Even as tired as I was, I can't see how I broke so badly," Vardon said that evening. "Why, I am sure I could go out now and do better by kicking the ball around those last few holes with my boot."

The beneficiary was 43-year-old Ray, who remained the oldest U.S. Open champion until Ray Floyd in 1986. (In 1990, 45-year-old Hale Irwin won.)

17TH HOLE

18TH HOLE

Had Vardon been able to hold on, he would have been the oldest winner of any major championship.

An affable fellow and one of the longest hitters of his day, Ray used a grip-it-and-rip-it philosophy, firing his tee shot over trees guarding the dogleg on the 320-yard seventh in all four rounds. He successfully hit the green or its vicinity every time to make four birdies. After being stretched to 400 yards before the 1957 Open, this hole was eliminated in the Fazio redesign.

Vardon wasn't the only one to wonder, "What if?" Leo Diegel was a high-strung 22-year-old from Detroit who appeared to have a great chance down the stretch, especially since the storm had abated. Diegel would finish his career with two PGA Championships, but might have won more majors if not for his nerves, which cost him at Inverness.

Diegel topped his tee shot on the 14th hole as a spectator coughed violently on his downswing. While he was walking to his ball, an acquaintance rushed up to him to tell him what he needed to shoot to win. Diegel threw his club to the ground and announced, "I don't care what scores anyone else had! I'm playing my own game!" He would make a double bogey and follow it with bogeys on 15 and 16. Pars on the last two holes left Diegel tied for second with Vardon, Jack Burke (father of 1956 Masters and PGA champion Jackie), and Jock Hutchison.

Diegel again contended in the 1931 Open at Inverness, finishing two strokes back in third place. Sportswriter Grantland Rice described this curious championship as "the most sensational open ever played in the 500-year history of golf." Yet it has come to be viewed as more of a farce. Each side holds some truth.

At the time, ties were settled by a 36-hole playoff. That year, Billy Burke and George Von Elm tied after 36 extra holes, which meant 36 more holes the next day. Ultimately, Burke had to play eight rounds to nip Von Elm by a stroke. The USGA reverted to 18-hole playoffs afterward.

Von Elm provided plenty of drama, making birdies on the 325-yard 18th at the end of regulation

An Open Moment

Leo Diegel's caddie for the last nine holes of the 1920 U.S. Open was Chick Evans, the great amateur who had won the Open four years earlier. Evans had just finished his own run at the title (his 298 total left him three back) and wandered back onto the course to check on the progress of Diegel, who had just had a disagreement with his caddie.

Diegel came to the last two holes knowing he needed a birdie to match Ted Ray. He had a chance on the tough 17th, hitting a great second shot to eight feet. Diegel and Evans spent a lot of time studying the crucial putt.

Finally, Diegel stroked the putt, and watched it hit the cup and stay out. When a long birdie putt failed to drop on the 18th, Diegel finished one back.

and in the first playoff to prolong the marathon. The second playoff, like the first, was a tense struggle and included several lead changes. Former U.S. Amateur champion Von Elm made more birdies, but missed from inside two feet three times in the final round. The steadier Burke, an ironworker before he joined the Tour, rarely found the rough flanking fairways that "had been contracted in such a way to make them the narrowest that they have ever been on any course on which the championship has been played," according to *Golf Illustrated*.

Crowds for the 1931 Open were disappointing, largely because this was the first year after Bobby Jones's retirement. But when organizers cut the cost of a ticket to $1 for the afternoon round of the second playoff day, players had to wait on a number of occasions for the gallery to be controlled. "It looks as though we had to play all week to draw a crowd," Burke said.

The scene of Von Elm's important birdies, the 18th hole again was key in the 1957 Open. While the short par four is hardly a pushover—its fairway is snaky, its green tiny and well-bunkered—it affords a realistic birdie possibility. In 1957, both Dick Mayer and Cary Middlecoff birdied it to move past Jimmy Demaret, the 47-year-old three-time Masters champion.

Middlecoff's birdie came right after Mayer made his. Middlecoff was a notoriously slow player, and the *Toledo Blade* joked that he took as much time

studying the putt as Burke and Von Elm did for their entire 72-hole playoff. "I looked the first time and thought I should give it about three inches of break," he said afterward. "Then I looked again and thought four would do it. Every time I looked, it got bigger. Finally, I decided not to let her out on the amateur side [low side] so I played it about eight inches."

Middlecoff shot 68-68 in the last two rounds, matching Gene Sarazen in 1932 for the best 36-hole finish ever. But he had nothing left for the playoff, which Mayer won by seven strokes with a 72.

The final round of the 1979 Open was dull by comparison. Irwin began with a three-stroke lead and won by two despite a double bogey-bogey finish on a course that played tough because the small greens were exceptionally firm.

The intrigue came earlier. In the first round, Lon Hinkle decided to take a shortcut on the par-five eighth hole. Neither the Fazios nor the USGA had noticed an opening to play the hole down the adjacent 17th fairway, leaving a shorter second shot to the green, albeit over trees.

Five other players took Hinkle's route, and the USGA feared more would try it the next day. So they planted a 24-foot Black Hills spruce early the next morning to block the opening. It didn't stop Hinkle or some others, who fired through the smaller gap.

By the 1986 PGA, more flora joined the "Hinkle Tree," cutting off that option for good. Both the 1986 and 1993 PGAs meant heartbreak for Greg Norman. Bob Tway holed from a greenside bunker on No. 18 to win in 1986, then Norman lipped out putts on the 18th in both regulation and a playoff to lose to Paul Azinger in 1993.

A 24-year-old Norman also had a bit role in Inverness history, making his first appearance at a major championship in the 1979 Open. His playing partners for the first two rounds were Hinkle and Chi Chi Rodriguez.

Teeing off first, Hinkle took his shortcut, and Rodriguez followed the same route. It may seem surprising considering Norman's later reputation for attacking play, but the man who would become known as the Great White Shark played the hole conventionally. The second day, Hinkle and Rodriguez both defied the USGA by hitting down the 17th fairway again. Norman played safe again, and showed why for him a shortcut wasn't necessary: He reached the green in two and made an eagle.

TED RAY

HALE IRWIN

1920 TOP FINISHERS

Ted Ray	74-73-73-75—295
Jack Burke Sr.	75-77-72-72—296
Leo Diegel	72-74-73-77—296
Jock Hutchison	69-76-74-77—296
Harry Vardon	74-73-71-78—296

Low round: Hutchison, 69

1931 TOP FINISHERS

*Billy Burke	73-72-74-73—292
George Von Elm	75-69-73-75—292
Leo Diegel	75-73-74-72—294
Wiffy Cox	75-74-74-72—295
Bill Mehlhorn	77-73-75-71—296
Gene Sarazen	74-78-74-70—296

*Burke won playoff, 149-148 to 149-149

Low round: Von Elm, 69

1957 TOP FINISHERS

*Dick Mayer	70-68-74-70—282
Cary Middlecoff	71-75-68-68—282
Jimmy Demaret	68-73-70-72—283
Julius Boros	69-75-70-70—284
Walter Burkemo	74-73-72-65—284
Fred Hawkins	72-72-71-71—286
Ken Venturi	69-71-75-71—286
Roberto De Vicenzo	72-70-72-76—290
Chick Harbert	68-79-71-72—290
Billy Maxwell	70-76-72-72—290
Billy Joe Patton	70-68-76-76—290
Sam Snead	74-74-69-73—290

*Mayer won playoff, 72-79

Low round: Burkemo, 65

1979 TOP FINISHERS

Hale Irwin	74-68-67-75—284
Jerry Pate	71-74-69-72—286
Gary Player	73-73-72-68—286
Larry Nelson	71-68-76-73—288
Bill Rogers	71-72-73-72—288
Tom Weiskopf	71-74-67-76—288
David Graham	73-73-70-73—289
Tom Purtzer	70-69-75-76—290
Keith Fergus	70-77-72-72—291
Jack Nicklaus	74-77-72-68—291

Low round: Irwin, Weiskopf, 67

Scorecard

Ross Course

Hole	Par	Yardage 1920 Open	Yardage 1957 Open
1	4	385	394
2	4	392	384
3	3	135	175
4	4	430	466
5	4	438	423
6	4	360	385
7	4	320	400
8	3	208	212
9	5/4	492	466
Out	35/34	3160	3305
10	4	346	400
11	4	359	380
12	5	522	527
13	3	150	167
14	4	417	479
15	4	443	468
16	4	410	412
17	4	430	451
18	4	332	330
In	36	3409	3614
Total	71/70	6569	6919

Ross/Fazio Course Today

Hole*	Par	Yardage 1979 Open	Yardage Today
1 (1)	4	398	395
2 (2)	4	385	385
3	3	185	200
4 (4)	4	466	466
5	4	401	450
6	3	220	231
7 (5)	4	452	481
8	5	528	569
9 (9)	4	420	468
Out	35	3455	3645
10 (10)	4	363	363
11 (11)	4	378	378
12 (3)	3	167	172
13 (12)	5	523	516
14 (14)	4	448	480
15 (15)	4	458	468
16 (16)	4	405	409
17 (17)	4	431	470
18 (18)	4	354	354
In	36	3527	3610
Total	71	6982	7255

*Hole number from Ross course in parentheses

BOBBY JONES PUTTING IN 1923. OPPOSITE: 2ND HOLE

INWOOD COUNTRY CLUB INWOOD, NEW YORK 1923

We live in an age in which a highly demanding media is quick to pin a tag on the best player who hasn't won a major. Recently, players like David Duval, Phil Mickelson, and Colin Montgomerie have worn that dubious badge. ¶ But there is nothing new about this phenomenon. More than 80 years ago, Bobby Jones came into the 1923 U.S. Open at Inwood Country Club without a victory in either the Open or the U.S. Amateur, the two biggest events of the era. He had contended a few times and posted a second-place finish in each. For this, he was labeled a talented player who didn't have the fortitude to win. Here's the kicker—Jones was just 21 years old at the time. ¶ "They said Bobby Jones couldn't win because he didn't have punch," wrote Jones's biographer and confidant O.B. Keeler in *The Bobby Jones Story.* "They said he was the greatest golfer in the world but he lacked the punch. We had heard it a thousand times, but we never had to hear it again. One stroke settled that little matter for ever and ever."

That stroke came at the 1923 Open, and it was one of the greatest shots—and gutsiest decisions—of all time. Jones and Bobby Cruickshank were tied during their 18-hole playoff when they arrived at the final hole, a 425-yard par four with a lagoon in front of the green.

Cruickshank half-topped his drive into the left rough, forcing a lay-up second. Jones let his drive slide to the right, and the ball finished in the rough, 190 yards from the hole. Did he dare risk a shot at the green over the water? Jones didn't hesitate, decisively grabbing a 2-iron from his bag. (He later wrote that he didn't remember the moment at all.) The shot not only carried the water, it flew straight at the hole, finishing six feet away. His par gave him the title.

At the awards ceremony, a relieved Jones said, "I don't care what happens now." He finally had his championship—12 others would follow.

Jones would have won his first major a day earlier if not for a collapse that seemed to prove his critics correct. He was four-over on his last three holes, including a double bogey on 18. Despite the finish, Keeler figured Jones's total would hold up and said, "Bob, I think you're champion."

"I didn't finish like a champion," Jones responded. "I finished like a yellow dog."

It took a shot just as great as the one Jones would hit in the playoff to force the extra round. Trailing by one, Cruickshank hit a 2-iron of his own to six feet and made the putt to tie Jones. The *New York Times* called it "one of the greatest shots ever made at any championship."

Considering Inwood's origins, it was an unlikely that the greatest golfers in the world would be competing there. The club was started by tobacco merchant Jacob Wertheim as a present to his fiancée, Emma Stern, who wanted to play golf but didn't have a place to do so.

In 1901, Wortheim and some associates rented a potato farm in Inwood, just outside Queens, and began the club. They hired Dr. William Exton to design nine holes, but, according to the club history, "In its new status as a golf course, it bore a striking resemblance to the original farm."

The next year, Inwood had a pro lined up from A.G. Spalding & Bros., but the morning he was supposed to go to the club for a meeting, the candidate showed up drunk at the Spalding office. Looking around, Spalding manager Charles Kirshner saw Edward Eriksen, an ex-baseball player who had thrown out his arm and was looking for a job as a coach. Kirshner suggested he go to Inwood to apply for the job.

18TH HOLE

BOBBY JONES PLAQUE ON THE 18TH HOLE

"But I know nothing about golf," Eriksen said.

"Neither do they," Kirshner replied.

Eriksen was hired, and it proved to be a good move for both sides. A quick study, Eriksen not only became a respected teacher, but he also laid out a new, much better, nine holes. By 1906, he laid out nine more.

Inwood was also fortunate in hiring English pro Herbert Strong in 1912. It turned out Strong had a flair for golf architecture, and he made many refinements to the course. After five years, Strong left to become a full-time course designer and was responsible for another Open site, Cleveland's Canterbury. The next pro, Jack Mackie, continued the refining process.

The first big event at Inwood was the 1921 PGA Championship, won by Walter Hagen but perhaps most noteworthy for an incident involving a tree. Hagen and others played the 11th hole by hitting drives down the 18th fairway because it set up a better approach to the green. One night, Mackie led a delegation into the woods adjacent to the 16th fairway, uprooted a 15-foot willow tree, and replanted it near the 11th tee to block the alternate route. "Hagen's Willow" is still there.

Situated less than a mile from the ocean and not far from Kennedy Airport, many of Inwood's holes have a links feel. The surrounding land, however, is marshy (if you play, bring insect repellant), so it isn't true links turf. Inwood was redesigned in 1926 by Mackie, with three holes eliminated and new ones built closer to the bay by filling marshland with sand. A quirky layout, with three consecutive par fives followed by two straight par threes on the front nine, it has been little changed since and still plays to about the same yardage. The hole that was the 12th in 1923, now the 10th, is the shortest hole in U.S. Open history at 108 yards (currently 106).

1923 TOP FINISHERS

*Bobby Jones	71-73-76-76—296
Bobby Cruickshank	73-72-78-73—296
Jock Hutchison	70-72-82-78—302
Jack Forrester	75-73-77-78—303
Johnny Farrell	76-77-75-76—304
Francis Gallett	76-72-77-79—304
W.M. Reekie	80-74-75-75—304

*Jones won playoff, 76-78

Low round: Hutchison, 70

Scorecard

1923 U.S. Open

HOLE	PAR	YARDAGE
1	4	343
2	4	371
3	5	522
4	5	530
5	5	519
6	3	177
7	3	223
8	4	318
9	4	360
Out	37	3363
10	4	295
11	4	421
12	3	108
13	4	420
14	5	497
15	3	173
16	4	425
17	4	405
18	4	425
In	35	3169
Total	72	6532

Post-1926 Course

HOLE*	PAR	YARDAGE
1 (1)	4	345
2 (2)	4	362
3 (3)	5	514
4 (4)	5	539
5 (5)	5	512
6 (6)	3	171
7 (7)	3	219
8 (8)	4	415
9 (11)	4	419
Out	37	3496
10 (12)	3	106
11 (13)	4	433
12 (14)	4	456
13	4	341
14	3	155
15	4	471
16 (16)	4	376
17 (17)	4	405
18 (18)	4	408
In	34	3151
Total	71	6647

*Hole numbers from 1923 in parentheses

HALE IRWIN CELEBRATES HIS 72ND-HOLE BIRDIE IN 1990. OPPOSITE TOP: 2ND HOLE. OPPOSITE BOTTOM: 13TH HOLE

MEDINAH COUNTRY CLUB (NO. 3 COURSE) MEDINAH, ILLINOIS 1949, 1975, 1990

It has become part of golf lore that the members of Medinah Country Club decided to redesign their No. 3 Course after Harry Cooper showed them it was too easy by shooting a 63 at the 1930 Medinah Open. It's a nice story, but it's not true. The real story is even better. ¶ Actually, the members already had decided to redesign the course in 1929, and the plans for the stronger layout were drawn up that same year, before Cooper ever set foot on Medinah. The reason for the change: The four founding members had perpetrated a land swindle and were planning to build a housing development on a portion of the property. When first building No. 3, they instructed architect Tom Bendelow not to use that block of land, which forced him to compromise on the layout. ¶ The club swept that untidy story under the rug for a long while. To their credit, the members revealed the deception in a recent club history, *The Spirit of Medinah,* by Timothy Cronin. Then there is another misconception. The common view is that the club was founded by the Chicago chapter of the Shriners (known as the Ancient Arabic

Order of the Mystic Shrine), the Medinah Temple. Actually, the temple merely gave its tacit endorsement and permission to use its name and symbol, but was not financially involved. (Only Shriners were allowed as members in the early years, contributing to the image.)

Four Shriners, Charles H. Canode, Theodore R. Heman, Frederick N. Peck, and William S. Barbee, started the club. For $65,000, they bought the first 260 acres for the club in 1923, acting as a four-man partnership called the Irving Lake Land Association. They also controlled the purse strings of Medinah Country Club and used $130,000 of club money to buy the land from their partnership—a quick profit of 100 percent.

That wasn't the end. Memberships were being sold at a rapid rate for between $750 and $1,450 for a club with grandiose plans, including a huge, ornate clubhouse designed by Ricard Gustav Schmidt in a distinctive blend of Byzantine, Oriental, Louis XIV, and Italian styles that would open in 1926. Within a few years there were 1,500 members, and the four partners took a healthy 30 percent from each member. Finally, in the course of buying more land, they secretly kept a parcel of 77 acres for themselves. They planned on using it for a luxury home development for club members to be called Medinah Forest.

Their scheme started to unravel when members decided their third course (No. 1 opened in 1925 and No. 2 a year later) should be 18 holes instead of nine. That caused the awkward initial design that skirted the property the partners were holding. The four founders didn't actually own Medinah Country Club, so when the club got around to electing officers and a board after the clubhouse opened, the members began to realize what was happening.

In April 1927, the club sued the four founders, asking for $576,814.30 in damages and clear title to all the land. A year and a half later, with the legal system moving slowly and attorney's fees mounting, Medinah Temple Potentate Edward H. Thomas urged the two sides to settle. The founders turned over the 77 acres to the club and resigned their memberships. In turn, the club agreed not to try to collect any of the money the four had diverted to themselves from the membership fees.

In 1929, the club sent Bendelow back to the drawing board to use that land for the No. 3 Course. Financial considerations, however, prevented the work from starting until 1931—after Cooper had torched the course with a 63, a virtually unheard-of score for that era. The timing of his round is what started the oft-told myth of the origins of No. 3's redesign.

The new and improved No. 3 included eight new holes and two modified ones. The current third, fourth, eighth, and last half of the seventh holes occupy the land that would have become Medinah Forest, while the extra room also allowed for several other improvements to the routing. The course grew from a modest 6,215 yards to a severe 6,820 yards.

Another bit of misinformed history had the changes being made by Harry Collis, a Chicago-area pro who dabbled in course design. This also turns out not to be true. Bendelow, in fact, was paid $1,000 for the job.

This incorrect version undoubtedly arose out of lack of regard for Bendelow, who had a reputation for laying out courses in a single walk-through during his long design career, which started in 1895 when the transplanted Scotsman was working as a linotype operator for the *New York Herald* and saw a classified ad asking for a golf teacher for a wealthy family. He not only got the job, but he also laid out a six-hole course on the family estate. Bendelow would eventually design more than 600 courses—many of which no longer exist.

Many of those were "quickies," but Bendelow wasn't the only architect to work that way in those days. (His "18 stakes on a Sunday afternoon" label was untrue in one respect: The deeply religious Bendelow never worked on Sunday.) In 1920, at age 52, Bendelow went to work for American Park Builders in Chicago. By then, he was paying more attention to detail, not only drawing up plans but also sometimes building plaster models of greens, showing the contours he wanted.

Bendelow got the Medinah job because American Park Builders was the low bidder. To that point, his only course of real note was Atlanta's East Lake, later redesigned by Donald Ross. But he would take advantage of the opportunity and build his best course, though in a roundabout fashion.

One true part of Medinah lore is that No. 3 was intended as a women's course that would become "famous the country over to and for women." But whereas the No. 1 and No. 2 courses sat mostly on farmland, the topography of No. 3 had the ingredients for a demanding course—it was densely wooded and included Lake Kadijah, a man-made body of water created by damming a stream to turn a wetland into a lake.

16TH HOLE

An Open Moment

The competitors in the 18-hole playoff in 1990 were two-time Open champ Hale Irwin and Mike Donald, who was seeking a second win of any kind. Donald was leading by two strokes when Irwin's drive on No. 16 finished in the left side of the fairway, setting up an uphill second shot from 207 yards that had to be drawn around trees. Irwin, who prefers to fade the ball, hit a perfect right-to-left shot with a 2-iron to six feet. He holed the putt for a birdie to move within one, pulled into a tie when Donald bogeyed the 18th, and won with a birdie on the first sudden-death hole. Irwin later called the 2-iron "the shot of my career. I may have hit other shots as well or better, but not under those nerve-wracking conditions."

Even the first version of No. 3 proved to be too strong for its original intention. No. 2 quickly became the women's course. The second version of No. 3 opened in 1932 and immediately earned a reputation as a Monster of the Midway. Wrote Arthur B. Sweet of the *Chicago Daily News*: "Let Mr. Harry Cooper try to shoot a 63 over this new course. It will never be done."

It still hasn't. In fact, the competitive course record at No. 3 is 65, by Skip Kendall in the 1999 PGA Championship and Tiger Woods and Mike Weir in the 2006 PGA. Cooper came back in 1935 for another Medinah Open, this time a 72-hole event. He won again, but with a total of five-over 289 for four rounds. The best score all week was 69.

While Medinah could provide the stern examination the USGA demands for an Open, it has a star-crossed Open history. There wasn't much wrong with the first Open in 1949, by which time the course had been lengthened to 6,936 yards. Cary Middlecoff, who had given up a career in dentistry to turn pro two and a half years earlier, won the first of his two Open titles without making a single birdie in a final-round 75 for a two-over 286 total. He parred the last eight holes to hold off Sam Snead, who made a costly bogey on the 17th hole to tie for second with Clayton Heafner.

It was 26 years before the Open returned to Medinah, in part because the Western Golf Association decided to make Chicago the annual home of the Western Open in 1962. At first, it rotated among some of the area's great courses, including Medinah in 1962 and 1966. Finally, the Western settled on Butler National as a permanent site in 1974 and Medinah held the Open in 1975.

Peter Andrews wrote in the June 1990 issue of *Golf Digest* that "old-time members of Medinah remember the U.S. Open of 1975 the way people downtown remember the Chicago fire of 1871." In his report for *Golf World,* Ron Coffman called Medinah "the stinkiest, wettest, noisiest, most dangerous, and craziest U.S. Open on record. It was also likely the most disorganized and might have been considered the hottest and most humid but for the memory of Congressional in 1964."

After heavy rains on Tuesday and Wednesday, 1,500 bales of straw from nearby Arlington Park racetrack were brought in to make the wet turf passable for spectators. When mixed with the mud and baked by the hot sun, the straw gave the grounds the aroma of a stable. Spectators still ended up with mud-caked ankles and often returned to parking lots to find their cars stuck in the mud.

The noise came from air traffic at nearby O'Hare, trucks rumbling down Lake Street adjacent to the 10th hole, and children having fun at an amusement park across the road. The danger came from lightning. Tom Watson refused to start his second round when he saw lightning. Just when USGA officials were trying to convince him to start, an even closer bolt struck, suspending play. There was also a lightning delay at a critical juncture of the final round.

Evidences of the disorganization were huge traffic jams and a too-narrow practice range on a hole from one of Medinah's other courses. As for crazy, how about Jack Nicklaus, in his prime at age 35 and coming off a Masters victory, bringing his final-round charge to a crashing halt by making bogeys on the last three holes? He missed the playoff by two strokes.

Nicklaus was hardly only the only player to give up strokes. In the last two hours of play, there was only one birdie by a contender—and there were plenty of contenders. The top three going into the final round, Watson, Frank Beard, and Pat Fitzsimons, shot 77 or 78. Ben Crenshaw double bogeyed the par-three 17th and lost by one. Lou Graham bogeyed the 18th hole to fall into a tie with John Mahaffey, who stormed from six shots back with a seemingly unspectacular even-par 71. Mahaffey would hit 16 greens in the playoff but not make a single birdie, shooting a 73 to lose by two to Graham, a 37-year-old who scored only his third career victory.

Neither Medinah nor the USGA was anxious for a reprise, and when the club did finally decide in 1982 that it was ready to consider hosting another Open, the USGA had little interest. The organization didn't like the 18th hole, a 406-yard dogleg that turned to the right so early the pros needed to hit irons off the tee—with a fade. Moreover, the hole afforded very little room for spectators, and the grandstand in 1975 was so close to the green that it led to numerous drops for players to take relief.

USGA Senior Executive Director Frank Hannigan explained in a letter to the club that the hole would be fine if it were any hole other than the 18th. "In most cases, and given the intensity of feelings on the matters, I would rather say to a man, 'Your wife needs fixing' than 'Your course needs fixing.' Medinah No. 3 'needs fixing' for our very singular purpose only as a venue for a U.S. Open Championship."

Hannigan was right about the intensity of feeling. Medinah enlisted architect Roger Packard for those changes, which needed to be approved by a two-thirds vote. The measure passed only after at first being voted down at two special meetings. At the second meeting, a new vote was held after some opponents of the changes left the building; this time, it got the necessary two-thirds of those present.

Changing the 18th created a domino effect. The new finishing hole was longer and turned slightly left, so the tee was far from the old 17th green. A new 17th was built and some holes, including the former No. 17, were re-sequenced. The 15th, a short par four, was extended to become the par-five 14th, turning the course from a par 71 to a 72. The old par-three 14th was abandoned. Holes 12, 13, 16, and 17 became, respectively, 15, 16, 12, and 13.

"We took out the weakest holes and made three new holes that are as strong as the other 15," said Packard at the time. But the 168-yard 17th became the new problem hole—the severe back-to-front slope of the green made pitches and putts from above the hole an adventure.

Just as in 1975, neither the membership nor the USGA was happy about the 1990 Open. The members' complaints involved the course setup. P.J. Boatwright, the USGA official in charge of competition, felt the 7,336-yard No. 3 course was too long and set the course at 7,195 yards.

Then came the Wednesday night deluge. With the course playing hard and fast in the practice rounds, Boatwright felt it might play too tough, so he ordered the rough to be cut on Wednesday. But two inches of rain made the course play much easier. The 36-hole cut came at one-over, a record for the Open, leading the members to complain that the pros hadn't played the "real" Medinah.

They had a point. On the other hand, the conditions helped provide an exciting finish. In the final round, Hale Irwin played the back nine in 31, including four straight birdies and a 45-foot birdie putt on the 18th, one of the most scintillating moments in U.S. Open history. He and Mike Donald finished at eight-under 280, with Irwin becoming the first sudden-death Open champion after the 18-hole playoff ended in a tie.

The outcome left the USGA unconvinced that Medinah was a truly great course. "Medinah is not a tried-and-true championship site," said executive director David Fay a decade later.

With the USGA losing interest, the PGA snatched it up for the 1999 and 2006 PGA Championships and 2012 Ryder Cup. Before the 1999 PGA, Medinah ripped up the 17th and had Roger Rulewich design a new one. He moved the green away from the water and up the hill, lengthening it to 206 yards. Tiger Woods won after yet another big rain just before the tournament led to soft conditions.

In 2002, the club hired Rees Jones, who rebunkered the entire course, lengthened four holes, re-graded five fairways to improve visibility, and rebuilt seven greens. The only unchanged hole was the 12th, which has no bunkers.

Jones built one new hole: the 17th, yet again. The green is now right behind the water, but the slope of the green isn't so severe. Jones also redesigned the par-three 13th. A new tee makes it play 244 yards, bringing long irons back into play for a shot over the water, though the hazard isn't as close to the green as on No. 17. In a way, it's a throwback. There was a "long tee" at 238 yards in 1949, but the USGA elected to play the "short tee" at 193.

Medinah tends to have a polarizing effect on those who judge it. The consensus is that it's a great course, ranked 15th in the U.S. by *Golf Digest.* Others think less highly of it because—take your pick—it's long and tough but not that interesting, three of its par threes are similar ones across the water, or it has too many trees.

Trees factor at Medinah more than at any of the nation's other top courses—many huge oaks loom close enough to the fairways to be in play after a slightly errant drive. Brad Klein, the architecture editor of *Golfweek* and no fan of heavily treed courses, has said, "The proliferation of trees

17TH HOLE

[at Medinah No. 3] masked the fact that the course was stunningly mediocre in the first place."

A tree played a conspicuous role in the 1999 PGA. On the nearly 90-degree dogleg-left 16th, which now plays 453 yards, Sergio Garcia's tee shot was sitting virtually against a tree. With a 6-iron, he lashed his approach shot to the elevated green, running after it to get a look at the result. Despite his great shot, he still couldn't catch Woods, who won again in 2006.

Trees also figure in one of Medinah's most humorous anecdotes. In his walk-through before the 1975 Open, Boatwright suggested that trees be planted to the left of the fifth fairway, at the time one of the few open areas on the course. In preparation for the 1990 Open, Boatwright asked that they be taken out. After being told that the trees were there at his request, he replied, "You planted them promiscuously." The trees stayed.

1949 TOP FINISHERS

Cary Middlecoff	75-67-69-75—286
Clayton Heafner	72-71-71-73—287
Sam Snead	73-73-71-70—287
Bobby Locke	74-71-73-71—289
Jim Turnesa	78-69-70-72—289
Dave Douglas	74-73-70-73—290
Buck White	74-68-70-78—290
Pete Cooper	71-73-74-73—291
Claude Harmon	71-72-74-74—291
Johnny Palmer	71-75-72-73—291

Low round: Middlecoff, 67

18TH HOLE

*Lou Graham	74-72-68-73—287
John Mahaffey	73-71-72-71—287
Frank Beard	74-69-67-78—288
Ben Crenshaw	70-68-76-74—288
Hale Irwin	74-71-73-70—288
Bob Murphy	74-73-72-69—288
Jack Nicklaus	72-70-75-72—289
Peter Oosterhuis	69-73-72-75—289
Pat Fitzsimons	67-73-73-77—290
Arnold Palmer	69-75-73-73—290
Tom Watson	67-68-78-77—290

*Graham won playoff, 71-73

Low round: Beard, Fitzsimons, Watson, Jerry Heard, 67

*Hale Irwin	69-70-74-67—280
Mike Donald	67-70-72-71—280
Billy Ray Brown	69-71-69-72—281
Nick Faldo	72-72-68-69—281
Mark Brooks	68-70-72-73—283
Greg Norman	72-73-69-69—283
Tim Simpson	66-69-75-73—283
Scott Hoch	70-73-69-72—284
Steve Jones	67-76-74-67—284
Jose Maria Olazabal	73-69-69-73—284
Tom Sieckmann	70-74-68-72—284
Craig Stadler	71-70-72-71—284
Fuzzy Zoeller	73-70-68-73—284

*Irwin won playoff, 74-3 to 74-4

Low round: T. Simpson, Mike Hulbert, Scott Simpson, Jeff Sluman, 66

CARY MIDDLECOFF

Scorecard

1975 U.S. Open

HOLE	PAR	YARDAGE
1	4	390
2	3	187
3	4	421
4	4	446
5	5	527
6	4	442
7	5	594
8	3	205
9	4	435
Out	36	3647
10	5	583
11	4	402
12	4	384
13	4	453
14	3	167
15	4	318
16	4	452
17	3	220
18	4	406
In	35	3385
Total	71	7032

Scorecard

Today

HOLE*	PAR	YARDAGE 1990 OPEN	YARDAGE 2006 PGA	AVERAGE**	RANK**
1 (1)	4	385	434	4.03	11
2 (2)	3	180	191	3.07	9
3 (3)	4	412	414	4.04	10
4 (4)	4	434	463	4.21	4
5 (5)	5	526	537	4.83	17
6 (6)	4	445	474	4.18	6
7 (7)	5	581	587	5.00	15
8 (8)	3	190	204	3.02	12
9 (9)	4	429	435	4.20	5
Out	36	3582	3739	36.57	
10 (10)	5	577	579	4.94	16
11 (11)	4	402	438	4.01	14
12 (16)	4	462	471	4.31	2
13 (17)	3	199	244	3.12	8
14	5	545	605	4.80	18
15 (12)	4	384	392	4.02	12
16 (13)	4	436	453	4.31	1
17	3	168	197	3.15	7
18	4	440	443	4.22	3
In	36	3613	3822	36.88	
Total	72	7195	7561	73.45	

*Pre-1986 holes in parentheses

**Average score and rank from 1990 Open

BEN HOGAN HITS HIS 1-IRON TO THE 72ND HOLE IN 1950. OPPOSITE TOP: 5TH HOLE. OPPOSITE BOTTOM: 11TH HOLE

MERION GOLF CLUB (EAST COURSE)

ARDMORE, PENNSYLVANIA   1934, 1950, 1971, 1981, 2013

Before Merion Golf Club hosted the U.S. Open in 1981, Charles Price wrote in *Golf Magazine* that "[the USGA] knew better than to ask the members to make architectural changes in the course. Merion wouldn't alter that course for the Second Coming." ¶ Times change, and so, finally, does Merion. Always long on charm, strategic interest, and shot values, if short on yardage, Merion was in danger of being left behind by the distance gains players have achieved due to improved equipment. It played at 6,544 yards in 1981, considered very short even at the time, when the average drive on the PGA Tour traveled 259.7 yards. By 2005, the average driving distance had jumped to 288.9 yards. ¶ Merion now plays 6,868 yards, but lengthening was the last of a four-step process, much of which came under the category of restoration. After hosting the 1989 U.S. Amateur, the club realized its conditioning, once a hallmark, had deteriorated. Ultimately, the greens were regrassed in 1996. At about the same time, a tree-removal

program moved into full swing, eliminating some unnecessary trees that had been planted either randomly by birds dropping seeds or ill-advisedly by green chairmen in the 1950s.

Those improvements put Merion back on the USGA's list of Open candidates, and the club was a finalist for the 2003 Open, eventually awarded to Olympia Fields. A lack of length and a surplus of logistical problems ultimately sank Merion's bid.

The club's next move was a thorough bunker restoration, using the design in 1930—when Bobby Jones won the U.S. Amateur at Merion to complete his Grand Slam—as a benchmark. Using old photos, the bunkers were rebuilt to the dimensions that existed then. Some bunkers that had been eliminated for maintenance reasons during World War II were restored, while others that had been added were taken out.

During this restoration period, the USGA awarded Merion the 2005 U.S. Amateur. Only then did the club address the distance issue. Tom Fazio, who had supervised the bunker work and whose uncle George had lost in a playoff at the 1950 U.S. Open at Merion, was called in to figure out a way to stretch the course.

It wasn't an easy assignment. Built on just 127 acres, Merion didn't have much room. With creative thinking and tree removal, Fazio found nine new tees that enabled Merion to maintain its character, which to a large degree comes from the variety of its holes. The course has always had a number of short holes that placed emphasis on accuracy and strategy, but also some longer holes that were extremely difficult.

"The overall concept hasn't changed," says Fazio. "The short holes are short and the long holes are long. You don't feel like you've played a short course." Over time, the long and intermediate holes had lost their challenge, and Fazio added to those. The shorter holes, which never asked for driver off the tee, hadn't become significantly easier.

There were only two truly long holes on the course—the last two. To retain that short-long mix, the par-three 17th has been extended from 224 to 246 yards, and the par-four 18th from 458 to 505, giving Merion back the fearsome finish it used to have. Now there are two long holes on the front nine. The fifth and sixth have been transformed from 426 and 420 yards, respectively, to 504 and 487.

The revamped course proved resistant to scoring in the 2005 U.S. Amateur, and that was a major fac-

tor in the USGA's awarding to Merion the 2013 U.S. Open. (The course will also host the 2009 Walker Cup.) The USGA also had to satisfy itself about other concerns, mostly involving a lack of space.

Merion's small acreage means the number of spectators must be limited. Also, the course is in the middle of a residential area in Philadelphia's Main Line suburbs, which means traffic and parking can be major headaches.

Then there is the question of facilities like corporate villages, merchandise tents, and television compound, all part of the modern Open. That was solved to a degree in 2000 after Merion bought six acres adjacent to the sixth fairway. Merion also has another course, the West, about a mile away. Since the East's range is too small, players use a fairway on the West Course for practice at Merion's championships, requiring a shuttle service.

Still, the USGA has shown that even in this era of a larger-than-life Open, it is willing to take the event to a truly great course if all of the accoutrements aren't present. And Merion has always been one of America's finest.

Opening in 1912, it was among the earliest of the truly outstanding courses built in America. Though Merion provides virtually the only evidence, designer Hugh Wilson may have been as much an architectural genius as Donald Ross, A.W. Tillinghast, and Dr. Alister MacKenzie.

Wilson was one of a committee of five members selected to lay out a new golf course for the club, then known as Merion Cricket Club, which was founded

LEE TREVINO

13TH HOLE

An Open Moment

When he came to Philadelphia for the summer of 1981 to star in a production of *The King and I*, Yul Brynner asked a real estate agent to find a house for rent in a quiet neighborhood. He settled into a home on Golf House Road, which runs adjacent to Merion's 14th and 15th fairways. Imagine his surprise in the third week in June, when his peace and quiet were shattered by 20,000 people swarming on the property across the street.

in 1865 and added golf to its activities in 1896. (The Golf Club split from the Cricket Club in 1942.)

The committee singled out Wilson, who had played golf at Princeton and was in the insurance business. He prepared for his assignment by making a seven-month trip to see the great courses of Scotland and England in 1910, stopping on the way at the new National Golf Links on Long Island.

Merion's L-shaped property was described at the time as "worn-out farmland, none too well adapted in dimension or topography for golf course purposes." The topography comment may have been off the mark—there were some significant slopes, a couple of creeks, and an abandoned quarry that had provided large stones for some of the buildings in the area. Wilson would make good use of that quarry, crisscrossing it to make a strong, memorable closing stretch.

He also incorporated the boundaries of the tight property as design features. On two holes, the seventh and eighth, Wilson gives the best angle of approach to the player who drives down the right side of the fairway, flirting with the boundary. The out-of-bounds stakes also are prominent on the second, sixth, 14th, and 15th holes.

Wilson used Ardmore Avenue, then a dirt road, as a hazard—the second, 10th, 11th, and 12th holes crossed it. The second tee was moved across the road shortly after the course opened; the other three holes were changed in 1922 when traffic became heavier. (The street now separates the second through 12th holes from the rest of the course.)

Unlike C.B. Macdonald, architect of Chicago Golf Club and the National Golf Links of America, Wilson didn't replicate particular holes from across the Atlantic. Instead, he integrated concepts into his own design, although Merion does have some old-world touches, including wicker flagsticks and Scotch broom in some of bunkers.

One aspect Wilson emphatically did not borrow was the invisible pot bunkers that so often dot Scottish links. He thought bunkers should be visible and had construction foreman Joe Valentine spread a sheet on the spot of proposed bunkers so Wilson could be sure players would see them. That's one reason the bunkers became known as the "white faces of Merion."

Valentine became the club's superintendent, a post he would keep for 52 years while becoming one of the most respected members of that profession. Two others involved in the construction were William Flynn and Howard Toomey, who formed a design firm together and built courses like Cherry Hills and the redesigned Shinnecock Hills.

Flynn and Toomey supervised a revision of the bunkers at Merion that Wilson had started before his death at age 45 in 1925. The only other courses Wilson designed were Merion's West Course, which opened in 1914, and Cobb's Creek, also in the Philadelphia suburbs. He also supervised construction of four holes at nearby Pine Valley after the death of its founder/designer, George Crump.

History, as well as design, has helped Merion become one of America's classic courses. Legends Bobby Jones and Ben Hogan enjoyed perhaps their greatest moments at Merion—Jones completed the Grand Slam there in 1930 and Hogan completed his comeback from a near-fatal automobile crash by winning the 1950 U.S. Open.

16TH HOLE

Jones had retired by the time of Merion's first Open in 1934. Olin Dutra, a genial 6-foot-3, 230-pounder whose ancestors were among the early Spanish settlers of California, became the first player from that state to win the Open. But he almost didn't make it to the first tee, having picked up a case of amoebic dysentery on the train ride east. A doctor recommended he check into a hospital, but he continued on to Merion, taking arsenic-based medicine and eating very little.

Two years earlier, Dutra had led by four strokes after one round at Fresh Meadow but finished seventh. This time he got better as the championship went on. Trailing by eight at the halfway point, he shot 71-72 in the 36-hole finish to shoot 293, handling the windy conditions better than anyone else.

The 11th hole knocked out two challengers, one literally and the other figuratively. In the third round, Bobby Cruickshank, the 36-hole leader, hit a bad second shot on the 11th. The ball appeared to be heading into the "Baffling Brook," but it bounced off a rock and onto the green. He tossed his club into the air, saying, "Thank you, Lord." But he forgot to keep his eyes on the club, which struck him in the head and knocked him to the ground. The shaken Cruickshank went on to shoot 77-76 to tie for third, two strokes behind.

Runner-up Gene Sarazen, who finished one back, was done in by a triple bogey on the 11th. Taking an iron from the tee for safety, Sarazen hooked it wildly into the part of the creek that guards the left side of the fairway.

In 1950, one of golf's greatest stories unfolded at Merion as Hogan limped to victory after a car crash that caused him to miss almost an entire year. When he returned, Hogan had to wrap his battered legs in elastic bandages and soak them in the evening. Many questioned whether he could make it through the 36-hole final day, and on several occasions it seemed doubtful. His knees buckled on the 12th tee and he bogeyed three of the next six holes to lose the lead.

Hogan then struck his iconic 1-iron to the 18th green, captured by photographer Hy Peskin of *Life*. He parred that hole to reach a playoff with Lloyd Mangrum and George Fazio. The next day, Hogan shot 69 to beat Mangrum by four strokes and Fazio by six.

17TH HOLE

Hogan developed a healthy respect for Merion's fierce rough, fast greens, and demands for accuracy. "It always has you on the defensive," he said. "You can never take the offensive against it." Indeed, although there were sub-par rounds early on, nobody broke 70 in a final round in which the leaders went backward and a seven-over 287 total made the playoff.

When the Open returned in 1971, some predicted low scoring. The players had gotten longer in two decades, while Merion had gotten shorter on the scorecard. A remeasuring showed the yardage to be 6,544 rather than the 6,694 listed in 1950.

Others weren't so sure Merion would yield. "Ninety-seven percent of the field, myself included, is not equipped to play this course," said George Archer. "They simply don't have the shots. I heard Byron Nelson say on television that 272 would win. Heck, I couldn't shoot 272 here if I got a mulligan on every hole."

Lee Trevino had his own take on Merion's difficulty. "Sure, there are 16 birdie holes here," he said. "But there are 18 bogey holes." Archer would make a respectable showing, tying for fifth at 283. Trevino would shoot even-par 280 for a playoff with Jack Nicklaus. Trevino won that battle of titans, 68-71.

Nicklaus fell behind early in the playoff when he failed to escape bunkers on the second and third holes. Still, he would have won in regulation if not for a double bogey on the fifth hole of the final round. There was some drama on the 18th in regulation, where Trevino made a bogey after missing the green with a 3-wood approach. Nicklaus, playing behind him, hit a 4-iron to 15 feet but missed the putt.

Lower scores finally materialized in 1981, when the greens were softer. But there were still just five sub-par totals. David Graham came from three strokes behind to pass George Burns and win by three with a round for the ages. It was only a 67, but Graham's precision was remarkable. He missed only one fairway (the first) and hit the green or fringe in regulation on every hole.

Graham finished with a seven-under total, marking a progression of winning scores in Merion Opens from 293 to 287 to 280 to 273. It's likely that progression will be interrupted when the Open comes to the revised Merion.

While many find it refreshing to see a course where accuracy is paramount, the main downside to Merion is that it doesn't test the pros' driving ability as much as other courses. In 1981, most used driver only about four times a round. The redesign might bring the driver back into play on the fifth and sixth holes, but today's bombers no longer may need it on 14, 15, or 16.

One area of Merion's resistance to scoring is the two par fives—neither is an easy birdie, even for the pros. The second is 556 yards, with Ardmore Avenue running all the way down the right side, while the fourth is 597 yards with a creek in front of the green.

The par threes are a demanding group, especially with new tees on three of them. The 219-yard third is tightly bunkered, the 206-yard ninth plays over a pond, and the 246-yard 17th is a narrow target. Although the 13th is just 120 yards, it plays over a yawning bunker to an elevated green.

Of the par fours, the fifth, with its creek-guarded fairway and severely sloping green, is one of Merion's best holes. Despite its length, the 325-yard 10th has been surprisingly troublesome. Nicklaus bogeyed the hole in the 1971 playoff when he chunked his second shot, and Burns bogeyed it in 1981 to lose sole possession of the lead for good.

Nos. 14 and 15, with new tees and typically demanding greens, begin to turn the screws on players as they enter the finishing stretch. The quarry-hole 16th has lost some of its challenge. With the tee sitting at the course's boundary, the hole couldn't be lengthened beyond 430 yards—it's a 3-wood and short iron for today's pros, which makes the quarry in front of the green less formidable.

The 16th mightily impressed architect A.W. Tillinghast, who reviewed the course shortly after it opened for *The American Cricketer.* He called No. 16 "a real gem...If your drive is a good one, before you stretches the old quarry, its cliff-like sides frowning forbiddingly. Just beyond, and sparkling like an emerald, is the green, calling for a shot that is brave and true. It seems almost like a coy and flirtatious maiden with mocking eyes flashing at you from over her fan, and as you measure the distance between, you are fired with the ambition to show off a bit."

The analogy might well apply to the whole course, although over the years, maid Merion has spurned numerous suitors enthralled by her charms.

18TH HOLE

DAVID GRAHAM

Scorecard

Hole	Par	Yardage 1981 Open	Yardage Today
1	4	355	350
2	5	535	556
3	3	183	219
4	5	600	597
5	4	426	504
6	4	420	487
7	4	350	345
8	4	360	359
9	3	195	206
Out	36	3424	3623
10	4	312	325
11	4	370	367
12	4	405	403
13	3	129	120
14	4	414	438
15	4	378	411
16	4	430	430
17	3	224	246
18	4	458	505
In	34	3120	3245
Total	70	6544	6868

1934 TOP FINISHERS

Olin Dutra	76-74-71-72—293
Gene Sarazen	73-72-73-76—294
Harry Cooper	76-74-74-71—295
Wiffy Cox	71-75-74-75—295
Bobby Cruickshank	71-71-77-76—295

Low round: Tom Creavy, 66

1950 TOP FINISHERS

•Ben Hogan	72-69-72-74—287
Lloyd Mangrum	72-70-69-76—287
George Fazio	73-72-72-70—287
Dutch Harrison	72-67-73-76—288
Jim Ferrier	71-69-74-75—289
Joe Kirkwood Jr.	71-74-74-70—289
Henry Ransom	72-71-73-73—289
Bill Nary	73-70-74-73—290
Julius Boros	68-72-77-74—291
Cary Middlecoff	71-71-71-79—292
Johnny Palmer	73-70-70-79—292

•Hogan won playoff with a 69, Mangrum 73, Fazio 75

Low round: Lee Mackey, 64

1971 TOP FINISHERS

•Lee Trevino	70-72-69-69—280
Jack Nicklaus	69-72-68-71—280
Jim Colbert	69-69-73-71—282
Bob Rosburg	71-72-70-69—282
George Archer	71-70-70-72—283
Johnny Miller	70-73-70-70—283
Jim Simons	71-71-65-76—283
Ray Floyd	71-75-67-71—284
Gay Brewer	70-70-73-72—285
Larry Hinson	71-71-70-73—285
Bobby Nichols	69-72-69-75—285
Bert Yancey	75-69-69-72—285

•Trevino won playoff, 68-71

Low round: Simons, 65

1981 TOP FINISHERS

David Graham	68-68-70-67—273
George Burns	69-66-68-73—276
Bill Rogers	70-68-69-69—276
John Cook	68-70-71-70—279
John Schroeder	71-68-69-71—279
Frank Conner	71-72-69-68—280
Lon Hinkle	69-71-70-70—280
Jack Nicklaus	69-68-71-72—280
Sammy Rachels	70-71-69-70—280
Chi Chi Rodriguez	68-73-67-72—280

Low round: Ben Crenshaw, 64

THE CLUB OPERATED ITS OWN RAIL LINE UNTIL 1912. OPPOSITE TOP: 18TH HOLE. OPPOSITE BOTTOM: 11TH HOLE

MIDLOTHIAN COUNTRY CLUB   MIDLOTHIAN, ILLINOIS   1914

Describing the 1914 U.S. Open at Midlothian Country Club, Max H. Behr wrote in *Golf Illustrated* that the course, "from the standpoint of golf architecture, belongs to the dark ages of the science. So far as punishment from misplaced shots, it was simplicity itself. There are no carries that deserve the name and the greens keep 'open house.'"   ¶   Although only 16 years had passed since the course was built, both the game and golf architecture had advanced greatly, in no small part due to the invention of the wound ball. In addition, there hadn't been any thought of challenging the game's best players when the club, the first in the south suburbs of Chicago, was founded in 1898.   ¶   The course was originally seen as a "playground for millionaires," an alternative to the summer retreats to the north, where there was little recreation. "Nothing except to be absolutely idle, and the business man found it hard to be that after his busy time in the office," wrote Alexis J. Colman in *Golf: A Turn of the Century Treasury.* "Now something has been found which will keep the business man busy in his idleness."

WALTER HAGEN

Anchored by the Midlothian layout, built at a remote site on rolling prairie land southwest of the city, a summer colony quickly developed, with some members lodging in the large clubhouse and others in cottages. Since the long carriage ride from the train station was inconvenient, the club built its own railroad line leading from a depot on the Rock Island line directly to the club. An engine and two passenger cars made 14 trips daily until 1912, when an electric streetcar took over until the service was discontinued in 1928.

The course was designed by Herbert J. Tweedie, who had been an avid golfer at Royal Liverpool in England before moving to the U.S. in 1887. A member of the original Chicago Golf Club in the early 1890s, Tweedie remained behind after the club moved to Wheaton in 1895, helping to form Belmont Golf Club and redesigning the course in 1898. The manager of A.G. Spalding & Bros. sporting goods store in Chicago, Tweedie went on to design a number of courses in the area around the turn of the century.

18TH GREEN AND CLUBHOUSE

The course was long enough for an Open, even if its greens were not as well defended as Behr would have liked. However, it played shorter than its 6,355 yards for the 1914 championship because hot weather burned out the fairways. Players were reaching the 520-yard 13th and even the 538-yard seventh in two strokes. They also nearly drove the green on the 277-yard finishing hole.

That makes the four birdies on the 18th hole by Walter Hagen, the only Open champion to accomplish that feat, somewhat less impressive. A more significant milestone was becoming the first of only six players to lead outright from wire to wire. His opening 68 matched the 18-hole championship record at the time—this after almost not making it to the course because of a case of food poisoning from dinner the previous night.

Hagen would later become one of the game's biggest attractions, but he was then a largely unknown 21-year-old. Attention was centered on another 21-year-old, amateur Francis Ouimet, who had scored a stunning victory the previous year at The Country Club. Attracting nearly the entire gallery, Ouimet was close behind Hagen after a 69 in the first round and entered the final round just three behind, but he couldn't summon the magic of the year before and finished fifth.

Hagen's biggest challenge came from another amateur, Chicago's Chick Evans. Playing on a bum ankle, Evans started slowly, but rounds of 71-70 on the final day nearly caught Hagen. Needing a two on the 18th to tie, Evans unleashed a mighty drive that stopped just a yard off the putting surface on the short par four. His putt from the fringe gave the fans a momentary jolt of excitement, but it stopped 10 inches left of the hole.

As the years went by, the area grew and the new village took the club's name in 1927. The U.S. Open never returned, but Midlothian did hold the Western Open in 1969 and 1973, both won by Billy Casper. By then, its shot values had been strengthened and the course lengthened to 6,654 yards. It remains virtually the same length today, though Chicago architects Ken Killian and Dick Nugent did some work in the 1980s, including adding a pond to the 18th, still a short par four at 332 yards. Another pond was added to the left in 2004, and a new clubhouse opened in 1999.

Anyone who visits Midlothian today would be shocked to learn there was not a single tree on the course when it opened, making its Scottish moniker appropriate. Early on, elm trees were planted. Then after they were lost to disease in the 1960s, the club went on a tree binge. The ensuing forest encroached so much that many fairway bunkers were lost in the trees. Faced with the option of cutting down hundreds of trees or moving the bunkers, the club chose the latter option, with Bob Lohmann completing a redesign and replacement of all 82 bunkers in 2004.

1914 TOP FINISHERS

Walter Hagen	68-74-75-73—290
Chick Evans	76-74-71-70—291
Fred McLeod	78-73-75-71—297
George Sargent	74-77-74-72—297
Mike Brady	78-72-74-74—298
James Donaldson	72-79-74-73—298
Francis Ouimet	69-76-75-78—298

Low round: Hagen, 68

Scorecard

Hole	Par	Yardage 1914 Open	Yardage Today
1	4	300	419
2	3	196	205
3	4	359	374
4	4	338	391
5	4	390	407
6	4	390	433
7	5	538	534
8	4/3	346	214
9	4	412	439
Out	36/35	3269	3416
10	4	437	429
11	4	382	373
12	3	122	150
13	5	520	521
14	4	300	316
15	3	158	179
16	5	490	518
17	4	400	427
18	4	277	332
In	36	3086	3245
Total	72/71	6355	6661

3RD HOLE

MINIKAHDA CLUB MINNEAPOLIS, MINNESOTA 1916

When the Minikahda Club was built in 1899, it was out in the countryside. The area around

the club is now highly developed, with the entrance to the club right off a busy street. Nonethe-

less, Minikahda is still in a beautiful spot overlooking one of Minnesota's thousand lakes, Lake

Calhoun. It also has a very good course that was redesigned by Donald Ross in 1917—a year

after holding its only U.S. Open. ¶ Clive T. Jaffray discovered the site during a picnic expe-

dition with his wife and two other couples. Deciding it was perfect setting for a golf course,

Jaffray founded the club, came up with the name, which means "by the side of the water" in

Sioux, and hired Willie Watson, fresh from Scotland, as the pro. With the help of another Scot-

tish pro, Robert Foulis, Watson laid out nine holes in 1899, the start of what would eventually

become a design career—he would be responsible for two more U.S. Open courses, Interlachen

and Olympic. He stayed at Minikahda only one year, to be replaced by Bob Taylor, who along

with Jaffray designed a second nine in 1907 after more land was purchased.

When the U.S. Open came to Minikahda in 1916, it marked the first time the championship was held west of the Mississippi River, if only by a few miles. Much like two years earlier at Chicago's Midlothian, many felt that the course wasn't challenging enough at only 6,175 yards. Many holes could be reached with a drive and a short approach. In addition, the course wasn't particularly tight, though the short par-three third, with a green that fell off steeply on all sides, drew complaints for its severity. Chick Evans won with a 286 total, breaking the record by four strokes and setting a standard that would last for 20 years.

Evans, who used only seven clubs, was perhaps the best ball-striker of his day, but he was held back by poor putting. The 25-year-old already had won the Western Open and Western Amateur, but had come up short in the U.S. Open and U.S. Amateur. He finished second at the 1914 U.S. Open, where he had missed a number of short putts, and was runner-up in the 1912 U.S. Amateur.

Evans putted well at Minikahda—it may have helped that the greens were slowed by rain before the first round. "One may say his education as a golfer has ended, for, like a good salesman he can now close an order," wrote Max Behr in *Golf Illustrated.* Tied for the lead with Wilfrid Reid after a first-round 70, Evans took control with a 69 in the second round and finished strong.

Pursued by Jock Hutchison and Jim Barnes in the final round, the long-hitting Evans struck the key blow at the 12th hole, a 535-yard par five. Boldly going for the green in two, his brassie shot cleared a creek and finished 18 feet from the hole, setting up a two-putt birdie that held off his challengers. Evans would remain hot, winning the U.S. Amateur to become the first to sweep the Open and Amateur in one year, a feat later matched by Bobby Jones in 1930. Shortly afterward, he endowed the Evans Scholarship Fund, which to this day provides caddies with money for college.

Evans called Minikahda "a championship course with a good golfing swing to the land, neither too severe nor too gentle...Playing shots to conform with the break of the ground is one of the chief difficulties at Minikahda."

Still, members came away from the Open feeling their course needed an upgrade and called in Ross in 1917. His changes, carried out over the next few years, were extensive, including four new holes. Minikahda landed the U.S. Amateur in 1927, with Evans losing in the final to Jones.

CHICK EVANS

The course never received further Open consideration due to its length (it currently plays 6,671 yards) and urban location. The club considered relocating to Chaska in 1957, but the proposal was voted down, and Minikahda member Totton Heffelfinger developed that suburban land as Hazeltine National. Minikahda hosted the 1988 U.S. Women's Amateur and 1998 Curtis Cup.

In 2003, Ron Prichard carried out a restoration to the Ross master plan. Hundreds of trees were cut down, greens that had shrunken were enlarged, and bunkers were rebuilt and relocated. Many of the shots players faced in the 1916 U.S. Open remain, including the treacherous tee shot to the par-three third and the second shot (if the player dares) over a creek on what was the par-five 12th hole then and is the 13th today.

1916 TOP FINISHERS

Chick Evans	70-69-74-73—286
Jock Hutchison	73-75-72-68—288
James Barnes	71-74-71-74—290
Gilbert Nicholls	73-76-71-73—293
Wilfrid Reid	70-72-79-72—293
George Sargent	75-71-72-75—293

Low round: Hutchison, 68

FRED MCLEOD. OPPOSITE TOP: 4TH HOLE. OPPOSITE
BOTTOM: 9TH HOLE

MYOPIA HUNT CLUB SOUTH HAMILTON, MASSACHUSETTS 1898, 1901, 1905, 1908

In the final round of the 1951 U.S. Open, Ben Hogan conquered an Oakland Hills course that was called a monster. In the early days of the U.S. Open, Myopia Hunt Club was a monster nobody could vanquish. It simply devoured and spit out every player in the field. ¶ The highest winning total ever at an Open was a whopping 331 by Willie Anderson at Myopia in 1901. The second highest: 328 by Fred Herd at Myopia in 1898. The third highest: 322 by Fred McLeod at Myopia in 1908. ¶ The reason for the high scores might have been that the course was simply more advanced than the players. The earliest American courses tended to be rudimentary, with greens that were fairly flat and not particularly fast. Myopia's greens were undulating and cut much closely than those at other courses. Myopia also made use of the natural terrain the way the courses of Scotland and England did. ¶ In 1907, the great amateur Walter J. Travis wrote that Myopia is "the best [course] in the country…Laid out originally on the long side with reference to the gutta ball, it just happened, with the advent of the rubber-cored ball, to

meet every requirement of the modern game by simply adding hazards where experience suggested. As a whole, it is beyond criticism, no two holes are alike, and there is not a single hole which is in any way unfair or which does not call for good play."

The course was the creation of Myopia member Herbert Corey Leeds, a baseball and football player at Harvard in the 1870s who took up golf when he was nearly 40 and developed a passion for the game. He built nine holes in 1896 to replace an existing nine and added another nine three years later. But his work was really never done. Much as Henry and William Fownes would do at Oakmont, Leeds was constantly looking for ways to make the course better—and harder.

Myopia historian Edward Weeks wrote that Leeds "never ceased digging new traps. It was his habit to carry small white chips in his pocket . . . When the drive of a long hitter was sliced or hooked Leeds would place a marker on the spot and a new trap filled with soft white Ipswich sand would appear."

Some thought Leeds overdid it. Harry Vardon and J.H. Taylor played Myopia Hunt on their exhibition tour in 1900, and Vardon later wrote that it is "a very fine course rather spoiled by an excess of hazards." And this was before Leeds added even more bunkers, bringing the total to nearly 200.

The 1898 U.S. Open at Myopia was won by Fred Herd, a recent transplant from St. Andrews, Scotland, whose brother Sandy was one of the top players back home. Fred judged that the best players of England and Scotland would have "walked away with [it]."

Herd never threatened in another Open, but in that championship he recorded one of the greatest rounds in the history of the event, though it is unrecognized in any discussion of best rounds. His 75 in third round was 10 strokes better than anyone

12TH HOLE

FRED HERD

else managed, propelling him from a six-stroke deficit to a six-stroke lead. He closed with an 84 and won by seven.

The 1901 Open would set an all-time standard for misery. Players complained about bad lies, as the turf was thin in many spots, while the wind blew shots off line and dried out the greens. Nobody broke 80 during the entire championship, but Alex Smith had a chance in the fourth round. He had a 10-foot birdie putt on the 335-yard 18th that not only would have given him a 79, but, more importantly, a one-stroke victory. He missed, sending him into a playoff with Willie Anderson.

Smith would make a six on the 18th in the playoff, turning a one-stroke lead into a one-stroke loss, 85-86. He missed a four-foot putt for a tie; maybe he just didn't want to come back for another round. Smith blew a five-stroke lead over the last five holes, which Anderson played, remarkably, in even par. Notwithstanding the exciting finish, the *Boston Herald* reported that "without belittling the pluck of the players, the performance of both was more a defeat for one than victory for the other."

The playoff, the first in U.S. Open history, was delayed two days since the members had the course for the weekend (the third and fourth rounds were played on Friday). That's the way it went in those days, when pros were second-class citizens. An information sheet for the 1898 Open at Myopia baldly proclaimed, "The privileges of the clubhouse and links are extended to all amateur contestants for one week previous to the tournament, and the privileges of the links to professional contestants for the same time."

Pros weren't allowed in the clubhouse in 1901 either, but it was too much for Anderson when a member told him pros would have to eat lunch in the kitchen between the first and second rounds. Anderson, swinging his mashie in the area near the clubhouse, became agitated and began swinging faster and faster, eventually taking a huge divot. The member went inside and hastily returned with word that a tent would be erected.

Anderson and Smith again finished 1-2 in 1905. With players now using the wound ball (1901 was the last year of the gutta percha), scoring came down and Anderson managed a 314 total even though the course had been lengthened to 6,300 yards. It was the fourth Open victory for Anderson and the third runner-up finish for a frustrated Smith, all at Myopia. He would finally claim the title the next year and again in 1910.

After the poor conditioning in 1901, Myopia was in superb shape four years later. The greens were still lightning fast, but very true. In *Golf*, a writer going by the name "Oldcastle" wrote of the players' complaints about the greens: "Granted, the greens were much faster than the majority of the men were accustomed to, it must not be forgotten that nearly everybody there had three days in which to acclimatise himself.... Myopia furnished a nearer approach to perfection in this respect than has been seen hitherto, and the club is to be congratulated upon its ability to provide a course where great golf is possible and where mediocre golf cannot win."

On the other hand, *Golfers' Magazine* stated, "Professional contestants had never suffered such utter humiliation as at Myopia and, judging from the talk by many of the most prominent, no self-respecting pro will ever take part in another national championship [there.]"

They did, though, in 1908, when Alex Smith's brother, Willie, continued the family tradition at Myopia by losing a playoff to Fred McLeod, 77-83. Like Alex in 1901, Willie lost six strokes to his opponent in the last five holes of the playoff.

The reasons for Myopia's not hosting any more Opens are unrecorded, but the players were undoubtedly grateful. The course has changed little since and is still regarded very highly by golf architecture aficionados. Now playing at 6,539 yards, it would no longer strike fear into Open competitors, but it's still a strong test for even scratch players.

WILLIE ANDERSON AND ALEX SMITH

18TH HOLE

Myopia features several holes that are considered classics. The great English golf writer Bernard Darwin wrote in 1913 that the fourth and fifth "are two as good consecutive holes as can be seen at any course in the world." The passing of nearly a century hasn't changed the verdict. Golf architect Tom Doak says the 392-yard fourth, which bends around a wetland on the left, "might very well be the best hole of its length in the free world." The story is told that a competitor in one of the U.S. Opens putted off the green on No. 4—and lost his ball in the swamp.

That hole is preceded by the third, a 253-yarder that used to be considered a par four but is now a brutal par three. The course opens with a short par four, the 274-yard first, but it's a steep uphill climb to a small green. Indeed, the short holes at Myopia have plenty of bite. The ninth is a par three of only 136 yards with a green that is 40 yards deep but only nine yards wide, flanked by fearsome bunkers. "Many a man has exploded back and forth from the five deep pits surrounding the narrow domino green," wrote Weeks in the club history.

The 446-yard 12th might be the toughest on the course. You can lose your ball on either side, in the woods on the left or knee-deep rough on the right, and the green repels any imprecise shot. Then again, the 349-yard 13th might be just as hard—its green sits 70 feet above the fairway.

Superintendent David Herioan restored many of Myopia's original features in recent years, bringing many bunkers back into play, which would no doubt please Leeds.

Golf, incidentally, wasn't the original purpose of Myopia. Nor, for that matter, was hunting. It was originally called simply the Myopia Club, formed officially in 1879 by recent Harvard graduates who comprised a baseball team known as the "Myopia Nine" because five of its members wore glasses. Early activities included any and all sports, including baseball, tennis, water sports, tug-of-war, rowing, and horse racing—but not golf, since the game had yet to be introduced in the U.S. A clubhouse was built in Winchester, but the club foundered because it was eight miles from Boston and didn't attract enough city people.

When The Country Club opened in 1883 closer to Boston, Myopia disbanded, with many of its members joining the Brookline club, which also featured horse racing. But some Myopia members formed the Myopia Fox Hounds, a hunting club, later renaming it Myopia Hunt Club.

The new Myopia settled into a clubhouse even farther from the city, 23 miles away in South Hamilton on the North Shore. This time, though, it was successful, and golf was one of the main reasons. The club laid out a rather primitive nine holes in 1894, and the first tournament on the course was won by Leeds, the club champion at The Country Club. Leeds soon joined Myopia and was asked to revamp the course, sending Myopia onto its U.S. Open path.

1898 TOP FINISHERS

Fred Herd	84-85-75-84—328
Alex Smith	78-86-86-85—335
Willie Anderson	81-82-87-86—336
Joe Lloyd	87-80-86-86—339
Willie Smith	82-91-85-82—340

Low round: Herd, 75

1901 TOP FINISHERS

*Willie Anderson	84-83-83-81—331
Alex Smith	82-82-87-80—331
Willie Smith	84-86-82-81—333
Stewart Gardner	86-82-81-85—334
Laurie Auchterlonie	81-85-86-83—335
Bernard Nicholls	84-85-83-83—335

*Anderson won playoff, 85-86
Low round: A. Smith, John Jones, 80

1905 TOP FINISHERS

Willie Anderson	81-80-76-77—314
Alex Smith	76-80-80-80—316
Percy Barrett	81-80-77-79—317
Peter Robertson	79-80-81-77—317
Stewart Gardner	78-78-85-77—318

Low round: Joe Lloyd, George Cummings, 75

1908 TOP FINISHERS

*Fred McLeod	82-82-81-77—322
Willie Smith	77-82-85-78—322
Alex Smith	80-83-83-81—327
Willie Anderson	85-86-80-79—330
John Jones	81-81-87-82—331

*McLeod won playoff, 77-83
Low round: McLeod, W. Smith, Gilbert Nicholls, Peter Robertson, 77

Scorecard

Hole	Par*	Yardage 1908 Open	Yardage Today
1	4	240	274
2	5	455	487
3	4/3	250	253
4	4	360	392
5	4	410	417
6	4	270	260
7	4	405	404
8	5	485	472
9	3	140	136
Out	37/36	3015	3095
10	4	400	406
11	4	320	339
12	4	415	446
13	4	320	349
14	4	350	392
15	5	520	525
16	4/3	265	192
17	4	380	391
18	4	350	404
In	37/36	3320	3444
Total	74/72	6335	6539

*Estimated for 1908

13TH HOLE AND CLUBHOUSE

NEWPORT GOLF CLUB NEWPORT, RHODE ISLAND 1895

The U.S. Open got off to a humble start in 1895 with a field of 11 going around four times on Newport Golf Club's nine-hole course, which measured 2,705 yards. Horace Rawlins, a 21-year-old recent arrival to the United States, became the first champion with a total of 173 for 36 holes. ¶ The event was held on the same site and a day after the conclusion of the U.S. Amateur, a much more heralded championship. American golf pioneer C.B. Macdonald won that event, becoming the first recipient of the Havemeyer Trophy, donated by the founder of Newport and first president of the United States Golf Association, Theodore A. Havemeyer. ¶ Havemeyer, known as the "Sugar King" because he was the head of the American Sugar Refining Company, was responsible for getting the wealthy Newport set into golf. After being introduced to the game in Pau, France, he built a primitive layout on 40 rented acres for himself and a few friends in Newport in 1890. Those friends, who owned summer "cottages" that were really mansions, included the likes of the Vanderbilts, the Astors, and the Whartons. In 1893, they organized the Newport Golf Club and the following year moved to a larger property,

Rocky Farm, which the club purchased. (A separate but related club, the Newport Country Club, was incorporated in 1894. Since a 1917 merger, the combined entity has gone by the name of Newport Country Club.) The elegant French-style clubhouse was designed by Whitney Warren, later the architect of Grand Central Station in New York City. Scottish pro Willie Davis, lured from Royal Montreal, the first course in North America, laid out nine holes.

The course wasn't much by the standards of just a decade or two later. The hazards included stone walls, a quarry, a bordering orchard, and "cop" bunkers, a feature on many early American courses created by placing the displaced turf from digging bunkers into piles of artificial-looking horizontal mounds. A local Rule from 1895 reads: "A ball lodging upon a cop shall be lifted and dropped a club length back in the bunker without penalty." Another Rule allowed a ball within one foot of a stone wall to be lifted and dropped three club lengths away from the wall, but that carried a one-stroke penalty.

Newport was one of the five founding member clubs of the USGA, formed in December 1894. Since Havemeyer was president, Newport was a logical choice to host the first Amateur and Open the next year. Originally scheduled for September, the championships were delayed a month to avoid conflict with the America's Cup yacht races.

With golf just gaining a foothold in the United States, the pros were nearly all transplanted Scotsmen. Rawlins, however, was from England and largely unknown. Recently employed as Davis's assistant at Newport, he remains the only host pro ever to win an Open.

Willie Dunn, winner of an unofficial Open the year before, was the favorite, but ended up second. (The *New York Times* reported that "lots of money was lost on him.") Willie Campbell led with nine holes to go, but ran afoul of the third hole, a 170-yarder where his first tee shot flew the green and was lost, and his second ended up against a stone wall. He took a nine and finished sixth.

Rawlins opened with a 91 for the first 18—not as bad as it sounds, since it was only two off the lead—then charged past the field with a pair of 41s. Laurence Curtis, vice president of the USGA, called it the best golf he had ever seen.

Havemeyer died in 1897 and Newport withdrew from the tournament scene, its governing committee rejecting the idea of hosting an Open in 1899.

The club did upgrade its course significantly, involving two of the biggest names in golf design. It expanded to 18 holes in 1897 and brought in Donald Ross for a thorough revision in 1915. There were complaints about poor drainage and in 1923–24 A.W. Tillinghast built seven holes (the current second through eighth) on newly acquired property while also rebuilding the greens on the 11 remaining holes.

Tournament golf finally returned to Newport in the 1980s with an event on the Senior PGA Tour. In 1995, it hosted the U.S. Amateur on the 100th anniversary of that event's inaugural playing—Tiger Woods won his second Havemeyer Trophy—and in 2006 it was the site of the U.S. Women's Open, won by Annika Sorenstam.

HORACE RAWLINS

THEODORE A. HAVEMEYER

1895 TOP FINISHERS

Horace Rawlins	91-82—	173
Willie Dunn	89-86—	175
James Foulis	89-87—	176
A.W. Smith	90-86—	176
Willie Davis	94-84—	178

Low round: Rawlins, 82

Scorecard

1895 U.S. Open

HOLE	YARDAGE
1	210
2	350
3	170
4	190
5	340
6	485
7	300
8	330
9	330
Total	2705

Today

HOLE	PAR	YARDAGE
1	4	450
2	4	390
3	4	324
4	3	221
5	4	450
6	4	381
7	5	551
8	3	190
9	4	440
Out	35	3397
10	5	537
11	4	295
12	4	455
13	3	160
14	3	208
15	4	434
16	4	335
17	4	441
18	4	407
In	35	3272
Total	70	6669

Note: 14th hole corresponds to 1st hole in 1895.

JOHNNY GOODMAN. OPPOSITE: 18TH HOLE

NORTH SHORE COUNTRY CLUB GLENVIEW, ILLINOIS 1933

Perhaps no club has benefited from real estate transactions more than North Shore Country Club.

Through a combination of shrewd thinking, timely investments, and sheer luck, North Shore

was able to move from a 40-acre tract with an ordinary nine-hole course to a 170-acre property on

which renowned architect Charles H. Alison built a course in 1924 that hosted the U.S. Open

less than a decade later. ¶ North Shore was formed in 1900 with a five-hole course northwest of

Chicago, near Lake Michigan, and in 1908 moved to the town of Kenilworth, where the club built

nine holes. Members were able to strike a deal with the local government and the owner to pay

the back taxes on the land in lieu of rent—$120 per year. ¶ By 1918, the club was paying $600 a

year, but with land prices rising the owner asked for $4,000 and gave the club a five-year option

to buy for $100,000—unlikely considering annual dues were then $24. But president Hobart

Marshall recommended raising the money to buy the property, and the club approved. Dues

skyrocketed to $75, there was a special assessment of $150, and a membership drive began.

They were wise moves, especially the five-year option. It gave the club time to come up with the $100,000; meanwhile real-estate prices took off. In 1923, not long after buying the land, the club received an offer of $262,000 from a developer who wanted to create a residential subdivision.

That left the question of where they would go. It happened that Edgewater Golf Club was holding an option on 170 acres in Glenview, a few miles inland from the lake, but decided not to move. North Shore bought the land with the profit they had just realized.

The club hired the esteemed English design firm of Colt, Alison, and MacKenzie to design the course. That's as close as Alister MacKenzie, author of such gems as Augusta National and Cypress Point, would get to laying out a U.S. Open course. He and Harry Colt, who helped design Pine Valley but then concentrated on working in Europe, had no involvement at North Shore, however. The job went to Alison, who handled all of the firm's work in U.S. in the 1920s, including Century and Old Oaks in New York's Westchester County and Milwaukee Country Club in Wisconsin.

He built a demanding course, long for its day—6,927 yards for the 1933 U.S. Open after a bit of lengthening. It played even longer, since North Shore installed one of the first underground watering systems, which helped the course avoid summer burnout and was one reason the USGA chose it for the Open.

3RD HOLE

Although it didn't go on to become one of the Open's classic courses, North Shore was a worthy site in its one shot at the event. It allowed players who were really on their game to shoot low numbers while still putting up plenty of resistance for the vast majority.

Tommy Armour, the 1927 Open champion who had just moved into town by taking a position at Medinah, shot 68 in the first round, with nobody else better than 73. The five-stroke lead after 18 holes still stands as the Open record.

His lead evaporated in the second round. Amateur Johnny Goodman tied the Open mark with a 66 for a 141 total, two ahead of Armour. The hot round of the 36-hole final day belonged to 40-year-old Walter Hagen, who moved up to fourth place with a closing 66 after a 77 in the morning.

Goodman was a 24-year-old who first came to prominence when he upset Bobby Jones in the first round of the 1929 U.S. Amateur. Born on the wrong side of the tracks in Omaha, Nebraska, and orphaned at 14, Goodman became a caddie. He was persuaded to play in the City Amateur at the age of 16 only when some members at the club where he caddied bought him some decent clothes; otherwise, he would have been too embarrassed to play. He won.

By 1933, Goodman was selling insurance, remaining an amateur because Jones was his idol and he didn't want to "turn the game into a business." Of course, there wasn't much money to be made in pro golf in those days anyway.

A third-round 70 gave Goodman a six-stroke lead, and when he started the final round with an eagle on the second hole and a birdie on the third, the tournament appeared over. "I sort of lost my head when I made that eagle," Goodman said after the round. He played the last six holes of the front nine in six over par, gathered himself on the back nine to finish with a 76, and retired to the clubhouse, exhausted. He was practically taking a nap when he heard a noise from the 18th green. Told that Ralph Guldahl needed a par at 18 to tie him, Goodman replied, "I hope he does it."

Guldahl followed a good drive on 18 by pulling an iron into a bunker. He came out to four feet but failed to hole the putt, making Goodman the last amateur to win the Open.

North Shore hasn't needed to add much length for regular play, but has introduced three new ponds to the layout. It lost a lot of elm trees to disease in the 1960s and 1970s, but replanted and remains a tree-lined course. The club hosted the 1983 U.S. Amateur, won by Jay Sigel.

1933 TOP FINISHERS

Johnny Goodman	75-66-70-76—287
Ralph Guldahl	76-71-70-71—288
Craig Wood	73-74-71-72—290
Tommy Armour	68-75-76-73—292
Walter Hagen	73-76-77-66—292

Low round: Goodman, Hagen, 66

Scorecard

HOLE	PAR	YARDAGE 1933 OPEN	YARDAGE TODAY
1	4	439	450
2	5	489	494
3	3	167	182
4	4	447	441
5	4	353	383
6	4	421	417
7	5	538	544
8	3	227	231
9	4	408	406
Out	36	3489	3547
10	4	446	428
11	4	349	363
12	5	552	561
13	3	185	201
14	4	375	378
15	5	511	515
16	3	160	183
17	4	423	426
18	4	437	429
In	36	3438	3484
Total	72	6927	7031

JULIUS BOROS

NORTHWOOD CLUB DALLAS, TEXAS 1952

Other than the earliest years of the championship, when golf in the United States was in its infancy, no course has ever hosted the U.S. Open as quickly as the Northwood Club—or disappeared as quickly from the national scene. The course was only four years old when the 1952 U.S. Open came to town, but it has never again served as a site for any USGA event. ¶ The club was the brainchild of four World War II veterans: William R. Moore, Hugh Prather Jr., John Pace, and E.S. Heyser Jr. Only Heyser was a member of a country club. The year was 1946 and the nation was entering a period of post-war expansion and prosperity, but no club had been built in Dallas since before the Depression, and waiting lists were long. The quartet resolved to build a club, and in a short time enlisted 100 member/investors, all but 10 of them veterans, to purchase property and build a course. ¶ They found a 160-acre tract north of the city that had been the country estate of oilman Buddy Fogelman. Conveniently, it had a house that could be expanded to serve as the clubhouse. The land was divided by Alpha Road, the southern half wooded and the northern half more open. All of it was gently rolling. ¶ The men hired architect William Diddel to design what would be his most notable course.

Like Pete Dye much later, Diddel was an Indiana Amateur champion (1905, '06, '07, '10, '12) who went into golf-course design. In fact, Diddel was a mentor to Dye early in the latter's career. When he was starting out, Dye told Diddel that he admired his low-profile style and would like to do the same kind of work.

"Do that and you'll starve," Diddel responded.

Diddel never worried about his next meal, but he didn't make much of a national splash. Most of his 90 or so courses were built in Indiana, Illinois, and Ohio. His design career lasted from 1922 to 1974, and before he died at the age of 100 in 1985, he had shot his age more than a thousand times.

One of Northwood's founding members was Jack Munger, the 1936 Southern Amateur champion and a competitor in three Masters from 1935 to 1937. He had some USGA connections and convinced some of the organization's officials to visit the course—and they were impressed enough to award Northwood the Open.

Compared to the "shock treatment" of Oakland Hills in 1951, Northwood seemed almost tame, and predictions for the winning total ranged from 273 to 283. (The record was then 276, set by Ben Hogan at Riviera in 1948.) But Northwood, even in a southern climate, featured bentgrass greens that Hogan described as "like glass," and a score of 281 by Julius Boros was good enough for a four-stroke victory.

That the championship was won by *anyone* other than Hogan was a stunner. The Hawk had won the last three Opens he had entered (1948, '50, '51). Playing just down the road from his home in Fort Worth, Hogan was as heavy a favorite as the Open had ever seen.

Everyone was ready to hand Hogan the title when he opened with a pair of 69s to tie the 36-hole record of 138 and take a two-stroke lead. On the 36-hole final day, however, the 39-year-old Hogan wilted in the 96-degree heat, shooting a pair of 74s to finish third. He didn't drive with his customary accuracy and made a costly course-management mistake, going over the green and out of bounds with a 4-wood second shot on the 448-yard par-four sixth hole in the final round.

Boros, meanwhile, rode a hot putter. The easy-going, slow-moving Boros had been an accountant until turning pro in 1950 at age 29. He hadn't yet won any tournaments (he would finish his career with 18 Tour wins and another Open), but had finished ninth and fourth in his first two Opens. Boros grabbed the lead with a 68 in the morning of the third day that included only 11 putts on the back nine. In the afternoon, he held off all challengers by holing putts of 35 and 25 feet for pars on the 15th and 16th holes.

This was the second of only three Opens that have been held in Texas, not a preferred location of the USGA because of its heat and the difficulty of maintaining greens that are both firm and fast. It was preceded by Colonial in 1941 and followed by Champions in 1969. Northwood hasn't changed much through the years, though it did get a facelift by Tom Weiskopf and Jay Morrish in 1990.

1952 TOP FINISHERS

Julius Boros	71-71-68-71—281
Ed Oliver	71-72-70-72—285
Ben Hogan	69-69-74-74—286
Johnny Bulla	73-68-73-73—287
George Fazio	71-69-75-75—290
Dick Metz	70-74-76-71—291
Tommy Bolt	72-76-71-73—292
Ted Kroll	71-75-76-70—292
Lew Worsham	72-71-74-75—292
Lloyd Mangrum	75-74-72-72—293
Sam Snead	70-75-76-72—293
Earl Stewart Jr.	76-75-70-72—293

Low round: Boros, Bulla, Al Brosch, 68

Scorecard

HOLE	PAR	YARDAGE 1952 OPEN	YARDAGE TODAY
1	4	365	354
2	5	577	564
3	4	435	454
4	4	450	446
5	3	153	161
6	4/5	448	468
7	4	420	418
8	4	445	453
9	3	220	210
Out	35/36	3513	3528
10	4	394	380
11	4	440	455
12	3	200	186
13	4	347	367
14	5	483	500
15	4	408	404
16	3	210	213
17	4	377	394
18	4	410	408
In	35	3269	3307
Total	70/71	6782	6835

CURTIS STRANGE. OPPOSITE: 1ST HOLE

OAK HILL COUNTRY CLUB (EAST COURSE) PITTSFORD, NEW YORK 1956, 1968, 1989

Oak Hill Country Club's East Course may bear only a passing resemblance to the course Donald Ross built in 1925, having undergone significant alterations by Robert Trent Jones Sr. in the 1950s, George and Tom Fazio in the 1970s, and Tom Fazio at the turn of the 21st century. What's more, a course that was nearly treeless when it opened has become a veritable arboretum, no doubt making the landscape more scenic—but less attractive to architectural purists, who see excessive tree planting as detrimental to the original strategic intentions of the designer. ¶ Oak Hill East has even been called a "Donald Trent Fazio" course. But no matter who is responsible for its various features, there's no denying that it has become one of the great championship tests in America. *Golf Magazine* now ranks Oak Hill 24th in the country. ¶ Oak Hill got the land for a nationally prominent course from a swap with the University of Rochester. Oak Hill was founded in 1901 as a nine-hole course, later expanded to 18, on a beautiful site overlooking the Genesee River. Two decades later, the university wanted that

land for an expansion. The club agreed to exchange its land for a larger property, 355 acres, just outside the city in Pittsford—the university sweetened the deal by paying for the construction of two 18-hole courses.

"We cannot do otherwise than give way to such a tremendous project for the good of the city," said Oak Hill president Clarence Wheeler. Although the land Oak Hill took over was worn-out farmland described as "barren, cheerless, and singularly lacking in beauty," the deal proved beneficial for both parties.

The land had enough topographical interest for Ross to create a pair of interesting courses. Oak Hill member Dr. John R. Williams almost single-handedly took care of the beauty. After a failed initial attempt to plant shrubbery between the fair-ways, Williams made himself a tree expert.

He established a couple of areas on the property as nurseries. He also used his own small backyard to grow saplings that would be transferred to Oak Hill. He planted all varieties of trees, but especially oaks—allowing the course to live up to its name.

"While there are only seven species of oak native to this country, ultimately we hope to have at least 50 varieties gathered from all parts of the world," Williams wrote in 1935. He ended up with "only" 30 varieties, but they included descendants of oaks planted by George Washington at Mount Vernon, Virginia, and the Shakespeare Oak at Stratford-on-Avon, England.

As the trees grew at Oak Hill, so did tournaments. First came the Hagen Memorial Open in 1934, honoring Rochester native Walter Hagen, won by Leo Diegel. Then Sam Snead and Ben Hogan won the 1941 and 1942 Times-Union Opens, establishing Oak Hill as a course that brought the cream to the top. That event didn't return after the war break, but the U.S. Amateur came to Oak Hill in 1949. USGA Executive Director Joe Dey was impressed, saying, "Where have you been for 20 years?" Soon afterward, the USGA awarded the club the 1956 U.S. Open.

There was some concern about whether Oak Hill was strong enough for the Open: Hogan had shot 64 there in 1942. In the 1950s, Trent Jones, the USGA's architect of choice and a native of Rochester, was given the assignment of redesigning Oak Hill. As it happened, an 18-year-old Trent Jones, just developing an interest in course design, had ventured to Oak Hill while it was being built and received some advice from Ross.

"He told me the green was the most important feature of every hole, and that every effort should be made to situate it in the most natural location possible," Trent Jones recalled many years later. "'Always remember, laddie,' he said, 'the green is the heart of the hole.'"

5TH HOLE

6TH HOLE

An Open Moment

It hadn't happened before and probably won't again. In the space of just 90 minutes, four players—Doug Weaver, Mark Wiebe, Jerry Pate, and Nick Price—made holes-in-one at Oak Hill's 167-yard sixth hole in the second round of the 1989 U.S. Open. The National Hole-in-One Association estimated the odds of four aces on the same hole on the same day in a pro event at 332,000-to-1.

Truthfully, those odds were reduced somewhat by a hole location that allowed players to use a ridge behind the hole as a backstop. Weaver's shot flew straight over the flag, landing 18 feet beyond the hole; Wiebe's landed eight feet to the left of it; Pate's and Price's landed slightly right and beyond, but all found the same destination—and all used 7-irons.

Trent Jones made changes to 17 holes—all but the 14th—but, possibly remembering Ross's words, left the greens untouched. The alterations included lengthening the course by 364 yards (while reducing par from 72 to 70), adding 26 bunkers, and rebuilding 27 others to give them a "flashed" look with sand faces.

Still, after a practice round, Hogan called Oak Hill "the easiest course I've ever seen for a National Open." His comment didn't reflect so much on the design as the course setup: He felt the fairways were too wide and the rough too forgiving.

Hogan later retracted his statement. He almost won his fifth Open at Oak Hill, finishing one stroke behind Cary Middlecoff, thanks to missing a two-and-a-half foot putt on the 17th hole of the final round.

Middlecoff won with a one-over 281 total with rounds of 71-70-70-70. In the final round, he followed birdies on 13 and 14 with bogeys on 16 and 17. He drove into the rough on 18, stayed in the rough with his second, then hit a pitch to two feet to save par.

"I thought I was going to die on those last three holes," he said. "The apple got in my throat so big I could hardly swallow." Oak Hill's last three holes, all par fours, earned a reputation as killers, especially with Middlecoff playing them in eight-over for the week.

After limping home, Middlecoff had to wait nearly two hours as first Hogan slipped up on 17, then Julius Boros lipped out his 15-foot birdie putt on the 18th to tie. Rochester legend Hagen, watching from behind the green, called it "the best stroked putt I have ever seen stay out of the hole." Finally came Ted Kroll, who needed three pars to tie but drove behind a tree on 16 and made a triple bogey.

There was one notable change when the Open returned in 1968. A new par-three fifth hole, built at a corner of the property, replaced the old par-three sixth to relieve gallery congestion. (The hole was later eliminated when the Fazios did their own routing changes in the 1970s.)

The 1968 Open was the coming-out party of Lee Trevino, the wisecracking eighth-grade dropout who entertained the gallery and the golf media on the way to his first victory and the first of six majors. The 28-year-old Trevino, who had served in the Army and spent time as a golf hustler, joined the Tour after a fifth-place finish in the previous year's Open but didn't merit a mention among the pre-tournament favorites.

At the end of 54 holes, it was almost a two-man race between Bert Yancey and Trevino, who was one behind but six clear of third place. One of the players in third was Jack Nicklaus, who made a final-round move with a 67 that could have been

13TH HOLE

much better. Nicklaus couldn't catch the winner, but he did catch the intense Yancey, who unraveled with a succession of bad drives and missed short putts to close with a 76. Trevino, on the other hand, didn't make a bogey after the first hole and birdied the 11th and 12th for the second straight day, waltzing to a four-stroke victory over Nicklaus.

Trevino became the first player to shoot four rounds in the 60s in an Open, and his total of 275 tied the record. Greens softened by rain aided the scoring, which really wasn't that low overall. (Nicklaus was the only other player to finish under par.) But Trevino's scoring and Yancey's 36-hole record of 135 left the impression that Oak Hill didn't exhibit major toughness, although the USGA never said so explicitly.

But it didn't say yes either several years later when the club offered to host another Open. So greens chairman Bob Hoff brought in George and Tom Fazio, whose work started in the winter of 1974–75. Most members were surprised to see bulldozers when they arrived in the spring. "The renovations committee was basically myself," Hoff said a few years later.

Hoff's instructions to the Fazios were "to put some muscle in the course." So while the Fazios would receive criticism for alterations that were out of character with the original layout, they were simply following directions.

They produced four new holes either from scratch or through modification. On the front nine, Team Fazio made greater use of Allen's Creek, which runs through the course. Ross was not a believer in placing water hazards very close to a green, and on many holes the creek crossed 40 or 50 yards in front of the putting surface (as it still does on Nos. 1 and 10). The Fazios ditched the par-three fifth built a decade earlier for a new par three, which would once again become the sixth. It was in the vicinity of Ross's old sixth, but now with the creek snaking to the front and left of the green.

The Fazios changed Ross's old fifth (the sixth for the 1968 Open), a controversial move because many considered it the best hole on the course. The original green was 40 yards past the creek; the Fazios moved it to the brink of the water and made it smaller, which also made room for their new sixth without the old congestion problem. They also moved the tee back about 20 yards, making the hole play at 419 yards instead of 440.

Another controversial change was the par-three 15th, which was relocated slightly. More importantly, a pond was installed to the right of the green—critics said it looked like a Florida golf hole. Finally, the 18th green, which was 40 yards beyond a swale, was moved so the dip was directly in front of the green, eliminating the run-up shot.

The changes helped the club land the 1980 PGA Championship, and the reviews, to put it very politely, were mixed. "I think the new holes are good, and they're more difficult than the old holes. But why did they do it? It's incongruous," said Nicklaus in one of the more diplomatic assessments.

Tom Weiskopf called for the establishment of a "Society for the Preservation of Donald Ross Courses." Joe Inman chimed in, "I just can't com-

15TH HOLE

prehend the masochistic tendency in these people. Look, if someone is breaking records in the 100-yard dash, do they extend it to 110?"

Ironically, Nicklaus won with a score of 274, one lower than Trevino's total in 1968. But he was the only player to break par, winning by seven strokes. While not quite a monster, its reputation as an "easy" course, deserved or not, was gone.

The U.S. Open returned in 1989, when a deluge on Friday night left parts of the course flooded. The conditions didn't lead to a stream of low scores, in part because the ground was so sloppy that it was hard to hit crisp, controlled iron shots, especially if the ball had mud on it, and the rough became terribly thick.

The best scoring came Friday before the rain, including a course-record 64 by Curtis Strange. It was Tom Kite, however, who took the 54-hole lead with rounds of 67-69-69.

But he was unable to match Trevino's feat of four rounds in the 60s as he came unglued on the fifth hole. Kite drove into the creek on the right and made a triple bogey that wiped out his three-stroke lead. Double bogeys on 13 and 15 knocked out his chances as he finished with a dismal 78, calling it "by far the worst round I've had in five or six years."

With Kite faltering, Strange's 15 straight pars to start the round amounted to a U.S. Open-style charge. In fact, Strange had gone 35 holes without a birdie until rolling in a 15-foot putt on the 16th to take a two-stroke lead. He was able to par the brutal 17th for the first time all week and a conservative three-putt bogey on 18 gave him his second straight Open title, with a one-stroke margin over Chip Beck, Mark McCumber, and Ian Woosnam.

Big-time golf has returned to Oak Hill twice since, with the Europeans surprising the U.S. in the 1995 Ryder Cup and Shaun Micheel pulling off an even bigger surprise by capturing the 2003 PGA Championship, clinching the title with a 7-iron to two inches on the final hole for a 276 total and a two-stroke win.

Between those two events, Tom Fazio came back to adjust the course for the recent onslaught of technology. He rebuilt all the bunkers, making them deeper, and built eight new tees, extending the course from 6,902 yards to 7,134—still not extremely long for the modern game, but a significant challenge when the rough is high and the greens are firm.

As proud as Oak Hill members are of their trees, they realized some of them had to go in order to improve the condition of greens that were not getting enough sunlight. Among the 800 trees cut down were several from the "Hill of Fame" next to the 13th green, where a row of trees was dedicated to various players and figures in the game, with each tree marked by a plaque. But there were plenty of remaining trees at various points on the course to both accommodate the plaques and get in the way of errant shots.

Except for the four Fazio greens from the 1970s, the rest of the putting surfaces are Ross's. The greens at Oak Hill are not severely contoured, but that makes them suited to modern green speeds.

Called the game's toughest opening hole by Hogan, Oak Hill's first hole has been extended to 460 yards. The third hole is a strong par three, little changed since Ross designed it, playing 214 yards to a small green.

Kite's waterloo hole, the fifth, now plays at 428 yards but still calls for accuracy, not length. Allen's Creek guards the right side of that fairway and the parallel seventh, a stern 461-yarder where trees are very much in play.

The back nine features an admirable variety of long, medium, and short holes. Two nice short par fours are the 372-yard 12th, where a unique oak grows at a 45-degree angle to cut off the right edge of the fairway, and the 323-yard 14th, where many players tried to drive the green in 2003 even though it plays uphill.

The 439-yard 16th, another hole with no room for extension, is not as difficult as it once was. But Nos. 17 and 18 pack as powerful a 1-2 punch at the finish as any in the game. Toughest is the 17th, a par five for members that played as a 495-yard par four in 2003, where long hitters have to worry about

18TH HOLE

driving through the fairway on the dogleg right and short hitters have to hit a smallish green with a long iron. The finishing hole isn't far behind in difficulty now that it plays 482 yards to its plateau green.

In time, the 1970s changes have come to be better accepted, especially for major championship play. The 18th hole, in particular, is a better hole for the modern pro, and while Ross's fifth was a fine hole, the new one might be even better. It took a while, but Oak Hill has shaken the critics who called it a good course spoiled.

Scorecard

Hole	Par	Yardage 1989 Open	Yardage 2003 PGA	Average*	Rank*
1	4	440	460	4.26	7
2	4	401	401	4.09	13
3	3	211	214	3.27	6
4	5	570	570	4.99	18
5	4	406	428	4.39	2
6	3	167	175	3.00	17
7	4	431	461	4.29	4
8	4	430	428	4.24	8
9	4	419	452	4.19	10
Out	35	3475	3589	36.72	
10	4	432	429	4.29	5
11	3	192	226	3.04	16
12	4	372	372	4.10	12
13	5	594	598	5.05	15
14	4	323	323	4.08	14
15	3	177	181	3.13	11
16	4	439	439	4.21	9
17	4	458	495	4.50	1
18	4	440	482	4.30	3
In	35	3427	3545	36.68	
Total	70	6902	7134	73.40	

*Average score and rank from 1989 Open

1956 TOP FINISHERS

Cary Middlecoff	71-70-70-70—281
Julius Boros	71-71-71-69—282
Ben Hogan	72-68-72-70—282
Ed Furgol	71-70-73-71—285
Ted Kroll	72-70-70-73—285
Peter Thomson	70-69-75-71—285
Arnold Palmer	72-70-72-73—287
Ken Venturi	77-71-68-73—289
Jerry Barber	72-69-74-75—290
Wes Ellis	71-70-71-78—290
Doug Ford	71-75-70-74—290

Low round: Hogan, Venturi, Bob Rosburg, 68

1968 TOP FINISHERS

Lee Trevino	69-68-69-69—275
Jack Nicklaus	72-70-70-67—279
Bert Yancey	67-68-70-76—281
Bobby Nichols	74-71-68-69—282
Don Bies	70-70-75-69—284
Steve Spray	73-75-71-65—284
Bob Charles	73-69-72-71—285
Jerry Pittman	73-67-74-71—285
Gay Brewer	71-71-75-69—286
Billy Casper	75-68-71-72—286
Bruce Devlin	71-69-75-71—286
Al Geiberger	72-74-68-72—286
Sam Snead	73-71-74-68—286
Dave Stockton	72-73-69-72—286

Low round: Spray, 65

1989 TOP FINISHERS

Curtis Strange	71-64-73-70—278
Chip Beck	71-69-71-68—279
Mark McCumber	70-68-72-69—279
Ian Woosnam	70-68-73-68—279
Brian Claar	71-72-68-69—280
Jumbo Ozaki	70-71-68-72—281
Scott Simpson	67-70-69-75—281
Peter Jacobsen	71-70-71-70—282
Paul Azinger	71-72-70-70—283
Hubert Green	69-72-74-68—283
Tom Kite	67-69-69-78—283
Jose Maria Olazabal	69-72-70-72—283

Low round: Strange, 64

LEE TREVINO

CYRIL WALKER ON THE 18TH HOLE IN 1924. OPPOSITE: CLUBHOUSE

OAKLAND HILLS COUNTRY CLUB (SOUTH COURSE)

BLOOMFIELD HILLS, MICHIGAN   1924, 1937, 1951, 1961, 1985, 1996

When the pros arrived at Oakland Hills Country Club for the 1951 U.S. Open, they couldn't

believe what they saw. The Donald Ross-designed South Course that had hosted two previous

Opens had been transformed by Robert Trent Jones Sr. into the harshest, most unforgiving test

of golf they had ever seen. ¶ Jones himself would later term his redesign of Oakland Hills the

"shock treatment." It involved building new bunkers in the landing zone of tee shots and replac-

ing obsolete ones built by Ross during the hickory-shaft era. ¶ That was just a first step. Trent

Jones flanked most of the fairways with bunkers on both sides of the entire driving zone, some-

thing Ross never did. And he didn't just build them along the edge of the fairway. He pinched

them into the fairway, often narrowing the landing to a width of 25 yards. At the time, USGA

guidelines for U.S. Opens stated that fairways should be 35 to 40 yards wide. Finally, Trent

Jones built new bunkers around the greens, defending every possible hole location with sand.

An Open Moment

Things were going so badly for Neal Lancaster through 27 holes of the 1996 U.S. Open that even his father abandoned him. Certain that Neal, who was seven over par, would miss the cut, Charles Lancaster said, "Don't worry about it; it's just a game," and drove home to Smithfield, North Carolina.

After saving par at the 10th hole, Lancaster reeled off a birdie at 11, an eagle at 12, and birdies at 13, 14, and 15, followed by pars on the last three holes for a 29 on the back nine, tying an Open record he himself had set the previous year on the back nine at Shinnecock Hills. Thus, a career journeyman who had gotten into only two Opens at that point (and just one more through 2006) owns the only two nine-hole scores of 29 ever shot in an Open.

"The game had outrun architecture," Trent Jones later said. "Development of two target areas made Oakland Hills unique. There was one on the fairway for the tee shot, one at the green demanding double accuracy. No mistake could be made without a just penalty."

It would seem such a course would be tailor-made for that paragon of accuracy, Ben Hogan. In fact, Hogan did win the championship with a final-round 67 that was one of the greatest Open rounds ever, considering the difficulty of the course. Hogan, however, was not a fan.

"I still think it is an unfair course in certain respects," Hogan said after the championship. "I'm not a machine, only a golfer, and Oakland Hills was designed for some sort of a super golfer that I've never seen yet. It's by far the toughest course I've ever played. And I hope I never have to play it again."

5TH HOLE

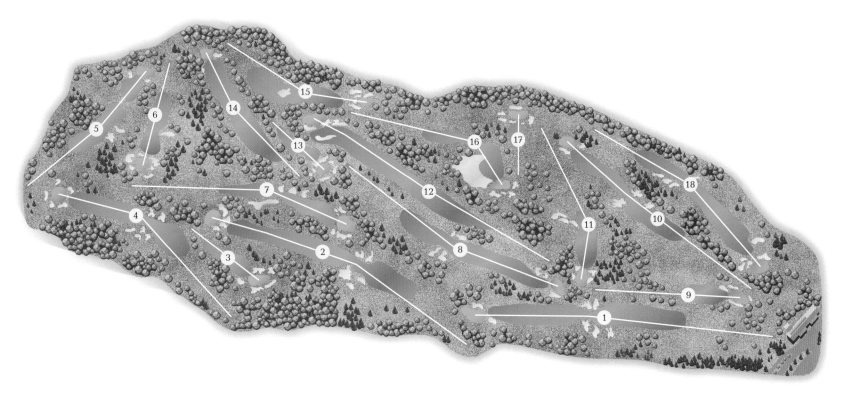

Hogan is often quoted as having said at the award ceremony that he was glad he "brought this monster to its knees." Research by Ron Whitten of *Golf World* turned up no contemporary accounts reporting any such statement, which first appears in Herbert Warren Wind's *The Story of American Golf,* published five years later, and seems to be an embellishment. Hogan did tell the press that "it was satisfying to bring the course to its knees," and others called the course a "monster." A faulty memory apparently led Wind to combine both thoughts as single memorable statement.

Willard Mullin of the *New York World Telegraph* was the first to call the course a "monster." Will Grimsley of the Associated Press called it "Frankenstein." Some dubbed it "Oakland Hells." Other labels, no doubt, were unprintable.

Hogan's frustration with the course began when he opened with rounds of 76-73 to stand in 16th place, five strokes out of the lead. It's been written that he started out conservatively and decided to attack in the final two rounds—an oversimplification. Hogan said after the championship, "I changed my style of play several times in each round."

In reality, he got mad and simply was determined to conquer the course. In the third round, he was three-under through 14 holes before a double bogey on the 15th sent him spinning to four-over on the last four holes and a 71. Afterward, a steamed Hogan told USGA Rules Committee chairman Isaac B. Grainger, "I'm going to burn it up this afternoon."

He did. Starting the final round two strokes behind the lead shared by Bobby Locke and Jimmy Demaret, Hogan shot even-par 35 on the front nine then hit what he termed his best shot of the tournament, a 2-iron to five feet to set up a birdie on No. 10. Birdies on the tricky 15th and terribly difficult 18th enabled him to play the last four holes in two-under, giving him an extraordinary 32 on the back nine for a round of 67 and a two-stroke victory. Hogan's 67 and a 69 by runner-up Clayton Heafner were the only sub-par rounds all week.

Although Oakland Hills in 1951 was almost as much a Trent Jones course as a Ross, the routing, at least, belonged to Ross, who said on his visit to the rolling property in 1916, "The Lord intended this for a golf course." His clients were Oakland Hills founders Norval Hawkins and Joseph Mack, both with connections to the auto industry. (Hawkins was the Ford Motor Company's first sales manager and Mack was involved in Ford's advertising business.)

The course opened in 1918 with Walter Hagen as its first pro. He stayed only a year, but Oakland Hills maintained a high profile and it didn't take long for the USGA to award it the U.S. Open, in 1924. The pre-tournament talk centered on the course's length—at 6,880 yards it shattered the previous Open record by more than 200 yards.

"This is a man's course—watch for the big hitters," was the buzzword of the week. Instead, the smallest man in the field, 118-pound Cyril Walker, emerged triumphant. The key turned out to be the ability to handle the strong wind on the 36-hole final day, a skill at which the transplanted Englishman was adept. His 297 total beat Bobby Jones by three.

Before the 1937 Open, architect A.W. Tillinghast said, "This course needs nothing to prepare it for the Open. What it needs is to be let alone." In truth, that Open showed the evolution of the game in just 13 years, as hickory shafts had been replaced by steel, which enabled players to hit both longer and straighter shots. The winning total was 16 strokes lower than in 1924, as Ralph Guldahl shot 281 to shatter the Open record by five on a 7,037-yard course, again the longest ever.

But the USGA gave the contestants a break by widening several fairways before the first round, in addition to moving up many tee markers and assigning accessible hole locations on the undulating greens.

That year, hot rookie Sam Snead was a favorite, and his 283 looked good enough. On the eighth hole when Snead's score was posted, Guldahl needed to play the last 11 holes in one-under to tie. He promptly holed a 65-foot eagle putt on the eighth and birdied the 215-yard ninth.

He then commented, "If I can't shoot 37 on the back nine, I'm a bum and don't deserve to win the Open." Guldahl's comment was tinged by the bitterness of already having blown one Open, missing a four-foot putt on the 72nd green to lose to Johnny Goodman by one stroke in 1933. He quit the game for a while to sell cars in 1935, but he came back with a revamped swing, which held up on the back nine, as he recovered from bogeys on 10 and 11 to birdie the next two holes and win by two.

Ross would have gotten a chance to update Oakland Hills himself if not for his death in 1948; in fact, he had already sketched out preliminary plans that involved moving the fairway bunkers. Ultimately, Trent Jones got the job, but his bunker work was undoubtedly more extreme than Ross's plan.

"I have some qualms about changing the work of great architects who are dead and unable to defend themselves," Trent Jones later wrote. "Still...there is very little in this world that can't be improved. Advances in technology...new ideas and techniques, the passage of time itself dictate change in almost everything."

Trent Jones didn't make drastic changes to Ross's greens, merely adding some tongue areas in places, guarded, naturally, by new bunkers. He added length to only two holes, the 13th and 16th. With two holes, the eighth and 18th, converted from par fives to par fours, the course actually played shorter in 1951 at 6,927 yards, but with a sterner par of 70.

When the Open returned in 1961, seven bunkers had been removed, and, more importantly, the rough was not as severe and the fairways not quite as narrow as a decade earlier. Also, the players were not surprised by the course they way they were in 1951.

10TH HOLE

BEN HOGAN ON THE 17TH HOLE IN 1951

Still, nobody broke par for 72 holes. Gene Littler, a 30-year-old Californian known for his rhythmic swing, claimed the title with a one-over 281 total, one ahead of Doug Sanders and Bob Goalby. An unflashy player known as "Gene the Machine," Littler quietly put together a great final round, a 68 consisting of three birdies against a lone bogey. It would remain the only major title among Littler's 29 career victories.

Oakland Hills hosted the 1972 PGA Championship, won by Gary Player, and the 1979 PGA, won by David Graham, before the Open returned in 1985. Graham punctured the "monster" legend with a score of 272, but Oakland Hills regained its bite in its fifth Open.

The course was vulnerable for the first two days, as T.C. Chen compiled a 134 total aided by a double eagle (he holed a 3-wood from 265 yards) on the second hole of the first round. But a chilly and rainy Saturday portended a miserable final round in which the contenders made a full-fledged retreat as frayed nerves and thick rough took a heavy toll. Nine players had been under par through 36 holes, but only one player finished under par, Andy North at 279.

North staggered home with a 74, following an outstanding 65 on Friday, which was overshadowed by Chen's early heroics. Similarly, the iconic memory of the event is not North's win but Chen's spectacular fall on Sunday. His four-stroke lead vanished in a few horrifying minutes with a double-hit on a pitch shot from next to the fifth green, leading to a quadruple bogey. Chen shot 77, tying for second with Dave Barr and Denis Watson, one behind North, who had been bothered by injuries and hadn't won anything since the 1978 Open.

The 1996 U.S. Open went to a player with an even bigger comeback story. Steve Jones missed virtually three entire years, from 1992 through 1994, due to an injury to his left ring finger suffered in a dirt-bike accident.

But appropriately enough for an Open at Oakland Hills, Jones was inspired by reading the biography *Hogan*, which a friend had lent him. "I couldn't put it down," Jones said. "I honestly don't think I could have won the Open if I hadn't read that book."

If no longer a monster, Oakland Hills still was one of the toughest Open tests. Only three players finished under par for 72 holes, Jones at two-under 278, and Tom Lehman and Davis Love III at 279.

Jones, Lehman, and Love all came to the 18th at two-under, but only Jones stayed that way. Love three-putted and Lehman's drive kicked through the fairway and into a bunker. Jones finished like a champion, nearly holing his 7-iron approach before it settled 12 feet behind the hole, setting up a winning par.

These days, the greens have replaced the bunkering as Oakland Hills's primary defense—and its most controversial feature. The greens are some of the most undulating in the country, and at today's Open speeds they can be scary. "Tee to green Oakland Hills is one of American's best tests," wrote Gary Van Sickle in *Golf World* in 1996. "But the greens? They're carnival golf."

Such comments are not new. After Oakland Hills's first Open in 1924, J. Lewis Brown wrote in *Golf Illustrated,* "I did not hear very much complaint about the texture of the greens, but I did about their structure. There is no question that some of them are radically wrong. Most of them had undulations running through them and often as not, sloped perilously away from the pin. It was these slopes that played the havoc."

That's not to say the bunkers are no longer a factor. They are, especially for amateurs. For one, they are visually intimidating, making the fairways look "so narrow that you have to walk down them single file," as Cary Middlecoff put it in 1951. The fairway on the 433-yard first hole pinches in to 26 yards, and the 523-yard second is just 24 yards wide.

The 455-yard fifth was the downfall of both Bobby Locke in 1951 and Chen 34 years later. Locke's nemesis was a blind fairway bunker on the right side that he found in both the third and fourth rounds to make bogeys. Chen avoided the bunker but missed the green by 30 yards, setting up his

double chip one shot later—his wedge struck the ball in the follow-through, shortly after the initial contact.

No. 10 has always been one of the strongest holes. The second shot is uphill to a green bisected by a ridge. Bobby Jones would have won in 1924 if he hadn't made three double bogeys and a bogey on this hole.

Holes 14, 15, and 16 offer a change of pace from all the flanking bunkers. The 471-yard 14th doesn't have a single fairway bunker, but it doesn't need any. Besides its length, the hole has trees down both sides and a green with a large swale and two terraces.

The 15th has just one bunker, which sits in the middle of the fairway and is not meant to be carried—although some players did so at the 2004 Ryder Cup. The choices are to aim for a narrow portion of the fairway to the right, boldly go for an even narrower portion to the left, or lay up short for a longer approach shot.

No. 16 is perhaps the most famous hole at Oakland Hills. Its salient feature is a pond fronting the

16TH HOLE

green. Ross didn't often make such penal use of water hazards, but the water was directly in front of the green in his original layout.

The hole produced a dramatic moment in the 1924 Open. Cyril Walker, a notoriously slow player, was between clubs for his approach. Consulting with his caddie, Gene Sullivan, he changed his mind several times. Although he had the lead, Walker went with the riskier shorter club and hit a beauty that finished eight feet away to set up a clinching birdie.

Gary Player made a similarly aggressive decision in the 1972 PGA Championship. From behind a willow tree in the right rough, Player's approach barely cleared the tree before settling four feet from the hole for a winning birdie.

On the flip side, many hopes have sunk along with shots into the water on the 16th—Walter Hagen in 1924, and Ernie Els and Payne Stewart in 1996.

The 17th is an uphill par three of 200 yards to a severe green divided by a ridge. From the wrong side of the green, two-putting can be considered an accomplishment. North clinched his Open here by getting up and down from a deep right bunker.

The toughest hole at Oakland Hills, and one of the toughest anywhere, is the 18th, a par four, extended to 494 yards for the 2004 Ryder Cup, that played to a 4.54 average in 1996. Long hitters need to shape the shot left-to-right on the dogleg right to avoid going through the fairway into bunkers or rough. (Bunkers await on the right, too, naturally.) Since this hole was designed as a par five and is still played that way by the members, it has a shallow green that is not very receptive to a long- or mid-iron approach.

For all the changes, one area that has remained pretty much the same is Oakland Hills's yardage—from 6,880 in 1924 to 6,974 in 1996. During that time, it has gone from being a long course to a shortish one for the modern game.

That won't be the case in the 2008 PGA Championship or in any future U.S. Opens. In a second-generation redesign, the club has called on Trent Jones's son Rees to update the course.

"When I went to interview for the job, I told them I probably wouldn't be sitting in that room if it hadn't been for my father's original success there," says the younger Jones, "I said, 'I've been waiting for this call for my entire career,' and they said, 'You're hired.'"

Many of the bunkers the father placed so carefully to bedevil the players have now become as obsolete as the Ross bunkers they replaced. The son will move tees back, stretching the course to more than 7,300 yards, and build some new bunkers beyond the existing ones. He will retain the character of the Trent Jones version of Oakland Hills by putting bunkers in play on both sides of most holes. Furthermore, he's extending water hazards on the seventh and 16th holes to bring them more into play on tee shots.

It may not be a monster anymore, but Oakland Hills will never be a pushover.

1924 TOP FINISHERS

Cyril Walker	74-74-74-75—297	
Bobby Jones	74-73-75-78—300	
William Mehlhorn	72-75-76-78—301	
Bobby Cruickshank	77-72-76-78—303	
Walter Hagen	75-75-76-77—303	
Macdonald Smith	74-72-77-75—303	

Low round: Abe Espinosa, 71

1937 TOP FINISHERS

Ralph Guldahl	71-69-72-69—281
Sam Snead	69-73-70-71—283
Bobby Cruickshank	73-73-67-72—285
Harry Cooper	72-70-73-71—286
Ed Dudley	70-70-71-76—287

Low round: Jimmy Thomson, 66

1951 TOP FINISHERS

Ben Hogan	76-73-71-67—287
Clayton Heafner	72-75-73-69—289
Bobby Locke	73-71-74-73—291
Julius Boros	74-74-71-74—293
Lloyd Mangrum	75-74-74-70—293
Al Besselink	72-77-72-73—294
Dave Douglas	75-70-75-74—294
Fred Hawkins	76-72-75-71—294
Paul Runyan	73-74-72-75—294
Al Brosch	73-74-76-72—295
Smiley Quick	73-76-74-72—295
Skee Riegel	75-76-71-73—295
Sam Snead	71-78-72-74—295

Low round: Hogan, 67

1961 TOP FINISHERS

Gene Littler	73-68-72-68—281
Bob Goalby	70-72-69-71—282
Doug Sanders	72-67-71-72—282
Jack Nicklaus	75-69-70-70—284
Mike Souchak	73-70-68-73—284
Dow Finsterwald	72-71-71-72—286
Doug Ford	72-69-71-74—286
Eric Monti	74-67-72-73—286
Jacky Cupit	72-72-67-76—287
Gardner Dickinson	72-69-71-75—287
Gary Player	75-72-69-71—287

Low round: Cupit, Monti, Sanders, Bob Harris, Bob Rosburg, 67

18TH HOLE

1985 TOP FINISHERS

Andy North	70-65-70-74—279
Dave Barr	70-68-70-72—280
T.C. Chen	65-69-69-77—280
Denis Watson	72-65-73-70—280
Seve Ballesteros	71-70-69-71—281
Payne Stewart	70-70-71-70—281
Lanny Wadkins	70-72-69-70—281
Johnny Miller	74-71-68-69—282
Rick Fehr	69-67-73-74—283
Corey Pavin	72-68-73-70—283
Jack Renner	72-69-72-70—283
Fuzzy Zoeller	71-69-72-71—283

Low round: Chen, North, Watson, 65

1996 TOP FINISHERS

Steve Jones	74-66-69-69—278
Davis Love III	71-69-70-69—279
Tom Lehman	71-72-65-71—279
John Morse	68-74-68-70—280
Ernie Els	72-67-72-70—281
Jim Furyk	72-69-70-70—281
Scott Hoch	73-71-71-67—282
Vijay Singh	71-72-70-69—282
Ken Green	73-67-72-70—282
Lee Janzen	68-75-71-69—283
Greg Norman	73-66-74-70—283
Colin Montgomerie	70-72-69-72—283

Low round: Lehman, 65

Scorecard

Hole	Par	Yardage 1996 Open	Yardage* 2008 PGA	Average**	Rank**
1	4	433	435	4.26	7
2	5	523	533	4.70	18
3	3	194	198	3.06	15
4	4	430	450	4.10	14
5	4	455	485	4.29	5
6	4	356	390	3.96	16
7	4	405	441	4.12	10
8	4	440	482	4.25	8
9	3	220	230	3.39	2
Out	35	3456	3664		
10	4	450	458	4.28	6
11	4	399	440	4.12	13
12	5	560	570	4.79	17
13	3	170	186	3.14	12
14	4	471	485	4.37	3
15	4	400	401	4.16	11
16	4	403	406	4.20	9
17	3	200	221	3.34	4
18	4	465	492	4.54	1
In	35	3518	3659		
Total	70	6974	7323		

*Expected yardage for 2008 PGA
**Average score and rank from 1996 Open

T.C. CHEN LOST THE LEAD IN THE 1985 OPEN WITH A DOUBLE HIT ON THE 5TH HOLE.

ARNOLD PALMER AND JACK NICKLAUS. OPPOSITE TOP: 4TH HOLE
OPPOSITE BOTTOM: 6TH HOLE

OAKMONT COUNTRY CLUB OAKMONT, PENNSYLVANIA 1927, 1935, 1953, 1962, 1973, 1983, 1994, 2007

"There's only one course in the country where you can step right out and play the U.S. Open,"

former USGA President Jim Hand once said. "And that's Oakmont." ¶ Lee Trevino has echoed

the statement, with an addendum. "You have to slow the greens down. You can't play the

course the way the members do. Man, those members are crazy." ¶ Through 2006, no course

has hosted the U.S. Open as many times as Oakmont Country Club's seven (Baltusrol has

hosted seven as a club, but on three different courses), largely because no course better satis-

fies the USGA's commitment to making the Open the ultimate challenge. Sometimes, Oak-

mont's members go too far for even the USGA. ¶ For its first 60 years, Oakmont used a special

rake to furrow the sand, making anything but a short blast impossible, even from a fairway bun-

ker. After playing two Opens that way, the USGA said no more in 1953, to the club's objection. A

compromise was reached in which the fairway bunkers remained smooth while the greenside

bunkers were moderately furrowed, an arrangement that also held in 1962.

8TH HOLE

In 1983, the rough became an issue, largely in response to Johnny Miller's record round of 63 in 1973. (For the 1978 PGA Championship at Oakmont, the members prepared a poster that read "No More 63s.") It was so long—nine inches in spots—that a drive into the rough automatically meant a wedge into the fairway. When the USGA told the club to cut the rough, the members responded by telling superintendent Paul Latshaw that if he cut it, he would be fired. It was finally trimmed Friday evening after the second round.

Oakmont's members come by their penchant for punishment naturally. In 1903, club founder Henry C. Fownes set out to build the hardest course around. Purely an amateur architect, Fownes did it without a single water hazard.

He didn't build deep bunkers, either, but not because he didn't want to. Fownes admired the deep pits found on Scottish courses, but couldn't replicate them in the clay-based soil near Pittsburgh because of construction and drainage issues. But he found a way to insure that his bunkers would embody his philosophy that "a shot poorly played is a shot irrevocably lost."

Fownes and his son invented a special rake to ensure the Oakmont bunkers provided the same penalty as the nastiest pot bunker. The enormous implement had long teeth that cut two-inch deep grooves into the sand. There were no regular rakes on the course, but a footprint was no worse—and maybe even better—than a lie in a furrow.

The most famous comment about the rake came later from Jimmy Demaret, who said, "You could have combed North Africa with it, and Rommel wouldn't have gotten past Casablanca."

The furrows disappeared for good in 1964 when the coarse river sand was replaced by finer white sand, which wouldn't retain the furrows. One diabolical bunker touch that remains, however, is the "Church Pew" bunker, with neat rows of three-foot high walls of turf, between the third and fourth fairways.

Fownes didn't take up the game until he was 39, but he became a good player. His son, W.C., was an even better player who won the 1910 U.S. Amateur. The older Fownes would often roam the course and watch the play, which gave him ideas about where to put new bunkers—by the 1930s there were 350 of them. He also installed a number of ditches for drainage, which doubled as new hazards.

But Oakmont's most salient feature was, and is, its greens. Built into the existing terrain, many have steep slopes, including a number that tilt from front to back, making approach shots especially challenging. Others, including the 18th, have enough swales and ridges to make a player seasick.

On top of everything, the club has always prided itself on having the fastest putting surfaces in the game. Emil "Dutch" Loeffler, the superintendent in Oakmont's early days, mastered the art of cutting

TOMMY ARMOUR

the greens as close as possible (3/32 inch, shorter than today's U.S. Open standard) while not losing the grass. He kept them firm, too, often with a roller.

W.C would stand at the back of the second green and drop a ball. If it didn't roll all the way down the slope and off the front of the green, he would tell Loeffler to speed things up.

The USGA likes to keep the green speed at a Stimpmeter reading of around 11 or 11½. For member-guest tournaments, though, Oakmont's members like to have them running at about 13. "The members here," said one of the club's veteran caddies in the 1990s, "want to see their guests in tears."

That's practically what players in the first two Opens at Oakmont did. The winning scores of 301 in 1927 and 299 in 1935 were the two highest in each decade. "Some of the players complained that the greens were skinned too fine and declared that a pair had no sooner passed than the putting sur-

faces were again being manicured and massaged," wrote Kerr N. Petrie in his 1927 tournament report in *Golf Illustrated*.

Thirty-five years after winning the 1927 Open, Tommy Armour wrote in the 1962 Open program, "Every hole was bordering on being a nightmare—not a single one that could even be called slightly easy. People reading this must think that I didn't like Oakmont. They are right, I didn't!"

You would think that Armour would remember the 1927 Open more fondly, considering his heroics both in regulation and in the playoff. Needing a birdie on the 72nd hole to tie Harry Cooper, Armour made one on the 457-yard 18th with a 3-iron to 10 feet. In the playoff, Armour sank a 40-foot par putt on the tough 15th and got up and down on the 234-yard 16th on his way to winning, 76-79.

On such a treacherous course, local knowledge and conservative strategy are assets. That's how Sam Parks Jr. won in 1935, becoming the biggest underdog ever to win an Open.

12TH HOLE

An Open Moment

Ernie Els, leading by two strokes, got off to a shaky start in the final round of the 1994 U.S. Open, hooking his drive on the first hole into deep rough to the left, where a moveable television crane blocked his line toward the green. The referee assigned to Els's group, however, gave him a free drop for line-sight-relief from a temporary *immoveable* obstruction.

Els gained a much better lie in an area trampled down by the gallery and hit the green with his second shot, although he ended up three-putting for the bogey he probably deserved in the first place, had the proper ruling—moving the crane so Els could play the ball as it lay—been enforced. Who was official making the improper ruling? None other than one of the foremost Rules experts in the country, chairman of the USGA Rules of Golf Committee Trey Holland.

ERNIE ELS GOT A BIG BREAK ON THE FIRST HOLE OF THE FINAL ROUND IN 1994.

The 25-year-old Parks grew up in Pittsburgh, attended the University of Pittsburgh, and became the pro at South Hills Country Club, not far from Oakmont. Parks played the winter tour for three years, but didn't have much success.

In the months before the Open, Parks played nine holes at Oakmont every morning before heading to work, deciding on a strategy and learning the breaks on the greens. "A lot of players back then just weren't familiar with fast greens like Oakmont had," Parks later said. "I knew how to deal with the greens better than most did. I wanted to minimize my chances of a huge error."

He did, though his winning total was 11-over-par 299 (the first hole then played as a par five, giving the course a par of 72). The runner-up, two strokes back, was long-hitting Jimmy Thomson, the John Daly of his day, who was hole high in two on the 621-yard 12th hole in the second round, albeit with a following wind.

Parks never won more than a regional event after his Open triumph. In 1942, he went to work for U.S. Steel and later became an Oakmont member, serving as co-chairman of the scoring committee in the 1962 U.S. Open and 1969 U.S. Amateur.

With the furrows gone from the fairway bunkers and moderated in the greenside bunkers, as the USGA wanted to establish consistency in Open setups, Oakmont was less fearsome in 1953. In addition, 60 bunkers had been eliminated. Still, the greens remained.

The Open was the middle leg of Ben Hogan's Triple Crown that year. He opened with a 67 and won by six strokes at five-under 283. Only one ahead of archrival Sam Snead entering the final round, Hogan pulled away with a 71 that included a 33 on the back nine and birdies on the last two holes.

The 1962 Open was also a battle of heavyweights and one of the game's seminal moments. Arnold Palmer, from nearby Latrobe, was at his best and at his most popular. Palmer, known as the King, won eight times in 1962, including the Masters and British Open. Between those two majors, he ran into the man who would dethrone him.

Jack Nicklaus was a PGA Tour rookie in 1962, but he had finished second and fourth as an amateur in the previous two Opens. Paired with Palmer for the first two rounds, Nicklaus was not intimidated as he started with birdies on the first three holes. Palmer recovered to beat Nicklaus in each round, shooting 71 and 68 to Nicklaus's 72 and 70.

Nicklaus caught Palmer at the end of regulation then beat him in the playoff, 71-74. The difference was Nicklaus's ability to handle Oakmont's greens. He had only one three-putt in 90 holes compared with 10 for Palmer, who had one of his best tee-to-green weeks ever but couldn't get the ball in the hole.

In 1973, Palmer also played with the eventual winner, Johnny Miller, in the first two rounds. Miller opened well with rounds of 71-69, but shot 76 in the third after leaving his yardage book at the hotel. That left him six strokes behind four players tied for the lead: Palmer, Julius Boros, Jerry Heard, and John Schlee.

That week, Oakmont wasn't as difficult as usual because a Tuesday rain had softened the greens, making approach shots easier, though they remained plenty fast. It rained again Saturday night and Miller, the best iron player of his generation,

IN ITS EARLY DAYS, THE OAKMONT GROUNDS CREW EMPLOYED A SPECIAL RAKE TO MAKE FURROWS IN THE BUNKERS.

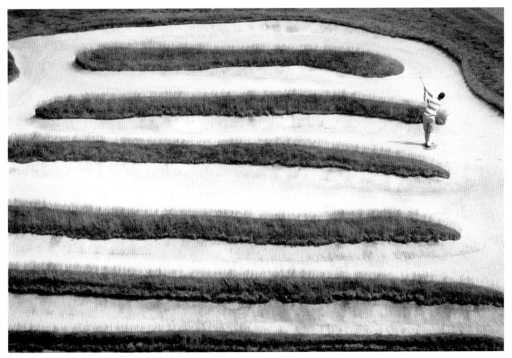

THE CHURCH PEW BUNKERS ARE IN PLAY ON THE THIRD AND FOURTH HOLES.

took full advantage. He hit 18 greens in regulation and had eight birdie putts of 10 feet or less as he broke the Open record with a 63. Miller birdied the first four holes, stalled momentarily with a three-putt bogey on the eighth, then birdied Nos. 9, 11, 12, 14, and 15.

At the 11th hole, 43-year-old Palmer was four-under, primed for a last hurrah in front of the home folks. He was stunned when he looked at the leader board.

"Who's that at minus-five?" he asked Schlee.

"Miller," came the answer. "Didn't you know?"

Palmer bogeyed the next three holes. It was left to Schlee to make the final challenge, but he fell one stroke short when his birdie chip just missed on the 72nd hole.

Miller's record round probably set the stage for the nasty rough at Oakmont's next Open, in 1983. *Golf World* editor Dick Taylor wrote, "It gets my vote after 35 years of golf watching as the most severe, most penal, most unfair [rough]."

So it's remarkable that Larry Nelson came from nowhere to close with rounds of 65-67 to beat Tom Watson by one stroke. Nelson's 132 total for the final 36 is the best in Open history and was six strokes better than anybody else managed that long weekend. (The last few holes of the final round were played on Monday morning due to a Sunday thunderstorm.)

Largely because of Miller's and Nelson's performances, Oakmont's reputation as the game's sternest test was gone by 1994, when Ernie Els, Loren Roberts, and Colin Montgomerie tied at five-under after four rounds. In the playoff, with difficult hole locations and the greens firmer than they'd been all week, Els won in sudden death after he and Roberts both shot 74. (Montgomerie shot 78.)

By this time, Oakmont had a different look than H.C. Fownes's vision as an inland American version of a Scottish links—early photographs show a treeless landscape dotted by countless bunkers. That scene began to change in the 1960s.

"Someone wrote that the U.S. Open was returning to Oakmont, 'that ugly, old brute,'" long-time Oakmont member Fred Brand Jr. recalled. "Well, I got to thinking, why can't it be a *beautiful* old brute." Brand spearheaded a tree-planting campaign to put the oak into Oakmont.

By the 1990s, those trees had grown up, giving it the look of many of America's parkland layouts. Too much so, according to some critics. "Oakmont should not be just another country club," wrote *Golf Digest*'s Ron Whitten in 1994.

An influential group of members agreed. Before the 1994 Open, an 18-member committee authorized a tree removal program, unknown to most of the membership. The removal was performed in the pre-dawn hours, starting at 4 a.m.

At one point, workers were tackling a group of 13 trees between the 12th fairway and 13th green. "We got down to three of them still standing when someone noticed what was going on," said former superintendent Mark Kuhns.

The issue divided the membership. There were threats of lawsuits for removing club property— the trees—without permission. There were even prayers for the trees at local churches. Grounds committee chairman Banks Smith, who became known as "Old Chain Saw," lost his position, but the cutting continued and the work was completed in the late 1990s.

Most of the members eventually came around to what was rightly seen as a restoration. Vistas once again have opened, agronomic conditions have improved, and there is no longer the double penalty of facing a shot from a fairway bunker and also being blocked by trees.

The next step was to turn to Tom Fazio in 1999 for changes to make the course stand up to today's long hitters. Fazio built six new back tees to give back to the course several really long par fours. It now has five that are longer than 480 yards: the 481-yard first, 486-yard seventh, 481-yard ninth, 502-yard 15th, and the 495-yard 18th. Fazio did not add any fairway bunkers, but he repositioned many of them to match the narrowing of the fairways.

Since the 2003 U.S. Amateur, one more new tee has been built, making the eighth the longest par three in championship golf at 275 to 280 yards. "It may be controversial," says the USGA's Mike Davis, "but that hole historically has always been a very long iron or fairway wood and it is played to probably the largest, flattest green on the course, a green designed to take that shot."

The 16th is another long par three at 233 yards, and with a pair of nearly unreachable par fives, the Fazio-lengthened 621-yard fourth and 626-yard 12th, the course has plenty of length.

Those are now the only two par fives on the course for championship play, making it harder to break the new par of 70. The ninth had become too short at 474 yards, even uphill, and there was no room to move the tee back because of the Pennsylvania Turnpike.

BEN HOGAN ON THE 18TH GREEN IN 1953

14TH HOLE

Oakmont is the only Open course with a major highway running through it, although it is below the level of most of the course and surprisingly unobtrusive. The turnpike divides the second through eighth holes from the rest of the course, but the roadway didn't necessitate major changes to the course when it was built in 1952 because it sat next to a railway line that already had run through the property.

The lack of a reachable par five is offset by a driveable par four, the 315-yard 17th, where Fazio worked on the greenside bunkering and redesigned the green so it falls off at the sides. If a player can somehow avoid the greenside bunkers and hold that green, he *deserves* his eagle putt.

The 17th has undergone some changes. Hogan drove the green in 1953, when the hole played 292 yards, and some smallish evergreens were planted near the green before the 1962 Open to make that route more difficult. In the first round, Phil Rodgers's ball got caught in one of those trees. He took three swings to extricate the ball, made a quadruple bogey, and ended up missing the playoff by two strokes.

Before the 1973 Open, Robert Trent Jones Sr. lengthened the hole to 322 yards and repositioned the tee, supposedly making an impossible angle to drive the green. Jack Nicklaus proved him wrong, but few, if any, others were capable of pulling it off. Before the 1994 Open, Arthur Hills restored the tee to its previous angle so it played 315 yards, encouraging players to take a gamble again.

The second is another interesting short par four, spiced by the smallest and most severe green on the course. Nos. 5, 11, and 14 are also less than 400 yards, giving Oakmont a great variety of par fours.

The toughest greens to hit are the first, 10th, and 12th—all slope away from the player. Since it was changed to a par four, the first has gained a reputation as one of the toughest opening holes in the world, with out of bounds to the right and a ditch to the left, combined with the fierce green. Oakmont

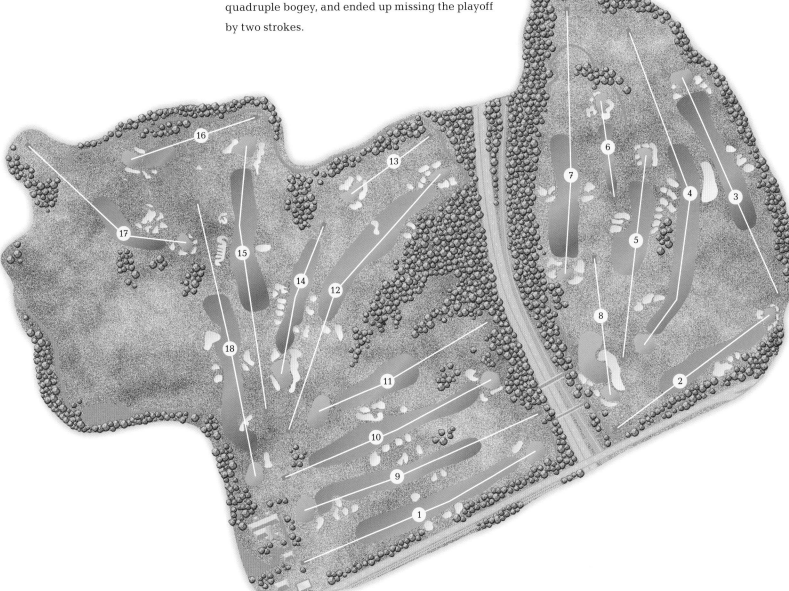

ends with an equally demanding hole. Now 495 yards and playing to one of the toughest greens to putt on the course, the 18th is a fitting finish worthy of the Fownes stamp.

After battling Oakmont's varied challenges for four—possibly five—rounds, the winner putting out on this green in the 2007 U.S. Open truly will have earned the title.

1927 TOP FINISHERS
•Tommy Armour	78-71-76-76—301
Harry Cooper	74-76-74-77—301
Gene Sarazen	74-74-80-74—302
Emmett French	75-79-77-73—304
William Mehlhorn	75-77-80-73—305

•Armour won playoff, 76-79
Low round: Al Espinosa, 69

1935 TOP FINISHERS
Sam Parks Jr.	77-73-73-76—299
Jimmy Thomson	73-73-77-78—301
Walter Hagen	77-76-73-76—302
Ray Mangrum	76-76-72-79—303
Denny Shute	78-73-76-76—303

Low round: Al Krueger, Ted Turner, 71

1953 TOP FINISHERS
Ben Hogan	67-72-73-71—283
Sam Snead	72-69-72-76—289
Lloyd Mangrum	73-70-74-75—292
Pete Cooper	78-75-71-70—294
Jimmy Demaret	71-76-71-76—294
George Fazio	70-71-77-76—294
Ted Kroll	76-71-74-74—295
Dick Metz	75-70-74-76—295
Marty Furgol	73-74-76-73—296
Jay Hebert	72-72-74-78—296
Frank Souchak	70-76-76-74—296

Low round: Hogan, 67

1962 TOP FINISHERS
•Jack Nicklaus	72-70-72-69—283
Arnold Palmer	71-68-73-71—283
Bobby Nichols	70-72-70-73—285
Phil Rodgers	74-70-69-72—285
Gay Brewer	73-72-73-69—287
Tommy Jacobs	74-71-73-70—288
Gary Player	71-71-72-74—288
Doug Ford	74-75-71-70—290
Gene Littler	69-74-72-75—290
Billy Maxwell	71-70-75-74—290

•Nicklaus won playoff, 71-74
Low round: Deane Beman, 67

17TH HOLE

1973 TOP FINISHERS

Johnny Miller	71-69-76-63—279
John Schlee	73-70-67-70—280
Tom Weiskopf	73-69-69-70—281
Jack Nicklaus	71-69-74-68—282
Arnold Palmer	71-71-68-72—282
Lee Trevino	70-72-70-70—282
Julius Boros	73-69-68-73—283
Jerry Heard	74-70-66-73—283
Lanny Wadkins	74-69-75-65—283
Jim Colbert	70-68-74-72—284

Low round: Miller, 63

1983 TOP FINISHERS

Larry Nelson	75-73-65-67—280
Tom Watson	72-70-70-69—281
Gil Morgan	73-72-70-68—283
Seve Ballesteros	69-74-69-74—286
Calvin Peete	75-68-70-73—286
Hal Sutton	73-70-73-71—287
Lanny Wadkins	72-73-74-69—288
David Graham	74-75-73-69—291
Ralph Landrum	75-73-69-74—291
Chip Beck	73-74-74-71—292
Andy North	73-71-72-76—292
Craig Stadler	76-74-73-69—292

Low round: Nelson, 65

1994 TOP FINISHERS

*Ernie Els	69-71-66-73—279
Colin Montgomerie	71-65-73-70—279
Loren Roberts	76-69-64-70—279
Curtis Strange	70-70-70-70—280
John Cook	73-65-73-71—282
Tom Watson	68-73-68-74—283
Greg Norman	71-71-69-72—283
Clark Dennis	71-71-70-71—283
Frank Nobilo	69-71-68-76—284
Jeff Sluman	72-69-72-71—284
Jeff Maggert	71-68-75-70—284
Duffy Waldorf	74-68-73-69—284

*Els won playoff with a 74-4-4, Roberts 74-4-5, Montgomerie 78

Low round: Roberts, 64

JOHNNY MILLER

Scorecard

HOLE	PAR	YARDAGE 1994 OPEN	YARDAGE TODAY	AVERAGE*	RANK*
1	4	463	481	4.43	2
2	4	342	341	4.04	14
3	4	421	426	4.26	7
4	5	560	621	4.99	15
5	4	378	383	4.08	13
6	3	195	196	3.18	11
7	4	431	486	4.25	9
8	3	249	253	3.32	6
9	5/4	474	481	4.62	18
Out	36/35	3513	3668	37.18	
10	4	458	463	4.48	1
11	4	378	382	4.23	10
12	5	598	626	5.26	7
13	3	181	185	3.12	12
14	4	356	360	3.93	17
15	4	467	502	4.37	4
16	3	228	233	3.37	3
17	4	315	315	3.94	16
18	4	452	495	4.36	5
In	35	3433	3561	37.04	
Total	71/70	6946	7229	74.22	

*Average score and rank from 1994 Open

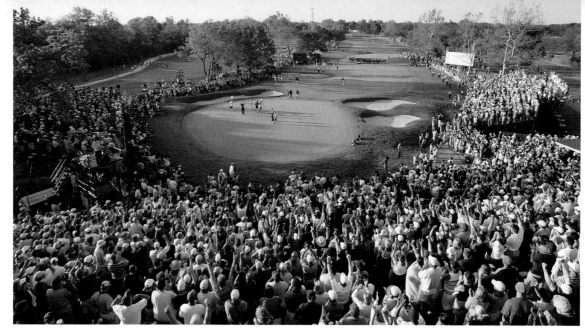

JIM FURYK WRAPS UP THE TITLE ON THE 72ND HOLE IN 2003. OPPOSITE TOP: 5TH HOLE. OPPOSITE BOTTOM: 7TH HOLE

OLYMPIA FIELDS COUNTRY CLUB (NORTH COURSE)

OLYMPIA FIELDS, ILLINOIS 1928, 2003

Never has the USGA waited so long to return to a course for a U.S. Open as the 75 years between the 1928 and 2003 Opens at Olympia Fields Country Club. True, 90 years (1896 to 1986) passed at Shinnecock Hills, but that wasn't really on the same golf course—by 1986, Shinnecock's original course was long gone. At Olympia Fields, Willie Park Jr.'s original design of the North Course remains very much intact, with no more than the usual updating for the modern game. ¶ Only the name has changed. When Park's course opened in 1923, it was known as the No. 4 Course at the sprawling complex south of Chicago. When the Nos. 2 and 3 courses were sold in 1943 for development, the remaining courses became known as North and South. ¶ The USGA's long hiatus wasn't a slap at the quality of Olympia Fields. There were many factors. For one, the club faced financial trouble through the Great Depression and World War II (hence the sale of half of its 72 holes), and harbored few tournament

ambitions. The club returned to national promi-nence with the 1961 PGA Championship and hosted the Western Open in 1968 and 1971, but in the following decades showed no inclination to bid for an Open, leaving Medinah as the USGA's primary Chicago site.

The wind began to shift in Olympia's direction in the 1990s. A group of young members pushed the club back into the championship picture, bid-ding for and receiving the 1997 U.S. Senior Open. Meanwhile, the PGA of America awarded the 1999 and 2006 PGA Championships, as well as the 2012 Ryder Cup, to Medinah, whose relationship with the USGA had cooled.

But the USGA didn't want to give up on holding the Open in Chicago. A number of metro Chicago courses had hosted the Open in the pre-war years, but only Olympia Fields had sufficient room—both to lengthen the course and for ancillary Open facili-ties such as corporate tents—to host a modern U.S. Open.

The other contender was Cog Hill No. 4, a public track that has hosted the Western Open since 1991. But the USGA was impressed by Olympia Fields at the 1997 U.S. Senior Open, won by Graham Marsh at even par, and decided to return on the 75th anniversary of Johnny Farrell's playoff win over Bobby Jones.

Although Olympia Fields is 32 miles south of Chicago's Loop, in an area lacking in hotels, a train station sits at the club's doorstep, enabling officials, media, and fans to stay downtown and commute by rail.

That's the same rail line Charles Beach took in 1913 to scout land for a country club. For three straight days, he took the train to Flossmoor and walked south. He found an area a mile long and a mile-and-a-half wide unmarred by roads but close to the railroad. It was just what he had in mind for a huge country club that would offer its members several courses. The land was covered by no fewer than 19 farms, which meant cobbling together a lot of purchases, and it took four years for Beach to accumulate 694 acres.

Once the courses were built, Beach persuaded the Illinois Central to build a station next to the club. Eventually, enough residences popped up around the club to incorporate a town, which took its name from the club. It now has a population of just under 5,000, many living in houses on land formerly occupied by the Nos. 2 and 3 Courses.

Those two abandoned courses were ordinary. The first course had been designed by Tom Ben-delow, the second by Willie Watson, and the third was a collaboration.

The club then made an inspired choice for the architect of its fourth course. Park had won the Brit-ish Open in 1887 and 1889, designed many courses in his native Scotland and in England, and moved to the United States in 1915 to make his mark in

10TH HOLE

JOHNNY FARRELL

the architecture business. Park's career, which included the design of Maidstone on Long Island, ended when he became ill in 1923, so Olympia Fields was one of his last projects. (He died in 1925.)

Park first came to Olympia Fields in 1919 to suggest changes to the No. 3 Course. Soon after, he drew up plans for the No. 4 Course, though work didn't get under way until 1922 and the course didn't open until spring of the following year. Park said that in Olympia Fields, he had "never seen a more natural setting for a championship course."

Park took up residence in the area and spent 40 days on the site during construction. A great putter in his playing days and known for the statement "A man who can putt is a match for anyone," Park took great care with the greens. He produced subtle slopes and undulations by building layers of sub-strata underneath the surface. The greens are still the strength of the golf course.

When No. 4 opened, the club newsletter *The Olympian* cautioned that "to the average player at Olympia, Number 4 will appear too severe and many a shock will be in store for the 90 player when he blazes around in a perfect 115, but even then his joy in overcoming certain obstacles of play will bring him back in preference to Numbers 1, 2, and 3."

No. 4 did indeed become the most popular among the members, and the game's governing bodies likewise recognized it as a gem. The course hosted the 1925 PGA Championship and the 1927 Western Open, both won by Walter Hagen.

Before the 1928 U.S. Open, Hagen's winning score of 281 in the Western Open led the USGA to request a lengthening of the course, which was stretched from 6,420 to 6,725 yards by building new tees on most of the holes.

Opinions of the course varied heading into the championship. William D. Richardson of the *New York Times* wrote, "Arriving here today one listened to many tales of woe regarding the course. Some express the unsolicited opinion that the course had been made too stiff by the lengthen-ing-out process...Others thought the greens were too fast. Still others would like to see a few of the bunkers and trees eliminated."

Bobby Jones, the perennial tournament favorite of the 1920s the way Tiger Woods is today, felt "the driver and the putter will win the National Open crown. The fairways are narrow and treacherous for the most part and drives must be placed exactly to

enable the player to get home readily. The greens are fairly large but undulations and rather fast turf put the good putter at a premium."

Guesses about the winning score ranged from 290 to 300 on the par-71 course, with Jones predict-ing "something around 294."

He was right on the money—294 got Jones into a playoff with Johnny Farrell, who had that score as his target down the stretch of a final-round 72 that would help him to wipe out a five-stroke deficit. With three holes remaining, sportswriter Grantland Rice asked Farrell how he was doing. "I need 3, 4, 4 [par, par, birdie] for 72," he replied. "But don't tell anyone."

Jones would have won if not for a horrid stretch at the end of the front nine of the final round, start-ing with a double bogey at the par-three sixth, where he pulled his tee shot into a creek 20 yards left of the green. He continued with bogeys on the next three holes. Jones recovered on the back nine, but his uncharacteristic 77 dropped him into a tie with Farrell.

It looked as if both would lose to an unknown 21-year-old North Carolinian, Roland Hancock, who torched the front nine with a 33 and needed to play the last two holes in one-over to win. That seemed likely, considering that the 383-yard par-four 17th and 490-yard par-five 18th weren't especially demanding. "Make way for the new champion!" yelled somebody in the crowd as Hancock made his way to the 17th tee.

The fan spoke too soon. Hancock drove behind a tree on 17 and made double bogey, then drove into the trees again on 18 and bogeyed to finish one behind. "Ah, well—he'll come again, will Roland Hancock; and next time, if any silly asses come bel-lowing up to him at the finish, and telling him he's champion, before the last putt is canned, by gum, I hope he takes a niblick and knocks their fool heads off!" wrote O.B. Keeler in *The American Golfer*. Alas, this was the only cut Hancock ever made at the Open.

The playoff wasn't the first time that Jones and Farrell played together that week. They had been put together for the first two rounds in the marquee pairing—Farrell had come off a seven-win cam-paign the year before. But it was Jones the galleries really came to see, and in the years before gal-lery ropes, Farrell, who shot 77 in the first round, found himself "jostled and jolted," according to the *Times*'s Richardson.

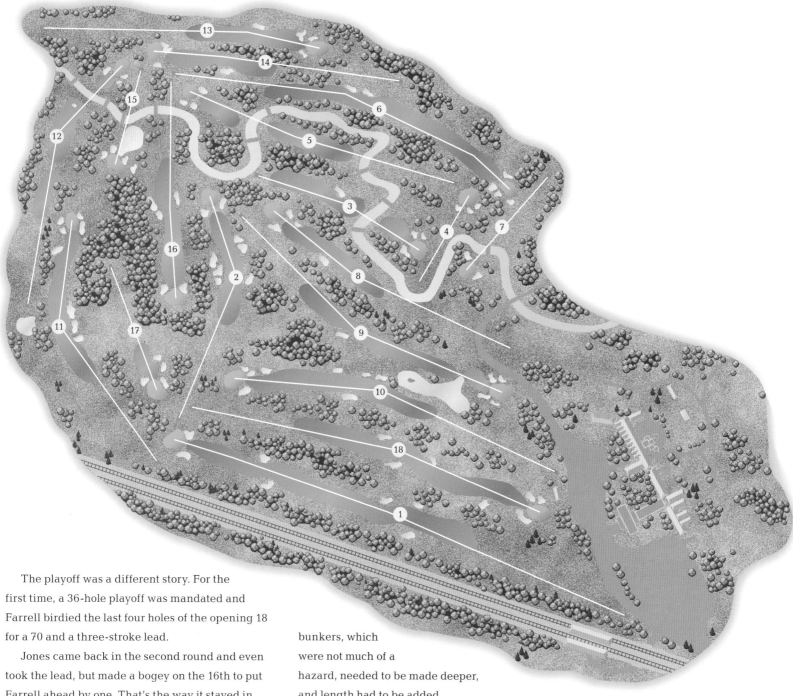

The playoff was a different story. For the first time, a 36-hole playoff was mandated and Farrell birdied the last four holes of the opening 18 for a 70 and a three-stroke lead.

Jones came back in the second round and even took the lead, but made a bogey on the 16th to put Farrell ahead by one. That's the way it stayed in a thrilling conclusion, with both making birdies on the last two holes. On 17, Farrell hit a brilliant approach from the rough to three feet, while Jones holed a 30-foot putt for his birdie. Farrell was in the rough again on 18, but pitched to eight feet. With Jones sitting three feet from the hole for a certain birdie, Farrell holed the putt to avoid another 36-hole playoff and claim his first and only major title.

The 1961 PGA Championship saw another fantastic finish, with Jerry Barber holing putts of 20, 40, and 60 feet on the last three holes, two for birdies, to force a playoff with Don January, which Barber won, 67-68.

When Olympia Fields re-emerged for the 1997 U.S. Senior Open, Arnold Palmer said it "absolutely" could host the U.S. Open. Actually, it needed some work before it could be Open-ready. The bunkers, which were not much of a hazard, needed to be made deeper, and length had to be added.

Mark Mungeam had done some restoration work on the course even before the club had bid for the Senior Open. So instead of hiring a high-profile architect to prepare the course for the U.S. Open, the club called on Mungeam again.

Length wasn't a problem. There was plenty of room to move tees back, and 13 holes were lengthened in extending the course from 6,907 to 7,190 yards. Mungeam was creative in borrowing the back of the sixth tee (all holes are referred to by their 2003 U.S. Open numbers) to make the 16th a more formidable 451 yards for championship play, while reducing the sixth from 570 to 555. He also used the middle tee on the second hole to bring No. 18 to 460 yards. The biggest change was on the eighth—a new tee back across the club's entrance road added 45 yards to make it 433.

An Open Moment

Brian Davis of England, playing in his first U.S. Open, started by holing a 75-yard wedge shot for an eagle on the par-five first hole, followed by birdies on the second, third, and fourth to get to five-under through four holes—the best start in U.S. Open history. "I think I'm going to wake up in a minute," Davis told his caddie while walking to the fifth tee. He did, making a double bogey on the fifth after hitting his tee shot into a creek to the right. Davis finished the day with a 71 and the week tied for 61st at 292.

Mungeam also showed some imagination in making the bunkers more punishing. Since Olympia Fields is built in a flood plain, there was worry about reaching the water table by going too deep. So the architect suggested digging only two feet and adding those two feet to the bank, effectively making a four-foot difference. (On top of the changes, the USGA tweaked the routing for the 2003 Open: The nines were reversed except for the first and 10th holes, which played normally.)

Despite the changes, Olympia Fields played like a pussycat in the first two rounds in 2003, thanks to a lack of wind and soft conditions caused by clay-based soil that does not drain as quickly as sand-based greens. There were 24 sub-par rounds on Thursday and 38 on Friday, the most ever on a par-70 layout and second only to the rain-softened first and second rounds at the 1990 Open at Medinah. On Friday, Vijay Singh became the fourth player to shoot 63 in the Open, and he and Jim Furyk established a new 36-hole mark of 133. The cut came at three-over 143.

Furyk added a third-round 67 for a 200 total that broke the 54-hole record by three strokes, and 20 players had sub-par totals through 54 holes. But Olympia Fields turned into a real Open course on Sunday, as the greens finally dried out and the USGA set up the course with more fire, virtually eliminating birdie opportunities on several holes—there was only one birdie all day on the 247-yard 17th.

The scoring average rose to 73.03 and four players finished under par for 72 holes—only Furyk (eight-under) and Stephen Leaney (five-under) were better than one-under. After his torrid start, Furyk ended up only tying the 72-hole mark of 272.

The final day was devoid of drama, as Furyk began the round three strokes ahead of Leaney, who never got any closer. Furyk reached 11-under for the championship with nine holes to play, but played the back nine in three-over with meaningless bogeys on the last two holes.

In truth, Olympia Fields is neither as easy as it appeared in the first three rounds nor as tough as it

JIM FURYK'S WINNING MOMENT

appeared in the last. It's a subtle layout that needs at least some help from the elements or course conditions to become a real challenge. It doesn't have many backbreaking par fours or memorable holes. It's "merely" a sequence of very good golf holes.

"It's not dramatic like Bethpage," said architect Mungeam. "It just feels like a country-club course. Even after working on it, I still think, 'Wow, this course is going to host a U.S. Open?'"

The newly deepened bunkers cause few problems for today's players. Butterfield Creek does not cut directly in front of any greens. It's most in play for catching errant drives to the right of the fifth and eighth fairways. The course was built partly in an open area and partly on more wooded terrain, so trees are sometimes a factor but not a constant presence.

The challenge lies mostly in the greens, all but four of which are Park originals. (The ninth and 12th were rebuilt by Mungeam because they had too much slope for today's greens speeds; two had been rebuilt earlier.) But like the rest of the layout, the putting surfaces are more subtle than dramatic, set into the landscape so the overall slope is not always noticeable, with built-in pitches and rolls that Park put in by hand.

The best hole on the front nine, and maybe on the course, is the fifth, a 440-yard par four. The tee shot must travel no more than 290 yards to stay short of the creek crossing the fairway; a miss to the right brings trees into play. The second shot plays uphill to a green that slopes severely from back to front. Another tough par four is the ninth, a 496-yarder that was the par-five finishing hole in 1928. Water to the right comes into play on the approach if the drive is poor.

The 11th is a 467-yard par four narrowed by large bunkers on the right, while the 458-yard 12th doesn't need any fairway bunkers thanks to trees on the right and a hard-sloping green with a false front.

The course has a tough finish. The slightly uphill 247-yard 17th is especially difficult when the hole is located behind the front bunker. The fairway on the 460-yard 18th snakes between fairway bunkers and the green features a host of little shelves along with an overall right-to-left/back-to-front slope. David Graham five-putted this green in the 1997 Senior Open; Furyk three-putted it to lose the 72-hole record.

Although Olympia Fields's return performance couldn't be termed a smashing success in the manner of Bethpage Black's 2002 debut, its showing on Sunday might have been enough to earn a return engagement, especially given the lack of viable options in Chicago, a desirable Open location.

15TH HOLE

1928 TOP FINISHERS

*Johnny Farrell	77-74-71-72—294	
Bobby Jones	73-71-73-77—294	
Roland Hancock	74-77-72-72—295	
Walter Hagen	75-72-73-76—296	
George Von Elm	74-72-76-74—296	

*Farrell won playoff, 143-144

Low round: Ed Dudley, 68

2003 TOP FINISHERS

Jim Furyk	67-66-67-72—272
Stephen Leaney	67-68-68-72—275
Mike Weir	73-67-68-71—279
Kenny Perry	72-71-69-67—279
Fredrik Jacobson	69-67-73-71—280
Justin Rose	70-71-70-69—280
Nick Price	71-65-69-75—280
Ernie Els	69-70-69-72—280
David Toms	72-67-70-71—280
Scott Verplank	76-67-68-70—281
Cliff Kresge	69-70-72-70—281
Billy Mayfair	69-71-67-74—281
Jonathan Kaye	70-70-72-69—281
Padraig Harrington	69-72-72-68—281

Low round: Vijay Singh, 63

Scorecard

2003 U.S. Open

Hole	Par	Yardage	Avg.	Rank	Fwy. %	Green %	Putts
1	5	576	4.87	17	39.0	73.0	1.59
2	4	400	4.01	14	49.8	66.4	1.63
3	4	389	4.07	12	63.9	63.0	1.65
4	3	164	2.95	16		86.5	1.80
5	4	440	4.29	3	61.0	53.4	1.72
6	5	555	4.75	18	43.0	77.1	1.69
7	3	212	3.21	9		50.9	1.64
8	4	433	4.24	7	50.9	47.3	1.61
9	4	496	4.27	5	66.4	57.0	1.79
Out	36	3655	36.65		53.4	63.9	1.68
10	4	444	4.28	4	51.3	51.8	1.74
11	4	467	4.20	10	55.6	50.7	1.66
12	4	458	4.37	1	51.8	39.5	1.64
13	4	397	4.11	11	65.7	66.1	1.74
14	4	414	4.24	6	51.1	45.3	1.56
15	3	187	3.00	15		74.7	1.72
16	4	451	4.03	13	52.7	64.1	1.64
17	3	247	3.29	2		39.7	1.64
18	4	460	4.21	8	44.8	60.1	1.76
In	34	3525	35.73		53.3	54.7	1.68
Total	70	7190	72.38		53.4	59.3	1.68

18TH HOLE

15TH HOLE. OPPOSITE: 8TH HOLE

OLYMPIC CLUB (LAKE COURSE) SAN FRANCISCO, CALIFORNIA 1955, 1966, 1987, 1998, 2012

Many courses are known for greens that are difficult to hold. At Olympic, the *fairways* are known for repelling shots. ¶ The Lake Course at the Olympic Club is built on a hill that falls from the clubhouse down to Lake Merced, which sits just off club property. Most of the holes slant to one side or the other, sometimes vigorously. Keeping the ball from running off those fairways into the rough is the biggest challenge at Olympic. ¶ A relatively short course, playing 6,797 yards to a par of 70 for the 1998 U.S. Open, Olympic doesn't have a single water hazard, no out of bounds, only one fairway bunker, and most of the greens are not terribly severe. Yet in four Opens, only four players have finished under par for 72 holes. In 1998, nobody finished under par and Lee Janzen won at even-par 280. ¶ It's a course where finesse, accuracy, and shotmaking trump the long ball. "You can never get up there and knock the crap out of the ball," said Bob Rosburg, who grew up playing Olympic before becoming a PGA champion. "It doesn't do you any good, except maybe on the first hole [a reachable par five]."

3RD HOLE

Shotmaking is important because the best way to hold the canted fairways is to work the ball against the slope—a right-to-left shot for left-to-right slopes and vice versa. Otherwise, those 28-yard-wide U.S. Open fairways play as if they were 18 or 20 yards wide, especially if the fairways are firm.

The fairways were *too* firm and too fast in 1998, when they practically played like greens and balls would trickle off the short grass. Only 58.5 percent of tee shots found the fairway on a course where players were hitting less than a driver on many holes. Still, Olympic has enough positives that the USGA has elected to go back in 2012.

All four Opens at Olympic have been dramatic affairs; in each case, the course wasn't kind to the game's legends, with Hall of Famers Ben Hogan, Arnold Palmer, Tom Watson, and Payne Stewart suffering painful setbacks from the heroics of the four players who beat them, Jack Fleck, Billy Casper, Scott Simpson, and Janzen, all of whom shot 33 or better on the last nine of regulation.

It's fitting that Olympic should be a stage for the greatest golfers, for the club has nurtured some great athletes. Started as a downtown athletic club in 1860, its members have included heavyweight boxing champion "Gentleman Jim" Corbett, basketball star Hank Luisetti, and Olympic shot-putter Parry O'Brien. The club got into golf in 1922 by purchasing Lakeside Country Club, but quickly tore it up and built 36 holes, the Ocean and Lake courses, designed by Willie Watson, with former Lakeside pro Sam Whiting, an Englishman, serving as construction foreman.

Those courses lasted only a year before earth slides destroyed eight holes. For the redesign, the club turned to Whiting, who showed the genius of a professional golf architect. Most of the damaged holes were on the Ocean Course, the showcase course of the two at the time. Unable to restore that track to its former glory because of land that was no longer available for golf, Whiting turned his attention to the Lake Course. He made extensive changes, including rerouting many holes. Whiting stayed on as superintendent, and had a great deal to do with the development of the Lake Course as a championship test by carrying out a tree-planting program.

Whiting planted some 30,000 cypress, cedar, pine, eucalyptus, and other species. Trees grow quickly in Northern California, and many sprouted to 60 feet. The trees added to the course's challenge and beauty without choking the fairways.

Its reputation growing as rapidly as its trees, Olympic hosted the 1955 U.S. Open. Robert Trent Jones Sr. was hired to prepare the course for the Open, though his work was nowhere near as extensive as it had been at Oakland Hills four years earlier. Mostly, he added length, turning a 6,433-yard par-71 layout into a 6,727-yarder with a par of 70. In contrast to his work at Oakland Hills, he actually took out some fairway bunkers, leaving only one on the entire course, to the left of the par-four sixth.

As is often the case, the members wanted their course to play as hard as possible, by any means available. They didn't cut the rough for a month beforehand, letting it grow to a foot long in many places. USGA officials ordered it to be cut, but the mowers at Olympic weren't up to the task. Fortunately, a nearby course had a new model that could handle the tall grass, to a point. Stories from that Open include a caddie losing his player's bag in the deep stuff and a player unable to find his ball after taking a drop over his shoulder.

Under those circumstances, straight-arrow Ben Hogan was the heavy favorite. As expected, Hogan led after three rounds and closed with a fine 70 to hold off rival Sam Snead, whose nearly annual bid for his first Open title came up short this time because his putter turned to ice on the back nine. Coming off the 18th green with a total of seven-over 287, Hogan handed the ball that would represent his record fifth Open victory to USGA Executive Director Joe Dey and said, "This is for Golf House."

"When I finished, I was sure I had won that tournament by at least two shots," Hogan later said. So was Gene Sarazen, then a television commentator. There were still players on the course (the leaders didn't go off last in those days) as the broadcast ended, but Sarazen proclaimed Hogan the winner.

At the time, there was one player with a ghost of a chance. Jack Fleck was eight-over and playing the 12th hole. But he was a long shot, a 33-year-old in his first season as a PGA Tour regular. Plus, *nobody* could be expected to mount a back-nine charge that year at Olympic, one of the harshest Open tests ever.

A friend in the gallery told Fleck on the 14th tee that he needed one birdie coming in. Littler, who

BILLY CASPER

ARNOLD PALMER LOST A SEVEN-STROKE LEAD ON THE LAST NINE HOLES IN 1966.

was playing with Fleck, chimed in, "He'll need some pars, too."

It truly seemed hopeless when Fleck bogeyed No. 14. The Iowa municipal-course pro got that stroke back at the 144-yard 15th, sinking a nine-foot putt. Equally vital was a par on the uphill 461-yard 17th, a par five that had been converted to a par four for the Open but was playing more like a par five. Fleck bounced a 3-wood second shot onto the green.

Fleck got a break at the 337-yard home hole when his tee shot stayed in the intermediate rough on the left, just missing the long stuff. From 100 yards, he feathered a soft 7-iron to eight feet and made the downhill putt to tie Hogan. Fleck had

played the back nine in 33 strokes for a 67—the only round of the day under par. In the locker room, Hogan said, "I was wishing he would make a two or a five. I was wishing it was over—all over."

Fleck was a huge underdog in the playoff, but he led most of the way. He birdied three straight holes starting at No. 8 and broke par again, shooting 69. The Olympic rough killed Hogan's last chance. Trailing by one on the 18th tee, his foot slipped and his tee shot flew well left of the fairway into some of the longest rough on the course. It took him three hacks to escape and he finished with a double bogey for a 72.

Olympic's second Open was more stunning. The winner, Casper, wasn't an outsider like Fleck. He

16TH HOLE

JACK FLECK

already had won the Open and was at the mid-point of a career in which he would win 51 times.

But he shocked the golf world by making up seven strokes to Arnold Palmer in the last nine holes. Although the tournament is largely remembered for Palmer's tragic collapse, one of the worst in major-championship history, Casper would not have won without a back-nine charge of 32 to Palmer's 39.

Palmer began the round three strokes ahead and figured he had wrapped it up after shooting a 32 on the front nine to extend the margin to seven. Playing partner Casper assumed it was over, too. Walking to the 10th tee, he said, "Arnie, it looks like I'm going to have to work hard to finish second. [He was two strokes ahead of third-place Jack Nicklaus at the time.]"

"Don't worry, Bill," Palmer replied. "If you need some help, I'll help you."

Palmer later admitted that he was most concerned at that point with trying to break Hogan's Open record of 276, which had stood since 1948. He needed to match par on the back nine to break it.

Strangely, the leader took risks and the challenger played it safe on the back nine, as each man stayed true to his own style. That was particularly true on the 15th and 16th holes, as Casper made up two strokes on each to cut the margin from five to one.

Playing first, Casper hit his shot on the short par-three 15th conservatively toward the center of the small green, 20 feet from the hole. Instead of doing the same, Palmer aimed for the flag on the right side of the green and ended up in a bunker. Casper made the putt; Palmer bogeyed. Suddenly, the margin was three with three to play.

"All I can think at this point is how irritated I am that Casper has been 'playing safe' and is catching up on me," Palmer wrote in *A Golfer's Life*. "I decide I will win or lose exactly the way I've won or lost every tournament I've ever played."

The 16th at Olympic is one of the hardest par fives in the world. At 609 yards (604 in 1966), it's not so much a dogleg as a crescent—the hole keeps turning left for its entire length. Palmer lashed at a driver, and his intended draw turned into an ugly snap-hook, which crashed into a tree 150 yards from the tee. Palmer then made a mistake he later called "ridiculous": He tried to hit a 3-iron out of the deep rough. It advanced only 100 yards, staying in the deep stuff. He hit a wedge into the fairway

An Open Moment

Harvie Ward was one of the top amateurs in the country in 1955; later in the year he would win the first of two straight U.S. Amateurs. A local who lived close to the club, Ward was threatening to become the first amateur winner of the Open since Johnny Goodman in 1933 as he held a share of the second-round lead with Tommy Bolt.

The beginning of the end came on the par-three eighth, where his tee shot into a 100-foot cypress tree never came down. The lost-ball penalty sent him to a double bogey that contributed to a 76-76 finish. Three decades later, Tommy Nakajima was among the leaders in the third round until his approach to the right of the 18th green got stuck in a tree.

PAYNE STEWART WATCHES AS HIS PUTT SLOWLY ROLLS DOWN THE 18TH GREEN IN 1998.

to a point from where he couldn't reach the green in four. He made bogey, and Casper holed a 15-foot putt from the fringe for a birdie. The lead was one with two holes remaining.

Each player missed both the fairway and the green on the extremely difficult 17th, but only Casper got up and down for par. Tied.

Palmer almost completed the giveaway on No. 18, hooking his tee shot into a thick patch of rough. He gouged a 9-iron onto the green, but his long putt was five feet wide and short, and he had to hole a nasty second putt for 278 and a playoff. After the round, a dazed Palmer sat in front of his locker and muttered the words that all who had witnessed the back nine were thinking, "It's hard to believe."

The extra session followed a similar pattern. Palmer led by two at the turn, 33-35, then fell apart on the back. Casper gained the lead with a 50-foot birdie putt on the par-three 13th, and the margin widened when Palmer made bogey, bogey, and double bogey on the next three. The final verdict was 69-73.

It was 21 years until the next Olympic Open, when Nicklaus, then an elder statesman, predicted that Olympic was the type of course where a "plodder" would win. In a way, he was right. Simpson was a plodder, not a long hitter, known mostly for steady play and excellent short game. But he hardly won in plodding fashion.

After playing six holes of the final round, Simpson was part of a five-way tie for the lead at one-over, with four players at two-over. He then played the final 12 holes in four-under, including a three-under 32 on the back nine marked by a burst of birdies on 14, 15, and 16, followed by an equally important par save on 17.

It came down to the 18th, where Watson, the 54-hole leader, trailed by one. The leading player of the late 1970s and early 1980s, Watson was seeking his first major since 1983. He watched his approach roll down a slope, leaving a 45-foot putt that he nearly holed. Instead of a return to glory, Watson joined Hogan and Palmer on the list of Olympic's victims.

Stewart joined them in 1998. Despite being cursed by bad luck earlier in the week, Stewart entered the final round with a four-stroke lead. On Friday, he was the most prominent victim of a misguided 18th-green hole location on the side of a slope, watching as his birdie putt from 10 feet just missed before trickling down the slope and finishing 25 feet away.

Stewart's bad luck continued in the final round, when he made a bogey after his tee shot on the 12th hole ended up in a sand-filled divot in the fairway. But luck was not the primary factor in a final-round 74; he simply did not play very well.

He still would have won it if not for an outstanding final round by Janzen. After bogeys on two of the first three holes, Janzen was four-under the rest of the way to shoot 68, the only man within eight strokes of the lead entering the round to do better than 73.

The key "blow" was actually a gust of wind on the fifth hole. Janzen's tee shot lodged in the branches of a tree—not unheard of at Olympic (see "An Open Moment")—and he was starting to walk back to the tee to play under a stroke-and-distance penalty when the wind blew the ball out of the branches. Janzen punched out, hit his third shot to the fringe, and chipped in for an adrenaline-rush par.

The fifth marks the end of "Quake Corner," the hardest four-hole stretch at Olympic. Although just 394 yards, the second hole is awkward—the approach shot must be played with the ball above the player's feet to an elevated green. Level lies are rare at Olympic, a big part of its resistance to scoring, especially when playing to the small greens.

The mirror-image fourth and fifth neatly encapsulate Olympic's challenges. First, they are two of the most severe greens on the course next to the 17th and 18th. The 438-yard fourth is a dogleg left with a fairway that slopes annoyingly to the right. An ideal tee shot is a draw; anything with a fade runs out of the fairway on the right. From the rough,

the green is nearly impossible to hit. The 457-yard fifth is just the opposite, a dogleg right that slopes to the left. A fade is the ideal approach shot to the firm green, but it must be played from a sidehill lie that promotes a draw.

The seventh and eighth both play uphill, but offer birdie chances at 288 and 137 yards, respectively. It's surprising how many bogeys are made, however.

If Olympic has a weakness, it's that most of the par fours are of a similar, medium length. From the ninth through the 14th, the five par fours measure between 416 and 433 yards. Under Open conditions, that means the driver stays in the bag for much of the round. While the lengths are similar, the holes offer a variety of terrain, green shapes, and bunkering.

Three of the Open winners (all but Janzen) birdied the 157-yard 15th in the final round, but No. 16 is anything but a birdie hole even though it's a par five. If you miss the fairway with either the first or second shot, par is a good score. Besides contributing to Palmer's demise, the 16th was the scene of Stewart's last bogey, which knocked him one behind in 1998.

For member play, Olympic concludes with a modest par five and a short par four. But the USGA

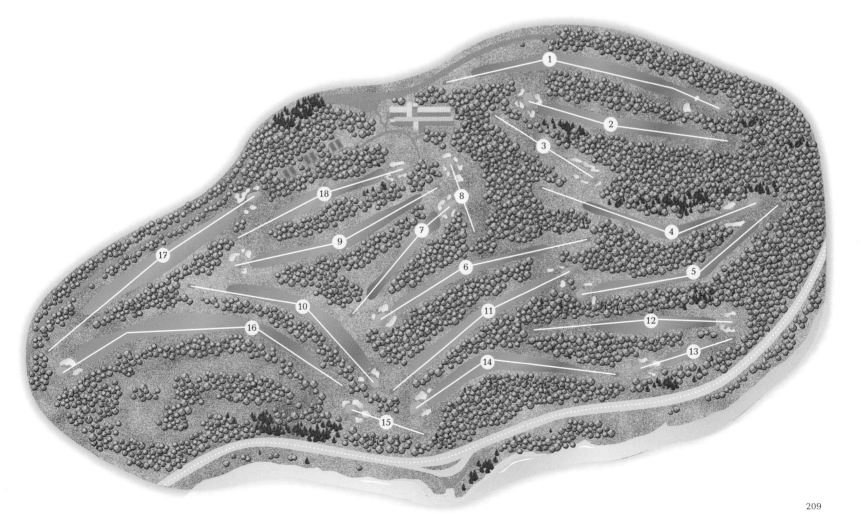

converts the 17th, which plays uphill with fairway sloping to the right, into a par four, even though it wasn't designed that way. They have tried different tee positions trying to find what distance works best—its yardages were 461, 435, 428, and 468 in the four Opens.

In 1955, there were only five birdies all week and the scoring average was 4.92. At a shorter distance in 1987, the landing zone for drives sloped sharply to the right. Nearly every drive that landed in the fairway took a right turn and ended up in the right rough. The field averaged 4.56.

In 1998, the tee was moved back 40 yards and the fairway moved slightly to the right in an effort to find a more reasonable landing area. That aspect worked, as 61.5 percent of the drives found the fairway. But a longer second shot to the elevated green resulted in a 4.72 scoring average. Janzen played the hole in five-over for three rounds before making a vital par on Sunday.

The 18th is an unusual finish for the U.S. Open at just 347 yards, generally an iron followed by a wedge. But the green's natural amphitheater setting, with a hillside leading up to the clubhouse, might be the best in golf. The sloping green assures that birdies aren't too easy, although this putting surface that caused so much trouble in 1998 has been rebuilt.

Since that Open, the second hole has been lengthened and after evaluating the situation at the 2007 U.S. Amateur, new tees might be added on a few other holes. Olympic has remained nearly unchanged since 1955, and those 420-yard holes that were considered medium length now have become short par fours.

Added length will ensure that Olympic remains the same challenge it has always been, a course that facilitated the development of shotmakers like Rosburg, Ken Venturi, and Johnny Miller.

"It really helped me learn to drive in the fairway and not be a wild slasher at the ball. Olympic teaches you good course management," said Rosburg. "I always felt that when you left the Olympic Club, everything else seemed kind of easy."

18TH HOLE

1955 TOP FINISHERS

*Jack Fleck	76-69-75-67—287
Ben Hogan	72-73-72-70—287
Tommy Bolt	67-77-75-73—292
Sam Snead	79-69-70-74—292
Julius Boros	76-69-73-77—295
Bob Rosburg	78-74-67-76—295
Doug Ford	74-77-74-71—296
Bud Holscher	77-75-71-73—296
Harvie Ward	74-70-76-76—296
Jack Burke Jr.	71-77-72-77—297
Mike Souchak	73-79-72-73—297

*Fleck won playoff, 69-72

Low round: Bolt, Fleck, Rosburg, 67

1966 TOP FINISHERS

*Billy Casper	69-68-73-68—278
Arnold Palmer	71-66-70-71—278
Jack Nicklaus	71-71-69-74—285
Tony Lema	71-74-70-71—286
Dave Marr	71-74-68-73—286
Phil Rodgers	70-70-73-74—287
Bobby Nichols	74-72-71-72—289
Wes Ellis	71-75-74-70—290
Johnny Miller	70-72-74-74—290
Mason Rudolph	74-72-71-73—290
Doug Sanders	70-75-74-71—290

*Casper won playoff, 69-73

Low round: Rives McBee, 64

1987 TOP FINISHERS

Scott Simpson	71-68-70-68—277
Tom Watson	72-65-71-70—278
Seve Ballesteros	68-75-68-71—282
Ben Crenshaw	67-72-72-72—283
Bernhard Langer	69-69-73-72—283
Curtis Strange	71-72-69-71—283
Bobby Wadkins	71-71-70-71—283
Lennie Clements	70-70-70-74—284
Tommy Nakajima	68-70-74-72—284
Mac O'Grady	71-69-72-72—284
Dan Pohl	75-71-69-69—284
Jim Thorpe	70-68-73-73—284

Low round: Keith Clearwater, 64

1998 TOP FINISHERS

Lee Janzen	73-66-73-68—280
Payne Stewart	66-71-70-74—281
Bob Tway	68-70-73-73—284
Nick Price	73-68-71-73—285
Steve Stricker	73-71-69-73—286
Tom Lehman	68-75-68-75—286
Lee Westwood	72-74-70-71—287
David Duval	75-68-75-69—287
Jeff Maggert	69-69-75-74—287
Phil Mickelson	71-73-74-70—288
Stuart Appleby	73-74-70-71—288
Stewart Cink	73-68-73-74—288
Jeff Sluman	72-74-74-68—288

Low round: Paul Azinger, 65

Scorecard

Hole	Par	Yardage	Avg.*	Rank*	Fwy. %*	Green %*	Putts*
1	5	533	4.85	18	54.7	77.9	1.62
2	4	394	4.33	4	67.0	45.7	1.68
3	3	223	3.26	6		51.5	1.74
4	4	438	4.42	3	46.7	31.5	1.66
5	4	457	4.44	2	41.9	31.7	1.63
6	4	437	4.25	9	58.5	56.6	1.76
7	4	288	4.02	16	59.2	72.0	1.71
8	3	137	3.01	17		78.3	1.73
9	4	433	4.25	8	45.0	48.3	1.73
Out	35	3340	36.83		53.3	54.8	1.70
10	4	422	4.16	13	63.2	59.0	1.68
11	4	430	4.27	5	56.6	49.0	1.71
12	4	416	4.19	12	55.0	46.4	1.66
13	3	186	3.20	11		43.8	1.62
14	4	422	4.26	7	68.8	46.4	1.69
15	3	157	3.07	15		66.4	1.76
16	5	609	5.25	10	68.5	52.4	1.67
17	4	468	4.64	1	61.5	21.9	1.74
18	4	347	4.15	14	72.5	66.9	1.81
In	35	3457	37.19		63.7	50.2	1.70
Total	70	6797	74.02		58.5	52.5	1.70

*Average score and rank cumulative from 1987 and 1998 Opens. Percentages of fairways and greens hit, and average number of putts from 1998.

4TH HOLE

ONWENTSIA CLUB LAKE FOREST, ILLINOIS 1906

The Onwentsia Club shares its roots with Chicago Golf Club. Both can trace their origins to the first primitive seven-hole course in the Chicago area, designed by C.B. Macdonald at the invitation of his friend Hobart Chatfield-Taylor. Laid out in 1892 on the estate of Senator Charles Farwell in Lake Forest, the course was intended to introduce people to the game of golf, which Macdonald had learned in St. Andrews, Scotland. ¶ The result was a golf course in name only; it was more akin to kids making a backyard course using tomato cans for holes, which is exactly what Macdonald did. The demonstration enabled Macdonald to round up some investors to form Chicago Golf Club and build a real course west of the city. Chatfield-Taylor led a contingent that would stay in Lake Forest, 28 miles north of Chicago, and eventually form Onwentsia. ¶ The group stayed on the estate course for a couple of years before moving to a slightly less primitive nine-hole layout on a nearby farm in 1894, calling it the Lake Forest Golf Club. In 1896, they made another short move to the 175-acre Cobb Farm and changed the name to Onwentsia, Iroquois for "meeting place."

Scorecard

1906 U.S. Open

HOLE	PAR*	YARDAGE
1	4	400
2	3	210
3	5	450
4	4	340
5	4	300
6	4	335
7	4	362
8	4	385
9	4	350
Out	36	3032
10	5	445
11	4	400
12	5	525
13	4	360
14	4	320
15	4	330
16	3	135
17	4	300
18	4	260
In	37	3075
Total	73	6107

*Par is estimated

Scorecard

Today

HOLE*	PAR	YARDAGE
1 (10)	5	497
2 (11)	4	400
3 (12)	5	516
4	4	414
5	3	171
6	4	371
7	4	418
8	4	419
9 (18)	3	198
Out	36	3404
10 (1)	5	510
11 (2)	3	193
12 (3)	4	449
13	4	437
14	3	181
15 (6)	4	345
16 (7)	4	376
17 (8)	4	329
18 (9)	4	421
In	35	3241
Total	71	6645

*Hole numbers from 1906 in parentheses

The 18-hole course, which still exists today in basically the same form, was built by committee—the first nine in 1896 and the second nine in 1898. Macdonald, a member at Onwentsia as well as at Chicago, was involved in designing the first nine along with Scottish professionals James and Robert Foulis, who had just come to the United States. Herbert James Tweedie, another leading figure in early Chicago golf, and H.J. Whigham, Macdonald's future son-in-law, worked with the Foulis brothers on the second nine.

Onwentsia hosted the 1899 U.S. Amateur, won by H.M. Harriman. An article in *Golf* stated, "What puzzled the visitors the most were the bunkers closely guarding a number of the greens. Opinions differed as to whether these were correctly placed, but I am decidedly of the opinion that in most cases they were correct. Some greens had been left open for running-up shots, but in most cases it was necessary to lay the ball dead immediately on carrying a rather formidable looking cop bunker. This shot is one of the most difficult in golf, so it is small wonder that some critics questioned the advisability of the plan in vogue."

When the U.S. Open came to Onwentsia in 1906, the course had been extended from 5,984 to 6,107 yards, and the club pro was Willie Anderson, who had captured four of the previous five Opens. He was in second place entering the final round, but faltered badly and would never be a factor in future Opens. The winner was Alex Smith, who had been three times an Open runner-up and was long overdue for a win.

Surrounded by a "bedraggled, umbrella-laden gallery" on a rainy last day, Smith finished 2-3-4 to post 75 for a 295 total, and said, "The man that beats that is welcome to it." Nobody came close. Alex's brother Willie, the 1899 champion, finished second, seven strokes back at 302.

The golfers shared the grounds with a polo tournament, which, according to *Golf*, "added to the gaiety of the occasion, and with the golfers' continuous march around the borders of the grounds, with their attendant galleries, and the polo field in the centre, with its fringe of spectators, brilliant equipages and automobiles, the whole spectacle formed a most pleasing picture of country club life, an emphatic answer that golf, the pastime really responsible for it all, is one of the greatest benefactors of modern civilization."

The polo field is gone from the interior of the course and the layout has undergone a couple of revisions; it now plays at 6,645 yards. Seven holes have been rerouted from the 1906 configuration, mostly to strengthen a stretch on what was originally the back nine. The nines were reversed in 1939 to fit better with a new clubhouse.

1906 TOP FINISHERS

Alex Smith	73-74-73-75—295
Willie Smith	73-81-74-74—302
Laurie Auchterlonie	76-78-75-76—305
James Maiden	80-73-77-75—305
Willie Anderson	73-76-74-84—307

Low round: Anderson, Maiden, A. Smith (2), W. Smith, 73

ALEX SMITH

TIGER WOODS WAS FAR ABOVE THE BEACH—AND THE FIELD—IN 2000. OPPOSITE: 9TH HOLE

PEBBLE BEACH GOLF LINKS   PEBBLE BEACH, CALIFORNIA   1972, 1982, 1992, 2000, 2010

If the measure of a golf course is the quality of champions it produces, Pebble Beach Golf Links is near the top. Its first U.S. Open, in 1972, was won by Jack Nicklaus, the game's best player. By 1982, Tom Watson had taken over as No. 1, and he beat out Nicklaus for the Open title. The 1992 Open came during an era without a dominant player, but Tom Kite was the leading career money winner on the PGA Tour when he scored a Pebble victory. During arguably the greatest season in golf history, Tiger Woods won at Pebble Beach in 2000 with the most dominating performance in the history of major championships. ¶ Why does Pebble Beach bring out the best in the best? Perhaps because it's a complete test of golf. Its small, sloping greens reward precise ball-striking and deft putting. There is enough room to reward power. It requires good thinking and course management. And when bad weather kicks in, as it often does, Pebble Beach tests fortitude and survival skills.

All that, plus beautiful views from its cliffside setting overlooking the Pacific Ocean, add up to a ranking of fifth in the United States by *Golf Magazine* and sixth by *Golf Digest*.

The man responsible for bringing golf to this spectacular spot on the Monterey Peninsula was Samuel F.B. Morse, a distant cousin of the telegraph inventor of the same name. This Morse was a 30-year-old Yale graduate who had found success in real estate. In 1915, he was hired to liquidate the holdings of the Pacific Improvement Company, founded nearly 40 years earlier by the men behind the Central Pacific Railroad. Those holdings included the land that would become Pebble Beach, which at the time was divided into residential lots the company was having trouble selling.

Morse decided the best way to make the property attractive to buyers would be a golf resort community. And the best spot for the course was along the ocean. A spectacular course would build excitement about the area, and the residential lots above would feature gorgeous views.

Morse set about buying or trading for the lots that had already been sold on what was now the golf-course site. He acquired all but one. William Beatty refused to sell his 5.5-acre parcel, and Pebble Beach had to be routed around it until 1998.

Morse approached C.B. Macdonald and Donald Ross, but neither was interested in traveling to California to lay out a course. So the job fell to locals Jack Neville and Douglas Grant, two of California's top amateur golfers but golf-design neophytes.

"Years before it was built I could see this place as a golf links," Neville said later. "Nature had intended it to be nothing else." Neville, who had sold real estate for the Pacific Improvement Company, quickly came up with the routing. Pete Dye, one of the top golf architects of the latter part of the 20th century, said he might have walked right past the small spit of land Neville utilized to create the 106-yard par-three seventh. Neville used another peninsula for the par-three 17th, and created an exhilarating second shot over a yawning chasm at the eighth.

After establishing the routing, Neville enlisted Grant to help with the rest. In truth, Pebble Beach was not a great course right away, in condition or design. It evolved into greatness over a decade, with many contributors.

Pebble Beach made its debut in April 1918 with a christening tournament. It didn't go well. Players found not enough turf and too many rocks on the fairways, and indentations on the greens from sheep that had been brought in to maintain the grass. The course was immediately closed to improve its condition.

The course and a new lodge opened officially in February 1919. In the interim, local landscape artist Francis McComas was asked to add some aesthetics. McComas, incidentally, is the one who called the Monterey Peninsula (specifically Point Lobos) "the greatest meeting of land and water in the world," a quote often incorrectly attributed to author Robert Louis Stevenson, who lived in the area. McComas's biggest change was creating the two-tiered 14th green.

The course hosted the California Amateur in September 1920. Although the event was successful, the California Golf Association wasn't happy with "a woefully poor finishing hole." They had good reason. The original 18th was a 325-yard par four that was uninspiring even with water on the left side.

The solution was to pile dirt on some rocks behind the 17th green to make a tee, lengthening the hole by 35 yards and creating an exciting tee shot across part of the cove. Now it was a better hole of 360 yards.

Research by Neil Hotelling for *Pebble Beach Golf Links: The Official History* revealed that English architect Herbert Fowler was responsible for creating the 18th hole as we know it today. Fowler, who was in Monterey to redesign the Del Monte course, came up with a plan that called for filling in a creek behind the original green and moving the green 175 yards up the coast to create a 535-yard par five that has long been acknowledged as one of the greatest finishing holes in golf

Another contributing architect was Alister MacKenzie. While designing Cypress Point next door, he suggested some changes to the bunkering on the eighth and 13th holes at Pebble Beach.

Prior to the 1929 U.S. Amateur, an event that had never been played west of St. Louis, Pebble Beach hired H. Chandler Egan, an outstanding amateur who had won the 1904 and '05 U.S. Opens before becoming a golf architect, for a final, extensive upgrade of the course.

Egan is responsible for the green complexes that turned Pebble Beach from a good course into a great one. He rebuilt, reshaped, and rebunkered no fewer than 16 greens. "Some of the old greens were rather old-fashioned, unattractive, and dull, some were a bit unfair in their slopes and lack of visibility and

JACK NICKLAUS

almost none of them offered a real target for an iron shot," Egan wrote. He also added length on nine holes, bringing the total yardage to 6,662.

Egan built a new ninth hole, moving the fairway closer to the ocean and the green back 50 yards, beyond the gully that used to be in front of the 10th tee to create the hardest par four on the course at 450 yards. A new 10th tee kept the distance of that hole almost the same at 406 yards, and the green was rebuilt "as close to the ocean as possible."

The course has remained much the same since 1929, but it has lost a striking feature of Egan's redesign: huge imitation sand dune bunkers, including ones surrounding the seventh green.

In addition to the 1929 Amateur, Pebble Beach went on to host the 1940 and '48 U.S. Women's

Amateur and the 1949 and '61 U.S. Amateur, the latter won by Nicklaus. The course was obviously a USGA favorite, so why didn't they award it an Open until 1972?

There were three main reasons. The first was the course's location, about 120 miles south of San Francisco. The fear was that it would not draw enough spectators—not a concern for the U.S. Amateur, but the U.S. Open is seen as a revenue maker. The second was that as a public course it didn't have a corps of members to serve as volunteers. The third was the question of whether the course's conditioning was worthy of an Open.

Two of the three issues were easy to overcome. Pebble Beach put up a financial guarantee to ease the USGA's concerns over ticket sales. (Of course, the concerns turned out to be unfounded.) Although

Pebble had no members, the annual Bing Crosby National Pro-Am demonstrated that members of area clubs would pitch in.

As for the conditioning—well, that concern was legitimate. But it turned out that nobody really cared. The spectacular setting, impressive layout, and dramatic action overshadowed any concerns about conditioning.

In retrospect, the 1972 Open could have been controversial if a journeyman had won instead of Nicklaus, or if ABC hadn't expanded its coverage to three hours, bringing the spectacular ocean holes to America. Instead, Pebble Beach instantly became *the* classic Open course.

For the first three days, Pebble Beach was very hard. Nicklaus held the lead through 54 holes at even-par 216. On Sunday, the course—and the weather—nearly blew everyone away.

The winds gusted to 35 m.p.h., leading Dan Jenkins to write in *Sports Illustrated*, "For a while it appeared that the winner wasn't going to be a man, but the course. Pebble—good old monstrous Pebble, Double-Bogey-by-the-Sea Pebble—won every battle, one-on-one, even with Nicklaus."

There are two enduring images of Nicklaus from the final round. The first is of a bedraggled warrior hitting two shots into the hazard on the 10th, making double bogey. The second is as a conquer-

7TH HOLE

TOM WATSON CHIPS IN ON THE 17TH HOLE ON THE WAY TO THE 1982 TITLE.

ing hero hitting a 1-iron tee shot that clanged off the flagstick on the 17th to clinch the victory. He finished with a 290 total, but his two-over 74 was the best final round among the contenders on a day the average score soared to 78.8.

The USGA contibuted to the nearly impossible conditions by not acting to preserve the greens, which by the final round were baked out and impossible to hold. After watching his ball bounce over the 12th green, Nicklaus asked USGA Executive Director P.J. Boatwright, who was serving as a referee, "What did you do with all the grass?"

In addition, so much new, white beach sand had been dumped into bunkers that balls were plugging and escape was difficult. Nonetheless, the only question was when, not if, the Open would return.

Ten years later, the championship produced one of the most thrilling finishes in U.S. Open history. The outcome hinged on a battle between giants Watson and Nicklaus. Watson had won five majors, including a head-to-head battle against Nicklaus at the 1977 British Open, but he was still looking for his first U.S. Open.

This time, they were in different groups in the final round as Nicklaus mounted a charge with five straight birdies on the front nine, shot a 69, and posted a four-under total as Watson was five-under on the 16th.

After driving into a deep fairway bunker on that hole, Watson fell back into a tie with a bogey. Ironically, that bunker had been installed by his good friend, former USGA president Sandy Tatum, a San Francisco resident who made minor changes before the 1972 and 1982 Opens.

On the 17th, site of Nicklaus's iconic 1-iron, Watson pulled his 2-iron and the ball finished in deep rough, 20 feet from the hole. The pitch was difficult, downhill all the way; a par would be a great save. Waiting behind the 18th green, Nicklaus contemplated the possibility—probability—of a record fifth Open title.

Watson, however, gained confidence when he saw a good lie. When his caddie, Bruce Edwards, told him he could get it close, Watson responded, "I'm not going to get it close, I'm going to make it." Aiming a foot left of the hole, Watson hit a shot that landed just past the fringe, bounced twice, and rolled into the hole, prompting a celebratory run by Watson and a look of disbelief from Nicklaus.

Bill Rogers, who was playing with Watson, later estimated that Watson wouldn't chip one in if were to drop 100 balls at that spot. Nicklaus responded, "Try a thousand." A birdie on the 72nd hole gave Watson a two-stroke victory with a total of six-under 282.

The 1992 Open began with calm conditions and low scoring, and ended with a stormy Sunday that sent scores and some tempers soaring. Through 43 holes, Gil Morgan was in uncharted territory with a seven-stroke lead at 12-under; he was the first player to reach double digits under par at the Open. Then, he played the next seven holes in nine-over. He finished at four-under 212, but his one-shot lead looked very shaky.

In the final round, Morgan blew up to an 81, not quite as terrible as it sounds. Unforecast high winds blew, surprising USGA officials, who later said they would have put more water on the greens and changed some hole locations had they known. The greens dried out and became cruelly treacherous, while some pins were impossible to approach in regulation.

Some players were livid. Ray Floyd, who shot 81, called the setup "a joke." Nick Faldo, who shot

77, said, "If they want greens like this, I'm going to take up topless darts, I think. It would be easier to catch them in your teeth today."

Conditions bordered on unplayable, especially on the ocean holes. When Colin Montgomerie, starting two-and-a-half hours ahead of the last pair, before conditions were at their worst, came in with a 70, Nicklaus declared him the winner on television. But somehow, two of the late starters shot par or better. Jeff Sluman's 71 gave him a 287 total to beat Montgomerie by one.

And Tom Kite's 72 gave him a 285 total and his first major championship. Kite made five birdies to offset the unavoidable slip-ups on such a day. The most dramatic was on the par-three seventh into the worst of the wind. Players were missing the green of the 107-yarder with middle irons. Kite didn't hit it either, but he pitched in for birdie that was the most memorable shot of the week.

Pebble Beach was again difficult in 2000, but for a different reason—thick rough. Or at least it was difficult for 155 of the field of 156. In a week in which the next-best score was three-over, Woods set an Open record for the most strokes under par for 72 holes, a 12-under 272 total on a course reduced to a par of 71. (The second hole played as a par four.) That week, in a sport in which a five-stroke win is considered a rout, his 15-stroke victory margin, the largest ever at a major, defies logic.

The lush rough at the 2000 Open reflects a change in Pebble Beach over the last couple of decades. Whereas the salty air and heavy traffic made conditions once spotty, it's now one of the best-manicured courses anywhere. The escalating green fees—now $450—have given management plenty of revenue for maintenance and also a responsibility to provide the best experience for that kind of money.

It's also made Pebble Beach more like an inland course that happens to border the sea, a less welcome change. "I think Pebble Beach is a much better golf course hard and fast with almost the old Pinehurst roughs, just nubby and sandy and not much there," says Nicklaus, who has called Pebble Beach his favorite course.

Nicklaus can partly blame himself. He was hired to restore the course before the 1992 Open, a job that revolved more around conditioning than design. He returned in 1998 to build a new fifth hole when Pebble Beach finally bought the last remaining beachfront property for $8 million.

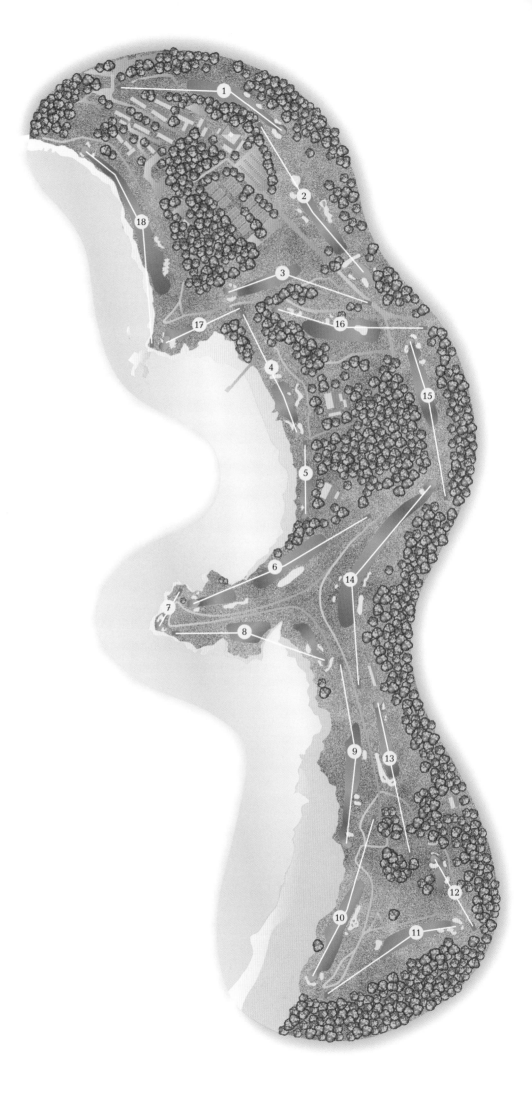

The acquisition allowed the company to abandon the awkward uphill par-three fifth for a beautiful downhill hole that gives the course an uninterrupted stretch along the coast from the fourth through 10th holes.

The first seven holes represent the most vulnerable part of Pebble Beach, even after the second has been changed from a par five to a par four (at least for Opens) and the addition of the new fifth, which plays harder than the old one. The Open record of six consecutive birdies has been accomplished twice, both times on this stretch—George Burns on the second through seventh in 1982 and Andy Dillard on the first six holes in 1992.

The tiny seventh can be included in the easy portion of the course under calm conditions, but the exposed hole is very demanding in the wind, despite its length. The 418-yard eighth features one of the most awe-inspiring approach shots in golf,

An Open Moment

If the USGA had known the wind would blow and dry the greens to a crisp in the final round of the 1992 Open, they wouldn't have located the hole on No. 12 on the shallow part of the green behind the left front bunker. Just as in 1972, there was no way to land the ball on that part of the green and keep it on the putting surface. Tom Kite didn't even try, playing to the right with a 4-iron and holing a long putt to take a four-stroke lead on the way to victory. "I hit it 30 feet from the hole and the gallery went absolutely crazy, like I hit it to within a foot," Kite later recalled. "I thought, 'My goodness, they haven't seen many balls on this green today.'"

17TH HOLE

18TH HOLE

over a chasm to a tiny green. Nicklaus calls it his favorite approach shot in golf.

That's followed by the toughest hole on the course, the 466-yard ninth. It's a difficult driving hole with a left-to-right sloping fairway and bunkers on the left. The 10th completes the Cliffs of Doom sequence. It's shorter than the ninth at 446 yards, but the hazard (cliffs leading to a beach below) is aggressively in play on both the tee shot and second shot.

A stretch of inland holes follows, and the highlight is the 14th, a sweeping uphill dogleg right of 573 yards to a small green made effectively smaller by its tiers—nothing on the front half stays on the green. It usually plays in the tougher half of holes on the course, rare for a par five.

The most noticeable feature of the 17th, aside from the Pacific behind and to the left, is a distinctive hourglass green divided by a large ridge. When the hole is on the back left portion, closely guarded by a large bunker, it's a challenge. If the shot is into the wind, it's nearly impossible.

The 18th is a thing of beauty, as well as a place of terror for wild drivers intimidated by the ocean left and out of bounds right. A few dissenters deem it overrated because it is nearly always played as a three-shot hole, with an unexciting lay-up followed by a wedge. This is one hole made better by equipment advances. It's now in range in two under many conditions for many players, adding a welcome risk/reward element.

The 18th has faced erosion and tree loss. The fairway, and especially the green, used to be farther from the water, but the sea had been eating into the land at several inches a year. In a big storm, large portions can disappear. An existing seawall was strengthened in 1997 to combat the problem, but a storm still took out a chunk of land just beyond the drive zone in 2005. The hole used to be distinguished by a large pine tree short and right of the green, complicating the second and third shots. The tree was lost to disease in 2001 and replaced the next year by a cypress transplanted from the first hole.

A tree replacement program is part of ongoing work at Pebble Beach under the aegis of RJ Harper, vice president of golf operations. Harper and his crew also are working on new bunkering on several holes, with all design ideas generated by the Pebble Beach staff and approved by Arnold Palmer, one of the four primary owners who took over in 1999. (The others are Peter Ueberroth, Clint Eastwood, and Richard Ferris.)

The changes include new tees on the second, ninth, and 14th holes that will add 18, 25, and eight yards respectively. It's unlikely any other holes will be lengthened—there simply isn't room. That will leave Pebble Beach at less than 6,900 yards, definitely on the short side for an Open in this day and age. Will the players tear it up? Not if the wind blows.

1972 TOP FINISHERS

Jack Nicklaus	71-73-72-74—290
Bruce Crampton	74-70-73-76—293
Arnold Palmer	77-68-73-76—294
Homero Blancas	74-70-76-75—295
Lee Trevino	74-72-71-78—295
Kermit Zarley	71-73-73-79—296
Johnny Miller	74-73-71-79—297
Tom Weiskopf	73-74-73-78—298
Chi Chi Rodriguez	71-75-78-75—299
Cesar Sanudo	72-72-78-77—299

Low round: Palmer, Lanny Wadkins, 68

1982 TOP FINISHERS

Tom Watson	72-72-68-70—282
Jack Nicklaus	74-70-71-69—284
Bobby Clampett	71-73-72-70—286
Dan Pohl	72-74-70-70—286
Bill Rogers	70-73-69-74—286
David Graham	73-72-69-73—287
Jay Haas	75-74-70-68—287
Gary Koch	78-73-69-67—287
Lanny Wadkins	73-76-67-71—287
Bruce Devlin	70-69-75-74—288
Calvin Peete	71-72-72-73—288

Low round: Koch, Wadkins, Peter Oosterhuis, Larry Rinker, 67

1992 TOP FINISHERS

Tom Kite	71-72-70-72—285
Jeff Sluman	73-74-69-71—287
Colin Montgomerie	70-71-77-70—288
Nick Faldo	70-76-68-77—291
Nick Price	71-72-77-71—291
Billy Andrade	72-74-72-74—292
Jay Don Blake	70-74-75-73—292
Bob Gilder	73-70-75-74—292
Mike Hulbert	74-73-70-75—292
Tom Lehman	69-74-72-77—292
Joey Sindelar	74-72-68-78—292
Ian Woosnam	72-72-69-79—292

Low round: Wayne Grady, Gil Morgan, 66

2000 TOP FINISHERS

Tiger Woods	65-69-71-67—272
Miguel Angel Jimenez	66-74-76-71—287
Ernie Els	74-73-68-72—287
John Huston	67-75-76-70—288
Padraig Harrington	73-71-72-73—289
Lee Westwood	71-71-76-71—289
Nick Faldo	69-74-76-71—290
Loren Roberts	68-78-73-72—291
David Duval	75-71-74-71—291
Stewart Cink	77-72-72-70—291
Vijay Singh	70-73-80-68—291

Low round: Woods, 65

Scorecard

2000 U.S. Open

HOLE	PAR	YARDAGE	AVG	RANK	FWY. %	GREEN %	PUTTS
1	4	381	4.15	12	77.1	57.7	1.70
2	4	484	4.42	4	62.4	27.5	1.58
3	4	390	4.22	10	63.1	53.0	1.67
4	4	331	3.95	17	78.4	75.5	1.67
5	3	188	3.38	6		40.8	1.63
6	5	524	4.83	18	61.5	73.9	1.59
7	3	106	3.03	16		73.9	1.73
8	4	418	4.53	2	78.2	30.5	1.64
9	4	466	4.56	1	52.8	26.1	1.60
Out	35	3288	37.06		67.6	51.0	1.65
10	4	446	4.38	5	75.5	44.0	1.64
11	4	380	4.16	11	63.1	51.6	1.63
12	3	202	3.36	8		25.0	1.51
13	4	406	4.12	13	68.1	49.1	1.55
14	5	573	5.38	7	60.8	35.1	1.61
15	4	397	4.06	15	64.7	68.1	1.72
16	4	403	4.31	9	62.2	49.3	1.69
17	3	208	3.44	3		19.0	1.50
18	5	543	5.09	14	60.6	70.9	1.71
In	36	3558	38.29		65.0	45.8	1.63
Total	71	6846	75.35		66.3	48.4	1.64

17TH HOLE (4TH HOLE IN 1939) OPPOSITE: 5TH HOLE (11TH HOLE IN 1939)

PHILADELPHIA COUNTRY CLUB (SPRING MILL COURSE)

GLADWYNE, PENNSYLVANIA 1939

Byron Nelson hit one of the greatest shots in U.S. Open history at Philadelphia Country Club's

Spring Mill Course in 1939 en route to a playoff victory and his only Open title, but that isn't what

the championship is remembered for. The enduring image is of Sam Snead hacking and slash-

ing his way to a triple-bogey eight on the 18th hole when a par would have given him the title

outright and a bogey would have earned a tie. ¶ Nelson and Snead, both 27, already had been

successful, Nelson with a victory at the 1937 Masters and Snead with an extraordinary 13 wins

in his first two years on tour, 1937–38. At Spring Mill, Snead led after each of the first two rounds,

then fell into a four-way tie for second, one behind Johnny Bulla heading into the final round. ¶

Philadelphia Country Club was the only par-69 course ever to host the Open. It was designed as

a par-71, but the USGA elected to call the 479-yard eighth and 480-yard 12th par fours instead of

par fives. That was strictly a matter of semantics, as the course realistically played to a par of 71

anyway. The only par five on the scorecard was the 558-yard 18th, the site of Snead's tragedy.

His collapse actually began on the 363-yard 17th hole, where he overshot the green and missed a five-foot putt for par. Standing on the tee, he thought he needed a birdie to tie Nelson, who had finished at 284 after a closing 68.

According to the tournament program, No. 18 "will furnish a lot of thrills for the galleries as well as the contestants. To be in perfect position a player must carry a trap or traps to the right center. This enables him to play a fine brassie or spoon over a wide, nasty trap similar to Hell's Bunker on the Old Course at St. Andrews."

After driving into the rough, Snead found Philadelphia's version of Hell when he gambled by hitting a 2-wood, which failed to clear the bunker. From a semi-buried lie and with birdie still on his mind, he tried to reach the green with an 8-iron. The shot slammed into the lip, lodging in a crack in the sod face. He could only hack the ball out nearly sideways, ending up in another bunker.

That's when somebody in the gallery told Snead he needed a bogey to tie Nelson. "Why didn't somebody tell me that back on the tee?" Snead bellowed. Still 80 yards from the green, he had to take an awkward stance with his feet out of the bunker, leaving him with no chance to get the ball close with his fifth shot. He did well to hit it on the green 40 feet from the hole, and narrowly missed the putt to tie. Demoralized, Snead missed the three-foot comebacker and took an eight that cost him his best chance for an Open victory.

"If I'd murdered someone, I'd have lived it down sooner than the '39 Open," Snead wrote later in *The Education of a Golfer.*

Craig Wood and Denny Shute later matched Nelson's 284, setting up a three-way playoff the next day. Wood and Nelson tied at 68, with some theatrics down the stretch. Nelson was one ahead going to the 17th, but one behind leaving it as he three-putted while Wood birdied. On 18 (which is the third hole today since the holes have been reordered), Wood went for the green in two but hooked it and hit a spectator on the head. The man was knocked out and was being carted away as the players arrived. Wood's ball had deflected into a better spot, and he was able to pitch to six feet. When Nelson made a birdie, Wood's putt was for the championship. He left it short.

Wood had been the victim of Gene Sarazen's double eagle in the 1935 Masters, and in the second 18-hole playoff he was done in by another amazing shot. Nelson holed a 1-iron on one of the strongest holes, the 453-yard fourth (the 17th in the course's current routing). More remarkably, it was Nelson's second eagle two of the week. In the third round, he had holed out on the 384-yard third. Nelson, one of the best iron players ever, also hit the flagstick with four other approaches during the week. He went on to win the second playoff by three strokes with a 70.

Philadelphia Country Club dates to 1890. It was formed for the purpose of horseback riding, but in 1891 a few members dug holes in the ground to play a makeshift course on the club lawn. The game caught

BYRON NELSON

SAM SNEAD LOST THE 1939 OPEN WITH A TRIPLE BOGEY ON THE 72ND HOLE.

on quickly and the club built a nine-hole course the next year, expanding to 18 holes in 1897. By the 1920s, that facility had become inadequate. With neighboring land unsuitable for golf, the club found 210 acres overlooking the Schuylkill River about 20 minutes away from its original site in Bala.

The new course was designed by William Flynn. Raised in Massachusetts, Flynn had moved to Philadelphia to assist Hugh Wilson in the construction of Merion in 1910, staying on as greenskeeper. Flynn eventually started a design business and was responsible for Open sites Shinnecock Hills on Long Island and Cherry Hills in Denver.

The Bala site was closed in the 1950s, and in 1991 the club opened nine new holes designed by Tom Fazio at the Spring Mill site. Shortly afterward, the greens and bunkering on the 18 holes that hosted the Open were restored to Flynn's design. The course has an outstanding set of par threes and very effective bunkering. It's still accorded plenty of respect, ranking 76th in *Golfweek's* Top 100 Classic (pre-1960) Courses, hosting the 2003 U.S. Women's Amateur, and serving as the second course for stroke-play qualifying for the 2005 U.S. Amateur.

1939 TOP FINISHERS
*Byron Nelson   72-73-71-68—284
Craig Wood   70-71-71-72—284
Denny Shute   70-72-70-72—284
Bud Ward   69-73-71-72—285
Sam Snead   68-71-73-74—286
*Nelson won playoff with a 68-70, Wood 68-73, Shute 76
Low round: Clayton Heafner, 66

Scorecard

Hole*	Par	Yardage 1939 Open	Yardage Today
1 (14)	4	450	477
2 (15)	3	234	225
3 (16)	4	384	403
4 (17)	4	453	472
5 (18)	4	425	392
6 (10)	4	447	437
7 (11)	3	191	192
8 (12)	4/5	479	580
9 (13)	4	350	380
Out	34	3413	**
10 (4)	4	454	470
11 (5)	3	169	167
12 (6)	4	480	491
13 (7)	3	206	211
14 (8)	4	394	391
15 (9)	4	421	416
16 (1)	4	328	325
17 (2)	4	363	353
18 (3)	5	558	580
In	35	3373	***
Total	69/70	6786	6967

*Holes in parentheses are numbers on current course
**Current front nine, par 35, 3409 yards
***Current back nine, par 35, 3558 yards

3RD HOLE (18TH HOLE IN 1939)

ALEX & MACDONALD SMITH

PHILADELPHIA CRICKET CLUB (ST. MARTINS COURSE)

PHILADELPHIA, PENNSYLVANIA 1907, 1910

Philadelphia Cricket Club not only has a fine A.W. Tillinghast course at its Flourtown site, but the legendary architect also was a member. Raised in a well-to-do Philadelphia family, Tillinghast, in his younger years, played the club's original course, which was on the short side (just less than 6,000 yards), but hosted the 1907 and 1910 U.S. Opens. ¶ At age 31, Tillinghast was on his way to becoming the low amateur at the 1907 Open on his home course when he had to withdraw on the 13th hole of the final round because he was overcome by heat. He finished 25th (second among amateurs) in 1910, when he was just getting into golf design by laying out the Shawnee-on-Delaware course at the request of a friend. Coincidentally, another top golf architect, George C. Thomas, was also a Cricket Club member, though he only dabbled in design before moving to California in the 1920s.

Scorecard

1910 U.S. Open

Hole	Par	Yardage
1	4	355
2	4	250
3	5	433
4	4	367
5	4	350
6	4	360
7	5	481
8	4	284
9	3	172
Out	37	3052
10	3	147
11	5	492
12	4	311
13	4	398
14	4	316
15	5	525
16	3	145
17	4	330
18	4	240
In	36	2904
Total	73	5956

Today

Hole*	Par	Yardage
1 (1)	4	343
2 (2)	4	257
3	4	322
4	4	289
5	3	110
6	4	316
7	4	368
8 (17)	4	326
9 (18)	4	243
Total	35	2574

*Hole numbers from 1910 in parentheses.

Donald Ross did some redesign work at the original course in 1914, but in 1920 the club, which was leasing the land, found it would no longer have use of the entire property. By this time, Tillinghast, who was well into his design career, laid out a new course six miles away just outside the city in Flourtown.

The club still maintains the original course, now known as the St. Martins Course, as a nine-holer on the smaller property. Located in the Chestnut Hill section of Philadelphia, it measures just 2,574 yards from the back tees and is played mostly by junior and senior golfers. The first, second, eighth, and ninth holes are basically the same as those that existed for the Opens—the latter two were the 17th and 18th.

Philadelphia was the leading spot for cricket in the United States, and William Roach Wister, known as the father of American cricket, founded the Philadelphia Cricket Club in 1854. Members actually played the sport in Camden, New Jersey, for nearly three decades before leasing the Chestnut Hill land in 1883. Golf was introduced in 1895 by member Samuel Heebner, who "borrowed" Philadelphia Country Club pro Willie Tucker to lay out nine holes. Nine more were added a few years later.

The 1907 Open was won by Alex Ross, brother of designer Donald, who finished 10th. In the second round, Jack Hobens made the first hole-in-one in Open history, on the 147-yard 10th. Hobens went on to hold the 54-hole lead of 224 before falling apart with an 85 in the final round.

In 1910, Fred McLeod was two shots off the lead when he reached the 240-yard 18th, considered a par four but reachable in one. McLeod drove the green and watched his 30-foot putt spin out "to the dismay of the gallery who had followed McLeod's plucky uphill fight," according to *American Golfer*.

Alex Smith's finish presaged Retief Goosen's final-hole plight in the 2001 Open. He needed a three to win outright, which seemed a certainty when he hit a marvelous tee shot to within 15 feet. Smith faced a tricky downhill putt, left it 18 inches short, then missed that one for the title. Like Goosen 91 years later, Smith gathered himself to win the playoff, shooting an excellent 71 to beat Macdonald Smith, his brother, and local lad John McDermott.

Oddly enough, the 18-year-old McDermott's parents did not know he was competing in the Open until they read in the newspaper that their son was in a playoff for the title. They knew about it the next year, when McDermott became the first homebred player to claim the Open, which had been the province of immigrant Scotsmen and Englishmen.

1907 TOP FINISHERS

Alex Ross	76-74-76-76	302
Gilbert Nicholls	80-73-72-79	304
Alex Campbell	78-74-78-75	305
Jack Hobens	76-75-73-85	309
George Low	78-76-79-77	310
Fred McLeod	79-77-79-75	310
Peter Robertson	81-77-78-74	310

Low round: Nicholls, 72

1910 TOP FINISHERS

*Alex Smith	73-73-79-73	298
John McDermott	74-74-75-75	298
Macdonald Smith	74-78-75-71	298
Fred McLeod	78-70-78-73	299
Tom McNamara	73-78-73-76	300
Gilbert Nicholls	73-75-77-75	300

*A. Smith won playoff with a 71, McDermottt 75, M. Smith 77

Low round: McLeod, 70

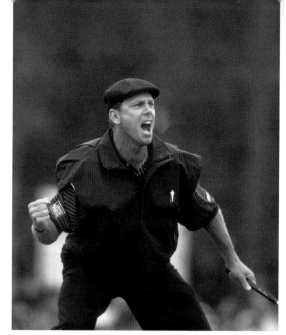

PAYNE STEWART CELEBRATES HIS WINNING PUTT IN 1999.
OPPOSITE TOP: 4TH HOLE. OPPOSITE BOTTOM: 5TH HOLE.

PINEHURST RESORT AND COUNTRY CLUB (NO. 2 COURSE)

PINEHURST, NORTH CAROLINA 1999, 2005

Pinehurst captures the essence of golf in such a way that it has been called the St. Andrews of America. Why, then, was it more than a century before it hosted its first U.S. Open, in 1999?

¶ The answer has mostly to do with geography. It was simply located in the wrong place: too far south and too far in the middle of nowhere. ¶ The village of Pinehurst was created in central North Carolina in 1895 and its first golf course built two years later. It quickly became a leading golf resort and its No. 2 Course was the masterpiece of Donald Ross, one of the true greats of golf design. But until the 1960s and the widespread use of air conditioning, Pinehurst was strictly a winter resort. It wasn't the right climate to host the Open, played in June.

¶ Geography also had a negative effect on agronomy. With summers too hot for the grasses that thrived in the north and winters too cold for those used in Florida, the course had sand greens until 1935. Pinehurst finally found a Bermuda strain that worked, but the USGA wanted the faster, smoother bentgrass greens for the Open.

That's why the Open had been to the Southeast only once before, at the Atlanta Athletic Club in 1976, and then only at the behest of Bobby Jones. Pinehurst installed bent in the 1970s, but the greens had to be watered so much in the summer that they became soft—a definite Open no-no.

In addition, the need for galleries dictated that the Open be played in metropolitan areas for most of its history, and Pinehurst is a small village that is not near North Carolina's cities. But by the latter part of the 20th century, the championship had become a big enough attraction that it didn't have to be in a population center to draw people.

As both the Open and Pinehurst evolved, it became apparent that the merits of the design, always a favorite of golf-course architects, were enough to overcome the logistical concerns of lodging and road systems.

"I know of no course, north or south, which provides a more thorough test or better golf, and none which give such diversity," wrote Walter Travis, one of America's great architects, in 1920.

"I've always thought Pinehust No. 2 to be my favorite course from a design standpoint," says Jack Nicklaus, who has become a leading architect.

The greens at No. 2 are unforgettable: rolling, heaving surfaces with pronounced fall-offs on the edges that provide perhaps the game's greatest approach-shot examination.

"Those green complexes give it a personality unlike anything I've seen," says architect Tom Doak. "I've always been amazed at what Donald Ross did there."

When the Open finally came to Pinehurst in 1999, it was a smash success. The unique setup, tailored to No. 2's singular challenges without the usual U.S. Open rough ringing the greens, won praise. It didn't hurt that the course brought the game's best players to the forefront and was the setting for one of the most dramatic U.S. Opens ever, with Payne Stewart winning by holing a 15-foot par putt on the 72nd hole.

Less than a year after the championship concluded, the USGA announced a return to No. 2 in

16TH HOLE

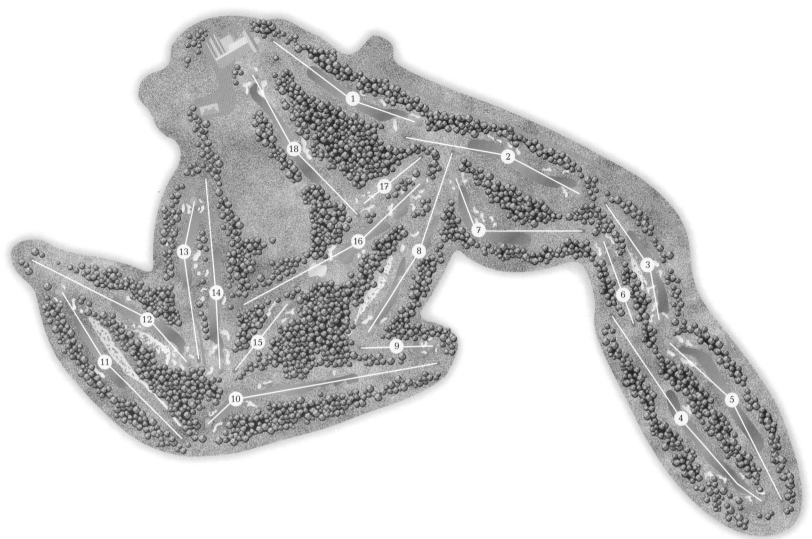

2005, the fastest return to the same site since the 1940s. USGA Executive Director David Fay had said before the 1999 event that "the Open at Pinehurst could be Tracy and Hepburnesque, a match made in heaven, the first of many."

Ironically, Pinehurst wasn't founded as a golf destination. In 1895, soda-fountain magnate James Walker Tufts founded the village, designed by landscape architect Frederick Law Olmsted and located near a rail line, as a place for northerners with health problems to rest during the winter. Tufts was not a golfer, but some of his guests were. In 1897, some of them began playing around a cow pasture. The next year, Pinehurst featured a nine-hole course, expanded to 18 holes in 1899.

The same year, a 26-year-old pro and green-keeper from the village of Dornoch in northern Scotland decided to strike off for America, based on a discussion with Harvard professor Robert Wilson, who on a visit to Dornoch described America as a land of opportunity, especially in golf. Soon afterward, Ross showed up at Wilson's doorstep with $2 in cash, a suitcase, and golf clubs.

Wilson set him up at Oakley Country Club, which needed not only a pro but also someone to

improve its design. Ross found a new calling, and soon a new benefactor in Tufts, who hired the Scotsman as Pinehurst's professional in 1900.

Ross handled all aspects of the golf operations in his early years. With the game rapidly becoming popular, his responsibilities included laying out a new course and modifying the existing one.

Nine holes of Course No. 2 opened in 1901 with a length of only 1,275 yards. In 1903, those nine holes were extended to 2,750 yards, and it wasn't until 1907 that the full 18 holes, at 5,860 yards, opened.

Writing in 1920, Travis took some credit for the leap forward in American golf design that No. 2 represented. "For some time I had been pouring into Donald's ears my ideas; in point of fact, I had urged him to take on the laying out of courses, as with the certain development of the game a fine future was assured for one having a bent in this line," Travis wrote.

Travis's ideas included a move away from the unimaginative method of installing artificial, artless cross bunkers and toward digging more carefully sculpted and reasoned bunkers flanking the fairways to catch off-line shots. Moreover, this kind of bunkering could create risk/reward scenarios for the better player who might be tempted to flirt with a bunker to create an easier shot to the green.

It's not known if Travis was exaggerating his role: Ross neither mentioned nor refuted it. In any case, Ross's views and talents were undoubtedly evolving during this development period. In 1910, he became a full-time architect, and success on a national level quickly followed. A virtuoso at fitting a course onto the existing land, finding the best routing, and creating layouts that were challenging without being unfair, Ross would ultimately design some 400 courses.

All the while, he retained his affiliation with Pinehurst, where he designed two more courses, Nos. 3 and 4. But No. 2 was his unquestioned masterpiece and the course on which he lavished the most attention, living in a house adjacent to the third hole.

No. 2 wasn't a classic from the start, however. The greens were flat, and at first had a permanent hole in the center. The sand/clay greens were so hard that the only way to hit the greens was to land short and bounce it on, so front bunkers were located some distance short of the putting surfaces.

Some holes were added and subtracted along the

An Open Moment

Payne Stewart trailed Phil Mickelson by one stroke on the 16th hole of the final round in 1999 and was staring at a 25-foot putt for a par. It was a downhill, double-breaker that was hard to read and could easily slide well past the hole. Mickelson, meanwhile, had a straightforward, uphill seven-footer for par. The situation looked bad for Stewart.

"You could take a small bucket of balls out there and maybe make one of 20," says course superintendent Paul Jett of Stewart's putt. But Stewart read both breaks correctly and his ball dived into the hole. It must have stunned Mickelson, who missed his par putt. The putt set up Stewart's later heroics—a birdie on 17 and par putt on 18.

way. The first two holes and the eighth through 18th of the current course have existed since 1907, but the third, sixth, and seventh were created in 1923 and the fourth and fifth were borrowed from a soon-to-be-abandoned nine-hole course in 1935.

When the resort found a strain of grass for the greens that was suitable for the climate and soil in 1935, Ross used the opportunity to redesign the course, and he addressed every aspect of No. 2,

10TH HOLE

including length (stretching it to about 6,900 yards) and bunkering. But he worked hardest on the green complexes, shaping the putting surfaces with a mule and drag pan. The idea was to make the greens hard to hit and to leave the players with challenging short-game shots.

"No. 2 has always been a pet of mine," Ross said. "In building these fine new greens, I have been able to carry out many of the changes which I have long visualized but only now have been able to put into practice. This contouring around a green makes possible an infinite variety in the requirements for short shots that no other form of hazard can call for."

It is fair to say Ross used Royal Dornoch, where he worked before emigrating, as an inspiration. The greens at that remote Scottish course are very similar to No. 2's surfaces.

The PGA immediately assigned the 1936 PGA Championship to No. 2. Said defending champion Johnny Revolta, "I don't see how a course could be any harder, but at the same time it's the most pleasant course I've ever seen. You have to play No. 2 with your head as much as your hands." In the final match, precise Denny Shute beat long-hitting Jimmy Thomson.

No. 2 annually hosted the North and South Open until 1951. Pinehurst chief executive Richard Tufts, grandson of Pinehurst's founder, served a stint as USGA president and didn't care for pro golf. The pros didn't care for the North and South's purse, one of the smallest on tour. After the 1951 Ryder Cup at No. 2, only five members of the U.S. team stayed around for the North and South the following week, and four withdrew before completing 72 holes, leading Tufts to pull the plug.

The Tour would return, but only after Pinehurst was sold in 1970. Tufts's two brothers, worried about inheritance taxes, outvoted him and elected to sell for $9.2 million to the Diamondhead Corporation.

In August 1972, the new management converted the greens to bent, which would make for smoother putting surfaces. But the move was done hastily, without rebuilding the greens for better drainage, because the PGA Club Professional Championship was coming in October.

The new management also changed the look and playing characteristics of the course by planting Bermuda rough between the fairways and the tree line, previously an unkempt area of hardpan sand and wire grass that was a distinguishing characteristic of Pinehurst.

MICHAEL CAMPBELL

Diamondhead thought big, but not always wisely. In 1973, it created a 144-hole tournament that aspired to be a world championship, with a blockbuster purse of $500,000. But very few of the top players, and hardly any spectators, turned up for the November event.

A 72-hole tournament with a smaller purse was held from 1974 through 1982. It was played in August or September, which meant either the greens were exceedingly soft or the tournament was overshadowed by football season. Still, luminaries such as Nicklaus, Johnny Miller, Ray Floyd, Hale Irwin, and Tom Watson won that event.

Red flags went up when Irwin blitzed a soft No. 2 for a 20-under 264 total in 1977. Approach shots stuck like darts, which meant Ross's greens did not function as intended. Nor did the green surrounds, grown with rough that prevented shots from running off the putting surface into Ross's chipping areas.

Management finally began to "get it." Tom Fazio was hired in 1978 to take out much of the Bermuda and restore the sandy areas. He also widened some fairways to bring bunkers more in play. Chipping areas were restored. In 1979, the greens were converted back to Bermuda.

But the Diamondhead era was soon to end, as the company couldn't pay its bills. From 1982 through 1984, banks owned Pinehurst. It ended up being purchased by Club Corporation of America, which eyed the prize of the Open almost from the outset of its 1984 purchase.

To have any chance, No. 2 would have to switch back to bentgrass greens, maintained with more firmness than those of the 1970s. Nicklaus was hired in 1987 to rebuild the greens and sod them with Penncross bent. But after the 1989 U.S. Women's Amateur, USGA agronomist Tim Moraghan and Boatwright told Pinehurst officials they would have to rebuild the greens again in order to host an Open.

The USGA struck a deal with Pinehurst early in 1993, awarding No. 2 the 1999 Open with the understanding that both parties would monitor developments in grasses over the next three years and decide on the best strain of bent for the rebuilt greens.

Ultimately, the choice was a new strain of bentgrass called Penn G-2 developed by a Penn State University professor. Pinehurst's greens are now among the firmest in the country, as G-2 can thrive in the heat even with little water. When the greens do get water, in the form of rain, they drain exceptionally well, as the 1999 Open proved.

In 1996, Rees Jones rebuilt the greens and lengthened the course. For the greens, Jones and his men relied on plans prepared for the 1962 U.S. Amateur by Richard Tufts, showing the dimensions of the putting surfaces. The greens had lost size due to mowing patterns, and those edges were a key part of Ross's design. Restoring them gave a boost to the greens' repelling nature as well as adding hole locations.

The lack of rough around the greens wasn't the only departure from the usual Open setup. In the

CLUBHOUSE

week before the championship, USGA officials decided to trim the rough to a mere three inches. The idea was to encourage players to have a go at the greens and, more often than not, watch as their balls failed to hold the putting surface.

The statistics from the 1999 Open tell the story of the relative difficulty of Pinehurst's targets. The players hit the relatively flat fairways at a 66.3 percent rate, but they hit only 47.1 percent of the greens in regulation.

"To win at Pinehurst, a player has to map out his strategy ahead of time and determine whether he will go for the flag or not depending on where the pin positions are," says Jones.

Before the 1999 Open, Stewart did that—and more. Arriving the previous weekend (missing the cut in the previous week's tournament proved to be a boon), he walked the course with just a couple of clubs and a putter, trying short-game shots. He usually didn't carry a yardage book, but he did at Pinehurst for one reason—he marked the places around the greens where it was imperative *not* to miss.

"He missed into one of those spots only one time in 72 holes," says Stewart's caddie, Mike Hicks. "That's an incredible statistic."

Tiger Woods and Vijay Singh were very much part of a tense final round, but in the end it came down to the final twosome, Stewart and Phil Mickelson. The outcome would be determined by one final putt on the 18th hole, and again Stewart's preparation paid off.

In practice rounds, Stewart and coach Chuck Cook had correctly guessed the final-round hole location, and Stewart tried this putt countless times. He had been surprised to find that it broke to the right. When it mattered most, Stewart trusted his preparation and rolled the 15-footer into the hole, setting off a wild celebration. Four months later, Stewart died in a plane tragedy when the cabin of a small jet failed to pressurize properly.

Unusual for North Carolina in June, the final round had taken place in eerie conditions, with the temperature around 60 degrees and a light rain that turned into a mist. "The atmosphere was almost ethereal," remembers Trey Holland, chairman of the USGA championship committee that year. "It's occurred to me it was like reading *Golf in the Kingdom*."

There was nothing as magical or dramatic about the 2005 Open, but the USGA again caught a weather break with temperatures that stayed mostly in the low 80s. New Zealand's Michael Campbell scored a surprise victory, thanks to an outstanding final-round 69, finishing two strokes ahead of Woods as the rest of the contenders were unable to handle the demands of Pinehurst on a U.S. Open Sunday.

Campbell's winning score was even par and only two players finished better than five-over, but once again No. 2 won plaudits from the players even as it punished them. Although the results were similar, the course played differently this time thanks to fairways that were narrower and firmer. Whereas 66.3 percent of the tee shots finished in the short grass in 1999, only 51.6 percent found the fairway in 2005, creating the challenge of trying to hold Pinehurst's greens from the rough.

18TH HOLE

The toughest hole during the two Opens has been the fifth, which played 482 yards in 1999 and 10 yards less in 2005. Its green falls off severely on the left side, and the target area where a ball will hit and stay on the green is very small for a middle- or long-iron approach. It is closely followed in difficulty by the two par fives that are converted into par fours for the Open, the eighth and 16th.

But there are no signature holes at Pinehurst No. 2—just a bunch of outstanding holes. Highlights include medium-long par fours like the second, 11th, and 18th, where angles of approach are important to set up easier shots from a particular side of the fairway depending on the hole location; a pair of short par fours with elevated greens, the third and the 13th; and any of the par threes. Of the one-shotters, the 175-yard ninth requires the most precision to get close and the 203-yard 15th features a green where the crown effect is most pronounced.

There are two ways of looking at Pinehurst's design. Bill Coore, one of today's "minimalist" designers in partnership with Ben Crenshaw, says

that its greatness is subtle. "It's the little things, the angles, dips, contouring work around the greens."

Then there's Pete Dye, who is known for building visually arresting courses, and equally a Ross admirer. "I wonder about all this talk about the 'subtleties' of Mr. Ross," Dye says. "I don't think when he built this thing in the early '30s that he felt the golf course was subtle at all. I think he thought he built a golf course that was severe and challenged the hell out of the great professionals at that time."

Both, in their way, are right. Pinehurst is built on terrain that isn't particularly dramatic. It has only one water hazard, which isn't really in play, on the 16th hole. The trees are well off the playing corridors. A mid- or high-handicapper can get around it using a single ball.

But the subtlety ends at the greens. Today's designers would be criticized for building those putting surfaces; the pros would likely circulate a petition insisting that the game's governing bodies never hold another tournament there. But Ross, the most beloved of Golden Age designers, could get away with it. Thankfully.

Scorecard

HOLE	PAR	YARDAGE	AVG.*	RANK*	FWY. %*	GREEN %*	PUTTS*
1	4	401	4.22	12	56.0	50.0	1.67
2	4	469	4.41	3	57.8	30.4	1.58
3	4	336	4.06	17	63.9	70.5	1.72
4	5	565	4.84	18	65.2	79.6	1.70
5	4	472	4.47	1	52.7	28.8	1.63
6	3	220	3.36	5		45.2	1.74
7	4	404	4.19	13	64.7	58.9	1.71
8	4	467	4.41	3	57.5	45.3	1.76
9	3	175	3.23	10		48.9	1.63
Out	35	3509	37.18		59.7	50.9	1.68
10	5	607	5.07	16	62.2	62.6	1.65
11	4	476	4.25	9	51.2	45.5	1.64
12	4	449	4.33	6	55.4	35.9	1.60
13	4	378	4.13	15	60.4	51.2	1.58
14	4	468	4.26	8	59.5	50.4	1.69
15	3	203	3.31	7		35.6	1.62
16	4	492	4.46	2	58.8	21.3	1.55
17	3	190	3.14	14		61.0	1.71
18	4	442	4.23	10	60.0	50.8	1.68
In	35	3705	37.18		58.2	46.0	1.64
Total	70	7214	74.36		59.0	48.5	1.66

*Statistics cumulative from 1999 and 2005 Opens
Note: Holes playing different yardages in 1999 were the second (447),
fifth (482), 11th (453), and 14th (436).

1999 TOP FINISHERS

Payne Stewart	68-69-72-70—279
Phil Mickelson	67-70-73-70—280
Vijay Singh	69-70-73-69—281
Tiger Woods	68-71-72-70—281
Steve Stricker	70-73-69-73—285
Tim Herron	69-72-70-75—286
Jeff Maggert	71-69-74-73—287
Hal Sutton	69-70-76-72—287
David Duval	67-70-75-75—287
Darren Clarke	73-70-74-71—288
Billy Mayfair	67-72-74-75—288

Low round: Duval, Mayfair, Mickelson, Paul
Goydos, 67

2005 TOP FINISHERS

Michael Campbell	71-69-71-69—280
Tiger Woods	70-71-72-69—282
Sergio Garcia	71-69-75-70—285
Tim Clark	76-69-70-70—285
Mark Hensby	71-68-72-74—285
Davis Love III	77-70-70-69—286
Rocco Mediate	67-74-74-71—286
Vijay Singh	70-70-74-72—286
Nick Price	72-71-72-72—287
Arron Oberholser	76-67-71-73—287

Low round: Peter Hedblom, 66

TIGER WOODS HAS COME CLOSE TWICE AT PINEHURST.

BEN HOGAN PLAYS FROM THE BUNKER IN THE MIDDLE OF THE 6TH GREEN. OPPOSITE: 2ND HOLE

RIVIERA COUNTRY CLUB PACIFIC PALISADES, CALIFORNIA 1948

Ben Crenshaw has called Riviera "the finest *made* golf course in the United States." By that he means that the architect, George C. Thomas, created it by moving earth on a relatively feature-less piece of land. ¶ Riviera Country Club was one of the first courses to be constructed in this manner. Until then, courses had been built using mule power, following the natural contours of the land. At Riviera, Thomas used 10 tractors and scrapers, and a crew that averaged 125 men, sometimes as many as 200. Fill dirt was imported from the San Fernando Valley to be used as Thomas saw fit. ¶ The result was terrain that appeared completely natural. "Nearly any stranger—golfer or non-golfer—would be hard pressed to detect any evidence of the hand of man," Crenshaw wrote in Riviera's club history. ¶ With Riviera, Thomas was a forerunner of the modern, earthmoving era of architecture. But in style, he was squarely a Golden Age archi-tect. Though not as well known as contemporaries like Donald Ross, Thomas built as much strategy into his courses as any of them.

The well-to-do Thomas designed courses in his spare time. A native of Philadelphia, he didn't get into architecture seriously until moving to California in 1919 to pursue his true passion—growing roses. But his new club, Los Angeles Country Club, asked him to construct a new 18. Soon, his creations were dotting the southern California landscape.

Los Angeles Athletic Club vice president Frank Garbutt gave Thomas the Riviera assignment on a site in the Santa Monica canyon, near an unpaved road that would become Sunset Boulevard. On looking over the flat site that sat in a flood plain between bluffs, Thomas reportedly told Garbutt that he could produce not a championship layout, but one that "would be good enough for the Los Angeles Athletic Club."

Garbutt still hired Thomas, who didn't accept any money for his work. Still, Riviera didn't come cheap: The architect insisted on an unlimited budget and on hiring Billy Bell to supervise construction. The course, complete with an irrigation system, ended up costing nearly $250,000, more than triple the typical amount for a golf course at that time.

2ND HOLE (FOREGROUND) AND 10TH HOLE

Thomas drew up 15 plans before deciding on one that suited him. Once he got started, Thomas changed his mind about the site, telling the club that the course would "vie with America's best in every detail."

He was right. After 18 months of construction, Riviera opened to acclaim in 1927. Twelve years later, when the National Golf Foundation compiled a list of the best courses in the country, Riviera was third, behind only New Jersey's Pine Valley and North Carolina's Pinehurst No. 2.

The club quickly attracted Hollywood celebrities, including Douglas Fairbanks and W.C. Fields. It also attracted the Los Angeles Open, which in its fourth year, 1929, moved to Riviera in order to "find a real test for the Hagens, Farrells, and Espinosas." The event was played at Riviera in 1929 and '30, then again in 1941 and 1945–53. It moved in permanently in 1973, and Riviera is now a favorite of Tour pros, who consider it one of the finest courses they play.

A sour note was struck in 1939, when a flood rushed through the barranca that borders the course. Sandbags saved the greens, but most of the fairways on Nos. 7, 8, 12, and 13 were washed away. The seventh and eighth were particularly affected. An alternate fairway on the right side of No. 8 was lost, as was a large bunker to the left of No. 7.

To prevent future erosion, an African grass called Kikuyu was planted on the slopes of the barranca. The Kikuyu quickly took over the course, giving Riviera's rough a distinctive difficulty because of the way it grabs the ball and club.

When the U.S. Open came to Riviera in 1948, USGA official Joe Dey reportedly wanted six-inch rough, but Riviera pro Willie Hunter convinced him that Kikuyu was tough enough at three inches. Maybe they should have compromised at four. Ben Hogan shattered the championship record by five strokes with an eight-under 276 in winning the first of his four Open titles, while Jimmy Demaret (278) and Jim Turnesa (280) also bettered the old mark.

Sam Snead led through two rounds and opened with an eagle on the downhill par-five first hole in the third round. After that, he couldn't make a putt and as *Golf World* rather cruelly noted, "Snead, who attracts universal sympathy with his tragic career [in the Open], had galleries calling 'Come on' at him as he pathetically tried to hold onto the lead." Snead finished 73-72 to Hogan's 68-69 over the final 36 holes.

Attendance was disappointing at the first Open west of Minnesota, which might be one reason the event went north to Olympic and Pebble Beach in its subsequent visits to California. Nor were the crowds huge for the 1983 and 1995 PGA Championships at Riviera, won by Hal Sutton and Steve Elkington, respectively.

The latter event was marred by greens that were very soft and terribly spiked up as Elkington set a PGA Championship record (since broken) of 267. So while Riviera annually plays as one of the toughest courses on the PGA Tour, it has been uncharacteristically vulnerable in majors.

The 1995 greens fiasco began with the best of intentions. The greens had shrunk due to encroachment of Kikuyu, and Crenshaw and Bill Coore were hired to restore them to their original sizes, as well as to restore the original shapes of many bunkers. The problem was that management decided to sod the greens rather than seeding them, as recommended, and the new grass never "took."

The USGA returned to Riviera for the 1998 U.S. Senior Open, won by Hale Irwin. The club has reportedly been under consideration for a future U.S. Open, but has yet to receive the nod.

A 2002 redesign by Tom Fazio restored some of the features lost in the 1939 flood, most notably the fairway bunker on the seventh and alternate fairway on the eighth. In ongoing work, he has added length on eight holes, though two of the new tees (Nos. 8 and 9) have not been used at the Nissan (L.A.) Open. In addition, Fazio enlarged four greens and revised the bunkering on four holes.

Thomas considered Riviera his masterpiece, and the layout is full of excellent holes that embody a number of his principles. One is that the ideal opening hole is a relatively easy par five—Riviera starts with a thrilling shot off of a very elevated tee—followed by a difficult par-four second that returns to the clubhouse.

The heart of the front nine is its two striking par threes. Hogan, who had two L.A. Open victories at Riviera in addition to his U.S. Open win, called the 236-yard fourth the greatest par three in America. It's certainly one of the hardest, playing into the prevailing wind and featuring a huge bunker at the front left of the green.

A bunker also grabs the player's attention on the 199-yard sixth. The hazard is small, but it sits in the middle of the green. This seeming gimmick actually works quite well, mainly by taking away the option of aiming for the center of the green no matter where the hole is located. Thomas never made a big deal about the bunker, simply saying

8TH HOLE

that the idea was to divide the green into two compartments.

The 10th is quite simply one of the greatest short par fours in the world—maybe *the* greatest. It plays 315 yards on the scorecard, but less if a player goes straight at it, which means Tour pros can shoot for the green with a driver or even a 3-wood. Many consider that a sucker play, however. The key to the hole is the tiny green angled to offer its full length to an approach from the left of the fairway. But it's very shallow from the angle of the tee and provides an extremely difficult pitch or chip from anywhere in the vicinity of the green.

The only existing features on the land before the course was built were a pair of washes, one that forms a boundary of the course and another that cuts across it. This wash crosses the fairway on the first, second, and 11th holes, but is a significant factor for the pros only on the 12th, where it cuts directly in front of the green. The 12th played at a fearsome 445 yards for the 1948 Open but was later reduced to 410 because it was felt the back tee was unfair. Fazio recently extended it back to 479.

The boundary wash (barranca) is in play on the second shot at the 459-yard 13th, sitting directly to the left of the green, making 12 and 13 a formidable gauntlet. The 487-yard 15th and 475-yard 18th also have been lengthened, giving the back nine a full quota of backbreakers. In between comes a different kind of challenge, the 166-yard 16th, with a small green ringed by bunkers.

No. 18 is one of the game's famous finishing holes, a long uphill climb to a green at the base of a natural amphitheater. *Los Angeles Times* columnist Jim Murray once wrote that the 18th doesn't need an ocean to be tough because it "keeps the riffraff out with its bare hands." Eucalyptus trees that have grown on the right of the fairway add to the challenge, and any player getting up and down from the Kikuyu on the hillside to the left of the green deserves a medal.

Although Riviera is no longer considered the third-best course in the country—it's currently ranked 22nd by *Golf Magazine*—it hasn't needed multiple U.S. Opens to remain in the upper echelon.

16TH HOLE

Scorecard

Hole	Par	Yardage 1948 Open	Yardage 2006 Nissan
1	5	513	503
2	4	466	463
3	4	415	434
4	3	245	236
5	4	432	434
6	3	166	199
7	4	402	408
8	4	385	433
9	5	422	458
Out	35	3446	3568
10	4	315	315
11	5	569	564
12	4	445	479
13	4	440	459
14	3	180	176
15	4	440	487
16	3	145	166
17	5	585	590
18	4	455	475
In	36	3574	3711
Total	71	7020	7279

1948 TOP FINISHERS

Ben Hogan	67-72-68-69—276
Jimmy Demaret	71-70-68-69—278
Jim Turnesa	71-69-70-70—280
Bobby Locke	70-69-73-70—282
Sam Snead	69-69-73-72—283
Lew Worsham	67-74-71-73—285
Herman Barron	73-70-71-72—286
Johnny Bulla	73-72-75-67—287
Smiley Quick	73-71-69-74—287

Low round: Bulla, Hogan, Worsham, 67

BOBBY JONES RECEIVES THE TROPHY FROM USGA PRESIDENT WILLIAM C. FOWNES JR. IN 1926.
OPPOSITE TOP: 8TH HOLE. OPPOSITE BOTTOM: 17TH HOLE

SCIOTO COUNTRY CLUB COLUMBUS, OHIO 1926

There are two places where the two greatest players of the 20th century, Bobby Jones and Jack Nicklaus, converge. One is Augusta National, founded by Jones and site of Nicklaus's six Masters victories. The other is Scioto Country Club, where Jones won the 1926 U.S. Open and Nicklaus learned to play the game. ¶ Another great name, Donald Ross, is prominent at Scioto. The architect was hired in 1915 by a group of Arlington Country Club members to build the first 18-hole course in Columbus. (Arlington and Columbus Country Club both had just nine holes.) The site was a former pasture near the Scioto River, a nice, rolling property with a couple of creeks flowing through it. ¶ Scioto's second pro was George Sargent, the 1909 U.S. Open champion. The well-connected Sargent, president of the PGA of America, was instrumental in landing the 1926 U.S. Open for Scioto. ¶ Jones arrived at Scioto nearly straight off the ship that brought him back to the United States after winning the British Open. Exhausted, he didn't think highly of his chances.

10TH HOLE

The pre-tournament talk was dominated by two subjects: Jones and Scioto's rough. "The rough did look terrifying," wrote A. Linde Fowler in *Golf Illustrated.* "Blue grass, so-called, but brown from the sun, heat and lack of moisture, stood about a foot high on either side of the fairways. It wrapped around the clubheads and so worried many of the contestants, some of the most prominent, too, that they made no bones about expressing their opinions of the USGA officials for allowing such an 'unfair' condition. Never have I seen such a worried and disgusted lot of golfers the day before a championship."

When the championship started, players had a new worry. The wind picked up and shifted, so the longest par fours played into it. "Right here was a break in favor of Jones," Fowler noted. "Counting distance and accuracy, hole for hole, no other man in the tournament was his equal, so I believe."

Jones eagled the 480-yard par-five eighth, which played into the wind in the first round, by hitting a

driving iron to three feet. That helped him to a 70, two strokes off Bill Mehlhorn's lead.

In the second round Jones posted 79, his worst score ever in the Open. A bad day turned worse on the 15th green, where his ball moved slightly at address and he called a one-stroke penalty on himself. His play on the reachable par-five 480-yard 18th summed up the round, as he went from the right rough to the left rough and ultimately three-putted for a seven that Jones described as "ghastly" in his book *Down the Fairway.*

The morning of the 36-hole final day, Jones lost his breakfast and paid a quick visit to a doctor to calm his stomach. It worked, as he shot a third-round 71 to pull within three strokes of leader Joe Turnesa. But Jones's chances didn't look good after playing the first six holes of the final round in three-over.

"If anybody told me, as I stood on the seventh tee, that I must finish with two 3's and ten 4's to win,

Scorecard

Hole	Par	Yardage 1926 Open	Yardage Today
1	4	410	418
2	4	425	459
3	4	350	381
4	3	175	188
5	4	445	439
6	5	500	527
7	4	360	378
8	5	480	509
9	3	140	160
Out	36	3285	3459
10	4	390	421
11	4	360	360
12	5	545	546
13	4	445	446
14	3	234	236
15	4	375	425
16	4	425	420
17	3	135	191
18	5/4	480	446
In	36/35	3390	3491
Total	72/71	6675	6950

I'd have laughed at him—if I'd had the strength," Jones wrote.

He did just that, grinding down Turnesa, playing just ahead. Jones moved into the lead after bogeys by his rival on 16 and 17, but when Turnesa recovered to birdie 18, Jones needed to match it for the win. On the same hole where he had finished so poorly the day before, Jones unleashed a drive that was paced at 310 yards. His mashie-iron second flew right at the hole, stopping 15 feet away to set up an easy two-putt birdie and victory.

Following Jones every step of the way was a 13-year-old named Charlie Nicklaus, who grew up to be a Scioto member and had a son named Jack. Charlie regaled his son with tales of Jones, who became young Jack's idol.

Jack learned the game from Scioto professional Jack Grout, who would remain his teacher throughout his career. "My well-documented left-to-right style of play developed strictly because of Scioto, where about 11 of 14 driving holes have either out-of-bounds right, serious trouble right, or at least encourage a left-to-right shot," Nicklaus wrote in *Nicklaus By Design*.

In the early 1960s, Scioto's members felt the need for a "facelift." Some of the low-lying greens didn't drain well and all the greens had gotten smaller through the years. They called in Dick Wilson, who put in new greens, most of them elevated for drainage, new bunkering, a lake for the par-three 17th, and a new tee for the 18th to make it a par four.

The changes were more extensive than the members were expecting. "He did not restore the course—he redesigned it," Nicklaus wrote of Wilson. "He delegated the front nine restoration to Robert von Hagge, who was working for him at the time. The back nine went to another associate, Joe Lee. The result was they turned what had been a great 18-hole golf course into two distinctly different nine-hole courses. It was still a nice golf course, but not the Ross course I had grown up on."

JACK NICKLAUS WITH HIS FATHER, CHARLIE

1926 TOP FINISHERS

Bobby Jones	70-79-71-73—293
Joe Turnesa	71-74-72-77—294
Leo Diegel	72-76-75-74—297
Johnny Farrell	76-79-69-73—297
William Mehlhorn	68-75-76-78—297
Gene Sarazen	78-77-72-70—297

Low round: Mehlhorn, Macdonald Smith, 68

LEE TREVINO (LEFT) AND RAY FLOYD IN 1986.
OPPOSITE TOP: 7TH HOLE. OPPOSITE BOTTOM: 9TH HOLE

SHINNECOCK HILLS GOLF CLUB

SOUTHAMPTON, NEW YORK   1896 (ORIGINAL COURSE), 1986, 1995, 2004

It isn't hard to find testimonials for Shinnecock Hills Golf Club. ¶ "I absolutely fell in love with the place the first time I saw it," says Lee Trevino. ¶ "The course is stunning, the nearest thing America has to a British links," says Frank Hannigan, former USGA senior executive director. ¶ "This is the Holy Grail of golf in America," wrote Johnny Miller in *Golf World*. "Shot for shot, based on shot values for testing skills, Shinnecock is America's best." ¶ In a letter to the club, Tom Lehman wrote, "If I were given one day to live, and could play any course that I wanted for my last round, I would choose Shinnecock!" ¶ The course raters agree. Shinnecock Hills ranks third on both the *Golf Digest* and *Golf Magazine* lists (behind Pine Valley and Augusta National in the former, and Pine Valley and Cypress Point in the latter), and is the highest-ranked U.S. Open course. ¶ Shinnecock Hills has a unique look and feel for an American course. Laid out on true links turf, its sinuous green fairways are framed by tall brown

fescue rough blowing in the wind. Its setting is completely natural, but it was cleverly devised by designer William Flynn to be a thorough examination, especially when the wind is blowing, as it usually is on eastern Long Island.

Here's what Tom Doak, who later designed the highly acclaimed Pacific Dunes in Oregon, wrote about Shinnecock Hills in *Golf Magazine* in 1995: "The true genius of Flynn's design lies in its changes of direction. Whereas most British links courses are confined to a narrow strip of linksland along the sea's edge, dictating that many of the holes run parallel and long stretches are played into (or with) the prevailing wind, Shinnecock is routed in a series of triangles, so that more than two consecutive holes never play in the same direction. The course takes as many different tacks as an America's Cup race.

"The truth is there are two or three common winds, and they come from such different angles that, combined with the complex routing, each changes the course completely. Virtually every hole on the course has two or three different characters,

depending on the wind of the moment." At no time was that more evident than the 1986 U.S. Open, where the wind blew from a different direction in all four rounds.

The 1986 Open was a landmark event that brought Shinnecock Hills into the national limelight. It also marked a new way to run the Open. Since Shinnecock Hills is largely a seasonal club, it couldn't count on year-round effort from its members to put on the event. So the USGA ran the Open itself, which worked so well that the USGA since has taken on more and more responsibility for running the Open at all sites.

After decades of hidden-gem status, that Open brought Shinnecock into the national spotlight. "Not to denigrate any of our other venues, but there are two showstopper sites," USGA Executive Director David Fay said in 1995. "Your heart beats a little faster when you go to Pebble Beach and Shinnecock."

On top of it all, Shinnecock Hills has history. One of the five founding member clubs of the USGA in 1894 with the first clubhouse designed and built

11TH HOLE

An Open Moment

No player loves Shinnecock Hills more than Ben Crenshaw, a classic-course buff who calls it "blessed golf terrain." He shot 65 in a casual round as an amateur, but it hasn't treated him so kindly in the U.S. Open. He grabbed the lead in 1986 with four straight birdies from the third to sixth holes in the final round, but bogeyed the seventh and slid to a sixth-place tie.

Crenshaw wasn't in contention in 1995, but he suffered some embarrassment on the 10th hole in the third round. After his approach shot came back down the hill in front of the green, he watched two bump-and-run attempts with a 7-iron roll back to his feet. The third try made the putting surface, but Crenshaw finished with a triple bogey on a hole where he had a sand-wedge approach.

10TH HOLE

for the purpose, Shinnecock had the second 18-hole course in the United States and hosted the second U.S. Open in 1896.

The club's genesis was an 1891 winter-holiday trip to Biarritz, France, by William K. Vanderbilt, Duncan Cryder, and Edward S. Mead, three members of the summer colony of Southampton, Long Island. Biarritz had a golf course, and the pro, Willie Dunn, showed the men how the game was played.

"Gentlemen, this beats rifle shooting for distance and accuracy," Vanderbilt is reported to have said. "It's a game that I think would go in our country." Vanderbilt was right, though the other two became the prime movers behind Shinnecock Hills while he never even became a member.

Shinnecock's founders were such novices at the game that they probably didn't appreciate just how perfect the terrain and turf at their Southampton site was for golf. They didn't even realize the game was taking root elsewhere in the United States—St. Andrew's Golf Club already had been founded in Yonkers, New York, and golf was being played at scattered locations around the country.

But they were familiar with Royal Montreal, founded in 1873, so they asked to borrow their pro, Willie Davis, to design a 12-hole course in the sum-

mer of 1891. They also hired one of the top architects in the country, Stanford White, to design the clubhouse.

Dunn came aboard as the pro in 1894 and that fall plotted six new holes to make the 18-hole course that would host the 1896 Open, in which he finished 12th after being one of the favorites. James Foulis, a Scotsman who was the pro at Chicago Golf Club, was the winner.

That Open is noteworthy for the participation of African-American John Shippen and Native American Oscar Bunn (the local Shinnecock tribe had helped build the course), both caddies at Shinnecock. USGA President Theodore Havemeyer headed off a threatened boycott by the rest of the players by making it clear that Shippen and Bunn would play regardless.

It should be pointed out, however, that the USGA did not then hold pros in high regard socially. It's not so easy to imagine Havemeyer making the same stand in the U.S. Amateur.

Shippen was tied for second after shooting 78 in the first round but fell to sixth after a second-round 81 that included an 11 on the 13th hole, where he had trouble escaping a sandy road. "I've wished a hundred times I could play that little par four again," Shippen later said. After Shippen, who played in four more Opens, the next black player in the Open was Ted Rhodes in 1948.

Despite Shippen's troubles, the championship demonstrated the shortcomings of the Shinnecock Hills course, which measured only 4,423 yards. Foulis's winning score of 152 was 21 strokes less the winning score the year before and 10 less than the following year.

In 1897, Shinnecock Hills became the first U.S. Open course to be redesigned, with changes on virtually every hole and three brand new holes, for a 5,493-yard course. This layout—and its predecessor—occupied land mostly south of the clubhouse, the opposite side of today's course.

Change came to the neighborhood with the opening of C.B. Macdonald's National Golf Links of America next door in 1910. The finest course in the country at the time, National immediately made Shinnecock look decidedly ordinary.

Six years later, Macdonald gave Shinnecock another makeover, precipitated by the Long Island Railroad's demand that the club change three holes that played over the tracks or pay an indemnity. The club decided to eliminate the railroad holes, and Macdonald extended the course north and west of the clubhouse, where he built six new holes. He changed the rest substantially, leaving only five holes intact.

It was a significant upgrade, but Macdonald didn't give the project the same effort he gave National. (His associate, Seth Raynor, probably did most of the work.) With its second redesign, Shinnecock progressed from a mediocre course to a good one. Greatness was still in the future.

In 1927, the club learned that Suffolk County planned to build a two-lane highway through the course. So a member, Lucien Tyng, bought 100 acres north and east of the clubhouse and arranged for the club to build holes on the new land. (The club eventually bought the property from Tyng in 1948.)

William Flynn and his partner, Howard Toomey, who handled the engineering, got the job. Flynn used the new land to build the back nine and the

14TH HOLE

COREY PAVIN

fourth, fifth, and sixth holes on the current course. He left intact only two Macdonald holes, the current par-four third and par-three Redan seventh, which were the 13th and 14th on Macdonald's layout. He also retained Macdonald's 18th green, now the ninth.

Whereas Macdonald was a believer in replicating particular holes from Scotland—there were seven or eight that popped up on nearly all his courses—Flynn was very good at using the existing terrain, and Shinnecock represents his finest work.

The back nine is on wonderful ground for golf, with fairways that have plenty of bumps and rolls. The fourth through sixth are flatter, so Flynn used more bunkering on those holes.

Hard to believe now, but Shinnecock members had second thoughts about Flynn's plan and called in another architect, C.H. Alison, to evaluate it. "We are entirely satisfied that Mr. Flynn's plans are as good as can be made on this site, and that the proposed course will be of the first order," Alison wrote in his report.

When the new course opened in 1931, Shinnecock had a course to rival National. But it took a long time for the word to spread. It hosted no tournaments, no exhibitions. Ben Hogan made it there for a casual round and later wrote in a letter to Paul Shields, a member, "Each hole is different and requires a great amount of skill to play it properly... All in all, I think it is one of the finest courses I have ever played."

The secret began to leak at the 1963 Lesley Cup, a competition between teams from New York, Pennsylvania, Massachusetts, and eastern Canada. The field included some USGA officials, who were impressed. Four years later, the USGA awarded Shinnecock the 1967 U.S. Senior Amateur.

Virgil Sherrill, the president of the club from 1972 to 1980, recognized that the Walker Cup, an amateur team competition between the U.S. and Great Britain and Ireland with a small field and small crowds, but with a great tradition and importance in golf, was a perfect fit for Shinnecock. The club bid for the 1977 Walker Cup and got it.

USGA President Harry Easterly was a houseguest of Sherrill's during the event, and at one point Easterly asked his host, "Wouldn't it be nice if we held the Open here?"

Nice, yes, but was it possible? PGA Tour Commissioner Deane Beman had asked the club to host the World Series of Golf, but was turned down because club officials felt the logistics were too difficult. The same reasoning would have shot down the Open, but in a 1981 meeting, the USGA's Hannigan broached the idea of having the organization run the championship. (Prior to that, the host club had handled most of the work for the Open.)

The notion was accepted, and Shinnecock was awarded the 1986 Open. At the time, Hannigan was working part-time as a director of special projects, but became senior executive director in 1983. He was now responsible for running the championship, "giving new meaning to the phrase 'hoist by his own petard,'" Hannigan says.

For the USGA, it wasn't just a question of running the Open for the first time; it had to stage a *difficult* Open, in an ill-suited area because of traffic and housing concerns. But the logistics went smoothly, thanks largely to a temporary spectator bridge erected over Route 27, which runs past the club.

The 1986 Open was an even bigger success inside the ropes, as everyone recognized the quality of the course and how appropriate—and unique—it was as an Open setting. Players weren't necessarily thinking that on the first day, as no player broke par in a forbidding combination of cold, rain, and wind. Jack Nicklaus, who lost a ball on the 10th hole and shot 77, called it "the most difficult day I have ever seen in American championship golf."

The weather was considerably better Friday, and a calm weekend allowed the players to attack the course. Lanny Wadkins and Chip Beck both finished with 65 to post one-over 281 and waited to see if anyone would better it. At one point, nine players—including Wadkins and Beck—were tied for the lead at one-over, but even without much wind Shinnecock punished those who weren't precise with their shots. Those other seven players all went the wrong way and finished worse, but Ray Floyd, who was two-over at the time of the big tie, shot 32 on the back nine to finish at 279 and claim the title.

Floyd was then 43 and didn't have a stellar Open record. "For years I have literally loathed playing the Open," Floyd told *Golf Digest* the next year. "While they have been played on some of the greatest golf courses in the country, I've always had a sour feeling about the way they've been set up... I remember playing Shinnecock the Monday before the tournament. I had never seen the golf course before and I came home with the biggest grin on my face. I told my wife, Maria, 'This is finally going to

16TH HOLE

be a great Open. They couldn't trick it up. It is out there in its natural state and there is nothing they can do about it.'"

Floyd's love affair with Shinnecock is ongoing. He is now a member and has built a home nearby.

Six new tees were built before 1986, including the finishing holes on both nines, to bring the course to 6,912 yards. Only two new tees were added before 1995, on the 15th and 17th holes. With the course playing firmer, nobody broke par for 72 holes as Corey Pavin won with a 280 total, beating Greg Norman by two shots.

Again, there was one tough weather day—a third round in which only three players broke par in 25 m.p.h. winds. The final round played out much like in 1986, with one player breaking away from a tightly bunched pack. Pavin played the last 10 holes in three-under to win. One of the shorter hitters on tour, Pavin finessed his way around the course and concluded with a memorable 4-wood to within five feet on the 18th. (It hardly mattered that he missed the putt.)

Shinnecock Hills's reputation as a perfect Open site was tarnished in 2004, when the USGA lost control of the course conditions on the weekend, especially in the final round in which the average score was 78.7—on a day the wind blew at no more than 15 m.p.h.

Officials blamed the *direction* of the wind— when blowing from the northwest, it brings dry air instead of moisture—which was a lame excuse. In reality, the USGA itself was to blame.

Though five new tees were added, the length gain was modest—the course now measured 6,996 yards—whereas the average PGA Tour drive since 1995 increased by more than 24 yards. So there was apparently concern that Shinnecock might be vulnerable and could only be protected by challenging players with rock-hard, super-fast greens. When rain before the championship followed by calm conditions led to low scoring in the opening rounds, the USGA was more concerned with attaining firmness than fairness.

The best example is the par-three seventh green, which slopes front-to-back and left-to-right. Early Sunday, it became impossible for the ball to remain on the green—with a *putt*. At that point, the USGA determined that the green needed to be watered, which was done periodically through the day. Another impossible green was at the 412-yard 10th. This drive-and-pitch hole played to an astounding scoring average of 5.03.

Instead of rewarding good play, these conditions only resulted in embarrassing displays by the best players in the world. Jerry Kelly summed it up best when he said about the USGA: "If they were smart, they'd realize they look really stupid."

The championship was saved by the brilliant play of Retief Goosen and Phil Mickelson, who battled the course and each other and came away with 71s. Mickelson made three birdies in a four-hole stretch on the back nine to take the lead before succumbing with a double bogey on the 17th. Despite missing fairways and greens down the stretch, Goosen stole the title by one-putting the last six holes—his biggest putt was a 20-footer for bogey on the 14th—to finish with a four-under 276 total.

Unfortunately, the controversy over the final round gave an undeserved reputation to Shinnecock Hills, which always had been known as a course that was difficult but fair. Shotmakers such as Pavin have won, while bombers Norman and Mickelson have prospered as well. Angles of play are important, helping players who can find the

proper side of the fairway. But the long hitters can benefit from risk/reward scenarios, where they can hit shorter shots into the small, firm greens.

The hardest hole on the course is usually the 474-yard sixth. The pros are able to make the long carry over sand and rough to the right side. The pond, the only water hazard on the course, is well short of the green and doesn't bother them either. The sixth's difficulty is the wind, which blows across the hole in the two most common scenarios.

The seventh was the nightmare hole in 2004, but it's normally not so fearsome. It's actually easier playing into the wind—it played downwind in 2004, adding to the difficult of holding the green—as it did most of the time in 1995, when it was only the ninth-hardest hole.

The 10th hole is only 412 yards but presents options off the tee: Lay up short of a downslope at the 250-yard mark or drive the ball to the bottom of the hill, leaving an uphill approach. Either way, a short second shot rolls back down a steep hill in front of the green. That's what made it so tough in

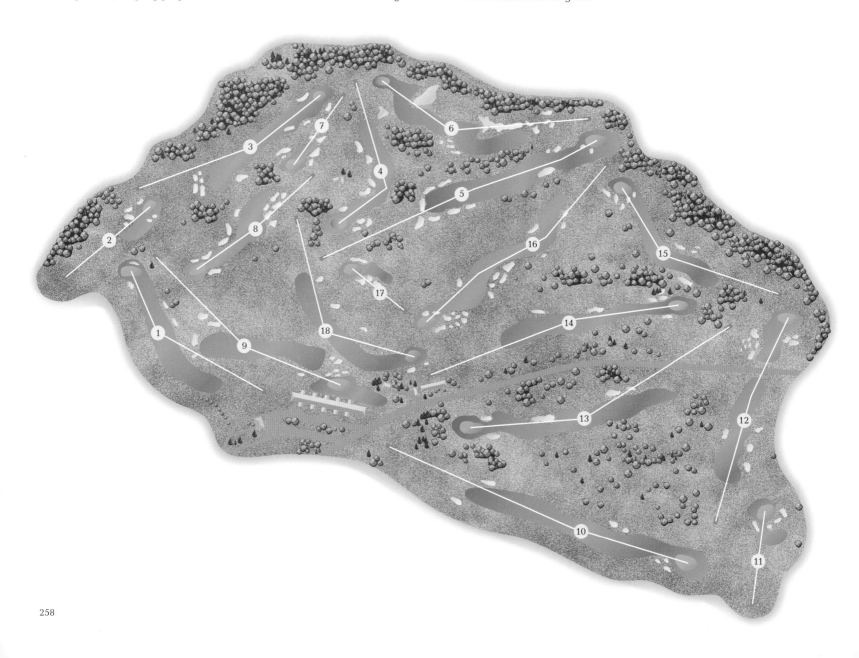

2004—there was no option of bouncing the ball onto the green with a low shot.

The 443-yard 14th plays to a tumbling fairway that is one of the hardest to hit on the course—and a drive in the rough means a struggle for par. The 540-yard 16th is another interesting fairway. Overall, the hole is straight, but the fairway snakes left, right, left, and right around clusters of bunkers. Floyd clinched his title with a knockdown 8-iron into the wind to set up a birdie, and Mickelson blew it in 1995 by playing it in six-over for the week to finish four back.

The 18th fairway takes a hard left turn in the last 80 yards, which means approach shots usually must carry rough and sand; that's why Pavin hit his 4-wood with a draw in 1995. Nine years later, when it played downwind, players were hitting 9-irons.

That's the kind of variety that makes Shinnecock so special. The same hole can play entirely differently from day to day. That's what keeps players wanting to come back—as long as they don't have to face anything like 2004's final round.

Scorecard

Hole	Par	Yardage	Avg.*	Rank*	Fwy. %*	Green %*	Putts*
1	4	393	4.13	15	46.7	61.6	1.71
2	3	226	3.24	10		43.1	1.66
3	4	478	4.23	11	46.7	43.8	1.60
4	4	435	4.28	6	53.3	48.1	1.74
5	5	537	4.70	18	45.1	82.8	1.58
6	4	474	4.40	1	47.2	44.2	1.74
7	3	189	3.31	5		33.4	1.67
8	4	398	4.12	16	70.7	55.1	1.67
9	4	443	4.32	4	52.4	49.2	1.71
Out	35	3573	36.71		51.7	51.3	1.67
10	4	412	4.39	2	58.2	41.8	1.71
11	3	158	3.26	8		49.9	1.68
12	4	468	4.22	12	69.5	50.8	1.57
13	4	370	4.19	13	47.6	49.7	1.63
14	4	443	4.26	9	41.5	46.0	1.66
15	4	403	4.27	7	54.1	50.9	1.69
16	5	540	4.98	17	35.5	82.1	1.73
17	3	179	3.18	14		44.6	1.59
18	4	450	4.35	3	43.7	49.3	1.73
In	35	3423	37.09		50.0	51.7	1.66
Total	70	6996	73.80		50.9	51.5	1.67

*Average and rank cumulative from 1995 and 2004 Opens.
Yardage and other statistics from 2004 Open.

1896 TOP FINISHERS

James Foulis	78-74—152
Horace Rawlins	79-76—155
Joe Lloyd	76-81—157
George Douglas	79-79—158
A.W. Smith	78-80—158

Low round: Foulis, 74

1986 TOP FINISHERS

Ray Floyd	75-68-70-66—279
Chip Beck	75-73-68-65—281
Lanny Wadkins	74-70-72-65—281
Hal Sutton	75-70-66-71—282
Lee Trevino	74-68-69-71—282
Ben Crenshaw	76-69-69-69—283
Payne Stewart	76-68-69-70—283
Bernhard Langer	74-70-70-70—284
Mark McCumber	74-71-68-71—284
Jack Nicklaus	77-72-67-68—284
Bob Tway	70-73-69-72—284

Low round: Beck, Wadkins, Mark Calcavecchia, 65

1995 TOP FINISHERS

Corey Pavin	72-69-71-68—280
Greg Norman	68-67-74-73—282
Tom Lehman	70-72-67-74—283
Bill Glasson	69-70-76-69—284
Neal Lancaster	70-72-77-65—284
Jeff Maggert	69-72-77-66—284
Phil Mickelson	68-70-72-74—284
Davis Love III	72-68-73-71—284
Jay Haas	70-73-72-69—284
Frank Nobilo	72-72-70-71—285
Bob Tway	69-69-72-75—285
Vijay Singh	70-71-72-72—285

Low round: Lancaster, 65

2004 TOP FINISHERS

Retief Goosen	70-66-69-71—276
Phil Mickelson	68-66-73-71—278
Jeff Maggert	68-67-74-72—281
Mike Weir	69-70-71-74—284
Shigeki Maruyama	66-68-74-76—284
Fred Funk	70-66-72-77—285
Robert Allenby	70-72-74-70—286
Steve Flesch	68-74-70-74—286
Jay Haas	66-74-76-71—287
Stephen Ames	74-66-73-74—287
Chris DiMarco	71-71-70-75—287
Ernie Els	70-67-70-80—287

Low round: Ames, Funk, Goosen, Haas, Maruyama, Mickelson, Angel Cabrera, Tim Clark, Tim Herron, 66

15TH HOLE

SKOKIE COUNTRY CLUB GLENCOE, ILLINOIS 1922

Gene Sarazen's most famous shot was the 4-wood he holed for a double eagle on the 15th hole

of the final round of the 1935 Masters, setting up his playoff victory over Craig Wood. At the

1922 U.S. Open at Skokie Country Club, Sarazen hit another second shot to a par five worthy

of being remembered. ¶ The setting was the 470-yard 18th hole. The 20-year-old Sarazen

had made a strong move as an early starter in the final round and played the last hole without

knowing what score he needed to win. ¶ "As I and my caddie walked to the ball, we debated

how to play the next shot," Sarazen later recalled. At first, Sarazen considered hitting a 4-wood

short of the green. "When we saw the perfect lie in the fairway, my caddie insisted I take my

driver and go for broke. I agreed." ¶ There was out of bounds to the left and water to the right,

but Sarazen's driver shot flew straight and true, stopping 15 feet from the hole. He two-putted

for a birdie and waited to see if anyone would catch him. Two players had a chance, but both

came to grief on the 17th hole, a 430-yard par four.

First came another 20-year-old, Bobby Jones, the 54-hole leader, who needed to play the last two holes in one-under to tie. His drive on 17, however, took an unfortunate kick to the left and finished in a shallow grass ditch, under some trees. He punched a fine recovery just short of the green but failed to get up and down.

Next it was 43-year-old John Black, an unheralded Scotsman by way of California. He led through two rounds and came to the last two holes needing two pars to tie Sarazen. He also hooked his drive on 17, so badly that it finished out of bounds to set up a crushing double bogey.

Although this was the first Open to charge for admission ($1), the fee didn't stop people from coming. Grantland Rice in the *New York Tribune* called the spectators "eighteen thousand of the wildest golf fanatics that ever raced over hill and hollow."

This was the third course to occupy this particular set of hills and hollows in the quarter century since Skokie was founded in 1897. The first was a member-designed layout, followed by a Tom Bendelow design in 1905. Members weren't happy with long walks between greens and tees, or that the ninth hole didn't come back to the clubhouse, so they hired Donald Ross to build a new course on the same ground.

Ross retained only one Bendelow hole, which he made his eighth, and ran a couple of holes in the opposite direction, from the old green to the old tee.

The course was one of the easier Open sites in the 1920s. Walter Hagen tied the Open record with a 68 in the first round, matched by Sarazen in the final round.

After the Open, there was some unhappiness among members about a stretch of short holes, the 12th through the 16th, on a narrow part of the property. Arguing for a redesign, grounds chairman Thomas McMahon said in 1938, "The golf course today is definitely not a championship course. It is satisfactory and provides adequate trouble for most of us. But there is unquestionably a certain value in attracting members and in being able to state, as some neighboring clubs can, that their courses are championship caliber."

The club had acquired some land in 1924 that was still unused. It resolved to utilize that property in a redesign and turn part of the unsatisfactory stretch of holes into a housing development. Respected architects William Langford and Bill Moreau were hired for a "rearrangement" that ended up with nine new holes—seemingly a questionable move considering Ross's stature in golf design.

Still, Golfclubatlas.com, a Web site that avowedly values classic architecture, states in a commentary on Skokie, "Whether Ross's 1922 course or Langford/Moreau's 1938 version was the design zenith is a matter of conjecture but the authors would side with the 1938 one."

Ironically, in the nearly seven decades since the redesign, Skokie hasn't held any championships other than the 1998 U.S. Senior Amateur. It also served as the second course for the stroke-play portion of the 1983 U.S. Amateur, hosted by North Shore. Rees Jones helped prepare Skokie for that Amateur.

The tradition of change at Skokie got a new twist in 1999 with a restoration project carried out by Ron Prichard with the idea of bringing the course back to the way it was in 1938, but with more length. Many trees were removed (the course started out as a prairie but was planted extensively) and bunkers restored to their original configurations.

The 17th and 18th, pivotal in 1922, are two of the Ross holes that remain. Since there was no room to lengthen the 18th and players were reaching it in two in the hickory-shaft era, the hole now plays as a par four.

1922 TOP FINISHERS

Gene Sarazen	72-73-75-68—288
John Black	71-71-75-72—289
Bobby Jones	74-72-70-73—289
William Mehlhorn	73-71-72-74—290
Walter Hagen	68-77-74-72—291

Low round: Hagen, Sarazen, 68

GENE SARAZEN

TOMMY BOLT. OPPOSITE TOP: 2ND HOLE. OPPOSITE BOTTOM: 4TH HOLE

SOUTHERN HILLS COUNTRY CLUB TULSA, OKLAHOMA 1958, 1977, 2001

When you think about what was happening in Oklahoma in 1935, the first thing that's likely to come into your mind is the Dust Bowl. Strangely enough, that's the year Southern Hills Country Club was formed. While farmers were hit hard by the drought and the Great Depression, the city folks in Tulsa were just beginning a mini-recovery after the oil business had bottomed out. ¶ The Depression was a difficult time for country clubs, which suffered from declining membership. The tough economic climate actually played a role in the birth of Southern Hills, which was started by members of Tulsa Country Club who were told their course was going to become public. (The switch never happened.) ¶ Two of those members, Bill Warren and Cecil Canary, asked Waite Phillips, a banker and the richest man in Tulsa, to finance the project. Cofounder of Phillips Petroleum, Phillips had sold all his oil holdings in 1925 and presciently not invested them in the stock market, which left him with a personal fortune estimated at $50 million during the 1930s. Around town, he was known as "Tulsa's Fifth National Bank."

Phillips listened to the proposal and termed it "ridiculous." But he came back with a proposal of his own. If the men could sign up 100 Tulsans willing to put up $1,000 each, Phillips would donate the land for a course. Unknown to the petitioners, golf-course architect Perry Maxwell already had approached Phillips about building a golf course on that land, around which Phillips would build houses.

Finding 100 people to put up that kind of money during the Depression was a tall task, but Warren and Canary pulled it off—or at least came close enough for Phillips to go ahead with the deal.

Maxwell, naturally, designed the course. Whereas Phillips was an oilman-turned-banker, Maxwell was a banker-turned-golf architect. After reading up on golf design and traveling to see some of the courses in the East, he bought 500 acres of land in Ardmore, Oklahoma, in 1913 and built Dornick Hills. After his wife died at the age of 40 in 1919, Maxwell traveled to Scotland. Upon returning, he quit banking and began designing courses professionally.

A sometime partner of Alister MacKenzie, Maxwell believed that "nature must precede the architect in the laying out of courses. The site of the course should be there, not be brought there. In this way it will have its own character, distinct from any course in the world." He wasn't beyond putting his own stamp onto the greens, however. His undulating surfaces became known as "Maxwell's Rolls."

Maxwell lived on the property as Southern Hills was built, supervising construction. True to his "naturalist" philosophy, he used only one tractor.

He placed the clubhouse, ninth and 18th greens, and first and 10th tees on the property's only large hill. The rest of the terrain lacked major elevation changes, but the ground featured many bumps and gentle rolls, so the fairways are anything but flat. In fact, playing from various sidehill, uphill, and downhill lies is one of the challenges at Southern Hills.

But not the only one. A couple of creeks, including one now known as Maxwell's Creek, come into play, as do the bunkers, trees, and heavy Bermuda rough. Accuracy is very important at Southern Hills.

When the club opened in 1935, the swimming pool was the bigger attraction. Only 29 members showed up for the course opening, and many found the course too hard.

12TH HOLE

13TH HOLE

Gradually, the condition of the course improved, as did the members' appetite for golf and their desire to hold pro and amateur events of a national stature. Through the years, Southern Hills has hosted three Opens, three PGA Championships, two Tour Championships, and five other USGA championships.

Southern Hills's first big tournament was the 1945 Tulsa Open, won by Sam Snead, followed by the 1946 U.S. Women's Amateur, which Babe Didrikson Zaharias won. Next up was the 1958 U.S. Open.

Although the course was only two decades old and not in need of a major makeover, Robert Trent Jones Sr. was called in to prepare it for the big event. He added some length, narrowed the fairways, and installed bunkers or grew rough in spots fronting likely pin positions.

If anything, the course was too tough for the Open, especially in a first round in which nobody broke par. The field of 162 players combined for 141 birdies and one eagle. It was a perfectly unpleasant day—the 90-degree heat was accompanied by a wind that felt like a furnace blast and dried out the greens. The rough had been grown to pitch-out proportions and, to top it all off, the hole locations were diabolical.

Herbert Warren Wind in *Sports Illustrated* called those positions "sometimes ludicrous...On a number of downwind holes they were at the deep front of the trapped green. On several terraced greens

they were set just above the crest of the upslope... Most of the players were overcome with a sense of grogginess after suffering through their first series of misfortunes, and after a while it just took the heart out of them and they could fight the conditions no more."

The conditions became more favorable for the last three rounds, except for the temperature, which hit a peak of 97 degrees. Still, the scoring average for the week on the par-70 course was 77.92.

Based on his reputation, the last player expected to handle the trying conditions was "Terrible" Tommy Bolt, known for his hair-trigger temper. But this was a new Bolt, who that spring, after a conversation with an old Army buddy, had decided to work on his self-control and maintain a positive mental approach.

His reading list included Bishop Fulton Sheen's *Way to Inner Peace* and Reverend Norman Vincent Peale's *Power of Positive Thinking*. The latter must have helped: After making a birdie on the first hole of the Open, he recalls, "I remember turning back to look at the first tee and saying out loud, 'I wonder who's going to finish second?'"

Bolt, born in Oklahoma and raised in Louisiana, felt at home in the heat, and his newfound equanimity helped him to avoid getting upset about the pin placements, rough, or anything else. He shared the lead after the first round, and he kept it for himself the rest of the way. His 283 total gave him a four-stroke margin over 21-year-old Gary Player, who was making his Open debut. Bolt's worst round was 72, an impressive feat considering every other player had a round of 75 or worse.

The 1977 U.S. Open followed a similar scenario, as Hubert Green was tied for the lead after the first round and was out front by himself after 36, 54, and 72 holes. Like Bolt, Green was a fine player who had yet to win a major. (Green would go on to claim one more.)

While Bolt had to overcome the heat, Green faced a much different source of pressure. After playing the 14th hole in the final round, USGA officials told him that a woman had called the FBI saying that two men were planning to shoot Green on the 15th hole. Offered the option of asking for play to be suspended, Green elected to play on, joking that it must be an old girlfriend.

Police watched the gallery and secured a couple of houses under construction outside the property that had a view of the 15th hole as Green played it. He hooked his drive but managed a par.

Meanwhile, Lou Graham had just completed a stretch of four birdies in five holes to pull within one of the lead. Green responded by hitting a pitching wedge to a foot from the hole to birdie the par-five 16th.

Green came to the brutish final hole with a two-stroke cushion, which almost wasn't enough after

his drive found the rough. Green said after the round that he told himself not to hit his approach in the left bunker, which is precisely where it ended up. He then told himself not to chunk it, which he did, leaving a 35-foot putt for par. His first putt pulled up three-and-a-half feet short, and now suddenly Green faced a pressure putt for the Open. "It was the hardest kind of putt for me to make—dead straight," he said, but he knocked it in for a total of 278.

Twenty-four years later at Southern Hills's third Open, Retief Goosen stood over an even shorter putt to win the Open—only two feet—and missed. Fortunately he recovered to beat Mark Brooks in the following day's 18-hole playoff, 70-72.

Of the six major winners at Southern Hills, only Bolt has made par on the 18th hole in the final round. (The PGA champions were Dave Stockton in 1970, Ray Floyd in 1982, and Nick Price in 1994.) Goosen appeared to be a lock to do so when he hit a 6-iron approach to 12 feet. He came to the hole tied for the lead with playing partner Stewart Cink, but Cink missed the green, left his chip outside of Goosen's ball, and just missed his par putt.

HUBERT GREEN

Feeling he'd blown his chance and with his concentration gone, Cink tried to tap in his 18-inch bogey putt to get out of Goosen's way—and missed. That left Goosen needing only to two-putt for the win. But he knocked his first putt two feet past, setting up one of the most shocking misses in Open history. He had to make a slightly longer putt just to tie Brooks at 276.

Paul Azinger called the Cink-Goosen debacle on the 18th green, "the saddest thing I've ever seen watching sports." Brooks, by the way, had three-putted the 18th from 45 feet.

During practice rounds, there had been big problems with the ninth and 18th greens—because of their back-to-front slopes combined with green speeds, any ball not reaching the back portion would trickle back, all the way off the green. So the USGA decided to stop mowing those two greens, slowing them down by a foot on the Stimpmeter compared with the other putting surfaces. That made them fairer as targets for approach shots, but confused players trying to figure out just how hard to hit the putts.

Few courses have had more trouble with greens than Southern Hills, often due to freakish circumstances. A hailstorm just five minutes after the award ceremony for the 1958 Open caused so much damage that ultimately the greens had to be rebuilt over a three-year period, starting in 1960.

Two years after the 1982 PGA Championship, the club decided to replant the greens with Penncross bentgrass. For several years, the greens were in poor condition. Finally, Dr. Joseph Duitch,

the developer of Penncross, visited in 1988 and concluded that the grass was a counterfeit. This time the greens were replanted with a new strain called Pennlinks.

That lasted until 1999, when vandals ruined a number of greens by pouring chemicals on them. They were regrassed with a still more modern version of bentgrass, which enabled the club to attain speeds that were too fast for the slope of the greens on Nos. 9 and 18. Maxwell certainly never envisioned the surfaces rolling so fast.

At the same time, the club embarked on a restoration project with architect Keith Foster. The Bermuda rough and fringe had encroached on most of the greens, making them smaller and taking away hole locations close to the edges. Foster restored the greens to their original sizes; for good measure, he also deepened the bunkers and built new tees on eight holes.

Only two of those tees added more than 13 yards, though, and at 6,973 yards Southern Hills suddenly had become a short course by modern standards. The driver stayed in the bag on many holes for most players in 2001 since hitting the 28-yard-wide fairways was crucial. Many used irons even on the 454-yard first, which plays downhill. Once considered a fearsome opener, it is now just a middling hole.

The fifth hole was extended by 35 yards before 2001, making it the longest hole in Open history at 642 yards. That didn't stop several players from reaching the green, or coming close, in two. Still, the field averaged 5.18 strokes, making it the 10th hardest hole—unusual for a par five.

17TH HOLE

An Open Moment

After making birdies at the 12th, 14th, 15th, and 16th holes in the final round of the 1977 Open, Lou Graham stepped on the tee of the 354-yard 17th, a legitimate birdie opportunity. Trailing Hubert Green by just one stroke, Graham badly hooked his tee shot into some trees. He had to punch a 3-iron hook under some branches and hope for the ball to hop through some rough and onto the green. The shot came off better than he could have imagined, finishing eight feet from the hole. The stroke of genius was wasted when Graham missed the putt, and he finished one shot behind.

18TH HOLE

Among Southern Hills's five par fours of less than 400 yards, the hardest is the 374-yard ninth, where the second shot is played with a wedge to an elevated green that slopes sharply toward the front, as described previously.

The 456-yard 12th is the best hole on the course, and both Ben Hogan and Arnold Palmer called it one of the best in the country. It's a dogleg left with a green site that came about almost by accident. Showing the tentative layout to one of the founding members, Don Bothwell, Maxwell pointed to a spot to the right of the creek where he planned to put the green. Bothwell dropped a ball in the fairway and couldn't get there. Seeing a shelf of land on the other side of the creek, he said, "Why not put the green there?"

"Why didn't I see that before?" Maxwell replied.

The 13th and 16th are parallel par fives for the members. In the first two U.S. Opens and two PGAs, the 13th was played as a par four, but in the 1994 PGA and 2001 Open that hole played as a par five and the 16th as a par four. It was a good move because, with twin ponds in front of the green, No. 13 sets up as a risk/reward par five of 534 yards.

Players need to bring their "A" games to the finishing stretch of five holes. The 215-yard par-three 14th has out of bounds on the left that doesn't usually come into play, but it did for Tom Purtzer in the final round of 1977. He was one shot out of the lead when his hooked tee shot knocked him out of it.

The 15th measures only 412 yards, but has such a difficult green that it played as the fifth hardest hole in 2001. The 491-yard 16th was the third toughest and the 466-yard 18th the toughest.

The finishing hole is awkward. Unless the ball finds a small flat area, the tee shot leaves a downhill lie for an uphill shot to the green. In 1977, it played to a 4.8 average in the first round at 449 yards, and was shortened by 30 yards for the last three rounds. The hole is difficult these days even with a mid-iron approach, and missing a drive to the right brings the trees into play.

The 18th hole *looks* hard, which can't be said about the entire course. Tom Fazio was brought in with his uncle George to make some changes before the 1977 Open, but they ended up doing little. "When I first saw Southern Hills, it wasn't striking," said Tom in a 1977 interview. "Then, as I studied it hole by hole, I knew it was a sleeper. It doesn't look severe, but watch out."

Southern Hills is a course that applies a lot of heat, and not just on the thermometer.

RETIEF GOOSEN RECOVERED FROM A 72ND-HOLE DEBACLE TO WIN IN 2001.

Scorecard

2001 U.S. Open

Hole	Par	Yardage	Avg.	Rank	Fwy. %	Green %	Putts
1	4	454	4.21	8	56.1	51.6	1.67
2	4	467	4.40	2	51.0	37.2	1.61
3	4	408	4.15	11	57.6	63.0	1.73
4	4	368	4.13	13	66.0	62.2	1.71
5	5	642	5.18	10	44.3	58.3	1.70
6	3	175	3.01	17		67.7	1.66
7	4	382	4.08	14	72.3	59.8	1.62
8	3	225	3.27	6		37.8	1.59
9	4	374	4.19	9	61.3	52.7	1.64
Out	35	3495	36.62		58.4	54.5	1.66
10	4	374	4.13	12	62.6	66.5	1.75
11	3	165	3.03	16		61.7	1.59
12	4	456	4.30	4	59.8	44.7	1.62
13	5	534	4.82	18	58.5	78.1	1.65
14	3	215	3.23	7		42.4	1.54
15	4	412	4.29	5	68.0	56.1	1.79
16	4	491	4.34	3	51.0	33.3	1.56
17	4	365	4.08	15	62.2	56.8	1.58
18	4	466	4.44	1	70.3	38.9	1.72
In	35	3478	36.65		61.8	53.2	1.65
Total	70	6973	73.27		60.1	53.8	1.65

LEW WORSHAM (CENTER) BEAT SAM SNEAD (RIGHT) IN A 1947 PLAYOFF.

ST. LOUIS COUNTRY CLUB LADUE, MISSOURI 1947

By 1912, Charles Blair Macdonald had moved from Chicago to New York and built his National

Golf Links of America on Long Island. Since designing courses was his avocation rather than

his vocation (he never accepted a fee), he did not take just any project. But when asked by St.

Louis Country Club to design a course on their new site, the opportunity to spread quality golf

to another Midwestern city was too good to pass up. ¶ The dramatically rolling property made

a wonderful canvas for someone of Macdonald's talents. Aficionados of his work consider St.

Louis to be among his best courses, and golf-course architects have been known to stop by to

pick up a few pointers. ¶ On all his courses, Macdonald's style was to make copies of particu-

lar holes in Scotland. The repertoire usually consisted of seven or eight models, including all

four par threes—a Biarritz, an Eden, a Short, and a Redan. St. Louis has some of the best

examples of those holes; the par-three holes are the course's strength. He even threw in an

extra par three, the Crater hole 12th, which plays over a depression that sits in the middle of

the course. ¶ Except for the 150-yard seventh, where the main defense is a fiercely raised

green, the par threes are plenty long. The toughest come back-to-back: The 213-yard second

(Biarritz) features a three-foot-deep swale in the middle of the green and the 207-yard third (Eden) has dramatically deep bunkers in the front and rear of a sloping green.

The course is short—just 6,532 yards for the 1947 Open and shorter today—because it lacks long par fours. But it is by no means easy. Many greens drop off to steep slopes or are guarded by deep bunkers. There is plenty of trouble to be found off the tees as well. Accuracy is vital at St. Louis.

Still, many predicted that the record of 281 would fall at the 1947 Open. They were close: Lew Worsham and Sam Snead tied at two-under 282. Worsham had a good chance at the record, but he staggered home with a 39 on the back nine of the final round, and Snead tied him with a 15-foot birdie putt on the 18th hole.

That putt has been forgotten because it led not to a title but to more heartbreak for the man who never won an Open. Instead, the 18th green is remembered for what occurred in the playoff.

Snead had just lost a two-stroke lead, thanks to Worsham's birdie on 16 and his own bogey on 17, but Snead was in better shape on the par-four 18th, facing a 20-foot birdie putt while his opponent missed the green. Worsham's chip hit the hole and stopped two-and-a-half feet away. Snead lagged his downhill putt, but in trying not to knock it too far past, he left it about two-and-a-half feet short.

Actually, it was precisely 30.5 inches away. That's because just as Snead was about to putt, Worsham stepped in to ask who was away. USGA official Isaac Grainger measured and determined that Snead was an inch farther from the hole. So Snead returned to his tricky downhill putt with a left-to-right break, but he failed to regain his focus.

"I changed my mind at the last instant on both speed and amount of break . . . and by just the amount of break I didn't allow, the ball missed," Snead wrote in *Education of a Golfer*. The 29-year-old Worsham, who had just turned pro after World War II, knocked in his uphill putt and was the winner. By shooting his fourth straight 70 in the playoff, Snead had become the first player with four sub-par rounds in an Open—yet he still couldn't win.

Both players were natives of Virginia and went on to become friends. Still, the circumstances

would forever rankle Snead: "Years of thinking over this incident makes me believe that Chin [Worsham] didn't do it deliberately, yet the needle was there just the same."

St. Louis is basically the same course today, with an exception that actually brings the course back to its roots. On the 505-yard par-five fifth, Macdonald built the green in a depression, calling it the Punch Bowl. In the 1920s, a member named Samuel C. Davis thought the downslope leading to the green made the hole too easy. He believed an elevated spot beyond would be a better site for the green—so he built one there and offered it to the club. The greens committee didn't agree and planted evergreen trees on the would-be putting surface.

Twenty years later, with the Open approaching, the greens committee decided that the pros would reach the Punch Bowl too easily in two and that the hole would be stronger with the Davis green. The trees were removed and the green put in play. Davis, no doubt, would have been pleased—but by then he was dead. In a 1991 restoration, the club went back to the original Macdonald green.

1947 TOP FINISHERS

•Lew Worsham	70-70-71-71—282
Sam Snead	72-70-70-70—282
Bobby Locke	68-74-70-73—285
Edward Oliver Jr.	73-70-71-71—285
Bud Ward	69-72-73-73—287
Jim Ferrier	71-70-74-74—289
Vic Ghezzi	74-73-73-69—289
Leland Gibson	69-76-73-71—289
Ben Hogan	70-75-70-74—289
Johnny Palmer	72-70-75-72—289
Paul Runyan	71-74-72-72—289

•Worsham won playoff, 69–70
Low round: James McHale, 65

Scorecard

Hole	Par	Yardage 1947 Open	Yardage Today
1	4	395	396
2	3	233	213
3	3	187	207
4	4	421	412
5	5	545	505
6	4	325	359
7	3	150	155
8	4	347	355
9	5	537	512
Out	35	3140	3114
10	4	349	350
11	4	399	405
12	3	180	176
13	5	576	580
14	4	416	419
15	5	500	496
16	3	188	184
17	4	365	376
18	4	419	410
In	36	3392	3396
Total	71	6532	6510

4TH HOLE. OPPOSITE: 3RD HOLE

TORREY PINES GOLF COURSE (SOUTH COURSE) LA JOLLA, CALIFORNIA 2008

Will Torrey Pines South be Bethpage West when it hosts the U.S. Open in 2008? The people in the San Diego area hope so. ¶ Torrey Pines will be the second daily-fee course to host the Open, after Bethpage Black's successful 2002 debut. (Pebble Beach and Pinehurst are resort courses.) In fact, the awarding of the Open to New York's Bethpage was the inspiration for Torrey Pines to seek an Open. ¶ There are some parallels between the courses, but also many differences. Hidden gem Bethpage was an inspired design of the Golden Age that was in a sorry state due to a lack of conditioning. Torrey Pines was a pretty good layout from the 1950s that was better known to a national audience and in good shape because it hosted a PGA Tour event every year. ¶ Bethpage was targeted as a U.S. Open site by the USGA, which recognized the course's potential and went to its owner, the State of New York, with a proposal to pump millions into the course. Torrey Pines is owned by the City of San Diego, but got its Open through the efforts of a local group called Friends of Torrey Pines, which raised millions in private funding.

A common denominator is Rees Jones, the golf architect who worked on both courses. He faced vastly different assignments. His task at Bethpage was to restore A.W. Tillinghast's classic. At Torrey Pines, he had to redesign the course to make it challenging enough for the U.S. Open.

There were no guarantees from the USGA that it would reward Jones's work with the U.S. Open. In fact, other than USGA's stated interest in adding another public site, there was no particular reason to think it would choose Torrey Pines. "It was actually a longshot that Torrey Pines would get an Open," Jones says. "We had to do it first and then see."

The courses at Torrey Pines (the complex also has the North Course) were designed in 1957 by William F. Bell, better known as Billy Bell Jr. His father, William P. Bell, had worked as the construction foreman for George C. Thomas before embarking on his own career in golf design. The younger Bell worked in partnership with his father in the early 1950s before taking over the business after his father's death in 1953.

Torrey Pines was one of his early efforts. The site, which sits on cliffs above the Pacific Ocean and provides spectacular views, had been an Army training center called Camp Callen during World War II before it reverted back to the city, which eventually decided to build the courses.

Although the land is well above the ocean, there are a couple of canyons on the edge of the property that plunge toward the water. They came into play at a few spots on the original course, but several holes kept their distance. Jones changed that with his 2001 redesign.

The third green, fourth fairway and green, and 14th green were all shifted to the edge, bringing the hazard dramatically into play. "Those are natural settings—and natural disasters," says Jones.

He also completely rebuilt every green and redesigned the greenside bunkering. He made the putting surfaces much more difficult, adding elevation and multiple terraces. Essentially, it's a new golf course on the same piece of property, with a slightly altered routing.

14TH HOLE

16TH HOLE

The change that generated the most attention was the addition of 500 yards, to 7,607. It seemed extreme at the time, but it was ahead of the curve. The truth is that even 490-yard par fours can be a drive and a middle iron for today's pros.

"Torrey Pines probably will be the model for future courses that will host tournaments, with the modern equipment," Jones says, referring to the green contours as well as the length. "The contours separate the men from the boys. It almost forces you to go for some of the hole locations, because you don't want a long putt up or down to another terrace."

Since the redesign, the five Buick Invitationals at Torrey Pines all have been won by major champions—Jose Maria Olazabal, John Daly, and Tiger Woods three times. The victory by Olazabal helps dispel the notion that only long hitters can win on such a long course. Although Daly is one of the biggest of bombers, the two other contestants in his playoff win were short hitters Chris Riley and Luke Donald, so all kinds of players have been able to perform at the new South Course.

Woods, who can win anywhere and played Torrey Pines when he was growing up, was at first skeptical about the course's suitability as a U.S. Open site, but he changed his mind after playing the new course. "They can definitely host an Open here," he said in 2002. "The changes are definitely more for the way the game is changing. Guys are getting longer and stronger, and for what they want to have here, a U.S. Open, they did the right thing because I think this is a wonderful venue for it."

The USGA agreed. Later that year, it chose Torrey Pines for the 2008 Open, a selection that has not been without controversy among local residents. Plans for a new clubhouse were tabled until after the championship, and there has been much public debate over green fees and access to tee times. A plan approved in 2006 calls for fees to increase sharply after the Open.

As for the pros, they know the course will play much differently for the Open. The USGA will narrow the fairways and grow the rough, and the course will play firmer than it does for the Buick Invitational in February. The USGA tentatively has decided that the sixth and 18th holes will be par fours instead of par fives at the Open. That will reduce the yardage to about 7,470, but with a very stern par of 70.

"It's going to be amazing how hard this course will play when the U.S. Open is here," Daly said after winning at Torrey. "I don't see anyone breaking par in 2008 if the rough is up like we think it's going to be."

Even without Open rough, the South Course is quite a challenge for the everyday Joes. At least they have the much shorter North Course as an option.

The scenery and the challenge are co-stars at South Course, and both are very much in evidence on the third hole, a 198-yard downhill par three that plays toward the ocean. Any shot left or long is in the hazard.

The cliffside 471-yard fourth has become one of the hardest holes on the PGA Tour. It features another green that was shifted so the canyon looms left and long. Jones also moved the fairway closer to trouble.

There's no letup in this early stretch, at least as it will play for the Open. The fifth has been lengthened by 45 yards to 453, the sixth is a birdie opportunity at the Buick Invitational but will be a hard par four at the Open, and the 462-yard seventh reintroduces the canyon, this time on the right.

The course doesn't ease much on the back nine either. The uphill 12th is 504 yards on the regular scorecard, but only 477 for the Buick. Expect it to

18TH HOLE

play to its full length for the Open. There's a birdie chance on the par-five 13th, though a new tee will make it play something like 600 yards to an elevated green.

The 14th was once a straightaway hole, but Jones turned it into a 435-yard dogleg by moving the green to the precipice of disaster (again, long and left are very bad). The 16th is the hardest par three at 227 yards, usually into the wind. The canyon has always been a factor on the left of the 442-yard 17th; Jones's main change here was building the most undulating green on the course.

The 18th plays at 571 yards for the Buick Invitational, and with a pond in front of the green it offers long hitters a chance to go for it in two under the right conditions. After some debate, the USGA decided to make it a par four for the Open because it didn't want the finishing hole to play driver, 6-iron, sand wedge for most of the field. It will play at about 500 yards and driving in the fairway will be vital. When the hole location is close to the water, expect very few birdies.

Is that the best way to end an Open? We'll find out the answer to that, along with a host of other questions about Torrey Pines, in 2008.

Scorecard

2006 Buick Invitational

Hole*	Par	Yardage	Average	Rank
1	4	452	4.35	T3
2	4	387	4.01	12
3	3	198	3.18	9
4	4	471	4.29	6
5	4	453	4.08	10
6	5	560	4.70	18
7	4	462	4.35	T3
8	3	176	2.93	14
9	5	613	4.72	17
Out	36	3772	36.61	
10	4	405	3.94	13
11	3	221	3.33	5
12	4	477	4.43	1
13	5	541	4.76	15
14	4	435	4.24	7
15	4	477	4.36	2
16	3	227	3.23	8
17	4	442	4.04	11
18	5	571	4.75	16
In	36	3796	37.08	
Total	72	7568	73.69	

*Holes 6 and 18 are expected to be converted to par fours for the 2008 Open

BOBBY JONES HOLES THE TYING PUTT ON THE 72ND HOLE IN 1929. OPPOSITE TOP: 1ST HOLE.
OPPOSITE BOTTOM: 3RD HOLE

WINGED FOOT GOLF CLUB (WEST COURSE) MAMARONECK, NEW YORK 1929, 1959, 1974, 1984, 2006

The founders of Winged Foot Golf Club gave only one instruction to course architect A.W.
Tillinghast when they hired him in 1921: "Give us a man-sized course." ¶ That's exactly
what they got. Actually, they got two of them: the East and West, both ranked among the top
50 in the United States. But it's the West that has hosted five U.S. Opens, including two that are
remembered as the hardest in the last 40 years. The book about the 1974 championship is titled
Massacre at Winged Foot, and the 2006 event was no picnic. ¶ The "man-sized" appellation
to Winged Foot refers to more than just its length. Sure, it's plenty long. Back when hitting long
irons was a part of the pro game, it had a lot of par fours that required approaches with those
clubs. But it's the targets for those irons that give Winged Foot its character. ¶ Winged Foot's
greens average 5,100 square feet in surface area, about two-thirds the size of a typical course
today. They are surrounded by deep, grasping, fear-inducing bunkers. The shape and contour
of the greens and the placement of those bunkers make Winged Foot a severe test of a player's
skill and thinking on approach shots.

7TH HOLE

Winged Foot has only 66 bunkers, but they are large, deep, and very effective. Many of the green complexes have only two bunkers, but they are placed to maximum effect. Most of the greens are narrow in front, where they are tightly guarded by bunkers, usually on both sides. The greens get wider in the back, so the "safe" play is toward the back of the green. The genius of Winged Foot is that nearly every green slopes sharply from back to front, so an approach to the back of the green leaves a downhill putt.

The lack of bunkers in front helps the average player get around the course, whereas bunkers are not really needed behind the greens, because from there the player usually faces a difficult downhill shot. The fairway bunkering is rather sparse, but rough and trees are more effective penalties for errant drives these days.

When the greens are firm and fast, as they are for the U.S. Open, Winged Foot is perhaps the best example of Tillinghast's stated maxim that "a controlled shot to a closely guarded green is the surest test of any man's golf."

Fortunately for golf historians and architecture buffs, Tillinghast was a prolific writer, contributing many articles to magazines and even serving as the editor of *Golf Illustrated* for a couple of years. When the U.S. Open came to Winged Foot six years after its 1923 opening, he wrote a preview article for the magazine.

"The contouring of the greens places great premium on the placement of the drives but never is there the necessity of facing a prodigious carry of the sink or swim sort," Tillinghast wrote. "In fact, every hole, barring the one-shotters, seems quite innocent and without guile from the teeing ground, and it is only the knowledge that the next shot must be played with rifle accuracy that brings the realization that the drive must be placed."

Winged Foot is a particularly impressive achievement because the site is less dramatic than most of the other great courses in the country. There is little elevation change and the only creek is near the corner of the property. Nor is there an inspiring view, though in the early days, when there were fewer trees, Long Island Sound could be seen about a mile-and-a-half away from the club's hilltop site in Westchester County.

A portion of the property once belonged to Alton B. Parker, the losing Democratic candidate for President against Theodore Roosevelt in 1904. It had since passed into other hands when some members of the New York Athletic Club purchased it for their planned golf course.

The course would not be affiliated with the Athletic Club, which turned down the proposal, leaving the men to start a club on their own. They did solicit much of their early membership from the Athletic Club, however, and took their name from the NYAC's winged-foot logo.

One thing the property had in abundance was rocks. A total of 7,200 tons of rock was blasted, and some of it used in the building of the clubhouse. This was no easy construction job: It required a crew of 220 workmen, utilizing 60 teams of horses and 19 tractors.

Tillinghast made a couple of prescient predictions in his preview article for the 1929 Open. He said that four 74s would place "close to the top" and that the lowest round "may possibly break 70, but it won't be done often—if at all."

Four 74s would have been two shots out of a playoff, and there was one round under 70 in regulation, a 69 by Bobby Jones in the opening round.

Jones would shoot another 69 in the second round of a 36-hole playoff as he won the championship with a wildly inconsistent performance. Even his opening round was a crazy ride that included two eagles and two double bogeys. Tillinghast saw one of the eagles, at the 497-yard par-five 12th, which Jones reached with an iron to within 10 feet. (Baked-out fairways enabled drives to cover prodigious distances.)

Jones lost the lead with a 75 in a second round that he played in heavy rain before he regained it with a third-round 71, the best round of the morning on a course that was no longer playing short. Through seven holes of the final round he had a seven-stroke lead, but what should have been a comfortable stroll turned into a harrowing finish, as Jones made two triple bogeys coming in.

Those triples demonstrated the difficulty of the shots around Winged Foot's greens. On the eighth hole, Jones's shot from the back of the right bunker caught the slope of the green and rolled all the way into the front of the left bunker. From there, he blasted it too hard and ended up in the same bunker he'd been in before, going back and forth like a common duffer.

"After my experience at the eighth . . . I became trap-shy," Jones wrote in *The American Golfer*. "My only thought after that was to avoid bunkers and I began guiding each shot, with the usual result."

At the 15th, Jones drove in the trees, punched

An Open Moment

Johnny Miller not only came into the 1974 Open as the defending champion, he had already won five tournaments on the year. His Open bid came to an abrupt end on the seventh hole of the second round. Miller's tee shot came to rest in a deep bunker to the right of the green, and his first attempt failed to escape. So did his second. And his third. The fourth try finally made it, and Miller had a quadruple bogey. Incidentally, many blamed the harsh conditions at Winged Foot as revenge for Miller's 63 at Oakmont the year before.

brutal finishing hole it would later become. Nonetheless, Jones pulled his iron shot and it finished in a bunker. After playing out to 12 feet, he needed to sink the putt for a tie.

It was a difficult downhill putt with a significant left-to-right break. Jones's friend and chronicler, O.B. Keeler, closed his eyes because he couldn't bear to watch. This is what he missed, as reported by William Henry Beers in *Golf Illustrated*. "The progress of the ball seemed to prematurely die within a foot of the hole, and it appeared to have stopped an inch or so from the hole, which caused an excited enthusiast to exclaim: 'He missed it!' This seemed to spur the ball to further effort and it made a final turn of its 1.62 inches in circumference and fell in the cup."

out, knocked his third over the green, then hit a pitch shot that failed to carry a slope and rolled back toward him. "That was a dub!" said a man in the gallery in a loud whisper.

Now Jones needed three pars to match Al Espinosa's 294 total, though he had his sights on bettering that since the 16th was a reachable par five. He did get home in two there, but three-putted for par, followed by a routine par on 17. The 18th played 419 yards in those days, so it was not the

In the playoff the next day, Jones overwhelmed Espinosa, 72-69—141 to 84-80—164. Both Keeler and famed sportswriter Grantland Rice believed Jones would not have gone on to win the Grand Slam the following year if he had not made that putt on the 72nd hole.

Jones returned to Winged Foot in 1954 for the 25th anniversary of his win. It was arranged for four past Open champions to try the same putt. Tommy Armour, Johnny Farrell, Gene Sarazen, and Craig Wood all missed it.

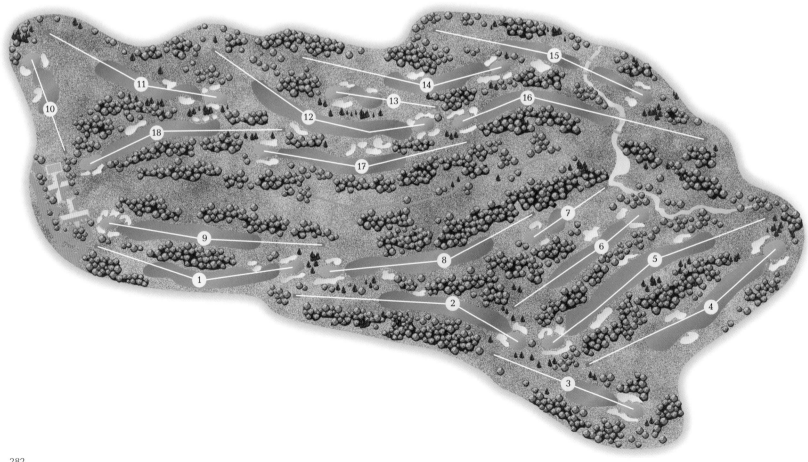

10TH HOLE

16TH HOLE

Ironically, Jones said he putted poorly that week, missing many putts in the four- to five-foot range. That wasn't the case at the next U.S. Open at Winged Foot in 1959, where winner Billy Casper displayed a sensational putting showcase. That Open, in fact, marked the beginning of Casper's reputation as a great putter, one that perhaps unfairly overshadowed the rest of his game.

Casper had 114 putts in four rounds with only one three-putt, outstanding on Winged Foot's greens. He was particularly uncanny in a stretch of nine straight one-putts, covering the last four holes of the third round and the first five of the final round. For the record, the putts were from 10, 8, 11, 4, 4, 8, 9, 7, and 18 feet.

The final round was the first time the Open concluded with a single round on Sunday. A stormy Saturday, with a delay in the morning and another stoppage in the late afternoon, turned the planned double round into a single one.

Casper led by three going into the final round, but his closest pursuers included Ben Hogan (three back), Arnold Palmer, and Sam Snead (both four back, along with Bob Rosburg). Casper stumbled in with a 38 on the back nine for 74, but his big-name pursuers fared even worse in the wind. Rosburg's 71 left him one short.

Casper's 282 total was two-over, as the ninth and 16th holes had been converted into par fours. Four holes were lengthened, bringing the yardage up to

18TH HOLE

6,873. Before the Open returned in 1974, George and Tom Fazio had built new tees on the fourth, 14th, and 18th holes to bring the yardage to 6,961. With seven par fours of at least 442 yards and two par threes of at least 212 players were complaining of wearing out their 2-irons. The Fazios also supervised the planting of trees on a number of holes to tighten the driving areas.

The bigger factor in the 1974 Open was the preparation of the course by superintendent Ted Horton. A few weeks before the championship, he said, "We'll try to make [the greens] as firm and fast as we possibly can, hoping we still have grass left when the members come to play the following Monday."

He wasn't kidding. The greens were like lightning, and the rough long and thick. Combined with Winged Foot's small greens, deep bunkers, and trees, that Open harkened back to torture tracks like Oakland Hills, Olympic, and Southern Hills in the 1950s.

Observed Dick Schaap in *Massacre at Winged Foot*, "Perhaps if A.W. Tillinghast had designed the Alamo, and the USGA had toughened it up, the Mexican siege would have failed."

On the first hole of the first round, Jack Nicklaus putted off the green on a 25-foot downhill putt. Instead of complaining, he said, "I wish we played a course like this every week. We'd learn how to putt."

The greens were so firm that even after somebody took a wrong turn trying to leave the club on Thursday night and drove his car right over the first green, the vehicle did so little damage that the players didn't even notice.

Hale Irwin had won only two tournaments at this point in his career, but he was already earning a reputation as a player who did well on tough courses. He cemented that reputation at Winged Foot, winning with a seven-over 287. Tom Watson, then a winless third-year player, led through 54 holes but closed with a 79, leaving Irwin to try to hold off Forrest Fezler.

Irwin's lead dwindled as he bogeyed 15 and 16, and he was in more trouble on 17, sitting 100 yards away from the green in two on the par four. From there, he finished like a champion, knocking a wedge to 10 feet and making the par putt, then hitting a 2-iron to 20 feet on 18 to clinch a two-stroke win.

The course wasn't quite as firm or formidable 10 years later. For some players, the biggest problem was getting there. The gallery was too large for the surrounding suburban road system and at times there were backups of nearly two hours getting into the club. On Thursday a number of players had to get out of their cars and walk—some carrying their clubs—to make their tee times.

Although the scoring was lower, this Open offered echoes of past championships at Winged Foot. As in 1974, the third-round leader shot 79 on Sunday, only this time the victim was Irwin. Winner Fuzzy Zoeller putted like Casper in making four straight birdies starting at the third hole of the final round. And like Jones, Greg Norman holed a dramatic putt on the 72nd hole to force a playoff—only his was a bomb from 50 feet for a third consecutive scrambling par.

Finally, there was another playoff blowout, with Zoeller beating Norman, 67-75. The two had tied at four-under 276, the only two players ever to break par over 72 holes at a Winged Foot Open.

Nobody came close to breaking par for the championship when the Open returned in 2006. Geoff Ogilvy won the survival test with a 285 total that was one ahead of Colin Montgomerie, Phil Mickelson, and Jim Furyk.

Along with Winged Foot's inherent difficulty, thick rough and relatively bumpy greens were the biggest factors in the high scoring this time as an over-par total won the Open for the first time in 28 years. In that sense, it was a fitting finish as only Ogilvy among the contenders parred the 18th hole on Sunday while the others failed to meet its various demands.

Furyk didn't get up and down from the left bunker, missing a five-foot putt and making a bogey. Montgomerie hit a poor iron shot short and right of the green, leaving a pitch that was impossible to get close, and he compounded the error by three-putting. Mickelson didn't come close to the fairway off the tee, hit a tree with his second shot, and couldn't find the green from the rough with his third. Both made double bogey.

While the finishing stretch is tough at Winged Foot, so is the opening sequence of four holes, especially since the second has been stretched to 453 yards. The first hole is one of the toughest openers in the game, 450 yards to the green that Nicklaus putted off in 1974. Like many holes at Winged Foot, a front pin is the most difficult.

The 216-yard third has a narrow green for such a long shot; Casper intentionally played short in every round here to avoid the right and left bunkers, and got up and down all four times. The 469-

yard fourth is another skinny green, this time with a narrow entrance between bunkers that wrap around the front.

The next three holes are birdie opportunities, especially the 515-yard fifth. The 321-yard sixth has a tiny green within range off the tee for long hitters, but the rough around the green holds some risk. The seventh is only 162 yards, but the deep bunker on the right is to be avoided at all costs.

The 188-yard 10th is Winged Foot's most famous hole and one of the best par threes in the world. Its length is unchanged since Winged Foot opened, which means it was especially tough in the early days. Tillinghast's description of the hole says the tee shot calls for a "high drifting iron, probably a 2, or a spoon," and in the 1950s Hogan described it as "a 3-iron into some guy's bedroom." (There is out of bounds, and a house, behind the green.) Today's players need less club, but they still need to be precise. The bunker to the right is cavernous and if your tee shot finds the green but is not close to the hole, three-putting is a strong possibility.

Tom Fazio has added 100 yards to the 12th to give the course a 640-yarder in keeping with Tillinghast's philosophy of building true three-shot par fives. Fazio's next-biggest addition was 40 yards to the 14th to bring it to 458, taking away what was a bit of a breather before the strong finish.

The 16th played at 478 yards for the 2006 Open. The hole bends to the left, but the drive should be played to the right center; a large maple tree near the green blocks approaches from the left.

The 449-yard 17th bends to the right and plays to a kidney-shaped green with typical Winged Foot bunkering. The 450-yard 18th completes a left-right-left sequence of doglegs at the finish. There are no bunkers to the right of the green, but a steep drop-off is just as effective. The green is one of the most treacherous on the course. "Missing this green with the second will likely run the score to one more than par for getting back dead is not easy," Tillinghast wrote.

There were two main reasons Winged Foot went 22 years between its last two Opens. (In the interim, the club hosted the 1997 PGA Championship, won by Davis Love III with an out-of-this-world 269 total.) One was the traffic problems of 1984. The second was that USGA officials felt the course had become choked by too many trees. The USGA could

HALE IRWIN

defuse traffic situations by moving parking away from the course. And though Winged Foot members were proud of their trees, they recognized that some of them had to go.

That was part of Fazio's redesign project in preparation for the 2004 U.S. Amateur. (Plenty of trees remain, as Mickelson's 2006 adventures attest.) The renovations also included restoring several greens to their original sizes to re-establish some lost pin positions close to the edges, rebuilding and reshaping all the bunkers, and adding yardage on a number of holes.

While Winged Foot now measures 7,264 yards, many of its par fours are no longer intimidating by virtue of their length. With no room to push back the tees on several holes in the 450-yard range, like the first, 17th, and 18th, pros were hitting middle and short irons into them in 2006 instead of the long irons they faced in 1974. Thanks to the genius of A.W. Tillinghast, however, that just makes it all the more frustrating when they can't make pars.

1929 TOP FINISHERS

•Bobby Jones	69-75-71-79—294
Al Espinosa	70-72-77-75—294
Gene Sarazen	71-71-76-78—296
Denny Shute	73-71-76-76—296
Tommy Armour	74-71-76-76—297
George Von Elm	79-70-74-74—297

•Jones won playoff, 72-69—141 to 84-80—164
Low round: Jones, 69

Scorecard

2006 U.S. Open

Hole	Par	Yardage	Avg.	Rank	Fwy. %	Green %	Putts
1	4	450	4.47	1	47.4	56.3	1.99
2	4	453	4.40	4	53.8	43.9	1.76
3	3	216	3.37	7		36.4	1.66
4	4	469	4.35	9	56.8	43.7	1.70
5	5	515	4.65	18	48.3	87.6	1.78
6	4	321	4.11	16	48.1	62.5	1.69
7	3	162	3.09	17		67.3	1.73
8	4	475	4.38	6	49.2	43.2	1.75
9	4	514	4.39	5	58.4	32.7	1.62
Out	35	3575	37.22		51.7	52.6	1.74
10	3	188	3.32	10		50.8	1.76
11	4	396	4.13	15	59.3	63.2	1.69
12	5	640	5.24	13	48.7	58.1	1.77
13	3	214	3.23	14		58.6	1.76
14	4	458	4.46	3	49.9	36.6	1.70
15	4	416	4.27	12	36.5	42.3	1.69
16	4	478	4.36	8	48.7	38.2	1.66
17	4	449	4.29	11	50.6	49.4	1.71
18	4	450	4.47	1	47.6	44.6	1.79
In	35	3689	37.77		50.2	51.2	1.73
Total	70	7264	74.99		51.5	49.2	1.75

GREG NORMAN AND FUZZY ZOELLER

1959 TOP FINISHERS

Billy Casper	71-68-69-74—282
Bob Rosburg	75-70-67-71—283
Claude Harmon	72-71-70-71—284
Mike Souchak	71-70-72-71—284
Doug Ford	72-69-72-73—286
Arnold Palmer	71-69-72-74—286
Ernie Vossler	72-70-72-72—286
Ben Hogan	69-71-71-76—287
Sam Snead	73-72-67-75—287
Dick Knight	69-75-73-73—290

Low round: Rosburg, Snead, 67

1974 TOP FINISHERS

Hale Irwin	73-70-71-73—287
Forrest Fezler	75-70-74-70—289
Lou Graham	71-75-74-70—290
Bert Yancey	76-69-73-72—290
Jim Colbert	72-77-69-74—292
Arnold Palmer	73-70-73-76—292
Tom Watson	73-71-69-79—292
Tom Kite	74-70-77-72—293
Gary Player	70-73-77-73—293
Brian Allin	76-71-74-73—294
Jack Nicklaus	75-74-76-69—294

Low round: Hubert Green, 67

1984 TOP FINISHERS

*Fuzzy Zoeller	71-66-69-70—276
Greg Norman	70-68-69-69—276
Curtis Strange	69-70-74-68—281
Johnny Miller	74-68-70-70—282
Jim Thorpe	68-71-70-73—282
Hale Irwin	68-68-69-79—284
Peter Jacobsen	72-73-73-67—285
Mark O'Meara	71-74-71-69—285
Fred Couples	69-71-74-72—286
Lee Trevino	71-72-69-74—286

*Zoeller won playoff, 67-75

Low round: Zoeller, 66

2006 TOP FINISHERS

Geoff Ogilvy	71-70-72-72—285
Jim Furyk	70-72-74-70—286
Colin Montgomerie	69-71-75-71—286
Phil Mickelson	70-73-69-74—286
Padraig Harrington	73-69-74-71—287
Nick O'Hern	75-70-74-69—288
Jeff Sluman	74-73-72-69—288
Mike Weir	71-74-71-72—288
Steve Stricker	70-69-76-73—288
Vijay Singh	71-74-70-73—288
Kenneth Ferrie	71-70-71-76—288

Low round: David Duval, Arron Oberholser, 68

18TH HOLE

WORCESTER COUNTRY CLUB WORCESTER, MASSACHUSETTS 1925

With few exceptions (Olympic comes to mind), the finishing hole of current U.S. Open

courses is a long par four. That often wasn't the case in the first few decades of the Open.

Worcester Country Club, for example, finished with a 335-yard par four in 1925. ¶ The little

hole provided plenty of drama, and more than its share of difficulty. Bobby Jones and Willie

Macfarlane had tied their first 18-hole playoff and were completing a second 18 in 100-degree

heat as they arrived on the 18th tee. Another tie seemed inevitable. ¶ But one hole earlier,

when writer/friend O.B. Keeler observed that a third playoff might be needed, Jones told him,

"There won't be another playoff. I'll settle it one way or another this round." After Macfarlane

hit his second shot safely 30 feet from the hole, Jones made a bold bid, trying to squeeze his

approach just over the front bunker to the front hole location. He came up just short, the ball

trickled into the bunker, and he lost to Macfarlane's par. ¶ At the end of the first playoff,

Macfarlane had a chance to win with a six-foot birdie putt; he missed the tough downhiller.

After a 30-minute meeting of USGA officials that ensued because they had no rule for a tied 18-hole playoff, they sent the players right back out for another round.

The 18th also proved a worthy finish in regulation play. Four players could have made birdie for a 291 total and a spot in the playoff. Johnny Farrell and Francis Ouimet made pars, Walter Hagen bogeyed, and poor Leo Diegel, who already had a reputation for throwing away tournaments, got caught in the rough and made eight.

Improbably, the 18th actually played easier for the Open, the result of a USGA suggestion after Open qualifying at Worcester in 1924—officials felt that the slope between the two levels of the green was too severe.

Macfarlane was a 34-year-old native of Scotland who preferred teaching to playing in tournaments. He shot an Open record 67 in the second round, blew the lead with a 78 in the final round, and made up a four-stroke deficit on Jones in the second playoff thanks to a 33 on the final nine. The victory helped convince him to become a more regular tournament player, and he would go on to record 21 victories.

This was the championship in which Jones famously called a penalty on himself when his ball moved slightly in the rough after he touched the grass with his club on the 11th hole of the first round. That penalty stroke cost him the title, but when praised for his sportsmanship, Jones responded that he might as well have been congratulated for not robbing a bank.

Because there were so many players with a chance on the final nine of regulation and both playoff rounds were drama-filled, William D. Richardson of the *New York Times* called it "easily the greatest Open championship of them all," a surprising assessment of a tournament that is overshadowed in today's history books by Ouimet's 1913 victory at the Country Club and Jones's 1923 triumph at Inwood.

Worcester was a short course even for the 1920s at 6,430 yards, but the Donald Ross design proved testing enough for the Open. Ross designed it in 1913 when the club, which had formed 13 years earlier, moved to its second site.

The club went on to host the inaugural Ryder Cup in 1927 and the U.S. Women's Open in 1960,

WILLIE MACFARLANE

Scorecard

Hole	Par	Yardage 1925	Yardage Today
1	4	375	380
2	5	570	558
3	4	375	372
4	3	235	232
5	5	450	478
6	3	180	179
7	4	400	398
8	3	175	177
9	4	405	410
Out	35	3165	3184
10	3	145	161
11	4	400	388
12	4	430	420
13	3	195	196
14	4	350	344
15	5	555	534
16	4	395	407
17	5/4	460	462
18	4	335	326
In	36/35	3265	3238
Total	71/70	6430	6422

becoming the only club to host those two events plus a U.S. Open. Donald Ross came back in 1929 with a plan for changes, including new tees and even some grading work on the fairways that he had been unable to carry out in 1913. Only some of the plans were implemented, so the routing from the 1925 Open remains intact.

The course is even shorter on the scorecard today at 6,422 yards, largely because of more accurate measurements. A few holes have been lengthened, though not by much. And the 18th, now listed at 326 yards, is essentially the same as when Jones made his costly bogey.

1925 TOP FINISHERS

•Willie Macfarlane	74-67-72-78—291
Bobby Jones	77-70-70-74—291
Johnny Farrell	71-74-69-78—292
Francis Ouimet	70-73-73-76—292
Walter Hagen	72-76-71-74—293
Gene Sarazen	72-72-75-74—293

•Macfarlane won playoff, 75-72—147 to 75-73—148
Low round: Macfarlane, 67

YEAR	WINNER RUNNER-UP	SCORE	SITE
1895	Horace Rawlins	173	Newport GC
	Willie Dunn		Newport, R.I.
1896	James Foulis	152	Shinnecock Hills GC (original)
	Horace Rawlins		Southampton, N.Y.
1897	Joe Lloyd	162	Chicago GC
	Willie Anderson		Wheaton, Ill.
1898	Fred Herd	328	Myopia Hunt Club
	Alex Smith		S. Hamilton, Mass.
1899	Willie Smith	315	Baltimore CC (Roland Park)
	George Low		Baltimore, Md.
	Val Fitzjohn		
	W.H. Way		
1900	Harry Vardon	313	Chicago GC
	J.H. Taylor		Wheaton, Ill.
1901	*Willie Anderson	331	Myopia Hunt Club
	Alex Smith		S. Hamilton, Mass.
1902	Laurie Auchterlonie	307	Garden City GC
	Stewart Gardner		Garden City, N.Y.
	Walter Travis		
1903	*Willie Anderson	307	Baltusrol GC (Old)
	David Brown		Springfield, N.J.
1904	Willie Anderson	303	Glen View Club
	Gilbert Nicholls		Golf, Ill.
1905	Willie Anderson	314	Myopia Hunt Club
	Alex Smith		S. Hamilton, Mass.
1906	Alex Smith	295	Onwentsia Club
	Willie Smith		Lake Forest, Ill.
1907	Alex Ross	302	Philadelphia Cricket Club
	Gilbert Nicholls		(St. Martins)
			Philadelphia, Pa.
1908	*Fred McLeod	322	Myopia Hunt Club
	Willie Smith		S. Hamilton, Mass.
1909	George Sargent	290	Englewood GC
	Tom McNamara		Englewood, N.J.
1910	*Alex Smith	298	Philadelphia Cricket Club
	John McDermott		(St. Martins)
	Macdonald Smith		Philadelphia, Pa.
1911	*John McDermott	307	Chicago GC
	Mike Brady		Wheaton, Ill.
	George Simpson		
1912	John McDermott	294	CC of Buffalo
	Tom McNamara		Buffalo, N.Y.
1913	*Francis Ouimet	304	The Country Club (Clyde)
	Harry Vardon		Brookline, Mass.
	Ted Ray		
1914	Walter Hagen	290	Midlothian CC
	Chick Evans		Blue Island, Ill.
1915	Jerry Travers	297	Baltusrol GC (Old)
	Tom McNamara		Springfield, N.J.
1916	Chick Evans	286	Minikahda Club
	Jock Hutchison		Minneapolis, Minn.
1917–18	No championships		
1919	*Walter Hagen	301	Brae Burn CC
	Mike Brady		W. Newton, Mass.
1920	Ted Ray	295	Inverness Club
	Harry Vardon		Toledo, Ohio
	Jack Burke Sr.		
	Leo Diegel		
1921	James Barnes	289	Columbia CC
	Walter Hagen		Chevy Chase, Md.
	Fred McLeod		
1922	Gene Sarazen	288	Skokie CC
	Bobby Jones		Glencoe, Ill.
	John Black		
1923	*Bobby Jones	296	Inwood CC
	Bobby Cruickshank		Inwood, N.Y.
1924	Cyril Walker	297	Oakland Hills CC (South)
	Bobby Jones		Bloomfield Hills, Mich.
1925	*Willie Macfarlane	291	Worcester CC
	Bobby Jones		Worcester, Mass.
1926	Bobby Jones	293	Scioto CC
	Joe Turnesa		Columbus, Ohio
1927	*Tommy Armour	301	Oakmont CC
	Harry Cooper		Oakmont, Pa.
1928	Johnny Farrell	294	Olympia Fields CC (No. 4)
	Bobby Jones		Olympia Fields, Ill.
1929	*Bobby Jones	294	Winged Foot GC (West)
	Al Espinosa		Mamaroneck, N.Y.
1930	Bobby Jones	287	Interlachen CC
	Macdonald Smith		Minneapolis, Minn.
1931	*Billy Burke	292	Inverness Club
	George Von Elm		Toledo, Ohio
1932	Gene Sarazen	286	Fresh Meadow CC
	Philip Perkins		Flushing, N.Y.
1933	John Goodman	287	North Shore CC
	Ralph Guldahl		Glenview, Ill.
1934	Olin Dutra	293	Merion Cricket Club (East)
	Gene Sarazen		Ardmore, Pa.
1935	Sam Parks Jr.	299	Oakmont CC
	Jimmy Thomson		Oakmont, Pa.
1936	Tony Manero	282	Baltusrol GC (Upper)
	Harry Cooper		Springfield, N.J.
1937	Ralph Guldahl	281	Oakland Hills CC (South)
	Sam Snead		Bloomfield Hills, Mich.
1938	Ralph Guldahl	284	Cherry Hills CC
	Dick Metz		Englewood, Colo.
1939	*Byron Nelson	284	Philadelphia CC (Spring Mill)
	Craig Wood		Gladwyne, Pa.
	Denny Shute		
1940	*Lawson Little	287	Canterbury GC
	Gene Sarazen		Cleveland, Ohio
1941	Craig Wood	284	Colonial CC
	Denny Shute		Fort Worth, Texas
1942–45	No championships		
1946	*Lloyd Mangrum	284	Canterbury GC
	Byron Nelson		Cleveland, Ohio
	Vic Ghezzi		
1947	*Lew Worsham	282	St. Louis CC
	Sam Snead		Ladue, Mo.
1948	Ben Hogan	276	Riviera CC
	Jimmy Demaret		Pacific Palisades, Calif.
1949	Cary Middlecoff	286	Medinah CC (No. 3)
	Sam Snead		Medinah, Ill.
	Clayton Heafner		
1950	*Ben Hogan	287	Merion GC (East)
	Lloyd Mangrum		Ardmore, Pa.
	George Fazio		
1951	Ben Hogan	287	Oakland Hills CC (South)
	Clayton Heafner		Bloomfield Hills, Mich.

Year	Player	Score	Venue
1952	Julius Boros	281	Northwood Club
	Ed Oliver		Dallas, Texas
1953	Ben Hogan	283	Oakmont CC,
	Sam Snead		Oakmont, Pa.
1954	Ed Furgol	284	Baltusrol GC (Lower)
	Gene Littler		Springfield, N.J.
1955	*Jack Fleck	287	Olympic Club (Lake)
	Ben Hogan		San Francisco, Calif.
1956	Cary Middlecoff	281	Oak Hill CC (East)
	Julius Boros		Rochester, N.Y.
	Ben Hogan		
1957	*Dick Mayer	282	Inverness Club
	Cary Middlecoff		Toledo, Ohio
1958	Tommy Bolt	283	Southern Hills CC
	Gary Player		Tulsa, Okla.
1959	Billy Casper	282	Winged Foot GC (West)
	Bob Rosburg		Mamaroneck, N.Y.
1960	Arnold Palmer	280	Cherry Hills CC
	Jack Nicklaus		Cherry Hills Village, Colo.
1961	Gene Littler	281	Oakland Hills CC (South)
	Doug Sanders		Bloomfield Hills, Mich.
	Bob Goalby		
1962	*Jack Nicklaus	283	Oakmont CC
	Arnold Palmer		Oakmont, Pa.
1963	*Julius Boros	293	The Country Club (Composite)
	Jacky Cupit		Brookline, Mass.
	Arnold Palmer		
1964	Ken Venturi	278	Congressional CC (Blue)
	Tommy Jacobs		Bethesda, Md.
1965	*Gary Player	282	Bellerive CC
	Kel Nagle		St. Louis, Mo.
1966	*Billy Casper	278	Olympic Club (Lake)
	Arnold Palmer		San Francisco, Calif.
1967	Jack Nicklaus	275	Baltusrol GC (Lower)
	Arnold Palmer		Springfield, N.J.
1968	Lee Trevino	275	Oak Hill CC (East)
	Jack Nicklaus		Rochester, N.Y.
1969	Orville Moody	281	Champions GC (Cypress Creek)
	Deane Beman		Houston, Texas
	Al Geiberger		
	Bob Rosburg		
1970	Tony Jacklin	281	Hazeltine National GC
	Dave Hill		Chaska, Minn.
1971	*Lee Trevino	280	Merion GC (East)
	Jack Nicklaus		Ardmore, Pa.
1972	Jack Nicklaus	290	Pebble Beach GL
	Bruce Crampton		Pebble Beach, Calif.
1973	Johnny Miller	279	Oakmont CC
	John Schlee		Oakmont, Pa.
1974	Hale Irwin	287	Winged Foot GC (West)
	Forrest Fezler		Mamaroneck, N.Y.
1975	*Lou Graham	287	Medinah CC (No. 3)
	John Mahaffey		Medinah, Ill.
1976	Jerry Pate	277	Atlanta Athletic Club (Highlands)
	Tom Weiskopf		Duluth, Ga.
	Al Geiberger		
1977	Hubert Green	278	Southern Hills CC
	Lou Graham		Tulsa, Okla.
1978	Andy North	285	Cherry Hills CC
	J.C. Snead		Cherry Hills Village, Colo.
	Dave Stockton		
1979	Hale Irwin	284	Inverness Club
	Gary Player		Toledo, Ohio
1980	Jack Nicklaus	272	Baltusrol GC (Lower)
	Isao Aoki		Springfield, N.J.
1981	David Graham	273	Merion GC (East)
	Bill Rogers		Ardmore, Pa.
	George Burns		
1982	Tom Watson	282	Pebble Beach GL
	Jack Nicklaus		Pebble Beach, Calif.
1983	Larry Nelson	280	Oakmont CC
	Tom Watson		Oakmont, Pa.
1984	*Fuzzy Zoeller	276	Winged Foot GC (West)
	Greg Norman		Mamaroneck, N.Y.
1985	Andy North	279	Oakland Hills CC (South)
	Denis Watson		Bloomfield Hills, Mich.
	Dave Barr		
	T.C. Chen		
1986	Raymond Floyd	279	Shinnecock Hills GC
	Lanny Wadkins		Southampton, N.Y.
	Chip Beck		
1987	Scott Simpson	277	Olympic Club (Lake)
	Tom Watson		San Francisco, Calif.
1988	*Curtis Strange	278	The Country Club (Composite)
	Nick Faldo		Brookline, Mass.
1989	Curtis Strange	278	Oak Hill CC (East)
	Ian Woosnam		Rochester, N.Y.
	Chip Beck		
	Mark McCumber		
1990	*Hale Irwin	280	Medinah CC (No. 3)
	Mike Donald		Medinah, Ill.
1991	*Payne Stewart	282	Hazeltine National GC
	Scott Simpson		Chaska, Minn.
1992	Tom Kite	285	Pebble Beach GL
	Jeff Sluman		Pebble Beach, Calif.
1993	Lee Janzen	272	Baltusrol GC (Lower)
	Payne Stewart		Springfield, N.J.
1994	*Ernie Els	279	Oakmont CC
	Loren Roberts		Oakmont, Pa.
	Colin Montgomerie		
1995	Corey Pavin	280	Shinnecock Hills GC
	Greg Norman		Southampton, N.Y.
1996	Steve Jones	278	Oakland Hills CC (South)
	Davis Love III		Bloomfield Hills, Mich.
	Tom Lehman		
1997	Ernie Els	276	Congressional CC (Blue)
	Colin Montgomerie		Bethesda, Md.
1998	Lee Janzen	280	Olympic Club (Lake)
	Payne Stewart		San Francisco, Calif.
1999	Payne Stewart	279	Pinehurst Resort & CC (No. 2)
	Phil Mickelson		Pinehurst, N.C.
2000	Tiger Woods	272	Pebble Beach GL
	Ernie Els		Pebble Beach, Calif.
	Miguel Angel Jimenez		
2001	*Retief Goosen	276	Southern Hills CC
	Mark Brooks		Tulsa, Okla.
2002	Tiger Woods	277	Bethpage State Park (Black)
	Phil Mickelson		Farmingdale, N.Y.
2003	Jim Furyk	272	Olympia Fields CC (North)
	Stephen Leaney		Olympia Fields, Ill.
2004	Retief Goosen	276	Shinnecock Hills GC
	Phil Mickelson		Southampton, N.Y.
2005	Michael Campbell	280	Pinehurst Resort & CC (No. 2)
	Tiger Woods		Pinehurst, N.C.
2006	Geoff Ogilvy	285	Winged Foot GC (West)
	Jim Furyk		Mamaroneck, N.Y.
	Colin Montgomerie		
	Phil Mickelson		

*Won in playoff

U.S. OPEN RECORDS

SCORING

LOWEST SCORE, 72 HOLES
272—Jack Nicklaus (63-71-70-68), Baltusrol GC (Lower), 1980
272—Lee Janzen (67-67-69-69), Baltusrol GC (Lower), 1993
272—Tiger Woods (65-69-71-67), Pebble Beach GL, 2000
272—Jim Furyk (67-66-67-72), Olympia Fields CC (North), 2003
273—David Graham (68-68-70-67), Merion GC (East), 1981

MOST STROKES UNDER PAR, 72 HOLES
12 under (272)—Tiger Woods, Pebble Beach GL, 2000
 8 under (272)—Jack Nicklaus, Baltusrol GC (Lower), 1980
 8 under (272)—Lee Janzen, Baltusrol GC (Lower), 1993
 8 under (272)—Jim Furyk, Olympia Fields CC (North), 2003
 8 under (276)—Ben Hogan, Riviera CC, 1948
 8 under (280)—Hale Irwin, Medinah CC (No. 3), 1990
 8 under (280)—Mike Donald, Medinah CC (No. 3), 1990

MOST STROKES UNDER PAR AT ANY POINT
12 under—Tiger Woods (fourth round), Pebble Beach GL, 2000
12 under—Gil Morgan (third round), Pebble Beach GL, 1992
11 under—Jim Furyk (fourth round), Olympia Fields CC (North), 2003

LOWEST SCORE BY NON-WINNER, 72 HOLES
274—Isao Aoki (68-68-68-70), Baltusrol GC (Lower), 1980
274—Payne Stewart (70-66-68-70), Baltusrol GC (Lower), 1993

MOST STROKES UNDER PAR BY NON-WINNER, 72 HOLES
8 under (280)—Mike Donald, Medinah CC (No. 3), 1990

LOWEST SCORE, FIRST 54 HOLES
*200—Jim Furyk (67-66-67), Olympia Fields CC (North), 2003
203—George Burns (69-66-68), Merion GC (East), 1981
203—Tze-Chung Chen (65-69-69), Oakland Hills CC (South), 1985
203—Lee Janzen (67-67-69), Baltusrol CC (Lower), 1993
203—Stephen Leaney (67-68-68), Olympia Fields CC (North), 2003
*Also most strokes under par, 54 holes (10 under)

LOWEST SCORE, LAST 54 HOLES
*203—Loren Roberts (69-64-70), Oakmont CC, 1994
204—Payne Stewart (70-66-68), Baltusrol GC (Lower), 1993
204—Steve Jones (66-69-69), Oakland Hills CC (South), 1996
204—Mark Brooks (64-70-70), Southern Hills CC, 2001
*Also most strokes under par, last 54 holes (10 under)

LOWEST SCORE, FIRST 36 HOLES
133—Jim Furyk (67-66), Olympia Fields CC (North), 2003
133—Vijay Singh (70-63), Olympia Fields CC (North), 2003
134—Jack Nicklaus (63-71), Baltusrol GC (Lower), 1980
134—Tze-Chung Chen (65-69), Oakland Hills CC (South), 1985
134—Lee Janzen (67-67), Baltusrol (Lower), 1993
134—Tiger Woods (65-69), Pebble Beach GL, 2000
134—Phil Mickelson (68-66), Shinnecock Hills GC, 2004
134—Shigeki Maruyama (66-68), Shinnecock Hills GC, 2004

MOST STROKES UNDER PAR, FIRST 36 HOLES
9 under (135)—Tim Simpson, Medinah CC (No. 3), 1990
9 under (135)—Gil Morgan, Pebble Beach GL, 1992

LOWEST SCORE, LAST 36 HOLES
*132—Larry Nelson (65-67), Oakmont CC, 1983
133—Chip Beck (68-65), Shinnecock Hills GC, 1986
134—Loren Roberts (64-70), Oakmont CC, 1994
*Also most strokes under par, last 36 holes (10 under)

LOWEST SCORE, MIDDLE 36 HOLES
*133—Loren Roberts (69-64), Oakmont CC, 1994
133—Jim Furyk (66-67), Olympia Fields CC (North), 2003
*Also most strokes under par, middle 36 holes (9 under)

LOWEST SCORE, 18 HOLES
*63—Johnny Miller, Oakmont CC, 1973, fourth round
63—Jack Nicklaus, Baltusrol GC (Lower), 1980, first round
63—Tom Weiskopf, Baltusrol GC (Lower), 1980, first round
63—Vijay Singh, Olympia Fields CC (North), 2003, second round
*Also most strokes under par, 18 holes (8 under)

LOWEST SCORE, 9 HOLES
29—Neal Lancaster, Shinnecock Hills GC, 1995, fourth round, second nine
29—Neal Lancaster, Oakland Hills CC (South), 1996, second round, second nine
29—Vijay Singh, Olympia Fields CC (North), 2003, second round, second nine

MOST CONSECUTIVE BIRDIES
6—George Burns, Pebble Beach GL (holes 2-7), 1982
6—Andy Dillard, Pebble Beach GL (holes 1-6), 1992

MOST CONSECUTIVE 3S
8—Hubert Green, Baltusrol GC (Lower) (holes 9-16), 1980
7—Hubert Green, Southern Hills CC (holes 10-16), 1977
7—Peter Jacobsen, The Country Club (Composite) (holes 1-7), 1988

LARGEST 54-HOLE LEAD
10—Tiger Woods (205), Pebble Beach GL, 2000
 7—James Barnes (217), Columbia CC, 1921
 6—Fred Herd (224), Myopia Hunt Club, 1898
 6—Willie Anderson (225), Baltusrol GC (Old), 1903
 6—Johnny Goodman (211), North Shore GC, 1933

LARGEST 54-HOLE LEAD, NON-WINNER
5—Mike Brady, Brae Burn CC, 1919

LARGEST 36-HOLE LEAD
6—Tiger Woods (134), Pebble Beach GL, 2000
5—Willie Anderson (149), Baltusrol GC (Old), 1903
*4—Tom McNamara (142), Englewood GC, 1909
4—James Barnes (144), Columbia CC, 1921
* Did not win

LARGEST 18-HOLE LEAD
*5—Tommy Armour (68), North Shore CC, 1933
*4—Olin Dutra (69), Fresh Meadow CC, 1932
* Did not win

BEST COMEBACK BY WINNER, FINAL ROUND
7 strokes—Arnold Palmer (65), Cherry Hills CC, 1960
6 strokes—Johnny Miller (63), Oakmont CC, 1973
5 strokes—Johnny Farrell (72), Olympia Fields CC (No. 4), 1928
5 strokes—Byron Nelson (68), Philadelphia CC (Spring Mill), 1939
5 strokes—Lee Janzen (68), Olympic Club (Lake), 1998

BEST COMEBACK BY WINNER, FINAL 36 HOLES
11 strokes—Lou Graham, Medinah CC (No. 3), 1975

BEST COMEBACK BY WINNER, FINAL 54 HOLES
9 strokes—Jack Fleck, Olympic Club (Lake), 1955

LARGEST WINNING MARGIN
15 strokes—Tiger Woods (272), Pebble Beach GL, 2000
11 strokes—Willie Smith (315), Baltimore CC (Roland Park), 1899
9 strokes—James Barnes (289), Columbia CC, 1921

FOUR SUB-PAR ROUNDS IN ONE CHAMPIONSHIP
4—Lee Trevino, Oak Hill CC (East), 1968
4—Tony Jacklin, Hazeltine National GC, 1970
4—Lee Janzen, Baltusrol GC (Lower), 1993
*4—Curtis Strange, Oakmont CC, 1994
*Did not win

FOUR ROUNDS IN THE 60S IN ONE CHAMPIONSHIP

4—Lee Trevino, Oak Hill CC (East), 1968
4—Lee Janzen, Baltusrol GC (Lower), 1993

LOWEST SCORE BY WINNER, FIRST ROUND

63 (7 under)—Jack Nicklaus, Baltusrol GC (Lower), 1980

HIGHEST SCORE BY WINNER, FIRST ROUND

91—Horace Rawlins, Newport GC, 1895
Since World War I
78—Walter Hagen, Brae Burn CC, 1919
78—Tommy Armour, Oakmont CC, 1927
Since World War II
76—Ben Hogan, Oakland Hills CC (South), 1951
76—Jack Fleck, Olympic Club (Lake), 1955

LOWEST SCORE BY WINNER, SECOND ROUND

64—Curtis Strange, Oak Hill (East), 1989

HIGHEST SCORE BY WINNER, SECOND ROUND

85—Fred Herd, Myopia Hunt Club, 1898
Since World War I
79—Bobby Jones, Scioto CC, 1926
Since World War II
74—Julius Boros, The Country Club (Composite), 1963

LOWEST SCORE BY WINNER, THIRD ROUND

65—Larry Nelson, Oakmont CC, 1983

HIGHEST SCORE BY WINNER, THIRD ROUND

83—Willie Anderson, Myopia Hunt Club, 1901
Since World War I
76—Bobby Jones, Inwood CC, 1923
76—Tommy Armour, Oakmont CC, 1927
76—Julius Boros, The Country Club (Composite), 1963
76—Johnny Miller, Oakmont CC, 1973

LOWEST SCORE BY WINNER, FOURTH ROUND

63—Johnny Miller, Oakmont CC, 1973
65—Arnold Palmer, Cherry Hills CC, 1960
65—Jack Nicklaus, Baltusrol GC (Lower), 1967

HIGHEST SCORE BY WINNER, FOURTH ROUND

84—Fred Herd, Myopia Hunt Club, 1898
Since World War I
79—Bobby Jones, Winged Foot GC (West), 1929
Since World War II
75—Cary Middlecoff, Medinah CC (No. 3), 1949
75—Hale Irwin, Inverness Club, 1979

HIGHEST SCORE TO LEAD FIELD, 18 HOLES

89—Willie Dunn, James Foulis, and Willie Campbell, Newport GC, 1895
Since World War I
73—Harry Hampton and Harrison Johnston, Oakmont CC, 1927
Since World War II
71—Sam Snead, Oakland Hills CC (South), 1951
71—Tommy Bolt, Julius Boros, and Dick Metz, Southern Hills CC, 1958
71—Tony Jacklin, Hazeltine National GC, 1970
71—Orville Moody, Jack Nicklaus, Chi Chi Rodriguez, Mason Rudolph, Tom Shaw, and Kermit Zarley, Pebble Beach GL, 1972

HIGHEST SCORE TO LEAD FIELD, 36 HOLES

173—Horace Rawlins (91-82), Newport GC, 1895 (Open played over 36 holes)
164—Alex Smith (82-82), Myopia Hunt Club, 1901 (Open played over 72 holes)
Since World War I
148—Mike Brady (74-74), Brae Burn CC, 1919
Since World War II
144—Bobby Locke (73-71), Oakland Hills CC (South), 1951
144—Tommy Bolt (67-77) and E. Harvie Ward (74-70), Olympic Club (Lake), 1955
144—Homero Blancas (74-70), Bruce Crampton (74-70), Jack Nicklaus (71-73), Cesar Sanudo (72-72), Lanny Wadkins (76-68), and Kermit Zarley (71-73), Pebble Beach GL, 1972

HIGHEST SCORE TO LEAD FIELD, 54 HOLES

249—Stewart Gardner (86-82-81), Myopia Hunt Club, 1901
Since World War I
224—Harry Cooper (74-76-74), Oakmont CC, 1927
Since World War II
218—Bobby Locke (73-71-74), Oakland Hills CC (South), 1951
218—Jacky Cupit (70-72-76), The Country Club (Composite), 1963

HIGHEST WINNING SCORE

331—Willie Anderson (84-83-83-81), Myopia Hunt Club, 1901
Since World War I
301—Walter Hagen (78-73-75-75), Brae Burn CC, 1919
301—Tommy Armour (78-71-76-76), Oakmont CC, 1927
Since World War II
293—Julius Boros (71-74-76-72), The Country Club (Composite), 1963

EVOLUTION OF THE 18-HOLE SCORING RECORD

*74—James Foulis, Shinnecock Hills GC (original), 1896
73—Gilbert Nicholls, Garden City GC, 1902; Willie Anderson, Baltusrol GC (Old), 1903
72—Willie Anderson, Glen View Club, 1904; Alex Campbell, Glen View Club, 1904; Gilbert Nicholls, Philadelphia Cr. Club (St. Martins), 1907
68—David Hunter, Englewood GC, 1909; Walter Hagen, Midlothian CC, 1914; Jock Hutchison, Minikahda Club, 1916; Walter Hagen, Skokie CC, 1922; Gene Sarazen, Skokie CC, 1922
67—Willie Macfarlane, Worcester CC, 1925
66—Gene Sarazen, Fresh Meadow CC, 1932; Johnny Goodman, North Shore CC, 1933; Tom Creavy, Merion Cr. Club (East), 1934; Jimmy Thomson, Oakland Hills CC (South), 1937; Clayton Heafner, Philadelphia CC (Spring Mill), 1939
65—James McHale, St. Louis CC, 1947
64—Lee Mackey, Merion GC (East), 1950; Tommy Jacobs, Congressional CC (Blue), 1964; Rives McBee, Olympic Club (Lake), 1966
63—Johnny Miller, Oakmont CC, 1973; Jack Nicklaus, Baltusrol GC (Lower), 1980; Tom Weiskopf, Baltusrol (Lower), 1980; Vijay Singh, Olympia Fields (North), 2003
*First championship contested on 18-hole course

EVOLUTION OF THE 72-HOLE SCORING RECORD

*328—Fred Herd, Myopia Hunt Club, 1898
315—Willie Smith, Baltimore CC (Roland Park), 1899
313—Harry Vardon, Chicago GC, 1900
307—Laurie Auchterlonie, Garden City GC, 1902
303—Willie Anderson, Glen View Club, 1904
295—Alex Smith, Onwentsia Club, 1906
290—George Sargent, Englewood GC, 1909
286—Charles Evans Jr., Minikahda Club, 1916
282—Tony Manero, Baltusrol GC (Upper), 1936
281—Ralph Guldahl, Oakland Hills CC (South), 1937
276—Ben Hogan, Riviera CC, 1948
275—Jack Nicklaus, Baltusrol GC (Lower), 1967
272—Jack Nicklaus, Baltusrol GC (Lower), 1980; Lee Janzen, Baltusrol GC (Lower), 1993; Tiger Woods, Pebble Beach GL, 2000; Jim Furyk, Olympia Fields CC (North), 2003
*First 72-hole championship

INDIVIDUAL

MOST VICTORIES

4—Willie Anderson (1901, 1903, 1904, 1905)
4—Bobby Jones (1923, 1926, 1929, 1930)
4—Ben Hogan (1948, 1950, 1951, 1953)
4—Jack Nicklaus (1962, 1967, 1972, 1980)
3—Hale Irwin (1974, 1979, 1990)

MOST CONSECUTIVE VICTORIES

3—Willie Anderson (1903, 1904, 1905)
2—John McDermott (1911, 1912)
2—Bobby Jones (1929, 1930)
2—Ralph Guldahl (1937, 1938)
2—Ben Hogan (1950, 1951)
2—Curtis Strange (1988, 1989)

MOST RUNNER-UP FINISHES

4—Bobby Jones (1922, 1924, 1925, 1928)
*4—Sam Snead (1937, 1947, 1949, 1953)
4—Arnold Palmer (1962, 1963, 1966, 1967)
4—Jack Nicklaus (1960, 1968, 1971, 1982)
*4—Phil Mickelson (1999, 2002, 2004, 2006)
3—Alex Smith (1898, 1901, 1905)
*3—Tom McNamara (1908, 1912, 1915)
*3—Colin Montgomerie (1994, 1997, 2006)
*Never won championship

MOST TOP-10 FINISHES

18—Jack Nicklaus
16—Walter Hagen
15—Ben Hogan
14—Gene Sarazen
13—Arnold Palmer
*12—Sam Snead
11—Willie Anderson
11—Julius Boros
11—Alex Smith
11—Tom Watson
10—Bobby Jones
*Never won championship

MOST OPENS STARTED
44—Jack Nicklaus
33—Hale Irwin
33—Gene Sarazen
32—Arnold Palmer
31—Sam Snead

MOST CONSECUTIVE OPENS STARTED
44—Jack Nicklaus, 1957–2000
33—Hale Irwin, 1971–2003

MOST OPENS COMPLETED 72 HOLES
35—Jack Nicklaus
27—Sam Snead
27—Hale Irwin

LONGEST SPAN, FIRST TO LAST VICTORY
18 years—Jack Nicklaus, 1962–80

LONGEST SPAN BETWEEN VICTORIES
11 years—Julius Boros, 1952–63; Hale Irwin, 1979–90

MOST SUB-PAR ROUNDS, CAREER
37—Jack Nicklaus

MOST CONSECUTIVE SUB-PAR ROUNDS
6—Sam Snead, 1947–48 (includes 18-hole playoff)
5—Brian Claar, 1989–90
5—Curtis Strange, 1993–94

MOST ROUNDS IN THE 60S, CAREER
29—Jack Nicklaus

MOST CONSECUTIVE ROUNDS IN THE 60S
4—Lee Trevino, 1968
4—Ben Crenshaw, 1986–87
4—Lee Janzen, 1993
4—Tiger Woods, 2001–02

MOST SUB-PAR 72-HOLE TOTALS
7—Jack Nicklaus

MOST CONSECUTIVE SUB-PAR TOTALS
3—Curtis Strange, 1988–90

MOST TIMES LED AFTER 54 HOLES
6—Bobby Jones
4—Tom Watson

MOST TIMES LED AFTER 18, 36, OR 54 HOLES
11—Payne Stewart
10—Alex Smith

START-TO-FINISH LEADERS (NO TIES)
Walter Hagen, 1914; James Barnes, 1921; Ben Hogan, 1953; Tony Jacklin, 1970; Tiger Woods, 2000

START-TO-FINISH LEADERS (INCLUDING TIES)
Willie Anderson, 1903; Alex Smith, 1906; Charles Evans Jr., 1916; Tommy Bolt, 1958; Jack Nicklaus, 1972, 1980; Hubert Green, 1977; Payne Stewart, 1991; Retief Goosen, 2001 (not including names from previous category)

PLAYERS WHO LED FIRST THREE ROUNDS BUT DIDN'T WIN
*Willie Smith, 1908; Mike Brady, 1912; *Mike Souchak, 1960; *Bert Yancey, 1968; Hale Irwin, 1984; Tze-Chung Chen, 1985; *Gil Morgan, 1992; *Payne Stewart, 1998
*No ties

WON FIRST TIME PLAYED IN OPEN
Horace Rawlins, 1895; Fred Herd, 1898; Harry Vardon, 1900; George Sargent, 1909; Francis Ouimet, 1913

OLDEST CHAMPION (YEARS/MONTHS/DAYS)
45/0/15—Hale Irwin, 1990
43/9/11—Ray Floyd, 1986
43/4/16—Ted Ray, 1920

YOUNGEST CHAMPION
19/10/14—John McDermott, 1911
20/4/12—Francis Ouimet, 1913
20/4/16—Gene Sarazen, 1922

COURSE

MOST U.S. OPENS HOSTED (COURSE)
7—Oakmont CC
6—Oakland Hills CC (South)
5—Winged Foot GC (West)
4—Myopia Hunt Club, Inverness Club, Merion GC (East), Baltusrol GC (Lower), Olympic Club (Lake), Pebble Beach GL

MOST U.S. OPENS HOSTED (CLUB)
7—Baltusrol GC*, Oakmont CC
6—Oakland Hills CC
*Four on Lower Course, two on Old Course, one on Upper Course

LONGEST COURSES
7,264 yards—Winged Foot GC (West), 2006
7,214 yards—Bethpage State Park (Black), 2002
7,214 yards—Pinehurst Resort & CC (No. 2), 2005
7,213 yards—Congressional CC (Blue), 1997
7,195 yards—Medinah CC (No. 3), 1990
7,191 yards—Bellerive CC, 1965

SHORTEST COURSES
4,423 yards—Shinnecock Hills GC (original), 1896
Since World War II
6,528 yards—Merion GC (East), 1971, 1981

LONGEST HOLES
642 yards—5th, Southern Hills CC, 2001
640 yards—12th, Winged Foot GC (West), 2006
630 yards—16th, Olympic Club (Lake), 1955
630 yards—17th, Baltusrol GC (Lower), 1993

FEWEST SUB-PAR ROUNDS, CHAMPIONSHIP
Since World War I
0—Brae Burn CC, 1919
1—Oakland Hills CC (South), 1924
1—Merion Cr. Club (East), 1934
Since World War II
2—Oakland Hills CC (South), 1951

FEWEST SUB-PAR ROUNDS, FIRST ROUND
Since World War II
0—Oakland Hills CC (South), 1951; Southern Hills CC, 1958; Winged Foot GC (West), 1974; Shinnecock Hills GC, 1986

FEWEST SUB-PAR ROUNDS, SECOND ROUND
Since World War II
0—Oakland Hills CC (South), 1951

FEWEST SUB-PAR ROUNDS, THIRD ROUND
Since World War II
0—Oakland Hills CC (South), 1951; The Country Club (Composite), 1963

FEWEST SUB-PAR ROUNDS, FOURTH ROUND
0—Merion GC (East), 1950; Northwood Club, 1952; Winged Foot GC (West), 1959; The Country Club (Composite), 1963

HIGHEST 36-HOLE CUT
Since World War II
155 (15 over)—Olympic Club (Lake), 1955

LOWEST 36-HOLE CUT
143 (3 over)—Olympia Fields CC (North), 2003

LOWEST 36-HOLE CUT, RELATIVE TO PAR
145 (1 over)—Medinah CC (No. 3), 1990

MOST SUB-PAR ROUNDS, CHAMPIONSHIP
124—Medinah CC (No. 3), 1990
83—Olympia Fields (North), 2003
76—Pebble Beach GL, 1992
76—Baltusrol GC (Lower), 1993

MOST ROUNDS IN THE 60S, CHAMPIONSHIP
83—Olympia Fields CC (North), 2003
76—Baltusrol GC (Lower), 1993
58—Merion GC (East), 1981
54—Oak Hill CC (East), 1989

MOST SUB-PAR 72 HOLE TOTALS, CHAMPIONSHIP
28—Medinah CC (No. 3), 1990
11—The Country Club (Composite), 1988
10—Baltusrol GC (Lower), 1993

MOST SUB-PAR ROUNDS, FIRST ROUND
39—Medinah CC (No. 3), 1990
29—Pebble Beach GL, 1992
24—Olympia Fields (North), 2003

MOST SUB-PAR ROUNDS, SECOND ROUND
47—Medinah CC (No. 3), 1990
38—Olympia Fields CC (North), 2003
33—Hazeltine National GC, 1991

MOST SUB-PAR ROUNDS, THIRD ROUND
24—Medinah CC (No. 3), 1990
22—Pebble Beach GL, 1982
18—Baltusrol GC (Lower), 1993

MOST SUB-PAR ROUNDS, FOURTH ROUND
18—Baltusrol GC (Lower), 1993
17—Pebble Beach GL, 1982
17—The Country Club (Composite), 1988

LOWEST SCORING AVERAGE, CHAMPIONSHIP

72.10 (2.10 over)—Baltusrol GC (Lower), 1993

72.38 (2.38 over)—Olympia Fields CC (North), 2003

73.14 (3.14 over)—Oakland Hills CC (South), 1996

73.27 (3.27 over)—Southern Hills CC, 2001

73.40 (3.40 over)—Oak Hill CC (East), 1989

LOWEST SCORING AVERAGE RELATIVE TO PAR, CHAMPIONSHIP

73.46 (1.46 over)—Medinah CC (No. 3), 1990

72.10 (2.10 over)—Baltusrol GC (Lower), 1993

72.38 (2.38 over)—Olympia Fields CC (North), 2003

74.80 (2.80 over)—Hazeltine National GC, 1991

73.87 (2.87 over)—The Country Club (Composite), 1988

LOWEST SCORING AVERAGE, FIRST ROUND

72.3 (2.3 over)—Baltusrol GC (Lower), 1993

72.7 (2.7 over)—Olympia Fields CC (North), 2003

72.9 (2.9 over)—Pinehurst Resort & CC (No. 2), 1999

LOWEST SCORING AVERAGE RELATIVE TO PAR, FIRST ROUND

73.7 (1.7 over)—Medinah CC (No. 3), 1990

72.3 (2.3 over)—Baltusrol GC (Lower), 1993

74.5 (2.5 over)—Pebble Beach GL, 1992

LOWEST SCORING AVERAGE, SECOND ROUND

71.9 (1.9 over)—Olympia Fields CC (North), 2003

72.4 (2.4 over)—Baltusrol GC (Lower), 1993

73.0 (3.0 over)—Oakland Hills CC (South), 1996

73.0 (3.0 over)—Shinnecock Hills GC, 2004

LOWEST SCORING AVERAGE RELATIVE TO PAR, SECOND ROUND

73.5 (1.5 over)—Medinah CC (No. 3), 1990

74.3 (2.3 over)—Hazeltine National GC, 1991

72.4 (2.4 over)—Baltusrol GC (Lower), 1993

LOWEST SCORING AVERAGE, THIRD ROUND

71.5 (1.5 over)—Merion GC (East), 1981

71.7 (1.7 over)—Shinnecock Hills GC, 1986

71.8 (1.8 over)—Baltusrol GC (Lower), 1993

LOWEST SCORING AVERAGE RELATIVE TO PAR, THIRD ROUND

72.3 (0.3 over)—Medinah CC (No. 3), 1990

73.0 (1.0 over)—Pebble Beach GL, 1982

71.5 (1.5 over)—Merion GC (East), 1981

LOWEST SCORING AVERAGE, FOURTH ROUND

71.6 (1.6 over)—Baltusrol GC (Lower), 1993

72.0 (2.0 over)—Shinnecock Hills GC, 1986

72.0 (1.0 over)—The Country Club (Composite), 1988

LOWEST SCORING AVERAGE RELATIVE TO PAR, FOURTH ROUND

72.0 (1.0 over)—The Country Club (Composite), 1988

71.6 (1.6 over)—Baltusrol GC (Lower), 1993

73.9 (1.9 over)—Pebble Beach GL, 1982

HIGHEST SCORING AVERAGE, CHAMPIONSHIP

Since World War II

78.72 (8.72 over)—Olympic Club (Lake), 1955

77.92 (7.92 over)—Southern Hills CC, 1957

77.79 (5.79 over)—Pebble Beach GL, 1972

77.55 (6.55 over)—The Country Club (Composite), 1963

77.23 (7.23 over)—Oakland Hills CC (South), 1951

HIGHEST SCORING AVERAGE RELATIVE TO PAR, CHAMPIONSHIP

Since World War II

78.72 (8.72 over)—Olympic Club (Lake), 1955

77.92 (7.92 over)—Southern Hills CC, 1957

77.23 (7.23 over)—Oakland Hills CC (South), 1951

77.10 (7.10 over)—Baltusrol GC (Lower), 1954

77.04 (7.04 over)—Northwood Club, 1952

HIGHEST SCORING AVERAGE, FIRST ROUND

Since World War II

79.8 (9.8 over)—Olympic Club (Lake), 1955

79.7 (9.7 over)—Southern Hills CC, 1957

79.1 (7.1 over)—Hazeltine National GC, 1970

HIGHEST SCORING AVERAGE RELATIVE TO PAR, FIRST ROUND

Since World War II

79.8 (9.8 over)—Olympic Club (Lake), 1955

79.7 (9.7 over)—Southern Hills CC, 1957

78.8 (8.8 over)—Baltusrol GC (Lower), 1954

HIGHEST SCORING AVERAGE, SECOND ROUND

Since World War II

78.9 (8.9 over)—Olympic Club (Lake), 1955

78.5 (8.5 over)—Southern Hills CC, 1957

77.9 (5.9 over)—Pebble Beach GL, 1972

HIGHEST SCORING AVERAGE RELATIVE TO PAR, SECOND ROUND

Since World War II

78.9 (8.9 over)—Olympic Club (Lake), 1955

78.5 (8.5 over)—Southern Hills CC, 1957

77.7 (7.7 over)—Northwood Club, 1952

HIGHEST SCORING AVERAGE, THIRD ROUND

Since World War II

78.2 (7.2 over)—The Country Club (Composite), 1963

77.1 (6.1 over)—Pebble Beach GL, 2000

76.8 (6.8 over)—Olympic Club (Lake), 1955

HIGHEST SCORING AVERAGE RELATIVE TO PAR, THIRD ROUND

Since World War II

78.2 (7.2 over)—The Country Club (Composite), 1963

76.8 (6.8 over)—Olympic Club (Lake), 1955

76.2 (6.2 over)—Winged Foot GC (West), 1974

HIGHEST SCORING AVERAGE, FOURTH ROUND

Since World War II

78.8 (6.8 over)—Pebble Beach GL, 1972

78.8 (8.7 over)—Shinnecock Hills GC, 2004

77.4 (6.4 over)—The Country Club (Composite), 1963

HIGHEST SCORING AVERAGE RELATIVE TO PAR, FOURTH ROUND

Since World War II

78.7 (8.7 over)—Shinnecock Hills GC, 2004

78.8 (6.8 over)—Pebble Beach GL, 1972

76.6 (6.6 over)—Olympic Club (Lake), 1955

HARDEST PAR THREES

Since 1986

3.46—Pebble Beach GL, 17th, 209 yards, 1992

3.44—Pebble Beach GL, 17th, 208 yards, 2000

3.41—Shinnecock Hills GC, 7th, 189 yards, 2004

3.40—Pinehurst Resort & CC (No. 2), 6th, 222 yards, 1999

3.39—Oakland Hills CC (South), 9th, 220 yards, 1996

3.37—Oakmont CC, 16th, 228 yards, 1994

3.37—Winged Foot GC (West), 3rd, 216 yards, 2006

HARDEST PAR FOURS

Since 1986

4.72—Olympic Club (Lake), 17th, 468 yards, 1998

4.60—Bethpage State Park (Black), 15th, 459 yards, 2002

4.56—Olympic Club (Lake), 17th, 428 yards, 1987

4.56—Pebble Beach GL, 9th, 466 yards, 2000

4.55—Pinehurst Resort & CC (No. 2), 5th, 482 yards, 1999

4.54—Oakland Hills CC (South), 18th, 465 yards, 1996

4.53—Congressional CC (Blue), 6th, 475 yards, 1997

4.53—Pebble Beach GL, 8th, 418 yards, 2000

4.52—Bethpage State Park (Black), 12th, 499 yards, 2002

4.50—Oak Hill CC (East), 17th, 458 yards, 1989

4.50—Pinehurst Resort & CC (No. 2), 16th, 489 yards, 1999

4.50—Pinehurst Resort & CC (No. 2), 8th, 485 yards, 1999

4.50—Bethpage State Park (Black), 10th, 492 yards, 2002

HARDEST PAR FIVES

Since 1986

5.38—Pebble Beach GL, 14th, 573 yards, 2000

5.29—Pebble Beach GL, 14th, 565 yards, 1992

5.26—Oakmont CC, 12th, 598 yards, 1994

5.25—Olympic Club (Lake), 16th, 609 yards, 1987

5.25—Olympic Club (Lake), 16th, 609 yards, 1998

5.24—Winged Foot GC (West), 12th, 640 yards, 2006

5.18—Southern Hills CC, 5th, 642 yards, 2001

5.13—Shinnecock Hills GC, 16th, 544 yards, 1995

COURSE STATISTICS

YEAR	COURSE (PAR)	ROUND 1	ROUND 2	ROUND 3	ROUND 4	AVG. SCORE	AVG. BY RD.	WINNER	SUB-PAR RDS.
1930s									
1935	Oakmont (72)	80.6 (+8.6)	81.3 (+9.3)	79.8 (+7.8)	79.3 (+7.3)	80.5 (+8.5)	80.3 (+8.3)	299 (+11)	3
1932	Fresh Meadow (70)	81.4 (+11.4)	79.1 (+9.1)	76.2 (+6.2)	75.7 (+5.7)	78.8 (+8.8)	78.1 (+8.1)	286 (+6)	9
1934	Merion (70)	79.2 (+9.2)	77.4 (+7.4)	78.9 (+8.9)	76.8 (+6.8)	78.2 (+8.2)	78.1 (+8.1)	293 (+9)	1
1938	Cherry Hills (71)	80.0 (+9.0)	77.7 (+6.7)	77.3 (+6.3)	77.5 (+6.5)	78.5 (+7.5)	78.1 (+7.1)	284 (E)	15
1931	Inverness (71)	79.2 (+8.2)	78.9 (+7.9)	77.5 (+6.5)	76.6 (+5.6)	78.3 (+7.3)	78.1 (+7.1)	292 (+8)	5
1939	Philadelphia (69)	76.9 (+7.9)	77.0 (+8.0)	74.4 (+5.4)	74.9 (+5.9)	76.2 (+7.2)	75.8 (+6.8)	284 (+8)	6
1930	Interlachen (72)	78.5 (+6.5)	78.5 (+6.5)	77.6 (+5.6)	77.5 (+5.5)	78.2 (+6.2)	78.0 (+6.0)	287 (-1)	10
1933	North Shore (72)	78.9 (+6.9)	77.9 (+5.9)	76.5 (+4.5)	76.1 (+4.1)	77.8 (+5.8)	77.4 (+5.4)	287 (-1)	18
1936	Baltusrol (Upper) (72)	76.2 (+4.2)	76.4 (+4.4)	75.2 (+3.2)	75.8 (+3.8)	76.0 (+4.0)	76.0 (+4.0)	282 (-6)	38
1937	Oakland Hills (72)	77.4 (+5.4)	76.7 (+4.7)	74.9 (+2.9)	74.6 (+2.6)	76.4 (+4.4)	75.9 (+3.9)	281 (-7)	36
	Decade avg. (71.1)	78.8 (+7.7)	78.1 (+7.0)	76.8 (+5.7)	76.5 (+5.4)	77.9 (+6.8)	77.6 (+6.5)	287.5 (+3.1)	14.1
1940s									
1941	Colonial (70)	77.6 (+7.6)	79.3 (+9.3)	76.6 (+6.6)	76.1 (+6.1)	77.8 (+7.8)	77.4 (+7.4)	284 (+4)	2
1949	Medinah (71)	77.2 (+6.2)	76.7 (+5.7)	73.8 (+2.8)	75.3 (+4.3)	76.4 (+5.4)	75.8 (+4.8)	286 (+2)	19
1947	St. Louis (71)	75.8 (+4.8)	76.9 (+5.9)	74.8 (+3.8)	75.1 (+4.1)	75.9 (+4.9)	75.7 (+4.7)	282 (-2)	33
1940	Canterbury (72)	77.4 (+5.4)	77.0 (+5.0)	75.8 (+3.8)	75.0 (+3.0)	76.7 (+4.7)	76.3 (+4.3)	287 (-1)	34
1948	Riviera (71)	75.8 (+4.8)	76.0 (+5.0)	74.5 (+3.5)	73.8 (+2.8)	75.5 (+4.5)	75.0 (+4.0)	276 (-8)	32
1946	Canterbury (72)	77.2 (+5.2)	76.4 (+4.4)	74.4 (+2.4)	74.4 (+2.4)	76.1 (+4.1)	75.6 (+3.6)	284 (-4)	42
	Decade avg. (71.2)	76.8 (+5.6)	77.1 (+5.9)	75.0 (+3.8)	75.0 (+3.8)	76.4 (+5.2)	76.0 (+4.8)	283.2 (-1.5)	27
1950s									
1955	Olympic (70)	79.8 (+9.8)	78.9 (+8.9)	76.8 (+6.8)	76.6 (+6.6)	78.7 (+8.7)	78.0 (+8.0)	287 (+7)	7
1958	Southern Hills (70)	79.7 (+9.7)	78.5 (+8.5)	74.7 (+4.7)	74.3 (+4.3)	77.9 (+7.9)	76.8 (+6.8)	283 (+3)	6
1951	Oakland Hills (70)	78.4 (+8.4)	77.2 (+7.2)	76.0 (+6.0)	75.2 (+5.2)	77.2 (+7.2)	76.7 (+6.7)	287 (+7)	2
1952	Northwood (70)	77.5 (+7.5)	77.7 (+7.7)	75.1 (+5.1)	76.0 (+6.0)	77.0 (+7.0)	76.6 (+6.6)	281 (+1)	8
1954	Baltusrol (70)	78.8 (+8.8)	76.7 (+6.7)	74.4 (+4.4)	75.2 (+5.2)	77.1 (+7.1)	76.3 (+6.3)	284 (+4)	7
1950	Merion (70)	76.1 (+6.1)	76.7 (+6.7)	76.1 (+6.1)	75.9 (+5.9)	76.3 (+6.3)	76.2 (+6.2)	287 (+7)	14
1956	Oak Hill (70)	77.0 (+7.0)	76.4 (+6.4)	74.6 (+4.6)	75.2 (+5.2)	76.3 (+6.3)	75.8 (+5.8)	281 (+1)	8
1959	Winged Foot (70)	76.7 (+6.7)	75.6 (+5.6)	74.0 (+4.0)	76.3 (+6.3)	75.9 (+5.9)	75.7 (+5.7)	282 (+2)	16
1957	Inverness (70)	76.7 (+6.7)	76.9 (+6.9)	73.7 (+3.7)	74.6 (+4.6)	76.2 (+6.2)	75.5 (+5.5)	282 (+2)	15
1953	Oakmont (72)	77.8 (+5.8)	77.1 (+5.1)	76.3 (+4.3)	76.2 (+4.2)	77.1 (+5.1)	76.9 (+4.9)	283 (-5)	20
	Decade avg. (70.2)	77.9 (+7.7)	77.2 (+7.0)	75.2 (+5.0)	75.6 (+5.4)	77.0 (+6.8)	76.5 (+6.3)	283.7 (+2.9)	10.3
1960s									
1963	Country Club (71)	77.5 (+6.5)	77.5 (+6.5)	78.2 (+7.2)	77.4 (+6.4)	77.6 (+6.6)	77.7 (+6.7)	293 (+9)	5
1965	Bellerive (70)	77.4 (+7.4)	76.6 (+6.6)	74.0 (+4.0)	74.5 (+4.5)	76.3 (+6.3)	75.6 (+5.6)	282 (+2)	8
1966	Olympic (70)	75.8 (+5.8)	76.7 (+6.7)	74.5 (+4.5)	74.8 (+4.8)	75.8 (+5.8)	75.5 (+5.5)	278 (-2)	15
1964	Congressional (70)	76.6 (+6.6)	75.4 (+5.4)	75.0 (+5.0)	74.8 (+4.8)	75.7 (+5.7)	75.5 (+5.5)	278 (-2)	9
1961	Oakland Hills (70)	76.0 (+6.0)	74.8 (+4.8)	73.5 (+3.5)	74.4 (+4.4)	75.0 (+5.0)	74.7 (+4.7)	281 (+1)	18
1962	Oakmont (71)	76.3 (+5.3)	76.2 (+5.2)	74.5 (+3.5)	75.3 (+4.3)	75.9 (+4.9)	75.6 (+4.6)	283 (-1)	19
1969	Champions (70)	75.4 (+5.4)	75.2 (+5.2)	72.8 (+2.8)	74.1 (+4.1)	74.7 (+4.7)	74.4 (+4.4)	281 (+1)	28
1968	Oak Hill (70)	75.4 (+5.4)	74.6 (+4.6)	73.7 (+3.7)	73.0 (+3.0)	74.5 (+4.5)	74.2 (+4.2)	275 (-5)	30
1967	Baltusrol (70)	75.2 (+5.2)	74.5 (+4.5)	73.3 (+3.3)	72.8 (+2.8)	74.3 (+4.3)	74.0 (+4.0)	275 (-5)	26
1960	Cherry Hills (71)	75.7 (+4.7)	74.6 (+3.6)	72.7 (+1.7)	74.3 (+2.3)	74.7 (+3.7)	74.3 (+3.3)	280 (-4)	45
	Decade avg. (70.3)	76.1 (+5.8)	75.6 (+5.3)	74.2 (+3.9)	74.5 (+4.2)	75.5 (+5.2)	75.1 (+4.8)	280.6 (-0.6)	20.3

Note: Courses are ranked by order of difficulty in each decade, based on an average score by round.

YEAR	COURSE (PAR)	ROUND 1	ROUND 2	ROUND 3	ROUND 4	AVG. SCORE	AVG. BY RD.	WINNER	SUB-PAR RDS.
1970s									
1974	Winged Foot (70)	77.8 (+7.8)	77.0 (+7.0)	76.2 (+6.2)	75.9 (+5.9)	77.0 (+7.0)	76.7 (+6.7)	287 (+7)	8
1972	Pebble Beach (72)	78.0 (+6.0)	77.9 (+5.9)	76.0 (+4.0)	78.8 (+6.8)	77.8 (+5.8)	77.7 (+5.7)	290 (+2)	23
1976	Atlanta Athletic (70)	76.3 (+6.3)	76.2 (+6.2)	73.2 (+3.2)	74.2 (+4.2)	75.5 (+5.5)	75.0 (+5.0)	277 (-3)	23
1979	Inverness (71)	77.1 (+6.1)	77.4 (+6.4)	73.9 (+2.9)	75.5 (+4.5)	76.5 (+5.5)	76.0 (+5.0)	284 (E)	24
1978	Cherry Hills (71)	77.1 (+6.1)	75.7 (+4.7)	74.3 (+3.3)	75.1 (+4.1)	75.9 (+4.9)	75.6 (+4.6)	285 (+1)	27
1975	Medinah (71)	75.9 (+4.9)	75.0 (+4.0)	74.8 (+3.8)	75.4 (+4.4)	75.3 (+4.3)	75.3 (+4.3)	287 (+3)	26
1970	Hazeltine Nat. (72)	79.1 (+7.1)	75.8 (+3.8)	75.0 (+3.0)	74.6 (+2.6)	76.6 (+4.6)	76.1 (+4.1)	281 (-7)	39
1977	Southern Hills (70)	74.9 (+4.9)	74.8 (+4.8)	72.7 (+2.7)	74.0 (+4.0)	74.4 (+4.4)	74.1 (+4.1)	278 (-2)	35
1973	Oakmont (71)	76.8 (+5.8)	75.4 (+4.4)	74.3 (+3.3)	73.8 (+2.8)	75.5 (+4.5)	75.1 (+4.1)	279 (-5)	40
1971	Merion (70)	74.1 (+4.1)	75.8 (+5.8)	72.2 (+2.2)	73.1 (+3.1)	74.2 (+4.2)	73.8 (+3.8)	280 (E)	30
	Decade avg. (70.8)	76.7 (+5.9)	76.1 (+5.3)	74.3 (+3.5)	75.0 (+4.2)	75.9 (+5.1)	75.5 (+4.7)	282.8 (-0.4)	27.5
1980s									
1983	Oakmont (71)	77.1 (+6.1)	76.5 (+5.5)	75.0 (+4.0)	74.5 (+3.5)	76.1 (+5.1)	75.6 (+4.6)	280 (-4)	27
1984	Winged Foot (70)	74.3 (+4.3)	75.2 (+5.2)	73.3 (+3.3)	73.5 (+3.5)	74.4 (+4.4)	74.1 (+4.1)	276 (-4)	30
1986	Shinnecock Hills (70)	77.8 (+7.8)	74.0 (+4.0)	71.7 (+1.7)	72.0 (+2.0)	74.7 (+4.7)	73.9 (+3.9)	279 (-1)	39
1985	Oakland Hills (70)	74.7 (+4.7)	73.3 (+3.3)	73.6 (+3.6)	73.0 (+3.0)	73.8 (+3.8)	73.7 (+3.7)	279 (-1)	41
1980	Baltusrol (70)	74.4 (+4.4)	74.3 (+4.3)	72.2 (+2.2)	73.4 (+3.4)	73.9 (+3.9)	73.6 (+3.6)	272 (-8)	51
1987	Olympic (70)	74.2 (+4.2)	73.1 (+3.1)	72.9 (+2.9)	73.6 (+3.6)	73.5 (+3.5)	73.5 (+3.5)	277 (-3)	47
1989	Oak Hill (70)	73.3 (+3.3)	73.6 (+3.6)	73.4 (+3.4)	73.2 (+3.2)	73.2 (+3.2)	73.4 (+3.4)	278 (-2)	54
1981	Merion (70)	74.0 (+4.0)	74.7 (+4.7)	71.5 (+1.5)	72.5 (+2.5)	73.6 (+3.6)	73.2 (+3.2)	273 (-7)	58
1982	Pebble Beach (72)	77.3 (+5.3)	75.7 (+3.7)	73.0 (+1.0)	73.9 (+1.9)	75.6 (+3.6)	75.0 (+3.0)	282 (-6)	63
1988	Country Club (71)	75.1 (+4.1)	73.9 (+2.9)	72.7 (+1.7)	72.0 (+1.0)	73.9 (+2.9)	73.4 (+2.4)	278 (-6)	64
	Decade avg. (70.4)	75.2 (+4.8)	74.4 (+4.0)	72.9 (+2.5)	73.2 (+2.8)	74.0 (+3.6)	73.6 (+3.2)	277.4 (-4.2)	47.4
1990s									
1999	Pinehurst (70)	72.9 (+2.9)	75.4 (+5.4)	76.0 (+6.0)	75.0 (+5.0)	74.6 (+4.6)	74.8 (+4.8)	279 (-1)	29
1998	Olympic (70)	74.9 (+4.9)	74.5 (+4.5)	74.2 (+4.2)	73.7 (+3.7)	74.5 (+4.5)	74.3 (+4.3)	280 (E)	27
1997	Congressional (70)	73.8 (+3.8)	73.7 (+3.7)	73.2 (+3.2)	73.7 (+3.7)	73.6 (+3.6)	73.6 (+3.6)	276 (-4)	51
1995	Shinnecock Hills (70)	73.5 (+3.5)	73.9 (+3.9)	74.2 (+4.2)	72.1 (+2.1)	73.5 (+3.5)	73.4 (+3.4)	280 (E)	43
1994	Oakmont (71)	75.2 (+4.2)	73.5 (+2.5)	73.4 (+2.4)	74.5 (+3.5)	74.3 (+3.3)	74.2 (+3.2)	279 (-5)	62
1996	Oakland Hills (70)	73.6 (+3.6)	73.0 (+3.0)	72.9 (+2.9)	72.9 (+2.9)	73.1 (+3.1)	73.1 (+3.1)	278 (-2)	51
1992	Pebble Beach (72)	74.5 (+2.5)	75.0 (+3.0)	73.7 (+1.7)	77.3 (+5.3)	75.0 (+3.0)	75.1 (+3.1)	285 (-3)	76
1991	Hazeltine Nat. (72)	75.0 (+3.0)	74.3 (+2.3)	75.7 (+3.7)	74.4 (+2.4)	74.8 (+2.8)	74.9 (+2.9)	282 (-6)	67
1993	Baltusrol (70)	72.3 (+2.3)	72.4 (+2.4)	71.8 (+1.8)	71.6 (+1.6)	72.1 (+2.1)	72.0 (+2.0)	272 (-8)	76
1990	Medinah (72)	73.7 (+1.7)	73.5 (+1.5)	72.3 (+0.3)	74.0 (+2.0)	73.5 (+1.5)	73.4 (+1.4)	280 (-8)	124
	Decade avg. (70.7)	73.9 (+3.2)	73.8 (+3.1)	73.7 (+3.0)	73.9 (+3.2)	73.9 (+3.2)	73.9 (+3.2)	279.1 (-3.7)	60.6
2000s									
2004	Shinnecock Hills (70)	73.4 (+3.4)	73.0 (+3.0)	73.5 (+3.5)	78.7 (+8.7)	74.1 (+4.1)	74.7 (+4.7)	276 (-4)	43
2006	Winged Foot (70)	76.0 (+6.0)	75.0 (+5.0)	73.7 (+3.7)	73.8 (+3.8)	75.0 (+5.0)	74.6 (+4.6)	285 (+5)	12
2002	Bethpage (70)	74.9 (+4.9)	76.5 (+6.5)	72.1 (+2.1)	74.4 (+4.4)	74.9 (+4.9)	74.4 (+4.4)	277 (-3)	25
2000	Pebble Beach (71)	75.0 (+4.0)	75.9 (+4.9)	77.1 (+6.1)	73.2 (+2.2)	75.4 (+4.4)	75.3 (+4.3)	272 (-12)	35
2005	Pinehurst (70)	74.7 (+4.7)	73.7 (+3.7)	73.7 (+3.7)	74.4 (+4.4)	74.2 (+4.2)	74.1 (+4.1)	280 (E)	29
2001	Southern Hills (70)	74.1 (+4.1)	73.1 (+3.1)	72.1 (+2.1)	73.1 (+3.1)	73.3 (+3.3)	73.1 (+3.1)	276 (-4)	49
2003	Olympia Fields (70)	72.7 (+2.7)	71.9 (+1.9)	72.1 (+2.1)	73.0 (+3.0)	72.4 (+2.4)	72.4 (+2.4)	272 (-8)	83
	Decade avg. (70.1)	74.4 (+4.3)	74.2 (+4.1)	73.5 (+3.4)	74.4 (+4.3)	74.2 (+4.1)	74.1 (+4.0)	276.9 (-3.5)	37.7

ACKNOWLEDGMENTS

This book wouldn't quite have been impossible to write without the existence of the USGA library in Far Hills, New Jersey, but it would have been considerably more difficult. The USGA's comprehensive collection of periodicals and books is a treasure trove to a researcher. When you also consider the helpfulness of its staff, consisting of Douglas Stark and Patty Moran, and the fact that I was allowed to make photocopies of the vast majority of the material instead of having to go through a tedious note-taking process, it was just about perfect. I lost track of how many trips I took to Far Hills, but it was somewhere between 20 and 25.

This story of the U.S. Open courses is stitched together from a wealth of source material. First and foremost were various periodicals, from publications like *Golf, The American Golfer,* and *Golf Illustrated* from the early decades of the Open, to recent ones like *Golf Digest, Golf Magazine, Golf World, USGA Journal,* and *Sports Illustrated.* I combed through them not only for championship reports, but also for championship previews, which usually contain informative stories about the host course. The USGA's collection of photocopies of *New York Times* articles about the Open was also helpful.

Naturally, the USGA has a complete collection of U.S. Open programs. I also utilized programs of other USGA championships like the U.S. Amateur or U.S. Senior Open that have been held at these courses. The library also has collections of *The Majors of Golf* previews and, showing no favoritism, PGA Championship programs, which sometimes came in handy for courses that have also hosted that event.

The files of U.S. Opens from the past quarter century or so contain all the course statistics that are part of the computer era, as well as press materials like interview transcripts. And where else but the USGA would I have been able to find copies of the Rules of Golf from decades past in order to better understand a few tricky Rules situations that arose in Opens?

Another major source was club histories. Nearly all of these courses have them, many of them written within the past decade or so, and they're all in the USGA collection.

All of this was supplemented by consulting relevant sections from various books: biographies and autobiographies of players, books on golf architecture and golf architects, general golf histories, and books on courses in a given region. For statistics from the pre-computer days of the Open, I relied on *The Official U.S. Open Almanac,* by Sal Johnson.

By using multiple sources, I hope I have been able to separate truth from myth in a number of cases and present the authoritative story of these great courses that have hosted the Open, and of the championships themselves. I have also tried to sprinkle the book with many of the amusing or instructive anecdotes I ran across.

In addition to the many writers who produced the articles and books that I read in my research, I also need to thank some people who gave me their insights or assistance. The list starts with David Fay, Mike Davis, Marty Parkes, and Rand Jerris of the USGA and also includes golf architects Rees Jones and Tom Fazio, who between them have renovated or redesigned nearly all the courses that have hosted Opens recently. Their thoughts were particularly important since updating the courses to cope with the onslaught of modern technology and modern players has become such an integral part of championship preparations. I also owe thanks to some who helped me tie up loose ends along the way: particularly Bill Iredale, RJ Harper, Rick Wolffe, and Laura Warner.

Stepping back to look at the big picture, I owe a major debt of gratitude to George Peper and Jim Frank, my former bosses at *Golf Magazine,* who not only hired me but assigned me to oversee or write numerous major championship previews during my time there, from 1985 to 2003. At Harry N. Abrams, thanks go to former managing editor Harriet Whelchel for bringing me aboard to edit several golf books and then to write this one. Contributing mightily to this project were Laurie Platt Winfrey and Cristian Peña at Carousel Research for the vast task of gathering photos, Hunki Yun for his masterful editing, Bob McKee for his artful design, and current managing editor Andrea Colvin for seeing it through to conclusion.

None of this would have been possible without generous support at home from my wife, Ludmila, and inspiration from my children, Michael and Sophia. To you go my deepest thanks.

David Barrett
White Plains, New York
September 2006

INDEX

Page numbers in italics refer to illustrations

303

PHOTO CREDITS

AP: 24, 28, 52, 63, 98, 106, 140 top, 184, 216,
240, 249, 262, 287; Kevork Djanzesian, 208;
Rusty Kennedy, 250; Charles Krupa, 40;
Susan Walsh, 78
Boston Public Library: 92
Aidan Bradley: 176
Charles Briscoe-Knight: 242, 244, 245
Corbis/Bettmann: 48, 145, 187 top, 226, 266;
Ralf-Finn Hestoft, 105; Tony Roberts,
29 bottom, 65 top, 241
Courtesy of Atlanta Athletic Club/Bob
Maynard: 12
Courtesy of Baltimore Country Club/Richard W.
Rochfort: 16, 17
Courtesy of Baltusrol Golf Club: 18, 19, 22
Courtesy of Bellerive Country Club: 29 top, 30
Courtesy of Colonial Country Club: 71
Courtesy of Glen View Club: 104
Courtesy of Midlothian Country Club: 146, 147
top, 147 bottom, 148 top, 148 bottom
Courtesy of North Shore Country Club: 160,
161, 162
Courtesy of Queens Public Library, Long Island
Division/Frederick W. Weber: 99
Pete Fontaine: 185 top, 185 bottom, 186, 187
bottom, 190 bottom, 192
Getty Images: AFP/Roberto Schmidt, 235;
AFP/Jim Watson, 239; David Alexander, 67;
Allsport/Hulton Archive, 66; David Cannon,
183, 188, 255; David Cannon/Allsport, 113;
Evening Standard, 205 top; Donald Miralle,
2; Hy Peskin, 138; Jamie Squire, 214; Rick
Steward/Allsport, 166
Matthew Harris/Golf Picture Library: 122, 123
Henebry Photography Inc.: 57 top, 57 bottom, 58,
60, 61, 195 top, 195 bottom, 196, 202, 203, 204,
210, 224, 225, 227, 232, 267
Historic Golf Photos: 137, 151, 164
Chris John: 44-45, 76-77
John R. Johnson/Golfphotos.com: 49 bottom, 260

Russell Kirk/Golflinks: 1, 19, 21, 32, 34, 36,
37, 41, 75, 80, 81 bottom, 86, 94, 101 top, 101
bottom, 102, 139 bottom, 167, 168, 169, 170,
171, 172, 200, 201, 206-207, 215, 231 top, 231
bottom, 234, 236, 238, 251 top, 251 bottom,
252, 256-257, 279 bottom, 280, 284
Mike Klemme/Golfoto: 49 top, 53 top, 53 bottom,
54, 119 top, 119 bottom, 120-121, 247 top, 247
bottom, 248, 263 top, 263 bottom, 264, 265
L.C. Lambrecht Photography: 4, 11, 14, 20, 33, 38-
39, 65 bottom, 68, 79, 93 bottom, 127, 128, 129,
131 top, 131 bottom, 133, 135, 136, 139 top, 140
bottom, 141, 144, 153 bottom, 154, 156, 158, 175,
178, 180, 182, 217, 218, 221, 253, 254, 272, 274,
275, 276-277, 279 top, 283 top, 283 bottom
Tom Pantages: 43, 153 top, 288
Nancy J. Parisi: 46
ProShots: 212
Evan Schiller/Golfshots: Endpapers, 89, 90, 142,
222, 273
Phil Sheldon/Golf Picture Library: 82-83;
Larry Petrillo, 268
Richard Hamilton Smith: 107 top, 111, 112,
114, 115
Sports Illustrated: James Drake, 125 center, 173,
193; Jonathan Ferrey, 199; Walter Iooss Jr., 81
top; Richard Mackson, 219; Bob Martin, 189
bottom; Tony Triolo, 13; Fred Vuich, 194, 269;
John G. Zimmerman, 56
USGA: 10, 26, 42, 50, 59, 64, 72, 74 top, 88, 91,
96, 100, 118, 125 top, 126, 152, 155 top, 155
bottom, 159 top, 159 bottom, 174, 179, 189
center, 190 top, 197, 205 bottom, 207 top, 213,
226 top, 228, 246, 261, 270, 278, 286, 289;
Kelly & Russell, 25; John Mummert, 230;
Larry Petrillo, 93 top, 130
Watson Publications: 70, 72 bottom
Western New York Heritage Press: 47
Peter Wong Photography: 107 bottom, 108 top,
108 center, 108 bottom, 116, 150

Editor: Hunki Yun
Designer: Robert McKee
Design Assistant: E.Y. Lee
Photo Research: Laurie Platt Winfrey, Cristian Peña,
Carousel Research, Inc.
Production Manager: Jane Searle

Library of Congress Cataloging-in-Publication Data
Barrett, David.
Golf courses of the U.S. Open / by David Barrett.
p. cm.
Includes index.
ISBN-13: 978-0-8109-3387-3 (hardcover with jacket)
ISBN-10: 0-8109-3387-X (hardcover with jacket)
1. Golf courses—United States—Guidebooks.
2. U.S. Open (Golf tournament)
I. Title. II. Title: Golf courses of the US Open.

GV981.B394 2007
796.352068—dc22

2006036180

Published in 2007 by Abrams, an imprint of
Harry N. Abrams, Inc. All rights reserved.
No portion of this book may be reproduced,
stored in a retrieval system, or transmitted in
any form or by any means, mechanical,
electronic, photocopying, recording, or
otherwise, without written permission
from the publisher.

Printed and bound in China
10 9 8 7 6 5 4 3 2 1

HNA ▪▪▪▪▪
harry n. abrams, inc.
a subsidiary of La Martinière Groupe
115 West 18th Street
New York, NY 10011
www.hnabooks.com